I0482818

Page 1

1   UNITED STATES DISTRICT COURT
2   DISTRICT OF SOUTH DAKOTA
3   . . . . . . SOUTHERN DIVISION . . . . . .
4   *
     UNITED STATES OF AMERICA,   *
5   *
        Plaintiff,   Volume I   *
6   *
     -vs-   *   CR. 94-40015
7   *   MOTION FOR NEW TRIAL
     DESMOND ROUSE, JESSIE ROUSE   *
8   GARFIELD FEATHER, RUSSELL   *
     HUBBELING,   *
9   *
10   Defendants. *
11   * * * * * * * * * * * * * * * * *
12
13   BEFORE: The Honorable Lawrence L. Piersol
               Chief United States District Judge
14   For the District of South Dakota
               Sioux Falls, South Dakota
15
16
     PROCEEDINGS: The above-entitled matter came on for
17   hearing on the 5th day of September, 2001
               commencing at the hour of 9:00 a.m. in the
18   courtroom of the Federal Building, Sioux
               Falls, South Dakota.
19
     Proceedings recorded by mechanical stenography, transcript
20   produced by computer.
21
22
23
24
25

Page 2

1   APPEARANCES:
2   Mr. Randy Seiler
         Ms. Michelle Tapken
3   Mr. Dennis Holmes
         Assistant United States Attorneys
4   Pierre, South Dakota
         Sioux Falls, South Dakota
5
6   Attorneys for the United States;
7   Mr. John Wilka
         Attorney at Law
8   Sioux Falls, South Dakota
9   Attorney for Desmond Rouse;
10
11   Mr. Steven Binger
         Attorney at Law
12   Sioux Falls, South Dakota
13   Attorney for Jessie Rouse;
14   Mr. David Carter
         Attorney at Law
15   Sioux Falls, South Dakota
16   Attorney for Garfield Feather;
17
18   Mr. Steve Haugaard
         Attorney at Law
19   Sioux Falls, South Dakota
20   Attorney for Russell Hubbeling.
21
22
23
24
25

Page 3

1   THE COURT: Good morning. Appearances, first for the
2   United States.
3   MR. HOLMES: Dennis Holmes appears on behalf of the
4   United States.
5   MR. SEILER: Randy Seiler from the Pierre United
6   States Attorney's Office also appearing on behalf of the United
7   States.
8   MS. TAPKEN: Michelle Tapken also appearing for the
9   United States.
10   THE COURT: Then for the defendant Desmond Rouse.
11   MR. WILKA: John Wilka appearing on behalf of Desmond
12   Rouse.
13   THE COURT: Then for Jessie Rouse.
14   MR. BINGER: Steve Binger appearing for Jessie Rouse.
15   THE COURT: Garfield Feather.
16   MR. CARTER: David Carter, Sioux Falls appearing for
17   Mr. Feather, he is also here personally.
18   THE COURT: And then for Russell Hubbeling.
19   MR. HAUGAARD: Steve Haugaard appearing on behalf of
20   Russell Hubbeling, he is seated behind me.
21   THE COURT: I was dealing with some preliminary
22   matters before I came out here, one of them is I have the
23   Deputy United States Marshal here, but Jerome Rouse was
24   requested to be here by a subpoena I received some time last
25   week, I sent it back saying that we had to have an appearance

Page 4

1   time, I didn't get the subpoena back again until five o'clock
2   on Friday when I wasn't here. Of course that is about two
3   weeks later than we are supposed to get subpoena requests. The
4   problem is, as I have understood from Marshal Whitelock, is
5   that all the Marshals here are occupied with the defendants
6   that are here, and the Marshal in Aberdeen is occupied with
7   Judge Kornmann up there, and not only that, we have two more
8   defendants tomorrow that are, frankly, considered by me to be
9   high risk defendants, doesn't have anything to do with this
10   case, but they are making appearances in Judge Simko's Court.
11   So, you know, at this date there isn't any Marshal personnel to
12   move Jerome Rouse, and probably what we will have to do is
13   either not have his testimony, or have it at a later time,
14   because frankly this thing has been scheduled for months and
15   you should have gotten your subpoena requests in, it is just
16   that simple. I don't know what else to do, you know. If the
17   Marshals had another person that could go up, because Jerome
18   Rouse is in the Bureau of Prisons custody in Dickinson, North
19   Dakota, I believe for a violation. Then that's one thing. Now
20   before I came on the bench I get a request an ex parte motion
21   for a subpoena duces tecum for the Children's Home Society for
22   production of records at 9:00 this morning. I didn't get it
23   until 9:00 this morning. Mr. Haugaard, you are the one that
24   signed that one. I realize there are different
25   responsibilities taken by different counsel. For instance, I

Page 5

1 read a brief by Mr. Carter that was submitted by different
2 people, and Mr. Wilka has been apparently taking care of the
3 subpoenas, except for this one. Now who this one, is this a
4 friendly subpoena, or not, because sometimes just simply
5 somebody says, well, I want the subpoena so that we can turn
6 the records over, they are all ready to go, or is this
7 something that is news to the Children's Home Society too, what
8 is the story?
9   MR. HAUGAARD: This will be news to the Children's
10 Home Society.
11   THE COURT: Ordering that it be produced at the time
12 that I received this, I am not going to Order it, I mean it is
13 not timely, it is not even close. If it were, I would, but to
14 request all of the records concerning any of the following
15 children, Thrista Rouse, Donovan Rouse, Rosemary Rouse and
16 Lucritia Rouse, and particularly where you are getting records
17 of this kind, you can anticipate that there might be problems.
18 They are juvenile records, they are sensitive records, and my
19 recollection of the trial, we had some issues, you know,
20 sometimes getting certain records with regard to the children.
21 This just isn't timely, I am not going to Order it. The moving
22 parties that are Desmond and Jessie Rouse, Garfield Feather and
23 Russell Hubbeling may proceed with their proof. Now at trial
24 we had, I didn't look back to see what the order of trial was,
25 and I don't remember, frankly. Can, does anybody remember for

Page 6

1 sure, would it be just a guess on your part too.
2   MR. WILKA: No, Your Honor, we remember and we have
3 also discussed the order with regard to the witnesses. I will
4 be examining our experts, and then we will be supplied with
5 suggestions and notes from co-counsel, but we anticipate just
6 one direct of our expert, and we, and Mr. Haugaard will be
7 examining the children who will be testifying and likewise we
8 will be supplying possibly with notes and/or suggestions.
9   THE COURT: Alright. That is fine with me. What
10 about other witnesses that aren't experts, that are not
11 children?
12   MR. HAUGAARD: That will be a division of labor, Your
13 Honor.
14   THE COURT: Alright.
15   MR. HAUGAARD: We expect just one attorney per
16 witness.
17   MR. WILKA: We, of course, reserve the right to have
18 all defense attorneys cross examine the government's witnesses.
19   THE COURT: Yes. Alright, well, so, and you had
20 indicated you figured out your order of witnesses.
21   MR. WILKA: Yes, Your Honor.
22   THE COURT: What is that, because it would be helpful
23 for me in terms of my preparing for witnesses.
24   MR. WILKA: We anticipate that first we would call
25 Dr. Maggie Bruck of Johns Hopkins University. Then we would

Page 7

1 call Kathleen Honomichl, then Julia Joseph.
2   THE COURT: Just a minute, I don't write that fast.
3 Then who after Kathleen Honomichl.
4   MR. WILKA: Then Julia Joseph. Then I believe we
5 would get into the children, and then Thrista Rouse, and then
6 Donovan Rouse, then Rosemary Rouse, then Lucritia Rouse, and
7 then Jessica Rouse.
8   THE COURT: Alright, thank you. Let's start off then
9 with Dr. Bruck.
10
11   MAGGIE BRUCK,
12 called as a witness, being first duly sworn, testified and said
13 as follows:
14
15 DIRECT EXAMINATION BY MR. WILKA:
16 Q. Would you please state your name?
17 A. Maggie Bruck.
18 Q. What is your occupation?
19 A. I am associate professor in child psychiatry at Johns
20 Hopkins University.
21 Q. What is your educational background starting with
22 college?
23 A. I have a Bachelor's degree from Wheaton College in
24 Norton, Massachusetts, and then a Masters Degree and a Doctoral
25 Degree, Ph.D. Degree in experimental psychology at McGill

Page 8

1 University in Montreal, Quebec.
2 Q. Currently you are an associate professor at Johns
3 Hopkins?
4 A. Yes, I am.
5 Q. What do you teach there?
6 A. Last semester I taught an undergraduate course pertaining
7 to issues of children's memory and the courtroom, and my major
8 duties teaching now involve teaching of psychiatry residents in
9 terms of aspects of memory, interviewing of children, as well I
10 run a post-doctoral training program where I am in charge of
11 mentoring and organizing programs for the various trainees that
12 come in.
13 Q. Are you involved in research activities?
14 A. Yes.
15 Q. If you could give us an example of some of the research
16 activities you are involved in?
17 A. Currently, or over my lifetime?
18 Q. Currently.
19 A. My major area of focus at this point is memory, and two
20 areas of memory. One concerns children's memory or their
21 reporting of experiences and the degree to which various
22 factors impinge on the accuracy of this reporting. I am also
23 doing research on adult's memory, conversations, of interviews
24 with children, and I am beginning a new area of research on the
25 association, on anxiety in children and a possible memory

Page 9

1 deficit.

2 Q. Do you peer review scientific articles?

3 A. Yes, I do.

4 Q. Approximately how many per year?

5 A. As of a few months ago up to about 50. It will increase

6 to probably 75 a year starting July 1.

7 Q. And have you published articles on children witnesses and

8 suggestibility in the courtroom on children witnesses?

9 A. I have published articles on children's testimony or

10 their recounting of the past, and these articles, most of which

11 have been co-authored with Steven CeCe, have appeared in peer

12 review journals, chapters in handbooks, in a book, we wrote a

13 book.

14 Q. Have you published any books?

15 A. Yes. Jeopardy in The Courtroom was published in 1995.

16 Q. Was that authored with Steven CeCe?

17 A. Yes.

18 Q. Are you a member of any editorial boards?

19 A. Yes, I am a member of three or four editorial boards of

20 journals in child development, in language, in psychology and

21 the law, and I think that covers the gamut.

22 Q. And what professional societies are you a member of?

23 A. Member of the American Psychological Socity, Society for

24 Research in Child Development, Psychonomics.

25 Q. Have you received any awards or honors for your work?

Page 10

1 A. Most recently we were, Steve and I were awarded the

2 William James prize for our contribution in writing Jeopardy in

3 The Courtroom. It was awarded by the American Psychological

4 Association as an example of scientific writings having an

5 impact in society. There was another one, the article that we

6 wrote that appeared in Psychological Bulletin in 1993 won, I

7 have to look, I think it is the Robert Chin award for the best

8 paper on sexual abuse for that year, scientific paper.

9 Q. Was the name of that paper The Suggestibility of the

10 Child Witness; An Historical Review and Synthesis?

11 A. That's correct.

12 Q. Have you been certified as an expert witness in a number

13 of jurisdictions?

14 A. I have.

15 Q. Do you recall how many?

16 A. Seven.

17 Q. Did you bring an updated curriculum vitae with you?

18 A. Yes, I have one.

19   MR. WILKA: May I approach the witness, Your Honor?

20   THE COURT: You may.

21

22   (Exhibit A marked For identification.)

23

24 BY MR. WILKA:

25 Q. I am showing you Defendant's Exhibit A, is that your

Page 11

1 updated curriculum vitae?

2 A. Yes.

3   MR. WILKA: We would offer Exhibit A, Your Honor.

4   MR. HOLMES: No objection.

5   THE COURT: Exhibit A is received.

6 BY MR. WILKA:

7 Q. Dr. Bruck, are you aware of literature currently being

8 published or published on recantation of child witnesses?

9 A. Yes, I am.

10 Q. What is meant by a recantation?

11 A. Recantation in its pure form means taking away of a

12 statement, changing it from an assent to a denial.

13 Q. In the context of sexual abuse how would you define a

14 recantation?

15 A. Well, as it is defined in the literature, I don't know if

16 it's ever really defined, it is just used. It refers to the

17 denial of a previous disclosure.

18 Q. When one looks at a recantation then, must one look at

19 the disclosure?

20 A. Unless there is a disclosure, there is nothing to recant.

21 And one must look at the whole, at the recantation in the

22 context of the disclosure, yes.

23 Q. Are you familiar, and again you are familiar with the

24 literature in this field?

25 A. In terms of patterns of disclosure of sexual abuse, yes.

Page 12

1 Q. You have been retained as an expert witness by the

2 defense in this case?

3 A. Yes.

4 Q. What did you review, just briefly, for your testimony

5 today?

6 A. I reviewed, I did a literature search on and reviewed

7 articles that passed certain degrees of scientific scrutiny

8 that examined rates of disclosure of sexual abuse among

9 different kinds of samples of children, and some of those

10 studies in fact contained information on recantation rates.

11 All studies of recantation rates I am pretty sure -- there are

12 studies of disclosures without information on recantation, but

13 there is no studies of recantation without disclosure, so that

14 was really the pie that I looked at. I reviewed articles that

15 appeared in journals that were accessible to the public that

16 passed some minor level of peer acceptance, and I mainly, with

17 one or two exceptions, I focused on articles that had been

18 published since the 1990's. I did that also for scientific

19 reasons.

20 Q. What were the scientific reasons?

21 A. I was concerned about cohort effects. Cohort effects

22 were the first effect that data or trends changed historically,

23 or over a period of time, and this could be due to a whole host

24 of factors. It could be due to methodological differences, so

25 that we become more savvy in terms of our measurements and so

Page 13

1 you want to look at the newer studies. A second possibility
2 really has to do with changes in rates that reflect actual
3 historical changes, interviewing practices. And so in the
4 disclosure/recantation literature, for example, interviewing
5 practices have changed greatly since the 1980's, and I think
6 that the sense that is coming through in the '90's is a much,
7 much better scientifically valid data set. And also there is
8 the real possibility, which is of interest for scientific study
9 but are not for the issues that we want to deal with here, and
10 that is that different kinds of symptoms were being reported in
11 the 1980's than in the 1990's. It's possible we are more
12 sensitive to different kinds of symptoms now, and that we are
13 getting a different pool of children. So I wanted to focus
14 mainly on the studies from the 1990's.
15 Q. In the case at hand, are you aware that there were four
16 child witnesses that are deemed victims at this time?
17 A. Yes.
18 Q. And are you aware that there is a fifth child witness who
19 was not, who did not make a disclosure of sexual abuse?
20 A. Yes.
21 Q. And have you been made aware that all five of these
22 witnesses are now allegedly recanting their accusations of
23 sexual abuse?
24 A. Yes, I am.
25 Q. Now in -- are you familiar with the proposition that

Page 14

1 recantation is a common thing amongst abused children?
2 A. I am familiar with the claim that is made by some people
3 that it is common.
4 Q. Do you agree, or disagree with that claim?
5 A. Well, it depends on what people want to claim is common.
6 Q. What does the science show about that?
7 A. We want to go right in to recantation?
8 Q. Yes.
9 A. Well, I was able to identify a number of studies, I have
10 them here. I think I identified six or seven different
11 published studies in which data are reported on recantation
12 rates of different kinds of samples of children where there is
13 a possibility, evaluation, treatment of sexual abuse,
14 recantation rates, and most of these studies involve
15 substantial numbers of children. The smallest is 65, some of
16 them contain 300, so these are very nice sized samples. The
17 recantation rates, which is based on the number of disclosures,
18 right, varies tremendously. It goes from a low of 3 percent to
19 a high of 27 percent.
20 Q. And what studies are those?
21 A. Okay. Actually I brought as many of them as I could, I
22 have to apologize sometimes for this for not being complete
23 here. I just moved from Montreal to Johns Hopkins and some of
24 my boxes got lost in transit where I had some of these papers.
25 There is one study by Jones and McGraw, 1987. Do you want me

Page 15

1 to tell you what they report the figures were.
2 Q. Yes?
3 A. Nine percent. Sorenson and Snow, one of the more
4 frequently cited studies, 22 percent. Gonzalez, Waterman and
5 Kelly, 27 percent. Gries, Goh and Cavanaugh, 15 percent.
6 Bradley and Wood, 3 percent. Elliott and Briere, 5 percent. I
7 think that is it.
8 Q. Say where there is 25 percent recantation rate, are those
9 amongst children that it has been substantiated there has been
10 abuse?
11 A. It's my professional opinion from carefully reading these
12 studies that there is high doubt that the rates of 25 and 27
13 percent are based upon substantiated cases.
14 Q. And why is that your --
15 A. I don't know what to call these, substantiated cases, or
16 really where these cases have been validated.
17 Q. And why is that?
18 A. What is my opinion based upon?
19 Q. Yes?
20 A. Shall I just talk about two of these studies?
21 Q. Yes?
22 A. These are two studies I chose where data were collected
23 before the 19 -- and these are the ones where one finds these
24 high rates of recantation, and they also are accompanied by
25 high rates of initial denial. And I chose these studies

Page 16

1 because, I decided to include them in this literature review
2 because they are commonly cited among clinicians as empirical
3 proof that sexually abused children don't disclose readily, and
4 that once they disclose they often recant. So we can start
5 with the Gonzalez study to begin with, and this is a study of
6 65 children, and I know the sample because it is described more
7 fully in a book called Beyond Nursery Walls or something, and
8 the sample of children that these people study are ones that
9 are brought in to a clinic for treatment, and the treatment is
10 for satanic and ritualistic abuse. It also turns out that most
11 of these children were in fact alleged victims in McMartin,
12 which was one of the early day care cases that took place in
13 the United States. Some of the other children are from other
14 schools in the area. When McMartin broke, there was a large
15 investigation of a lot of different kinds of nursery schools in
16 that area on the assumption that there was some kind of cult
17 ritualistic abuse going on. A number of nursery schools were
18 in fact closed down and there were a number of children who
19 came to make allegations of abuse. So I have two major
20 problems with this study. The first is that I don't know what
21 substantiated is, we know there were no convictions in
22 McMartin, there were never any confessions. The jurors who saw
23 the transcripts, saw these children being interviewed were,
24 they felt that there was really no evidence on which to convict
25 on, and so this is a group of children who are being studied

Page 17

1 where there is no outside substantiation. The second point is,
2 is that the claims of these children are ones that involved
3 very horrific terrorizing and ritualistic claims such as
4 murder, organized religious rituals, and certainly since 1993
5 there have been a number of very significant reports that have
6 come out including one from the FBI which all have failed to
7 find any evidence what so ever for the kinds of disclosures
8 that came out in cases like McMartin. So the other -- so that
9 is number two. Number three, when I look at the disclosure
10 data for these children, what the authors report in table 3 and
11 4 is the kinds of disclosures that each child made and the
12 number of weeks of therapy in which it took to make the
13 disclosure, and when you, for example, terrorizing acts, 54 --
14 I am sorry, 45 percent of the children in the sample made
15 claims of acts involving abuse of animals, dead bodies,
16 monsters, death of a child, children -- children use of feces
17 or urine. So 45 percent of the sample made these claims, but
18 when you look further down, in fact it looked like, it doesn't
19 look like, I am sorry, it is that it takes eight weeks of
20 treatment in order to get to these claims, and then the next
21 type of claims, ritualistic acts made by 43 percent of the
22 children involved acts involving churches, magic, satanic
23 rituals, and so on, took an average of twenty weeks of therapy
24 to emerge. So on the basis of these all very related points,
25 my conclusion on this paper is that one can look at the rates

Page 18

1 of recantation, but one has to be, think very hard about what
2 are these children actually recanting. Are they recanting
3 something that really happened, and now they are taking it
4 back? Given the evidence we have now on the likelihood of
5 those children's disclosures really happening and on the fact
6 that there was no evidence brought forward at trial, we are
7 left in a very uncertain hole, space about what to make of
8 this. So this is one study where what I think, my conclusion
9 is, is that high rates of recantation are associated with long
10 periods of interviewing children, and not necessarily, does
11 not, in this study does not necessarily, and in fact most
12 probably does not include children with substantiated cases of
13 sexual abuse, but it is often quoted in the literature, not in
14 the literature, in the clinical field.
15 Q. That is the study where there was a 25 percent
16 recantation, right?
17 A. I think this was 27 percent.
18 Q. 27 percent.
19 A. Um-hum, and the other interesting thing that happened in
20 this study was that the claim was that the finding was that 27
21 percent of the children, so it is 27 percent of 68, someone can
22 do the math, and that most of these children then reinstated
23 their earlier disclosures. And when they reinstated the
24 earlier disclosures, what happened was it wasn't just a
25 statement of, you know, I told you it didn't happen but it

Page 19

1 really did. What happened was that the disclosures expanded
2 and there were additional details. So this study provides
3 evidence for a pattern of disclosure that we haven't really
4 talked about, which is why we are doing all these studies, but
5 that it is very hard for children to tell about sexual abuse.
6 When you first ask them they deny, then they kind of dribble
7 out disclosures, they dribble these disclosures back in again,
8 that's called recantation, and then there is reinstatement.
9 This paper is certainly very supportive of that position, but I
10 think that its scientific validity is very poor given the fact
11 that there is huge doubts about the sample. So that is the
12 first study, that's when we get this high rate of 27 percent.
13 The next study is Sorenson and Snow. Now this study has,
14 shares all the same problems.
15   THE COURT: Which one is this?
16   THE WITNESS: The second study?
17   THE COURT: Yes.
18   THE WITNESS: It is called How Children Tell: The
19 Process of Disclosure in Child Sexual Abuse by Teena Sorenson
20 and Barbara Snow, and this was published in 1991. Again I made
21 an exception in including this in my review of the literature,
22 because it is something that I see quoted all the time, and I
23 see used in the courtroom, and as evidence again of the rates
24 of initial denial and significant rates of recantation.
25 BY MR. WILKA:

Page 20

1 Q. With the Sorenson and Snow article, what, you stated you
2 have the same problems with the scientific validity as you did
3 the first article?
4 A. Very similar problems.
5 Q. And just briefly what are they -- first of all, what was
6 the percent of disclosure in Sorenson and Snow?
7 A. According to Sorenson and Snow they all disclosed at some
8 point.
9 Q. Recantation, excuse me?
10 A. Recantation, 22 percent, and then they say that 93
11 percent reaffirm. So again you have this dribbling out, this
12 dribbling back in, this dribbling back out again.
13 Q. What is wrong with the science of this article?
14 A. Well, if you read the paper by itself, it looks pretty
15 okay, except that one is not really sure about why the sample
16 was selected that was selected. But now let's start to go
17 through the problems. The first problem which relates to every
18 other one is that they pick from their case load of 600
19 children who they have evaluated and treated for sexual abuse,
20 they selected 116 children, and it is not clear why they
21 selected those children. Maybe they selected them because they
22 showed the pattern, there is no explanation in the paper. The
23 second thing is, is that these are children that they treated
24 and evaluated. And in order to then come to understand what
25 the sample is all about, one has to know something about the

Page 21

1 history of these mental health professionals, and the kinds of
2 samples that they have treated and evaluated in the past. In a
3 previous year these same authors published an article, I don't
4 have it with me, on ritualistic abuse. And this article
5 described, I am sorry, I just don't have the numbers with me,
6 because that was in my suitcase that is not here. They
7 described approximately 30 to 40 cases involving ritualistic
8 abuse that they had assessed and evaluated over the past couple
9 of years. We know something of some of those cases because
10 they are in the case literature and have come up on appeal. So
11 just by --
12   MR. SEILER: I object to the testimony regarding
13 ritualistic abuse. There is no evidence in the record that any
14 of that was present in this particular case, and I think it is
15 irrelevant for the purposes of the issue of recantation which
16 this Court in its order indicates we need to focus on.
17   THE COURT: The objection is overruled, because I
18 think that the point that the witness was getting to, as I
19 understood it, was that this other article caused her in her
20 own opinion to have some doubt about these authors, that's what
21 I guessed it was about, not about the ritualistic abuse itself.
22 For that reason, I mean that's where you are going, the
23 objection is overruled.
24   THE WITNESS: I am sorry to interrupt and talk when I
25 shouldn't have.

Page 22

1   THE COURT: That's alright.
2 A. I am not, this is not about ritualistic abuse, and I
3 don't want to make any claims about that, but just simply that
4 when you study, when people come to make claims about the
5 science of recantation and it is based upon clinicians who have
6 samples of these children in the study and themselves have
7 believed that this has happened, I think that you have to
8 reconsider the validity or the reliability of their statistics,
9 nothing really to do with the ritualistic abuse. So Sorenson
10 and Snow were known to treat these kinds of cases to garner
11 them, and a number of these cases were included in the 116 that
12 are in the paper. The second problem again is when you have
13 studies that are based upon treatment and evaluation of one or
14 two people, then one wants to know something about treatment or
15 evaluation of those people. Most of the other studies that I
16 reviewed came from larger clinics, CPS agencies where there
17 were lots of different people interviewing children, and so
18 even though there might have been uniformally standard
19 interviewing practices that were questionable, at least, you
20 know, the rates would not reflect the practices of one or two
21 people. In several appeals we know that Barbara Snow testified
22 that she never believed children when they said it didn't
23 happen. And it is in the record, there are several cases where
24 she said this, and she was firmly castigated by an Appeals
25 Judge for this opinion and for being an expert in terms of the

Page 23

1 reliability of these children's allegations. As a result, we
2 also know that she was deliberately fed information by the
3 police, because they began to suspect that --
4   MR. SEILER: I object again, I think it is irrelevant
5 in terms of what is before the Court in terms of whether the
6 police, to question the scientific validity and attack the
7 authors.
8   THE COURT: I am going to let the witness go on, I am
9 going to overrule your objection. I would say that when one
10 talks about when an Appeal Court Judge did this or that, it's
11 always more impressive for the Court when I actually have the
12 citation, but go ahead.
13   THE WITNESS: Yes. Hadfield, was the citation, but I
14 am sorry I don't have it. Anyway, I don't have to continue on
15 this vein, I feel quite uncomfortable about doing it.
16   THE COURT: Also the assassination without the
17 documents in hand.
18   THE WITNESS: Right. I do have the documents, but I
19 think the point should be made that this is not a sample of
20 substantiated cases that would pass muster today, and there is
21 lots and lots of concern about the kinds of disclosures that
22 these children made and about the validity of their
23 disclosures, and therefore when we talk about recantation
24 rates, in this study one wonders what the children are actually
25 recanting.

Page 24

1 BY MR. WILKA:
2 Q. After the Sorenson and Snow what article did you review?
3 A. Well, then we get into the newer studies, and I think
4 that the newer studies are characterized by a number of points.
5 The first is that the samples are usually bigger. The second
6 is that the children do come from clinics or agencies where
7 there have been a number of different kinds of interviewers.
8 And the third is, is that in most, in all but one of the
9 studies which I cited in terms of recantation rates, the
10 authors classify the children in terms of their degree of
11 certainty that abuse had actually happened. So, and this is
12 based upon their review of the records and the interviews and
13 the medical evidence and so on. The children are classified
14 depending on the study as either, you know, high probability of
15 abuse, to improbable, to possible. And others such as the
16 Bradley and Wood study only selected cases from CPS which were
17 substantiated by CPS.
18   THE COURT: What is CPS?
19 A. I am sorry, Child Protection Services. Now when one
20 looks at these studies, what one finds is that the rates of
21 recantation are much, much lower, and in fact these rates of
22 recantation are based upon criteria of substantiation that
23 would probably pass muster by most people. These rates, as I
24 cited before, 3 per cent Bradley and Wood, that was the
25 Child Protection Service agency. Elliott and Briere, 5 percent

Page 25

1 of their samples with clear diagnoses of abuse recanted. Jones
2 and McGraw in 1967, their sample was not as well defined, but
3 again it was cases reported to Denver for the year of nineteen
4 eighty something, and 9 percent of those cases recanted.
5 Finally there is one study that I think actually has a number
6 of problems, because they don't talk about criteria for
7 including the children or whether or not they were
8 substantiated, and furthermore, the description of how the
9 interviews went make it seem as though these were quite
10 suggestive interviews, but nevertheless, in this study the rate
11 is 15 percent.
12 Q. Which study was that?
13 A. This is Gries, G-R-I-E-S.
14 Q. In the Bradley and Wood study how many children were in
15 the sample?
16 A. Two hundred thirty-four.
17 Q. And in the Elliott study?
18 A. That was a very big one. It started off -- it was around
19 400. I am coming up to it, sorry. 320. Okay, well, they
20 started off with a sample of 400, and then removed 79 who were
21 unclear, and that was a sample of 320 left.
22 Q. In the Jones study?
23 A. That was 500 plus.
24 Q. How about the Gries?
25 A. Ninety-six.

Page 26

1 Q. In any of these studies where we have the 3 percent, the
2 5 percent or the 15 percent is there any data about the
3 reinstatement rates?
4 A. The only two studies that provide data on reinstatement
5 are the Sorenson and Snow, and the Gonzalez study, and there
6 they state that most of the children who recanted reinstated.
7 Q. If I understand you correctly, Doctor, the Bradley and
8 Wood, the Elliott, the Jones and Gries studies, put it in
9 layman's terms, you find the science of about how they went
10 about these studies to be superior to that of Sorenson and Snow
11 and Gonzalez?
12 A. The Gries study I have more concerns about. The Bradley
13 and Wood, and the Elliott and Briere I think are well written,
14 I think that they present a lot of data for the reader to
15 consume or to get to know the paper, and I think that they are
16 very fair in terms of discussing what actually the sample is
17 all about. The Jones and McGraw study, the 9 percent, you
18 know, as the studies get older they become a little bit more
19 problematic, only because I think that standards of scientific
20 reporting have changed over the years, but the 9 percent is
21 just based on their county, and it is the same kind of sample
22 that Bradley and Wood used where they got their 3 percent, so
23 the figures are similar.
24 Q. In the instant case again you have been made aware that
25 it is alleged that 100 percent of the child witnesses had

Page 27

1 recanted?
2 A. That's correct.
3 Q. And that is five witnesses?
4 A. That's correct.
5 Q. Based even upon the Gonzalez study, what would the
6 probability be, based even just upon the Gonzalez study of 100
7 percent, of five universal recantations?
8 A. Well, I did the math last night on a piece of paper, and
9 just to make it easy, because I didn't have my calculator, I
10 used a 25 percent recantation rate, and so what you do is that
11 the rate, the probability of a child recanting is one out of
12 four, and the probability of two children recanting is going to
13 be one out of four times one out of four. So if you multiply
14 these point two five percent by five, or the factor of five, it
15 is one in a thousand. So you go to 27 percent, it is probably
16 going to be one in nine hundred the probability.
17 Q. With the Bradley and Wood study that was performed by
18 Child Protection Services?
19 A. Right.
20 Q. If you have one, have you performed that calculation?
21 A. No. The other one I did is I tried to be -- let's take
22 the rest of the ones that are left, the 3, 5, 9 and 15. I sort
23 of ballparked it an average rate might be 10 percent. If you
24 do 10 percent, then it is one out of a hundred thousand.
25 Q. One in one hundred thousand would be the probability?

Page 28

1 A. Yes, unless I did it wrong.
2 Q. Are you aware that it has been alleged that family
3 pressures and social pressures come in to play to bring about
4 recantation?
5 A. In the scientific literature?
6 Q. First of all, have you been made aware that that has been
7 alleged in this case?
8 A. Yes.
9 Q. What does the scientific literature say about that?
10 A. Well, I couldn't really find very much.
11   THE COURT: I am sorry, you can't put your hand over
12 your mouth because we can't hear you.
13 A. I couldn't find very much about recantation and the
14 factors associated with recantation. The only factor that I
15 found in my search that was related was that high recantation
16 is associated with a lot of previous interviewing, and with
17 dubious initial allegations, that's from the scientific
18 literature. In terms of recantations and family pressure, I
19 really couldn't find anything.
20 Q. So if a claim was made that -- if the claim is made that
21 recantations largely come about due to social and family
22 pressure, has that scientific technique or that claim been
23 tested?
24 A. Not to my knowledge.
25 Q. And this claim of social or family pressure, has it been

Page 29

1 subject to a peer review and publication?
2 A. In terms of recantation?
3 Q. In terms of the family pressure, yes.
4 A. Not to my knowledge.
5 Q. Are there any known rates of error in existence of
6 control standards when one talks about claims that family
7 pressure and social pressure bring about recantation?
8 A. Not to my knowledge.
9 Q. And then the last question I have to ask, is that
10 generally accepted in the scientific community?
11 A. Not to my knowledge.
12 MR. WILKA: If I may have one moment, Your Honor.
13 THE COURT: Certainly.
14 BY MR. WILKA:
15 Q. Are you familiar with an individual by the name of
16 Dr. Ralph Underwager?
17 A. Yes, I know his name.
18 Q. And did you review the, are you aware that I believe in
19 1999 that taped interviews of the children with Dr. Underwager
20 were made?
21 A. I was told that, yes.
22 Q. Did you review those?
23 A. I did not.
24 Q. And why is that?
25 A. Well, I was asked to talk about recantation, and my

Page 30

1 understanding was that these children's first recantation was
2 not during that interview, that it was several years previous
3 to that, and I just didn't know what good it would serve, you
4 know, I didn't think that was an efficient use of my time.
5 Q. And are you aware that the government, a possible
6 government witness, Dr. Mindy Mitnick was critical of
7 Dr. Underwager's interviewing techniques?
8 A. Yes, I actually read her report.
9 Q. And do you have any problem with her report?
10 A. Well, I haven't seen the tapes, but her report seems to
11 me to be fair. If those things actually happened on the tape
12 as she reported them, I think that she was correct in talking
13 about these breaking of common standards and in terms of her
14 comment of the quality of that kind of interview, but I haven't
15 seen the tapes. So if that is what it is.
16 Q. Is there any significance -- strike that.
17 Are you aware that it is alleged that the recantations took
18 place while the children were still under the custody of the
19 Indian Social Services?
20 A. Yes.
21 Q. And are you aware that it has been alleged that the
22 recantations have remained unchanged over the past number of
23 years?
24 A. Yes.
25 Q. Do you attach any significance to that?

Page 31

1 MR. SEILER: I object, inadequate foundation.
2 THE COURT: Well, we will see about the foundation,
3 the question as stated, it is alleged, we will see about that,
4 but I consider it a hypothetical question. We will see if the
5 foundation meets up with the hypothetical. If it doesn't in
6 subsequent proof, then the opinion doesn't mean anything, but
7 it is a hypothetical question, you can answer on the basis of
8 that hypothetical.
9 A. Well, based on very few reports we have in the literature
10 it is my understanding that when children recant, not making
11 any judgment about what the recantation means, whether it is a
12 real take away, or telling the truth, most of them reinstate,
13 they come back and say didn't mean to say that, it really
14 happened.
15 Q. Does the literature say anything as to how soon the
16 children would reinstate?
17 A. Not to my knowledge.
18 MR. WILKA: That's all I have for this direct, Your
19 Honor.
20 THE COURT: Cross.
21 MR. SEILER: Thank you, Your Honor.
22 THE COURT: Yes.
23 CROSS EXAMINATION BY MR. SEILER:
24 Q. Ms. Bruck, you are currently an associate professor at
25 Johns Hopkins University?

Page 32

1 A. That's right.
2 Q. It's a true statement, isn't it, that most of your work
3 including your articles has been done or accomplished in
4 Canada?
5 A. Yes, yes.
6 Q. Both your Masters and Ph.D. were obtained from a Canadian
7 University?
8 A. Yes.
9 Q. And just so I am clear, in terms of the ranking of
10 professors, associate professor is that the lowest level of
11 professor?
12 A. No.
13 Q. There is something below that?
14 A. Instructor and assistant below an associate.
15 Q. Pardon me?
16 A. There is instructor, assistant, associate, full.
17 Q. And are you still in adjunct professor at McGill
18 University in Canada, then?
19 A. That's an honorary position. When I left McGill I was a
20 full professor, and in order for me to be able to return and
21 have a place to work at different times and to continue my work
22 there, I was given the appointment as adjunct professor.
23 Q. Your postgraduate study is in experimental psychology?
24 A. That's true.
25 Q. You are not licensed in any state or country to practice

Page 33

1 psychology, are you?

2 A. No, I am not.

3 Q. You are not licensed or qualified to do child sex abuse

4 examinations or interviews, are you?

5 A. No.

6 Q. Not licensed as a clinical psychologist?

7 A. No, I am not.

8 Q. Throughout the course of your career you have not

9 conducted one child sexual abuse examination in a clinical

10 setting?

11 A. That's correct.

12 Q. All of your experiments and all of your opinions are

13 based upon basically a review of the literature?

14 A. That I did today?

15 Q. Generally and today?

16 A. Well, a lot of it is based on research that I have done.

17 Q. You are not an expert on child sexual abuse in terms of

18 the symptoms, or the findings, or anything like that, are you?

19 A. Well, I am not a clinician, but I am an expert in terms

20 of the scientific literature.

21 Q. Well, you are an expert because you know what literature

22 is out there, that's what an experimental psychologist does, it

23 reviews literature, isn't that correct?

24 A. No, not necessarily. Experimental psychologist is one

25 who conducts studies and publishes them.

Page 34

1 Q. All of your work and all of your studies have been done

2 in a quote ivory tower setting, you have never done anything

3 out in the field with victims of child sexual abuse?

4 A. That's correct.

5 Q. And the emphasis of your background is more the language

6 and linguistics, isn't it, than child sexual abuse?

7 A. My background is in child development and developmental

8 psychology.

9 Q. Well, your dissertation for your Ph.D. was in social

10 class differences in children's language, wasn't it?

11 A. Yes, it was, 1972.

12 Q. When I review some of these peer reviewed scientific

13 articles, the overwhelming majority seem to deal with for

14 French immersion programs, comparison of the effects of the

15 instruction of English readings at different levels, isn't that

16 correct?

17 A. Well, the early part of my career, yes.

18 Q. I mean you list as an article for example Fortysomething:

19 Recognizing faces at one's 25th reunion?

20 A. Yes. That was --

21 Q. That's not much of a scientific study, is it?

22   MR. WILKA: Objection, argumentative, Your Honor.

23   THE COURT: Overruled.

24 A. It wasn't a scientific study, it was a study on face

25 recognition and the degree to which people could recognize

Page 35

1 people that they hadn't seen each other for a long time, and it

2 was published in a peer reviewed journal, and it in fact

3 addressed important forensic issues.

4 BY MR. SEILER:

5 Q. Another article The syllable's role in the processing of

6 spoken English, that's correct?

7 A. One of my fields of expertise is speech perception,

8 bilingualism. It is associated with my work in learning

9 disabilities and dyslexia, and it was a field that I was very

10 active in.

11 Q. And you talked I think on direct examination about being

12 an expert in seven jurisdictions, those were all State Court

13 jurisdictions, were they not?

14 A. I believe so.

15 Q. So when you say in your professional accomplishments that

16 you have worked in federal courts, you haven't been certified

17 as an expert witness in any federal court, have you?

18 A. Not to my -- I don't think so.

19 Q. So when you have federal courts on the last page of your

20 resume, that's kind of a misnomer, isn't it?

21 A. Well, you know, I have to go talk to the lawyers who told

22 me how to write my resume, but I think that some of the amicus

23 briefs that I wrote actually were written for federal court.

24 Q. You don't know that, do you?

25 A. I do know that.

Page 36

1 Q. And your thirteen page resume here is based on in part

2 work that you have done with graduate students in terms of like

3 supervising or mentoring them, isn't that correct?

4 A. Is that the CV that you have, okay.

5 Q. It isn't dated, the one that I have.

6 A. That's not usually the one I give out for legal purposes,

7 but anyway, you have it, that's my full CV.

8 Q. So that's a correct statement, isn't it?

9 A. That's a very important part of my professional

10 appointment.

11 Q. That's right, and that's kind of what an experimental

12 psychologist does, too, isn't it, it trains students to be

13 researchers?

14 A. If you are a member of the university, yes.

15 Q. With respect to Johns Hopkins, they are currently in some

16 trouble in terms of their research program as far as the

17 federal government has cut off all funding to Johns Hopkins,

18 hasn't it?

19 A. That's not true.

20 Q. How about the psychology department, as I understand it

21 they are impacted by the cut off of funding including your boss

22 Paul McHugh?

23 A. I haven't heard of any of that. My understanding is that

24 it was a really unfortunate, terrible situation in which a

25 human subject died for participation in an asthma study, and

Page 37

1 this happened in May, and there was an internal investigation.
2 And some time in the summer the government came along and said
3 we are closing down all medical research in the hospital until
4 you can clear this up. And then within two or three days the
5 ban was lifted, and they have now, just released, my
6 understanding is, an internal and external report on how
7 medical research will undergo more stringent ethical, you know,
8 review.
9 Q. Ethical review?
10 A. Not ethical.
11 Q. Isn't that what you just said?
12 A. No, I made a mistake.
13 Q. You made a mistake?
14 A. It really has to do with informed consent, risks of
15 research.
16 Q. So the point is, Ms. Bruck, that there were some
17 inappropriate, sloppy, and even potentially unethical research
18 projects that were going on at Johns Hopkins University that
19 resulted in the death of an individual?
20   MR. WILKA: I object to the form of the question,
21 assuming facts not in evidence, and also the relevance to the
22 testimony at hand, Your Honor.
23   THE COURT: Well, it's cross examination, overruled.
24 The witness can answer.
25 A. You know, I know that there was one death due to research

Page 38

1 the last thirty years at Hopkins.
2 BY MR. SEILER:
3 Q. Let's talk about who hired you at the department of
4 psychology at Johns Hopkins, Paul McHugh?
5 A. I am not in psychology, I am in psychiatry.
6 Q. Who hired you in psychiatry?
7 A. Dr. McHugh.
8 Q. Dr. McHugh is a member of the FMSF, False Memory Syndrome
9 Foundation, isn't he?
10 A. I don't know.
11 Q. That's the same organization that Mr. Underwager was a
12 member of the board of directors of, isn't that correct?
13   MR. WILKA: Your Honor, the witness testified she
14 doesn't know what her boss does on nights and weekends.
15   THE COURT: This is a different question, overruled.
16 BY MR. SEILER:
17 Q. Isn't it true that Mr. Underwager was an original member
18 of the board of directors of the FMSF?
19 A. Possible, I don't know.
20 Q. I thought on direct examination you indicated in response
21 to a question that you were familiar with Ralph Underwager?
22 A. I know who he is.
23 Q. In fact, you cited his work in your book?
24 A. Did we?
25 Q. Page 165.

Page 39

1 A. Okay.
2 Q. Most of his work has been discredited based on some views
3 he has taken with respect to suggestibility, memory,
4 pedophiles, and similar subjects, isn't that correct?
5 A. I don't know if his work has been discredited. What
6 work?
7 Q. So you don't know?
8 A. Not really.
9 Q. You know Mr. Underwager's views on pedophilia?
10 A. I have read the controversy, yes.
11 Q. And as a result didn't he, was asked to resign from the
12 FMSF board of directors?
13 A. It's possible.
14 Q. Do you agree that with his views on pedophilia that it is
15 just a natural expression of God's love in a sense?
16 A. Well, that's my personal opinion, not a professional
17 opinion, but I don't agree with him.
18 Q. You don't agree with him?
19 A. I don't agree with him, no.
20 Q. Were you aware that he was involved in a lawsuit where he
21 sued a person because they were critical of his work?
22   MR. WILKA: Now, Your Honor, I am going to object.
23 We are not here talking about Dr. Underwager, we are here
24 talking about recantation.
25   THE COURT: Well, except that to an extent we are

Page 40

1 here talking about Underwager, because as a part of getting
2 ready for this hearing I have reviewed all of his interviews,
3 and so in a sense we are, so I am going to allow that. If this
4 were just on the bare record of what the witness has testified
5 to, I would sustain it, but Dr. Underwager is in a sense
6 involved since he was in the interviews that were presented to
7 me as a part of the motion. So it is overruled for that
8 reason.
9 BY MR. SEILER:
10 Q. You remember the question?
11 A. No.
12
13   (Whereupon, the requested portion of the Record was
14   read by the Reporter.)
15
16 A. Is this the one where he was called, he lost because he
17 was called a public figure or something?
18 BY MR. SEILER:
19 Q. Are you aware of that lawsuit brought in 1994 by him and
20 his wife against psychologist Anna Salter, S-A-L-T-E-R,
21 defamation because she was critical of his work?
22 A. Her name is Anna Salter, S-A-L-T-E-R. I didn't know she
23 was involved in it, I knew something about the case. Can I
24 just make a general comment about --
25 Q. No, just answer the questions, please, Ma'am.

Page 41

1 A. Okay.

2 Q. In fact, Ms. Salter indicated that their books have not
3 been well received in the medical and scientific press, were
4 you aware of that?

5 A. No.

6 Q. And review of the, first in the Journal of the American
7 Medical Association concluded that the authors took a one sided
8 approach, that they simply misstated their conclusions, they
9 used a quotation out of context, they made unsupported
10 statements, some of which were probably untrue and others
11 simply unprovable. Were you aware that she made those comments
12 about Ralph Underwager's works?

13 A. No.

14 Q. And he lost the lawsuit, didn't he?

15 A. I guess.

16 Q. I am not sure when you said it was a personal opinion,
17 when Mr. Underwager said pedophiles can boldly and courageously
18 affirm what they choose with boldness, they can say I believe
19 this is in fact part of God's will, do you agree with that,
20 that pedophilia is part of God's will?

21 A. I don't know what God's will is, but I mean no, I don't
22 support pedophilia, and I don't support any statements that try
23 to rationalize it by going to a greater deity. And he
24 certainly was extricated, or isolated, or thrown out of any
25 community because of those statements.

Page 42

1 Q. How about are you familiar with James Randi, R-A-N-D-I, a
2 magician known as the Amazing Randi?

3 A. The Amazing Randi. Keep going.

4 Q. You recall, you know him, apparently also a member of the
5 FMSF board of directors of which your boss is also a member?

6 A. No.

7 Q. He is involved in a lawsuit in which his opponent
8 introduced a tape of sexually explicit telephone conversations
9 Randi had with teen-age boys.

10   MR. WILKA: I am going to object, because she doesn't
11 know anything about this person.

12   THE COURT: Sustained.

13 A. I am not a member of FMSF, and I am not involved in their
14 politics and I am not involved in their issues, so I really
15 don't know very much about that organization.

16 BY MR. SEILER:

17 Q. On direct examination you talked about and held out I
18 think as one of your more prouder accomplishments your
19 involvement recently in the writing of a book Jeopardy in the
20 Courtroom: A scientific analysis of children's testimony, you
21 remember that?

22 A. I said I wrote the book, yes.

23 Q. I assume you are proud of that work?

24 A. Yes.

25 Q. Isn't it a true statement, I think that Mr. CeCe is an

Page 43

1 expert in the field and you are maybe his protege, he allowed
2 you initially early on in your career to cooperate with him on
3 some works and now you have written this book together?

4 A. Well, you should ask him that question.

5 Q. I am asking you.

6 A. That's not my understanding.

7 Q. You consider yourself on an equal level with him?

8 A. At least.

9 Q. Oh, higher?

10 A. At times, depending on the project we are working on,
11 yes.

12 Q. In what respect?

13 A. What respect what?

14 Q. In what respect do you consider yourself quote higher
15 than he is?

16 A. In terms of the responsibility we take for different
17 projects, on knowledge about different areas. You know, when
18 you have a colleague, you don't really think about, if it is a
19 working relationship, you don't really think about who is
20 higher or who is lower, you just split the work and you do it.

21 Q. Well, do you agree with his statement that he made on
22 Nightline that you have to work at creating false memories in
23 children, that's what he said on Nightline during the Nightline
24 interview, isn't that right?

25 A. I have heard, I know that he said that, yes.

Page 44

1 Q. Would you like to see the transcript of this Nightline
2 interview?

3 A. No.

4 Q. That's what he said on Nightline, right, you have to work
5 at creating false memories in children?

6 A. Okay.

7 Q. You agree with that?

8 A. No, I don't.

9 Q. Do you think it just happens routinely?

10 A. Okay, can you define false memories for me?

11 Q. So in any event, you disagree with your colleague, your
12 fellow author here, Steven CeCe, on his conclusion about
13 creating false memories in children?

14 A. First of all, that statement was not made in a scientific
15 venue, it was made to the media, and a situation in which he
16 felt incredibly uncomfortable, and was pushed in to making that
17 statement, as it turns out.

18 Q. So you are blaming the media that he made that statement,
19 is that what you are saying?

20   MR. WILKA: I object, we are not here talking about
21 Steve CeCe's interview on Nightline.

22   THE COURT: Overruled.

23 BY MR. SEILER:

24 Q. You are blaming the media for that statement?

25 A. You should ask Dr. CeCe about why he made that statement.

Page 45

1 Q. I note in reviewing your book that on the cover of your
2 book you put in fact a recreation of the Salem, Massachusetts
3 witch trials as the creation on the cover of your book?
4 A. That's incorrect.
5 Q. What does that depict then?
6 A. That is a picture called when was the last time you saw
7 your father, it is a 19th century painting done in England, and
8 it recreates the Cromwellian days when children would be
9 questioned by the round heads about where their father's were.
10 Q. You do cite, however, the Salem, Massachusetts witch
11 trials in your book, do you not?
12 A. Yes.
13 Q. And your book has been criticized in certain professional
14 journals concerning the approach that you took to research in
15 your book, hasn't it?
16 A. You have to read it to me.
17 Q. You are not aware of any criticism of your book?
18 A. I know that there is, has been some criticism, yes.
19 Q. And the criticism has to do with your research methods,
20 doesn't it?
21 A. I don't think the criticism has to do with our research
22 methods.
23 Q. What does the criticism have to do with then?
24 A. Well, I can't talk about our book, but I can talk about
25 the kinds of criticism that are generally leveled against our

Page 46

1 writings and those of many of our other colleagues in the
2 field.
3 Q. You think you are being unfairly criticized by colleagues
4 in your field, is that what you are saying?
5 A. I don't think I am criticized by colleagues in my field.
6 Q. They criticize your work?
7 A. If you could just, you know, tell me who it is, where it
8 appeared, what it is, I could talk about it.
9 Q. I am asking you what you know about the criticism of the
10 work by your colleagues?
11   MR. WILKA: Your Honor, I have to ask that there be
12 more foundation to bring up a specific article as opposed to
13 just kind of a general, nebulous bad feeling by certain
14 individuals allegedly about Dr. Bruck's work.
15   THE COURT: Overruled. I will tell you why. Because
16 when you write something, I know, at least I certainly haven't
17 forgotten any negative comment about anything I have written,
18 and you don't have to have as a cross examiner every document
19 there ready to nail somebody with it. I think it is fair cross
20 examination to ask somebody about negative criticism even
21 though you may not have all of them sitting right there in
22 front of you, that's the reason I am overruling your objection.
23 A. I think that's a major criticism of our work from certain
24 factors, certain areas has been that we have devoted too much
25 time to looking at the frailties of children's reporting, and

Page 47

1 have failed to include relevant, we have failed to in fact
2 include literature on how good children's memories actually
3 are. That has been one of the pervasive claims.
4 Q. That's true, isn't it, in terms of your book?
5 A. Yes, but our book was not --
6 Q. That's true in terms of your book? The answer is yes?
7 A. Our book was written to highlight the weaknesses of
8 children's memory, and the kinds of circumstances that those
9 things occur in, yes.
10 Q. You admit in the preface to the book that it is biased,
11 don't you?
12 A. Well, I have heard this one before from prosecutors, so I
13 think that there is a misinterpretation in terms of our use of
14 the word bias.
15 Q. You use the word bias in the preface to your book, don't
16 you?
17 A. We use the word bias, but we didn't use it in terms of
18 our interpretation of the literature, but we used it in terms
19 of the issues and the questions that we wanted to ask.
20 Q. I think this is a quote from your preface, at the outset,
21 we wish to acknowledge some of the biases in this book.
22 A. Um-hum.
23 Q. That's correct, isn't it? These biases become
24 immediately evident in our selection of the seven actual cases
25 presented. In six of the cases there are reasons to be

Page 48

1 skeptical about the reliability of the children's reports. So
2 you admit bias to the information, to the case studies that you
3 selected in your book, isn't that correct?
4 A. Yes, we selected --
5 Q. Okay, thank you.
6 A. Yes.
7 Q. You do also say in the preface to your book that we focus
8 disproportionately on cases where the children's testimony is
9 questionable?
10 A. That's correct.
11 Q. You don't go on the positive side and look at cases where
12 children's testimony has been reliable, instead you choose case
13 studies that prove it was unreliable, isn't that correct?
14 A. Well, we did that, one reason was we said because it is
15 very hard to get the records of, in fact it's impossible to get
16 the records.
17 Q. I understand why you say you did it, my point is you did
18 it, right?
19 A. We did it. In our revision of the book.
20 Q. Okay, so you chose case studies that were deliberately
21 focused disproportionately on cases where there were children's
22 testimony was questionable, and then you make the statement,
23 quote, is it because we believe that in the vast majority of
24 cases in which children's testify their testimony is tainted?
25 Our answer to this question is a resounding no, close quote.

Page 49

1 A. That's correct.

2 Q. So you do admit that in the vast majority of cases in
3 which children, in which children testify, they testify
4 truthfully and accurately, and there are no questions
5 concerning the tainting of their testimony?

6 A. If, depending upon the circumstances in which they are
7 questioned.

8 Q. And that's what you say in the preface to your book,
9 right?

10 A. Yes.

11 Q. But when you refer to your bias, you basically bury the
12 bias in the preface where only a careful reader would be able
13 to pick it out, you don't put it in the actual body of the
14 book, isn't that correct?

15 A. I disagree.

16 Q. Well --

17 A. I think our interpretation of the case studies in light
18 of the scientific data we try to hedge, we try to bring up
19 different kinds of hypotheses.

20 Q. You try to hedge, what does that mean?

21 A. We don't say this is definitely what happened, what we
22 say is it's possible.

23 Q. So you are hedging your research in this book.

24 A. Well, our research doesn't make any claims about the
25 truth or accuracy of any one child's statements in an actual

Page 50

1 case.

2 Q. Your book and your research doesn't make any claims about
3 the truthfulness or accuracy of a child's testimony in any
4 particular case?

5 A. Of any one specific child.

6 Q. Well, when you talk about bias, there is no subheading,
7 there is no bold or out sized type, no capitalization, no
8 reference to the index on the bias, it is just buried in the
9 preface, isn't that right?

10 A. I don't know. I would disagree. I would think that when
11 you read the book, that our interpretations are even handed.
12 that we say on the one hand it could be this, on the other hand
13 it could be this, it could be this, and we try to present the
14 scientific literature to substantiate some of these challenges.

15 Q. That's why you say you hedge?

16 A. What I meant by hedge was we never directly come out and
17 say this child definitely got it right and this child
18 definitely got it wrong.

19 Q. You do make two additional caveats in your book, you
20 indicate at page 82, for example, the materials we have
21 reviewed may not be representative of many of the interviews
22 carried out with children in forensic or therapeutic
23 situations, right?

24 A. That's true, but since that's been written we know a lot
25 more about the representativeness of these materials.

Page 51

1 Q. Well, it's in your book, isn't it, that they are not --

2 A. The book is written in 1995. published in 1995, it was
3 put to bed in 1994. At that point that was our opinion. It is
4 for a lot of these reasons we are now in the process of
5 revising this book.

6 Q. Again you took cases where the children's testimony
7 appeared suggestive, and that's what you put in your book?

8 A. No.

9 Q. That's what your book says, you go on to explain that the
10 interviews that came to your attention are those that appear
11 suggestive.

12 A. I guess those are the cases that came to our -- we were
13 brought, in most of these cases, one of us or some of us had
14 some involvement, and the involvement was because the attorneys
15 asked us to review materials that they felt were suggestive.

16 Q. But those were the case studies you picked for your book,
17 the suggestive ones?

18 A. Exactly. I mean at that time we really hadn't been asked
19 to review non-suggestive materials.

20 Q. The second caveat you make in your book is the
21 descriptions are not based on a quantitative analysis of all of
22 the interviews we have reviewed, right?

23 A. That is true.

24 Q. The data that you presented, your descriptions, you
25 didn't count the number of times that each type of the element

Page 52

1 occurs in an interview?

2 A. That's correct.

3 Q. That's at page 82 of your book, isn't it?

4 A. That's correct.

5 Q. And it is a fair statement that this is a basic violation
6 of scientific procedure in terms of not quantifying the type or
7 times each element occurs?

8 A. That's incorrect.

9 Q. Well, counting ensures objectivity, doesn't it?

10 A. Our research --

11 Q. Doesn't counting insure objectivity?

12   MR. WILKA: I ask the witness be allowed to answer
13 the question.

14   THE COURT: The question I think is outstanding.

15 A. The case literature was not the object of our scientific
16 study.

17 BY MR. SEILER:

18 Q. By using descriptive data instead of counting, or
19 empirical data, you got to add your own biases and opinions as
20 opposed to just counting in an empirical fashion, isn't that
21 correct?

22 A. I disagree.

23 Q. You disagree with the fact that counting insures
24 objectivity in terms of any kind of scientific analysis?

25 A. I disagree that we were attempting to do a scientific

Page 53

1 analysis of these cases.

2 Q. So you weren't trying to do a scientific analysis of the
3 cases, okay. You were just presenting that in these seven
4 cases which you picked because they were suggestive, you
5 weren't doing a scientific analysis?

6 A. We used these cases as an example of how science can
7 inform issues that come into the courtroom.

8 Q. But Ms. Bruck, isn't that misleading, didn't you try to
9 create an impression that the use of these suggestive type
10 interviews was more wide spread than it is, and that's why you
11 close those seven cases instead of including cases where there
12 was not suggestibility?

13   MR. WILKA: Your Honor, I will get back to the
14 compound form of that question later, but first I would ask
15 that the witness be allowed to answer her question before the
16 next question comes.

17   THE COURT: That's right. I don't know that the
18 witness had finished her last answer, and she is entitled to
19 that courtesy, so I want it accorded to her.

20 A. First the purpose of our book was to present the
21 scientific literature at it stands in terms of suggestibility.
22 The purpose of our book was not to write a book on the strength
23 of children's memories. That has been covered by a number of
24 other authors in a number of different ways. The purpose of
25 our book was to address issues that have come up in previous

Page 54

1 cases that involved questions of the accuracy of children's
2 statements when there is suggestive interviewing practices, and
3 we selected cases where there were suggestive interviewing
4 practices, and display examples of those practices in the book.
5 We didn't go through and say how many times each of these
6 things occurred for several reasons. One is that our research
7 is not involved counting or dissecting in a quantitative way
8 these interviews. Second of all, even if we did count, it
9 would be imprecise because we would never have the total
10 universe of all the interviews that were done with those
11 children. And so we have used these as examples of information
12 that is available to the Court, and what the scientific
13 evidence has to say about this. I mean, you know, I mean is
14 there any concern about using these practices based upon what
15 we know about science, and that is simply what the book was
16 about.

17 Q. The book was simply about the fact that there was a
18 concern about interviewing practices, is that what you are
19 saying?

20 A. That there was concern?

21 Q. That's what you just said. No?

22 A. No, the book was about what happens when there are
23 suggestive interviewing techniques used to elicit reports from
24 children.

25 Q. Well, suggestive interviewing practices is a two edge

Page 55

1 sword in a sense in that it can also lead to false recantations
2 as well as to false allegations, isn't that correct?

3 A. When I have used the word double edged sword, my
4 understanding is that suggestive interviewing techniques can
5 lead to true disclosures as well as to false disclosures.

6 Q. It can also lead to, if you use suggestive interviewing
7 techniques, it can also lead to false recantations?

8 A. Of getting children to renounce?

9 Q. To recant?

10 A. Renounce previous claims that they made before coming
11 into the interviewing room?

12 Q. Sure, I mean it doesn't apply on one hand, it also
13 applies on the other?

14 A. I am seeing what you are saying, but I am thinking about
15 has anyone ever done any real science on this of getting
16 children to retract statements, and now to say what, it didn't
17 happen?

18 Q. Are you saying that suggestive interviewing techniques
19 cannot lead to false recantations with children?

20 A. My understanding is from the literature that it is very
21 difficult to do that.

22 Q. So it can only lead to false disclosures, it can't lead
23 to false --

24 A. I am not saying that it can't, I am saying the one or two
25 studies that I know of that have been done where suggestive

Page 56

1 techniques have been used to elicit false recantations have
2 found this to be a relatively difficult, unproductive way. I
3 think we talked about this at the end of this book, I am not
4 sure. I am not sure.

5 Q. But in your expert opinion, suggestive interviewing
6 techniques, not based on the scientific literature, based on
7 your opinion, can suggestive interviewing techniques apply at
8 both ends of the spectrum in terms of false allegations
9 initially and also later on also to false recantations?

10 A. Well, my opinion that is based on the existing
11 literature.

12 Q. So you don't have an opinion exclusive of the literature
13 that is out there?

14 A. No.

15 Q. And in your book you don't set forth any criteria to
16 identify children who are more likely to be prone to
17 suggestibility, do you?

18 A. I am forgetting now when we have written what, because
19 this was a while ago. I think when we wrote the book age was
20 the major factor. Since that time this has been an active
21 field of inquiry.

22 Q. I am talking about your book, and your book you do not
23 set forth any criteria to identify children who may be more
24 likely to be suggestive?

25 A. I think that the two factors that we talked about in our

Page 57

1 book, and that was based on the evidence available at that
2 time, which was more than six years ago, was age and IQ. I
3 don't know if IQ, how much it made it in there.
4 Q. You are not sure about IQ, are you? In fact, well, you
5 are not sure about IQ being in your book?
6 A. I know IQ is in the book.
7 Q. Not with respect to the impact of suggestibility on
8 children with high IQ versus medium IQ versus low IQ?
9 A. No, that's in the book, those are the earlier studies
10 that have been done.
11 Q. You reference those studies?
12 A. I think we wrote a chapter on them.
13 Q. And also in your book you conclude that younger children
14 are more susceptible to suggestibility than older children?
15 A. That's true.
16   THE COURT: I think we will take a recess now. We
17 will be in recess for, it is four after 11:00 now, we will be
18 in recess until 11:15.
19 (Ten minute recess)
20   THE COURT: You may proceed.
21 BY MR. SEILER:
22 Q. We talked a lot about suggestibility, and the opposite is
23 also true, isn't it, Ms. Bruck, in that children who were
24 sexually abused can now come in occasionally in the literature
25 and say that they were not abused, and that's referred to as

Page 58

1 repressed memory?
2 A. My understanding of the literature is that the term
3 repressed memory is rarely used with children. Certainly not
4 in the scientific literature. I haven't in my review of the
5 literature, maybe it is used in the clinical literature, but in
6 the scientific literature there are no classifications of the
7 studies that I reviewed in which the term repressed memory has
8 been used.
9 Q. So as I understand what you are saying, that the
10 repressed memory, at least according to you, is not widely used
11 in the scientific community to make reference to children's
12 memories or testimony?
13 A. In terms of presenting, not reporting sexual abuse?
14 Q. What I am saying is that it is true that these repressed
15 memory children who actually were sexually abused can repress
16 that memory and come in and testify that they were not sexually
17 abused?
18 A. Because they can't remember the abuse?
19 Q. Because it is repressed, they repress it based on a
20 number of factors?
21 A. I know of no scientific evidence to support that
22 statement.
23 Q. No scientific evidence. It is contained in the
24 Diagnostic and Statistical Manual of Mental Disorders, the
25 DSM-IV in 1994, it talks about repressed memory, isn't that

Page 59

1 right?
2 A. In children?
3 Q. Yes?
4 A. The DSM-IV is not really a scientific document, it is one
5 that is based on consensus of clinicians. And I would like to
6 see the scientific literature that is in peer review journals
7 on the frequency of actual repressed memories in children of
8 sexual abuse. I know that there is a literature on adults
9 where, you know, adults are -- but not using samples of
10 children, and examining their memory or their reports. This is
11 a very complicated issue. I mean we can talk about it, but I
12 have to be given, I just need a minute or so, because I am just
13 surprised that it is an issue that is being brought up.
14 Q. You are not trying to discredit the DSM-IV, are you? I
15 mean this is the manual used by psychiatrists to define mental
16 diagnostic categories published by the American Psychiatric
17 Association and addresses the concept of repressed memory?
18 A. DSM-IV, DSM changes every few years, new things come in,
19 old things go out. There are different kinds of categories
20 that are put in, a lot of times it is for billing purposes.
21 The kinds of diagnoses that are often made are not because this
22 is really what the clinician sees, but it fits the best, it
23 fits the billing purposes, it has a very political and
24 financial role, and there are many, many critiques of DSM-IV.
25 I mean just in terms of multiple personality disorder was not

Page 60

1 in one, it comes in to another one, it disappears in another
2 one. And just because, you know, it talks about repressed
3 memory for sexual abuse in school age children, I just don't
4 know of any evidence that has ever been reported to say that,
5 you know, we know that 20 percent of children who come to Court
6 can't report it because they can't remember it, but we know it
7 really happened. I just don't know of that scientific
8 evidence.
9 Q. So much of what we have talked about here this morning
10 with respect to your book basically comes from laboratory
11 research and is not a perfect analog to real life sexual abuse
12 cases and real life questions, isn't that a true statement?
13 A. I disagree.
14 Q. And isn't it also true that in your book there is very
15 little agreement among the studies that there is a disparity in
16 the studies with respect to suggestibility, with respect to
17 children's memory, as you say it's a very complicated area?
18 A. I disagree.
19 Q. Well, when we talk about recantation, Dr. Summit in his
20 seminal work in 1983 on the child sexual abuse accommodation
21 syndrome basically says that recantation is part of the normal
22 evolution of children disclosing instances of sexual abuse,
23 isn't that right?
24 A. He said that, that's correct.
25 Q. And this was also verified by Sorenson and Snow in their

Page 61

1 study in 1993 where they also slightly modified the factors,
2 but did indicate that recantation was again part of this normal
3 process that children go through in the disclosure of sexual
4 abuse?
5 A. They found that 25 percent of their samples who they
6 claimed were sexually abused made recantations.
7 Q. And that this is part of a response that victims go
8 through, and part of this response can be to a number of
9 external factors including pressure from adults?
10 A. Snow -- Snow and --
11 Q. Isn't that true?
12   MR. WILKA: Excuse me, Your Honor, the witness should
13 be able to answer the question.
14   THE COURT: Yes, and there is a question outstanding
15 now.
16 A. Well, I didn't get to answer the least question, so --
17 Roland Summit's model is a model, purely speculative, not based
18 on any scientific data, purely based on his attempt to try to
19 explain why some children might in fact have a hard time
20 disclosing and why they might recant. The Snow and Sorenson
21 study was probably the first, the first to provide data to
22 address this issue. It is not great data, there is a lot of
23 other better data to address the issue.
24 Q. Well, both of those studies were early works on the area
25 of recantation and disclosure, and both of them talk about

Page 62

1 family and social pressures in the recantation process, isn't
2 that right?
3 A. Roland Summit was not a study, it did not do a study.
4 Q. Both of their articles in the American scientific
5 journals talk about recantation, and talk about family and
6 social pressures and how they impact recantation?
7 A. Well, I am only here to talk about the scientific
8 literature, not the clinical literature. Roland Summit, you
9 talk about his model, that's been tested, but it was his
10 intuition, it was his clinical intuition, it was an idea he put
11 forward.
12 Q. Well, in response or in preparation for your testimony
13 here today, as I understand it, what you did is you reviewed
14 five or six of these articles dealing with recantation rates,
15 is that correct?
16 A. Well, I reviewed more than those articles, but today I
17 presented the ones that had recantation rates in them, yes.
18 Q. And your testimony on direct basically is you tried to
19 discredit those articles that had the higher recantation rates?
20 A. I don't think that was the purpose of my testimony. My
21 testimony was to examine how come there was so much variability
22 in recantation rates where you get lows of 3 to highs of 27,
23 and when I reviewed the literature and the scientific
24 techniques and methodology, my conclusion was, was that it was
25 the weaker science and the weaker methodology that yielded the

Page 63

1 higher recantation rates.
2 Q. And you are not trying to prove that any of those
3 circumstances existed in this case, are you?
4 A. No.
5 Q. In fact, in preparation for your testimony here today you
6 didn't talk to any of the children involved, did you?
7 A. No, I didn't.
8 Q. You don't even know their names, do you?
9 A. I know their names, some of them.
10 Q. You don't know how old they are, you know their dates of
11 birth?
12 A. I know now how old they are, I know there are some 12
13 year olds and some 15 or 19, 21.
14 Q. Some 12, 15, 19, 21's, is that what you are saying? You
15 don't know what kind of influences these children have been
16 exposed to after they were returned to their families on the
17 Yankton Reservation, do you?
18 A. No, I don't.
19 Q. You don't know what kind of social pressures they were
20 exposed to?
21 A. No, I don't.
22 Q. Don't know what kind of family pressures they were
23 exposed to?
24 A. No, I don't.
25 Q. You don't know who transported them to see Ralph

Page 64

1 Underwager where they gave these recantation interviews, do
2 you?
3 A. I don't know that.
4 Q. You don't know if that aunt was present in the room when
5 those kids were interviewed, do you?
6 A. I do not.
7 Q. You don't know if those tapes were edited, do you?
8 A. I have never seen the tapes, so I don't know.
9 Q. The defense supplemental notice of witness list dated 29
10 June, 2001 says that you are familiar with the witnesses, is
11 that a true statement then?
12 A. I am, I have been sent some materials to review for the
13 case so that I could get a general feeling about what the facts
14 were, if I thought I could be an appropriate witness, but I do
15 not know, you know, every single sequence of details. I know a
16 picture. I didn't come to testify about the facts of the case.
17 Q. For example, you don't know the IQ scores of these
18 children, do you?
19 A. No.
20 Q. Certainly IQ is a factor in terms of their susceptibility
21 to suggestibility, and the IQ is a factor in memory, isn't that
22 true?
23 A. It is unclear. It is a new area topic of research
24 actually I am just starting to undertake now.
25 Q. Isn't one of the factors in recantation also the passage

Page 65

1 of time in terms of how much time has elapsed since their
2 initial testimony until the recantation?
3 A. You know, I don't have, I really wasn't able to find any
4 scientific data on that.
5 Q. So no scientific data is your testimony I think on the
6 issue of recantation factors?
7 A. The one study that I do know of, and I was actually
8 thinking about it last night, was a study that Gail Goodman and
9 her colleagues did, they wrote a monograph on children's
10 reactions to testifying in Court. I think it was written in
11 '94 or something. Recently they have followed up those
12 children to ask them if they remembered their abuse, and they
13 did all these kinds of questions, you know, did it happen and
14 so on, and my understanding, my memory of that study that I
15 heard reported about two or three years ago was that most of
16 those children remembered the abuse, and the few that didn't,
17 you know, that didn't were boys. So there was kind of a
18 question about maybe the boys didn't want to kind of reinstate
19 it. But I think that is, I have to actually speak to
20 Dr. Goodman about this, but I think that actually is an
21 important piece of data, because you do know exactly what the
22 records of these children were, what they testified to in
23 Court, and the consistency of what they testified to in Court
24 and what they said four or five years later.
25 Q. You are not aware of the factors?

Page 66

1 A. Her findings are that there is high consistency between
2 what they said in Court and what they said on follow-up.
3 Q. As I understand your testimony on direct examination, you
4 said when you did your literature search that you basically
5 were not able to find any articles that talked about factors in
6 recantation or the impact of family and social pressures on
7 recantation?
8 A. Not in the scientific studies, and this is on
9 recantation, right?
10 Q. Yes?
11 A. I mean I might have, it's possible I missed something,
12 but I looked.
13 Q. Well -- I am sorry.
14 A. I think part of the problem is, with many of these
15 studies, is the rates are so small to begin with that it is
16 just a hard thing to study. And I also think that a lot of
17 these are studies that involve charts, and going back and
18 looking over, you know, hundreds of charts, and that is
19 information is just not available at the time. Probably would
20 be a really interesting study to do.
21 Q. Would you agree that there are factors that may lead to
22 recantation in children? You are just saying that you are not
23 aware of any scientific studies that have been done on this?
24 A. Well, I mean I certainly, my expert opinion is that
25 recantation does occur. I am not quite sure what it means, but

Page 67

1 I must, I mean to be conservative I would say at least half the
2 cases the kids are probably recanting true disclosures, and the
3 question comes up but why are they doing it? And we have a lot
4 of questions about why they are doing it, but I don't know of
5 any scientific evidence that provides support for any of those
6 hypotheses. I think there is a lot of kind of, well, probably
7 because this, because this, but when you look at the 3 percent
8 or the 20 percent, do those hypotheses account for any of those
9 changes, what percentage, I simply don't know the answer.
10 Q. But you do admit that there are, I think you said at
11 least half of the cases that it's your expert opinion that
12 children recanted true disclosures?
13 A. It's not my expert opinion, I am just sitting here doing
14 a mind exercise with you. What I am saying is when people
15 report there has been a disclosure, the, I am sorry, a
16 recantation, there are two interpretations to that recantation.
17 One is, is that they are recanting a true disclosure; or the
18 other is, is that they are denying a previous false report.
19 When you see, this is the real problem, I mean I think the most
20 we can do at this point is just look at these rates, and then,
21 you know, maybe do more work with them. But I don't know what
22 the recantations mean. I don't know if it is because the kids
23 finally decided to tell the truth, or it is because the kid all
24 of the sudden has had enough, doesn't want to do this any more,
25 and so says it never happened. We just simply don't know. We

Page 68

1 just have these rates available to tell us about the frequency
2 that this actually happens in these different samples, and
3 that's it.
4 Q. Well, with respect to the rates, wouldn't it be an
5 important factor to take into account in recantation, for
6 example, if the child was questioned, that would have some
7 impact on what the child was going to do if a child was
8 threatened by a family member?
9 A. Threatened that if you don't say it didn't happen I won't
10 love you any more?
11 Q. Sure.
12 A. Well, we have this very uncertain literature on the
13 effects of threats on children's disclosure patterns. And as
14 far as I can tell, I tried to do, I tried every word I could
15 think of to do a search on for this area of work, it's another
16 one I am interested in, and I know of two studies. One is by
17 Sauzier which is a funny kind of clinical sample, I am not
18 really sure about who these kids were, but she says that
19 threats actually resulted in delayed disclosures. She didn't
20 talk -- or denial. She doesn't talk about recantation rates,
21 and there is a much larger study by Gray where she says that
22 these are cases of kids who come in to Court, or in forensic
23 arenas, and she says that when you look at the relationship
24 between threat and disclosure, there is no relationship at all.
25 So I don't, you know, it is probably not enough to talk about

Page 69

1 in the courtroom. Those are the data that are available, I
2 don't think we really know what the effect of these threats are
3 on disclosures or on recantation rates. It is a hypothesis
4 with such data, I think these are all very interesting
5 questions, and I am not sure that these are answers that are
6 based on common sense, because a lot of what we have found in
7 this field of inquiry has really not been common sense. I
8 mean, you know, there have been some very surprising findings.
9 So on the common sense ground I would say yeah, maybe, but I am
10 not here to bring my common sense into the courtroom.
11 Q. You left your common sense at the courthouse door?
12 A. You tell me.
13 Q. Let me just run through a list of factors that may lead a
14 child to recant and if you could answer yes or no if you are
15 aware of any literature or if you have an opinion on whether
16 this is a factor that could lead to recantation. One, the
17 abuser is a family member. Is that a factor that may lead the
18 child to recant; yes, no, I don't know?
19 A. I know of no literature. Could be wrong.
20 Q. The abuser has threatened the child?
21 A. In terms of recantation?
22 Q. Sure.
23 A. Okay, the child has disclosed, right, and then the abuser
24 is still out there and says if you don't say it didn't happen
25 then I will hurt you, right?

Page 70

1 Q. Yes?
2 A. Don't know.
3 Q. The family, specially the child's mother, is not
4 supporting the child since the disclosure, is that a factor
5 that can lead to recantation?
6 A. I know of two studies that talk about the role of
7 maternal support in disclosure, but I am not aware that this
8 was related to recantation. So I would have to say I don't
9 know. I really want, I don't want to say no, because I don't
10 know, you could be sitting on a pile of studies as far as I
11 know, but in terms of the ones I reviewed, I just couldn't see
12 anything that jumped out.
13 Q. How about is it a factor that the abuser is being openly
14 supported in the child's presence by other family members, that
15 be a factor in recantation?
16 A. It could be, but I don't know of any scientific evidence.
17 You see, I think Roland Summit's model was based on all this
18 very good common sense, and he wrote this model in order to
19 explain specifically in intrafamilial cases why it might be so
20 that it eludes a guy and not disclose for such a long time and,
21 yeah, why in fact they may recant. And it's been a long time
22 since I have read this article, so I can't say this with
23 certainty, but my guess is these are the kind of claims or the
24 kinds of things that he brought up to say, you know, these are
25 in fact possible explanations that clinicians might want to

Page 71

1 consider when children recant. But again, it was like, it was
2 really meant to be a kind of, I thought, my understanding was,
3 almost a support for clinicians to understand sometimes these
4 conflicting behaviors, and for him just to throw out these
5 different kinds of ideas. But I don't think it was based on
6 his own clinical observations, and I don't think that any of
7 these have ever been subjected to acceptable scientific
8 scrutiny.
9 Q. You were talking about Summit, I just want to know in
10 your opinion yes, no, or I don't know, that these are factors
11 that may lead a child to recant. We talked about the abuser
12 was a family member, talked about threats to the child, we
13 talked about if the family, especially the child's mother, is
14 not supporting the child since the disclosure, or the abuser is
15 being openly supported in the child's presence?
16 A. But again I am giving my opinion based on my knowledge of
17 scientific literature, right, not about whether it could be?
18 Q. So you don't know, is that what you are saying?
19 A. I am saying I don't know of any scientific evidence to
20 support that claim one way or another.
21 Q. So if the abuser continues to deny the alleged abuse, you
22 think that is a factor in recantation?
23 A. Based on my review of the scientific literature, I
24 haven't seen a report.
25 Q. What about the other forms of family violence in the

Page 72

1 home, do you think that may be a factor that may lead to
2 recantation?
3 A. I don't know of any literature, scientific literature.
4 Q. How about there is no ongoing mental health intervention
5 for the child, and that the child must deal alone with victim
6 issues such as self-blame and continuing feelings toward the
7 abuser, you think that can be a factor in recantation?
8 A. In recantation. The lack of therapy? That is kind of a
9 weird thought, but I don't know of any evidence.
10 Q. The child is removed from the home at disclosure, is that
11 a factor in recantation?
12 A. I don't know of any scientific literature.
13 Q. The child has been directly pressured to recant?
14 A. When I read the scientific literature, I think that Jim
15 Wood maybe at the end of his article goes through these
16 different kinds of possibilities, and I just don't think there
17 is any sense that we have any evidence to say that is it, or
18 that is important. Sounds good.
19 Q. On the studies you talked about in terms of the rates and
20 numbers, you are not aware, are you, in your review of the
21 literature that you testified to previously, whether there was
22 medical evidence present in any of those cases?
23 A. Yes, I could go back and get that information for you,
24 but in terms of the, the cases, the studies that I felt were
25 scientifically acceptable, the medical evidence was used as one

Page 73

1 of the criteria for substantiation of abuse. So this large
2 bunch of kids, and the different interviews, different
3 information from family, from schools, from the kids, medical
4 examiners, from psychiatrists who have interviewed them, and
5 the medical evidence is definitely used as one indicator of
6 substantiation. It turns out, and we notice that in many, many
7 cases, there just simply isn't medical evidence, and, you know,
8 it doesn't mean anything. Lack of medical evidence doesn't
9 mean abuse or not abuse. Most times the medical evidence means
10 something, but the cases that I have talked about where I
11 focused on the rates for the substantiated samples, there is
12 medical evidence for some of these, not all. Is that clear?
13 Q. No, but we will go on. Again, talking about recantation,
14 and from your review of the literature, what percentage of the
15 children initially disclose during their medical examination?
16 A. Oh, during the medical examination. There is an article
17 on that. Here it is. Predictors of Disclosure During Medical
18 Examination. This is the DiPietro and Fredrickson, alright.
19 Seventy-six percent, I have to go through this carefully, but
20 my understanding is, I wrote this on the top, 76 percent of
21 children with definite diagnoses disclosed in the first
22 interview in medical examinations.
23 Q. Not talking about disclosure, talking about recantation
24 now?
25 A. I thought you asked me about disclosure.

Page 74

1 Q. I said recantation, what percentage?
2 A. They don't talk about recantation in here.
3 Q. And with respect to recantation, are you aware of what
4 the percentage is as far as the children that were abused by a
5 family member? Are there higher rates for recantation for
6 children abused by family members than non-family members?
7 A. Well, most -- okay.
8 Q. If you know?
9 A. What I can tell you is this, the CPS agency studies, the
10 ones done by Bradley and Wood and by McGraw and Jones, CPS
11 handles mainly intra-familial abuse, that's, those are the
12 substantial part of those cases, and so those rates are 3
13 percent and 9 percent recantation.
14 Q. In your review of the literature, what percentage of the
15 children recanted after they were returned to their home
16 environment?
17 A. I have no idea.
18 Q. And in any of your studies or research, Ms. Bruck, as I
19 understand it, you haven't worked with Native American
20 children, have you?
21 A. No, I haven't.
22 Q. It's also true that there are sociological phenomenon
23 that are culturally sensitive, isn't that correct?
24 A. It's possible. This is not an area of my expertise.
25 Q. Pardon me?

Page 75

1 A. This is not an area of my expertise.
2 Q. That you don't have any experience with Native American
3 children and how they remember, or suggestibility with respect
4 to Native American children, or anything directly related to
5 the Native American culture, you don't have any experience?
6 A. That's correct.
7 Q. So you don't know if Native American children are
8 susceptible to a wider variety of influences regarding
9 recantation than non-Native American children, do you?
10 A. That's correct.
11 Q. And Native American children are returned to their home
12 Reservation, this setting, you don't know if they would be
13 susceptible to further and increased societal and family
14 pressures than a non-Indian child?
15 A. That's correct, but based on my review of the scientific
16 literature I didn't find any, I didn't find anything specific
17 to Native Americans.
18 Q. And again, your research focused on understanding
19 suggestibility with respect to children in experimental
20 settings as opposed to real life interviews and those kinds of
21 things, laboratory studies only, basically?
22 A. My research that has been conducted on children's
23 suggestibility has been conducted in laboratory settings.
24 Q. In laboratory studies, okay?
25 A. Settings.

Page 76

1 Q. This weird math that you calculated earlier, there is no
2 scientific studies or anything based on the probabilities you
3 established here regarding recantation, is there?
4   MR. WILKA: Objection, argumentative.
5   THE COURT: Overruled.
6 A. The process that I went through is a statistical process
7 of how people use published data to make statements of
8 probability.
9 BY MR. SEILER:
10 Q. It is just a bare, mathematical probability based on
11 numbers, isn't that right, it doesn't factor anything else in?
12 A. Not what I did, no.
13 Q. Doesn't factor in environment concerns, does it? Doesn't
14 factor in cultural concerns, doesn't factor in pressure on the
15 children to recant, doesn't factor in --
16   MR. WILKA: Objection, compound.
17   THE COURT: Sustained.
18 BY MR. SEILER:
19 Q. Does it factor in environment concerns?
20 A. The rate that I took, I took two rates, I took 25 percent
21 recantation rate and a 10 percent recantation rate, you know,
22 whatever, those account for whatever the range of children were
23 that were in each of those studies, and, you know, sum up those
24 studies, probably a couple thousand children. And so it
25 doesn't directly, as we have talked about before, none of these

Page 77

1 studies actually looks at any of these kind of factors, but
2 they are probably involved negatively or positively with these
3 recantation rates. So I would think that it is factored in. I
4 mean it is not as though I am basing these on a very pure
5 sample of children who came to one setting, who had these very
6 clean records, that went all on these standard procedures, that
7 all recanted at seven months, whatever. These numbers are
8 based on a large variety of different kinds of circumstances.
9 So I don't know what the weighting is, but some of these issues
10 that you are dealing with must be reflected in these numbers.
11 I mean given the wide range we are dealing with.
12 Q. I think you indicated your numbers were just the bare
13 mathematical probability, they didn't factor in any of these
14 other external factors that we talked about?
15 A. Well, but I think the recantation rates that are obtained
16 from these studies do in fact mirror the factors that you are
17 talking about.
18 Q. So what is the recantation rate when children are
19 returned from a safe environment to their home?
20 A. I don't know.
21 Q. What is the recantation rate when Native American
22 children are taken from a safe environment of foster care or a
23 group home placement and returned to the Reservation with
24 family members, what is the recantation rate then?
25   MR. WILKA: I object, it is assuming that the homes

Page 78

1 are not safe, it is assuming facts not in evidence, it is a
2 foundation objection, Your Honor.
3   THE COURT: Overruled.
4 A. Again let's just go back to this issue of recantation.
5 At this point I don't want to make any judgments about what the
6 recantation means. I mean the recantation could be one where
7 the child is finally feeling the truth, or the recantation
8 could be of when the child is taking the truth back, and, you
9 know, we are not, we are never going to know that. We will
10 never know that, it's not my job to know, no one will ever
11 know. In these studies, you know, we sort of have, you know,
12 some kind of clinical judgment about the probability that it
13 happened, and so I mean all we have are rates.
14 Q. No one will ever know statistically is what you are
15 saying?
16 A. No, I mean no one will ever know in their own minds.
17 Q. As your colleague Dr. CeCe said, there is no Pinocchio
18 type tests for determining whether children are telling the
19 truth, their nose doesn't grow or anything like that?
20 A. Exactly. Did he say that or did I say that?
21 Q. Well, I have no further questions.
22   THE COURT: Redirect. I am not inhibiting you in any
23 way, if it will be long we will go to lunch and then come back.
24   MR. WILKA: We should go probably to lunch then.
25 (Recess from 12:00 until 1:00)

Page 79

1   THE COURT: Redirect, Mr. Wilka.
2   MR. WILKA: Thank you, Your Honor.
3 REDIRECT EXAMINATION BY MR. WILKA:
4 Q. Dr. Bruck, have you ever testified on the side of
5 children?
6 A. Yes. I have been hired as an expert, the cases were
7 settled before we went to trial.
8 Q. Have you ever declined testimony on behalf of defendants?
9 A. Yes, I have.
10 Q. What were the circumstances, for instance, surrounding
11 those?
12 A. Usually people call me and say, you know, can you review
13 materials of the case, we know you are an expert in
14 suggestibility, we would like your advice about whether these
15 interviews are suggestive, and would you be interested in being
16 an expert? And so I asked them to send me the materials or to
17 discuss the details on the phone, and there are many cases
18 where I just say to them I don't see any evidence of suggestive
19 interviewing, and I cannot be of help to you on this case.
20 Q. Are there criteria for suggestibility?
21 A. Are there criteria for defining?
22   MR. SEILER: I object to going in to this whole area
23 of suggestibility again. I believe the Court's Order dealing
24 with this issue of March 28, 2001 says that the purpose of this
25 hearing is to focus on the claimed recantations and Brady

Page 80

1 issues. Going back into the whole issue of suggestibility as
2 it affects the children's testimony is irrelevant, has already
3 been litigated at the trial, and dealt with by the Eighth
4 Circuit, and so we would object.
5   THE COURT: Let me hear from Mr. Wilka.
6   MR. WILKA: Thank you, Your Honor. The United States
7 opened the door when they are talking about the pressures and
8 the suggestibility that would lead to a recantation, and it was
9 testified to by Dr. Bruck on direct that with a recantation
10 there has to first be disclosure, we realize we are not going
11 to retry the case, but we have to look at some of the
12 criterion, and they did open the door by asking Dr. Bruck about
13 a number of factors of suggestibility. If one were to look
14 through the transcript or the notes of cross-examination where
15 suggestibility came up many times.
16   THE COURT: Just a moment. Factors that were
17 primarily talked about were factors which can lead to
18 recantation after disclosure. But I am interested in
19 suggestibility not with regard to the testimony initially
20 given, because it is true that that was decided by a jury,
21 that's behind us, but with regard to suggestibility now, or
22 suggestibility for the recantation, I am interested in that,
23 because of course that is one of the claims that these mothers
24 and other relatives have one way or another gotten the kids to
25 recant. So I am interested in it from that perspective. Go

Page 81

1 ahead.

2 A. Well, let me answer the Judge's, your specific interest,

3 and I looked at it in terms of that. They are suggestible in

4 terms of recantation, what does it tell you about them in

5 general? One of the patterns that I noticed in the literature

6 was that it took a couple of studies to find that children have

7 to be interviewed a lot of times to get them to disclose abuse,

8 and those are the very same studies that find that there is a

9 high rate of recantation. My conclusions from that literature

10 was that when you get high rates of denial and high rates of

11 recantation, that is symptomatic of the repeated interviewing

12 and suggestive interviewing. Now on a logical side, to go back

13 to your question, suppose you accept the premise that these

14 children recanted because of pressure. Well, then you also

15 have the other side of the coin, which we know from the

16 studies, and as I see it, it is symptomatic of many cases, is

17 there was pressure, allegedly pressure to recant. There is

18 also pressure to disclose, and logically I don't know how you

19 can say that the pressure to disclose led to true allegations

20 whereas the pressure to recant led to false recantations. I

21 mean that the most that you can say is that these are children

22 who are very sensitive to pressure, and that once they are

23 pressured to give a certain kind of, to give a certain kind of

24 testimony, they are going to do it. But what we know from the

25 suggestibility literature is that once these practices go into

Page 82

1 effect in terms of the disclosure side, that those children's

2 testimony is tainted and, you know, it is gone. You are never

3 going to really know whether what they said is true or false,

4 because the goods have been ruined. So if you want to talk

5 about suggestibility in terms of recantation, it is correlated

6 with suggestibility in terms of disclosure, and the literature

7 is very clear that under moderate suggestive conditions this

8 can have damaging effects on children's testimony.

9 MR. SEILER: We request the answer be stricken as

10 non-responsive. On cross examination Ms. Bruck testified that

11 she was not aware of and did not know of any of the

12 circumstances that existed in this case with respect to the

13 children's initial interviewing and with respect to the initial

14 testimony by the children. Therefore she is unqualified and

15 has no basis to enter any opinions with respect to that. The

16 recantation or the suggestibility issue should be limited only

17 to recantation issues without harkening back to anything like

18 spoiled goods.

19 THE COURT: Well, I will tell you how I viewed the

20 answer, and why I am overruling your objection, because the

21 spoiled goods, I didn't take it to be a comment one way or the

22 other on the witnesses in this case, but rather an observation

23 where if there was a significant amount of suggestive or

24 coaching of the children before testifying, in a conceptual

25 sense, not these children, but just children in general that

Page 83

1 testify, that then what she says with regard do recantation

2 follows through. I don't view it as a comment at all upon the

3 evidence in this case, but rather a reflection of her opinion

4 from the literature, because the witness has already said that

5 she doesn't know, you know, about the different interviews of

6 the children. The jury heard that, they have already decided

7 that. But none-the-less, I am overruling the objection,

8 because the answer gives an opinion with regard to the

9 literature on this expert's, and I find her to be an expert,

10 opinion concerning suggestibility as it relates to recantation,

11 which in order to give her opinion she has to go back to the

12 initial declaration, but it isn't case specific. That's how I

13 am viewing the evidence so everybody knows. You may proceed.

14 MR. WILKA: Thank you, Your Honor.

15 BY MR. WILKA:

16 Q. On cross examination you were asked a series of questions

17 about Dr. Underwager, you recall that?

18 A. Yes.

19 Q. And you stated on direct examination that you did not

20 review the interviews that Dr. Underwager conducted with the

21 children, is that correct?

22 A. That's correct.

23 Q. Why did you not review those taped interviews?

24 A. Because my understanding of the facts of the case were

25 that those, there were children who were taken in to custody by

Page 84

1 the police, and who were questioned over a period of time, and

2 after that period of time some of them came to make

3 disclosures. Then there was a trial at which they testified,

4 and then shortly after, or a year to two years after the trial

5 they recanted their trial testimony and their initial

6 allegations. And it is those recantations, it is that period

7 that signifies the recantation. I mean from there my

8 understanding as to Dr. Underwager's interview is a period of

9 two to three years, and, you know, so he interviews them, and

10 allegedly it is a terrible interview. That doesn't change what

11 these children said two to three years previously, and so, you

12 know, it's too bad it wasn't a great interview, because maybe

13 you could have gotten some great information, but it just was

14 not within the proper analysis of this case to include that

15 interview.

16 Q. There was a statement on cross examination that I believe

17 it was something to the effect that your work is in an ivory

18 tower and you have never worked with sexually abused children,

19 do you recall that general area of cross examination?

20 A. Yes, these are general criticisms, yes.

21 Q. What, if any, significance do you place upon those

22 general criticisms when it comes to your empirical review of

23 the scientific data out there in the field?

24 A. I am sorry, my empirical review of the literature on

25 what?

Page 85

1 Q. Of the scientific literature.
2 A. So in terms of what I personally do in my own research
3 and in terms of my review of the literature?
4 Q. Yes?
5 A. Well, I don't think it makes any, I mean it makes me a
6 more astute reviewer of that literature maybe. But I think one
7 of the things that Dr. CeCe and I are known for is our ability
8 to synthesize and to summarize the existing literature in the
9 field, all different kinds of areas of child development, not
10 only this, and this ability has been recognized in terms of the
11 Psychological Bulletin article we wrote was very little of our
12 joint research in there, some of Steve's earlier studies, but
13 mainly recitation of other people's studies. In terms of our
14 book, again we try to synthesize the relevant literature, and
15 also I think it is demonstrated in terms of the kinds of
16 requests or invited requests we get to submit articles to state
17 of the art reviews. So annual review of Psychology, for
18 example, we have the definitive article on children's memory.
19 And the Handbook of Child Psychology, the definitive article on
20 children's suggestibility. And there is another one in the
21 American, I am sorry, I forget the name, what is it called.
22 Anyway, I will think about it in a minute. The Journal of the
23 American Psychological Association where there was a special
24 issue on children and we were asked to write that article.
25 Most of that really doesn't include our literature, but it is

Page 86

1 based upon people's consideration that we are able to fairly
2 collect, digest, integrate, think about the existing
3 literature, and think about where we should be going or where
4 we shouldn't be going. So I don't really see that, you know,
5 when you do research, it does make you much more critical and
6 have a clear understanding of other people's science, but it
7 doesn't necessarily have to be within your own field. I don't
8 think, I couldn't review anything on astrophysics, but in terms
9 of social science, there are lots of things that I can do
10 because I have had a lot of research experience. I know about
11 statistics, I know about sampling, I know a lot about theories
12 of child development and so on.
13 Q. To a particular question on cross examination I recall a
14 phrase called, that was stated as weird math, do you recall
15 that question?
16 A. Yes.
17 Q. Is this math weird?
18 A. I think what we were referring to is the logical
19 manipulation we got to from using the numbers in the scientific
20 literature to figure out what the probability is of the
21 children showing the same kind of pattern, and this is the
22 plausibility theory following the first chapter of statistics
23 for dummies, or the first chapter of any statistical book, a
24 basic probability theory.
25 Q. In that area we were talking about the probability where

Page 87

1 all five witnesses have a universal recantation?
2 A. That's right.
3 Q. You stated on cross examination that you knew of no
4 scientifically valid studies dealing with a family member
5 causing a recantation?
6 A. Of the association between recantation and family member
7 pressure.
8 Q. There were factors, one was family member pressure?
9 A. Right.
10 Q. So there is no studies out there that you know of?
11 A. That I know of.
12 Q. That have been subjected to peer review?
13 A. Well, no. My guess is that people have tried to do, as
14 we were waiting here today I looked back at one of the
15 articles, the Bradley and Wood one, where they actually
16 describe the cases of recantation they get, and they said they
17 tried to figure out what the correlation with recantation was
18 with these different variables. I don't think family support
19 was one, a whole host of ones, and there was no correlations.
20 But as I point out, one of the problem is because you only have
21 ten subjects who are recanting, it is not a lot of subjects to
22 do research on, because you can't really get statistical
23 patterns. And I have a feeling that's probably the case with
24 many of these published studies, that they tried but couldn't
25 do it. I could be wrong.

Page 88

1 Q. A factor where I believe you stated on cross examination
2 you know of no scientifically valid studies where one of the
3 factors were that the abuser has had wide support in the
4 family?
5 A. I know of no studies that that has been shown for that to
6 correlate with recantation.
7 Q. So there would be, so that type of statement, would it be
8 a fair statement to say, cannot be tested as to whether there
9 is a known rate of error, or whether that type of statement
10 would be subject to peer review?
11 A. Exactly. It is a hypothesis.
12 Q. I believe you also stated on cross examination that you
13 had found no scientifically valid studies out there where the
14 alleged victims had no support within the family structure,
15 that that would be a factor in recantation?
16 A. The alleged victims were not supported within the family,
17 that that would affect recantation, right?
18 Q. Correct.
19 A. Well, it doesn't matter if it is a yes or a no, but I
20 have not come across these data in my literature search.
21 Q. So would it be a fair statement to say then that such a
22 statement would lack a known rate of error of the technique and
23 existence in maintaining standards?
24 A. Yes, with one caveat, it's possible there is a study out
25 there and I missed it. I tried really hard lots of places.

Page 89

1 Q. If such a statement is made, would it be a fair statement
2 then that it would not be a subject, that you know hasn't been
3 subjected to peer review?
4 A. Right.
5 Q. Have you ever come across any studies where there were
6 four or five child witnesses where they all recanted?
7 A. Well, within the same case, they are never reported that
8 way. So I wouldn't know. My guess is that --
9   MR. SEILER: Objection, speculative.
10   THE COURT: Sustained.
11   MR. WILKA: That's all I have, Your Honor.
12   THE COURT: Redirect.
13 RECROSS EXAMINATION BY MR. SEILER:
14 Q. Ms. Bruck, you talked about your understanding of the
15 facts of the case in terms of taken in to custody by police,
16 then they made these disclosures over time, and they testified,
17 and there was recantation. Where did you get that information
18 from?
19 A. Okay. I got the information for some of this from the
20 briefs that were written in the appeal, and then I got the
21 recantation information from the attorneys.
22   THE COURT: I am going to tell both sides right now
23 so that you know in case there is more record that should be
24 made that I don't consider this witness's testimony to have
25 been fact specific with regard to this case, because the

Page 90

1 foundation hasn't been shown. And I don't believe that she
2 purported to testify on a factually specific basis, because in
3 order to do that we would be going in to a lot of other factual
4 information that hasn't been established in the record, so that
5 both sides know how I am taking the witness's testimony.
6 BY MR. SEILER:
7 Q. So again your testimony is based upon your review of
8 these six or seven articles that you read prior to coming to
9 trial, prior to coming to this hearing, and then kind of a
10 search of the literature in these other areas, like
11 recantation, that's basically what you did to prepare for this?
12 A. Yes.
13 Q. And is it a fair statement that there probably are no
14 perfect interviews?
15 A. Yes.
16 Q. Certainly Dr. Underwager didn't do one?
17 A. I don't know. Sound to me like not, but there are no
18 perfect interviews.
19 Q. Again, just so we know where you are coming from, your
20 statement in your book, which I believe you stand by, you
21 indicate much of the time children statements are reliable and
22 credible, and in such situations the cases are quickly settled
23 obviating the need for further investigative procedure and
24 hence for documenting the child's testimony.
25 A. Yes.

Page 91

1 Q. Are you aware of the Margaret Riser (sp) study in 1991
2 regarding recantation and child sex abuse cases in which she
3 sets forth a number of factors about why children recant?
4 A. Is it a study?
5 Q. Well, at least a quote scientific article that was
6 published in Child Welfare, November-December, 1991.
7 A. I have to look at the article, but my guess is that it is
8 not a unique collection of new data.
9 Q. I think the question was were you aware of it. Don't
10 guess about what it said.
11 A. What I have to tell you is when I did my review I took
12 out articles that I have read before, looked through their
13 bibliographies, did a search on the computer, and then looked
14 at the abstracts, or the contents, when I could, of the
15 articles to determine whether in fact they contained empirical
16 data that had not been analyzed before, and also if they had,
17 whether it met mild standards of scientific acceptability. I
18 mean there are a number of studies, I mean I don't know how
19 many, but there are a few that I did not include because I felt
20 that the standards for admission of the sample were, made the
21 findings invalid.
22 Q. Maybe you just didn't agree with them or didn't agree
23 with the position that you were told to take this morning when
24 you testified?
25 A. No, I made all these decisions before I looked at the

Page 92

1 results.
2 Q. So your position seems to be although I have never been
3 involved in child abuse cases and although I have never done
4 any interviews of children, I am the authority on how it should
5 be done even though I have never done it?
6 A. I don't believe these studies are on how it should be
7 done, I believe the studies are on once, while it is being
8 done, what are children doing. And I think it is the matter of
9 looking at the studies. I mean I could probably teach some of
10 you how to do it really quickly. I mean if you had more
11 research experience you probably would learn very quickly how
12 to do this.
13 Q. Somebody that's never performed brain surgery would go to
14 a person whose never been in the operating room for techniques
15 on how to do it?
16 A. This is not brain surgery.
17   MR. SEILER: No further questions.
18   THE COURT: Redirect.
19   MR. WILKA: No, Your Honor.
20   THE COURT: I do have some questions. Since this is
21 a Court proceedings and not a proceeding in front of a jury, I
22 can make comments. Before I ask you this series of questions I
23 have to say that it seems to me that you are an academician
24 that has come here that went over the literature and tried to
25 testify on the basis of your expertise as to what you believe

Page 93

1 the literature shows, and that's helpful to the Court. But
2 there is one area I am troubled about, having said that,
3 because one area I know something about is statistics. I
4 question that you do. I want to ask you now, because in your
5 testimony, I am not saying you don't know anything about them,
6 I just know enough to be dangerous, if that. But you did in
7 redirect to Mr. Wilka's redirect questions after lunch say I
8 know about statistics, sampling, theory of probability and so
9 on. Well, I am troubled with your statistical analysis. First
10 of all the mathematics, I think it is wrong. Ten times 10 is a
11 hundred, ten times a hundred is a thousand, ten times a
12 thousand is ten thousand.
13 A. Right.
14   THE COURT: Maybe I misheard you, I thought you said
15 the ten times probability is one in a hundred thousand?
16 A. It was a factor of five, right.
17   THE COURT: I thought you went out to a factor of
18 four.
19 A. I was told the question was five.
20   THE COURT: Then if it is five, it is a hundred
21 thousand. But I would like to know frankly what formal courses
22 you have had in statistics?
23 A. My formal courses?
24   THE COURT: Right.
25 A. When I was in undergraduate I took an undergraduate

Page 94

1 course, when I was a graduate student I taught a undergraduate
2 course, I took a graduate course, and I am pretty sure I taught
3 an undergraduate course.
4   THE COURT: Well, I am referring to --
5 A. You don't like my probability theory?
6   THE COURT: Not at all. Modern Elementary
7 Statistics, 8th Edition, by John Freund and Gary Simon, page
8 145 under the multiplication rules, because what you have done
9 is you have taken independent events and multiplied them out.
10 A. Right.
11   THE COURT: But that isn't the way to do this,
12 because I mean it is clear, because this is something that is
13 suggestive to be fact specific to this case, and the problem I
14 have with that is that these are dependent in that you have a
15 family situation, these are not independent events. This isn't
16 a child in South Dakota in Clay County and another one in
17 Shannon County and another one in Jackson County that were
18 unrelated cases, these are people all in a family unit, and you
19 cannot use the independent event formula.
20 A. Well, I mean, you know what, the fact of the matter is
21 that it is still with a replacement, I mean it is that, you
22 know, it is if you say you have twenty pennies or you have
23 twenty marbles, and half of them are black and half of them are
24 red, and you pick one out, what is the probability of it is
25 being black or red. It is going to be 50 percent. So you pick

Page 95

1 out a red one. Now the probability is going to change because
2 you have taken something out. So is that the way you see it
3 with this case, is that you have changed the denominator?
4   THE COURT: I don't usually answer questions, I ask
5 them.
6 A. You said were you the expert, so I don't really know.
7 People that I have talked to about this, Debra Pool (sp) for
8 example, and Jim Wood who has written a lot about basing it on
9 statistics, and actually did some of these formulas for me for
10 other cases, that was, those are their estimations, and it was
11 the estimations I came up with independently. So if you want
12 to give me a different estimation, I would be glad to research
13 it and tell you my opinion of it.
14   THE COURT: Well, you believe that simple
15 multiplication which is what you do with independent events
16 then can be applied to this situation, is that your opinion?
17 That's what the hundred thousand did.
18 A. Right, yes, I mean because their recantations are
19 independent. I mean I guess unless you are making the
20 assumption if one recanted then the other one would go down
21 also, is that right?
22   THE COURT: You can't assume that they are not
23 dependent.
24 A. Because they have words with each other.
25   THE COURT: Because you don't know the facts.

Page 96

1 A. Because I don't know the facts, okay. I mean it's an
2 interesting intellectual question issue, and I would just like
3 to know where you think I have gone wrong.
4   THE COURT: Because it is a misleading statistic to
5 treat these as independent events when they are clearly not.
6 A. They are not independent.
7   THE COURT: No, or at least you can't assume they are
8 independent, because that's the only way you get your
9 statistics.
10 A. So then your lowest rate, the worst case scenario is if
11 you take the Snow one, it is going to be, there is a chance of
12 one in four that there would be a recantation, and if you took,
13 I think the more sensible rates, then there is a chance in one
14 in ten there would be a recantation.
15   THE COURT: Still using the independent formula.
16 A. No, I am saying for the first child to recant it.
17   THE COURT: That is, obviously can't be with regard
18 to relationship to this case, you are just taking the
19 statistical analysis from the --
20 A. In terms of the studies I am extracting these numbers
21 from, I mean it's possible some of those, one would think some
22 of those recantations in fact do bear similarities to this
23 case. There is never going to be a perfect replication of any
24 scientific study that mirrors every single, I mean this was a
25 logical exercise, that's all.

Page 97

1   THE COURT: Well, alright, I just wanted to tell you
2 where there is a soft spot in your testimony.
3   A. I will take your point and think about it.
4   THE COURT: You had indicated that with regard to
5 suggestibility factors of age and IQ that were the ones that
6 you primarily focused on in 1995 in your book, but you said
7 that you were doing additional research now on trying to
8 identify other factors. Has that research gone to a point
9 where you are confident you have an expert opinion as to what
10 the factors are that you believe are --
11   A. I am an ultimate consumer of this literature, because
12 personally I would like to include some of these data in my
13 studies. I have had a graduate student who just did a huge
14 amount of work looking at predictors of suggestibility. I have
15 talked to people in lots of labs who are working on this. At
16 best once in a while something comes out that is related to
17 memory or that is related to personality. Rarely does it
18 replicate across lab, and when these effects do come out, they
19 are very, very small. It might account for 5 percent of the
20 variance or something like that. So I think people have been
21 very, very unsuccessful in accounting for these individual
22 variations that involve mental cognition, child's feelings
23 about themselves, and so on. I think that, you know, age is
24 really important, and it is a continuum. I mean we are all
25 suggestible, but the biggest effect you get with the younger

Page 98

1 kids. Then there are these external factors. It mean it has
2 to do with the delay between the alleged event and the
3 interview, the number of interviews, the type of interviewing.
4 I mean that's where all the meat and gravy is. We have been
5 very unsuccessful in trying to identify what are the
6 characteristics of an individual child that would make them
7 susceptible to suggestion.
8   THE COURT: I can understand the problem as a lay
9 person and as a academician, but not as a clinician then, you
10 wouldn't be a person then that would make the observation that
11 I might make as a layman that, having had contact with quite a
12 few kids, this is, and it would be a clinician probably would
13 say this, but it seems like for whatever reason maybe IQ is
14 part of it and age part of it, but there are other factors too,
15 the two kids seem pretty similar that one is much more
16 susceptible to suggestion than the next one.
17   A. Absolutely.
18   THE COURT: But it's hard to say why?
19   A. I haven't figured out why yet.
20   THE COURT: A problem that I am faced with, which you
21 are not because you have already indicated that you haven't
22 worked separately with Native American children, but given the
23 difference in family structure and traditions and so on of
24 Native American children, they may, although nobody knows,
25 might be more or less susceptible, we don't know.

Page 99

1   A. Absolutely. I know of, there has not been a lot of work
2 in terms of cross cultural, racial, ethnic differences in
3 suggestibility. You know, that would make this, you know, I
4 think it is a really interesting question, because obviously
5 the way we can talk about ourselves and our willingness to talk
6 about ourselves is dependent on how we are brought up; do you
7 tell people, how do you tell people. But again this is a
8 question, because as you say, you know, there are, sometimes
9 you see exactly, you see two kids from exactly the same
10 background who look very much alike and yet one will say "X"
11 and one will say "Y", and, you know, these are from exactly the
12 same background. So these are all really interesting
13 questions, and I hope one day we will have answers to them.
14   THE COURT: In talking about the literature that you
15 reviewed you made a clear distinction between the scientific
16 literature and clinical literature.
17   A. Yes, sir.
18   THE COURT: Explain that to me a little bit more,
19 because at least in the case of the Daubert test, for example,
20 that we apply in Federal Court cases, I believe the clinical
21 literature would normally be considered within the broader
22 category of scientific literature, and you have made a much
23 narrower distinction. I would like to have you explain the
24 distinction a little bit more to me.
25   A. You know, again this is your field of expertise, but my

Page 100

1 understanding is the clinical studies are allowed in, but not
2 clinical intuition. A clinical study is one that --
3   THE COURT: I was talking about publications.
4   A. Right. So in the articles that are reviewed there were a
5 number of studies that were clinical in nature in that the kids
6 came from clinics. In fact, my guess is that these are all
7 clinical studies, so that is just a way of defining where your
8 population comes from. One of the things one has to be careful
9 of in doing clinical studies is just to make sure that it is
10 representative of the population, and that you are not over
11 stepping generalizations. You know, in this field, people have
12 done the best they can. There are a number of studies -- I am
13 sorry, they are not studies, they are papers that appear in the
14 literature that are discussions of patterns of disclosure or
15 recantations, and to some degree it is based on a rehash of the
16 literature, but I must say, you know, when we wrote our book in
17 '93, '94, there were very few studies on disclosure and
18 recantation patterns at that point. And so I think that a lot
19 of the articles that are in the literature are ones that are
20 much more thought pieces of why this might happen, if it does
21 happen, but it is really based upon my experience in my clinic
22 with these kinds of kids. But again there is really, these are
23 very good hypotheses, but they are not necessarily right, and
24 for all the reasons that you are not allowed to bring this
25 evidence in to Court they don't withstand scientific scrutiny

Page 101

1 at all.

2   THE COURT: Thank you. Do the Court's questions give
3 rise to questions by either side?

4   MR. WILKA: No, Your Honor.

5 RECROSS EXAMINATION BY MR. SEILER:

6 Q. When you talk about younger children you are generally
7 talking about five and younger, aren't you?

8 A. I am very slippery with that term. You know, if you are
9 talking about correlations, and I just say there is a
10 correlation between suggestibility and age, in younger, I mean
11 whoever is in that sample, the younger ages.

12 Q. Your book makes reference --

13 A. My book is seven and under. I think now the literature,
14 we are getting to know a lot more about eight and under, and we
15 are getting to know a lot more of eighteen and older. We have
16 this funny gap in here where it's been hard to fill for lots of
17 reasons.

18   MR. SEILER: Nothing else, Judge.

19   MR. WILKA: Nothing.

20   THE COURT: Thank you, you may step down. Call your
21 next witness.

22   MR. WILKA: Call Kathleen Honomichl.

23

24   KATHLEEN HONOMICHL,

25 called as a witness, being first duly sworn, testified and said

Page 102

1 as follows:

2

3 DIRECT EXAMINATION BY MR. HAUGAARD:

4 Q. Kathleen, please state your name and spell your last
5 name?

6 A. Kathleen Honomichl, H-O-N-O-M-I-C-H-L.

7 Q. Where are you employed?

8 A. At the Fort Randall Casino and Hotel.

9 Q. How long have you been employed there?

10 A. Four years.

11 Q. And were you previously employed by Tribal Social
12 Services?

13 A. Yes, I was.

14 Q. When was that?

15 A. I started the job there in 19, June of 1995.

16 Q. And when did you leave that employment?

17 A. In June of '97.

18 Q. Tell us about your education?

19 A. I went to two and a half years at Mitchell for nursing,
20 RN.

21 Q. Do you have any other training or education besides that?

22 A. I took a course in social work. No, that's about it.

23 Q. When you were hired on at Tribal Social Services did you
24 attend any workshops?

25 A. Yes, I did.

Page 103

1 Q. Do you recall which types of workshops those might have
2 been?

3 A. It was for social services and working with children.

4 Q. When employed by Tribal Social Services what were your
5 responsibilities?

6 A. Working with families and trying to unite parents with
7 their children.

8 Q. What kind of situations would take them away from their
9 parents, children away from their parents?

10 A. Child neglect, child abuse, sexual abuse. Then they
11 would be taken out of the home.

12 Q. Were you eventually assigned to the Rouse case?

13 A. Yes, I was.

14 Q. Which children were you responsible for overseeing?

15 A. Lucritia Rouse, Jessica Rouse, Jerome Rouse, Fury Rouse,
16 Thrista Rouse, and Donovan Rouse.

17 Q. I don't recall, did you mention Rosemary too?

18 A. I wasn't Rosemary's case worker.

19 Q. Are you related to the Rouse family?

20 A. No, I am not.

21 Q. What were your specific duties in regard to that case?

22 A. When I got the case I was just to work with the children
23 and their mothers and to try to get the children back into the
24 home.

25 Q. What kind of things would that involve?

Page 104

1 A. It involved a lot of traveling here to Sioux Falls,
2 sometimes two, three times a week I would be up and meet at
3 Children's Home Society.

4 Q. That's where some of the children were placed?

5 A. Yes.

6 Q. Were they all placed there?

7 A. Lucritia and Jessica were placed there.

8 Q. Where were Thrista and Donovan?

9 A. Thrista was also there, too, and they all of them were
10 except for Fury, she wasn't.

11 Q. When you first became involved what did you know about
12 the claimed abuse?

13 A. I just know that the men were convicted of sexual
14 molestation of these kids, and that was, when I took the case
15 that was all over with. I just worked with the children and
16 their mothers.

17 Q. What did you believe personally to be the facts at that
18 time when you received the case?

19 A. I believed the facts to be true of what was in the
20 papers, what I have heard.

21 Q. That was based on your reading the newspaper articles?

22 A. Yes.

23 Q. What prompted you to -- well, this presupposes some
24 things. Did there come a time when you changed your view of
25 the claimed abuse in this case?

Page 105

1 A. Yes.
2 Q. What prompted that?
3 A. The reports I received from the Children's Home Society,
4 and just knowing the children.
5 Q. Tell me what reports did you receive from Children's Home
6 Society that caused you to question this?
7 A. I had received a report from the Children's Home Society
8 on the children's therapy, and their therapist was Mary Weber
9 at the time. She had faxed me an incident report, what had
10 happened in their group in that Jessica had made the statement
11 that none of that had ever happened.
12 Q. Do you recall approximately when you received that
13 report, or when that statement would have been made by Jessica?
14 A. I would say probably February or March of '96 maybe.
15 Q. What did you do with that report when you received it?
16 A. I faxed it to Michelle Tapken.
17 Q. Did you speak with her about it then?
18   MR. HOLMES: Objection, this is beyond the scope of
19 the Court's Order as far as Brady issues in this case, it's all
20 after the trial.
21   THE COURT: Sustained.
22 BY MR. HAUGAARD:
23 Q. So this statement by Jessica came out in the course of
24 discussion with the case worker or counselors, or do you
25 recall?

Page 106

1 A. The therapist at the Children's Home Society.
2 Q. Did you discuss that report with anyone?
3 A. I discussed it in the office with some of my co-workers.
4 Q. And who would that have been?
5 A. Ida Ashes, Deena LaPointe.
6 Q. And when would you likely have discussed that with them?
7 A. When I received the reports.
8 Q. What was decided as to action that should or should not
9 be taken with regard to that report?
10 A. On my part you mean, what I should have done with it?
11 Q. Well, no, was there a discussion between you and any of
12 your supervisors as to what you should do with the report?
13 A. Maggie Cavender was the director then, and I had to fax
14 it to Michelle Tapken.
15 Q. Did you have discussions with the people at Children's
16 Home Society about the report?
17 A. I discussed it with Mary Weber.
18 Q. Was there any action decided upon during that discussion
19 as to what should take place from that point forward?
20 A. No. I just faxed it on.
21 Q. Did the Children's Home Society staff indicate that they
22 intended to pursue that in any way?
23 A. No, they didn't.
24 Q. Did you have any meetings with others in the Tribal
25 office about this report?

Page 107

1 A. Just with my co-workers.
2 Q. Did you ever speak with Victor Provost about it?
3 A. Yes.
4 Q. Do you know, or tell me what was Victor Provost's
5 position at that time?
6 A. I think he was the CEO officer at that time, it was just
7 over all the programs there.
8 Q. Is that something like a president of the organization at
9 that point?
10 A. Yeah, over programs.
11 Q. Do you know if he had any discussions with anyone from
12 Children's Home Society about that report?
13 A. No, I don't know.
14 Q. You know if he spoke with the U. S. Attorney about it?
15   MR. HOLMES: Objection, calls for speculation.
16   THE COURT: Sustained -- overruled, it doesn't call
17 for speculation. She can say if she knows or not, not what the
18 answer is. It is preparatory to foundation, overruled, you may
19 answer.
20 A. No, I don't.
21 Q. Did anyone from the Tribal office consider the
22 possibility of doing a new interview with these kids?
23 A. Not that I remember, no.
24 Q. Tell me about the relationship you had with the kids as
25 far as on an ongoing basis, how often would you see them?

Page 108

1 A. The children I would see at least probably three times a
2 week.
3 Q. Did you ask them specific questions about the claimed
4 abuse?
5 A. No, I didn't.
6 Q. Did you ever prompt them to have a discussion with you
7 about the claimed abuse?
8 A. No.
9 Q. So did you just see your role as trying to reunite the
10 family, the children with their mother in this case?
11 A. Yes.
12 Q. How did it, or did there come a time when the children
13 brought this discussion up to you?
14 A. Yes.
15 Q. Who was that?
16 A. Thrista Rouse, Donovan, Rosemary.
17 Q. What exactly took place?
18 A. I was in my office doing paperwork, and in come the kids,
19 and they were sitting there visiting, just talking, and Thrista
20 started to cry, and I asked her why --
21 Q. Let me back up, they came into your office to visit about
22 what?
23 A. Just came down to see me.
24 Q. Okay, then what happened?
25 A. We were just visiting in general, and Thrista started to

Page 109

1 cry, and I asked her why she was crying, and she said our
2 uncles didn't do that.
3 Q. Had you been talking about the case at all at that point?
4 A. No.
5 Q. When she said our uncles didn't do that, what did that
6 mean to you?
7 A. I didn't say anything, I just went around and hugged her,
8 and I didn't ask any questions, and I just told her it was
9 okay.
10 Q. Approximately when did this take place?
11 A. I know the weather was nice, it would have had to have
12 been in the summer.
13 Q. Was this before or after you had received this report
14 about Jessica?
15 A. That was afterward.
16   THE COURT: Which was afterward?
17 A. When Thrista began to cry.
18 BY MR. HAUGAARD:
19 Q. That was after you received the report about Jessica?
20 A. Yes.
21 Q. Do you think it was within a matter of several months of
22 that same time?
23 A. I am not sure of the timeframe how long it was.
24 Q. Tell me what went on, what took place then in your office
25 that day?

Page 110

1 A. The children had left, and I went in to Ida Ashes' office
2 and talked with her about it.
3 Q. Let's back up. The comments, the extent of the comments
4 that were made were what, was it just Thrista?
5 A. Yes, and she started to cry.
6 Q. And she said, again what did she say exactly?
7 A. She said her uncles didn't do that.
8 Q. Did you ask her anything about didn't do what?
9 A. No, I didn't.
10 Q. Did Donovan or Rosemary say anything at that time?
11 A. No.
12 Q. What was their response to her comment?
13 A. Neither one said anything, they just sat there, and
14 Rosemary was standing up by the desk.
15 Q. So after you lent comfort to Thrista at that point?
16 A. Yes.
17 Q. For how long do you think they were probably in your
18 office?
19 A. Probably about fifteen minutes.
20 Q. After they left, then what did you do?
21 A. I went in and talked with Ida Ashes.
22 Q. And what did you discuss with her?
23 A. I just had told her what Thrista had done.
24 Q. Was there any action decided upon at that time?
25 A. No.

Page 111

1 Q. What else did the kids ever say to you about this claimed
2 abuse?
3 A. They never really talked about any of that abuse with me.
4 Q. Did you have any more discussions with them about it?
5 A. No.
6 Q. You had access to the various reports about the kids and
7 the foster care, did you review those things as you received
8 the Rouse case?
9 A. Yes.
10 Q. What did you find in there that helped you to understand
11 the case?
12 A. I read the reports when the kids were first taken and
13 what had all happened. I got to know the kids pretty well.
14 Then just in the reports that were in the file I just found it
15 unbelievable that this all had happened.
16 Q. Why did you find it unbelievable?
17 A. Because of what the children said had happened.
18 Q. Which was what?
19 A. That they were tied to bed posts, carried up and down the
20 stairs, that Grandmother had done stuff to them, it was just on
21 and on and on.
22 Q. Were these reports that had already been compiled by the
23 time you received the case?
24 A. Yes.
25 Q. How long have you lived in that community?

Page 112

1 A. How long have I lived there?
2 Q. Yes?
3 A. I lived there all my life.
4 Q. So you have known of the Rouse family all the time you
5 have been growing up?
6 A. Yes.
7 Q. And when you read these claims in the reports, why did
8 you question the accuracy of those claims?
9 A. There was just the things they had said in there what had
10 happened, I just found it very hard to believe.
11 Q. Had you received any training about sexual abuse cases?
12 A. When I went to Pierre, yes.
13 Q. Was it consistent with the training you received?
14 A. No.
15 Q. In what ways was it not consistent?
16 A. Just there are certain behaviors and things children will
17 show when this has happened to them. From my knowledge working
18 with these kids, they never showed no signs of behavior any
19 different from any other children. If children are being
20 sexually abused, they have a lot of anger, they have a lot of
21 difficulty, and their behavior seemed to be normal like another
22 child that has not been sexually abused.
23 Q. So did you have those thoughts before Thrista made the
24 comment to you?
25 A. That they weren't?

Page 113

1 Q. That there was a possibility that they weren't abused?
2 A. Yes.
3 Q. Did you have that thought or consideration of that
4 possibility before you received the report about Jessica?
5 A. Yes.
6 Q. Throughout your time in dealing with the kids did they
7 ever demonstrate behaviors that you would have found to be
8 consistent with victims of child abuse?
9 A. No.
10 Q. You were familiar with their home life, were you not?
11 A. The children's home?
12 Q. Yes?
13 A. Yes.
14 Q. Generally, I mean the Rouse household?
15 A. Yes.
16 Q. What was that characterized by?
17 A. I knew there was a lot of alcoholism in the home, quite a
18 bit of it.
19 Q. Who seemed to demonstrate the most of the alcoholic
20 behavior, or was it just generally a problem with the family.
21   MR. HOLMES: Objection, this isn't relevant.
22   THE COURT: Sustained.
23   MR. HAUGAARD: Your Honor, it is relevant in the
24 sense that the basis for removal of Rosemary Rouse was in
25 essence based along these lines that there was difficulties in

Page 114

1 the home.
2   THE COURT: The objection is sustained. Proceed.
3 BY MR. HAUGAARD:
4 Q. After these comments from the kids, how did you change
5 your interaction with the kids, or did you?
6 A. No, I did not change my interaction with the children.
7 Q. Did you try to influence them in any way to tell this to
8 anyone else?
9 A. No.
10 Q. Did you go back and ask them more questions about this
11 claimed abuse?
12 A. No.
13 Q. When you reviewed the reports through the case file, what
14 did you observe about the reports in regard to the sexual
15 activity of the kids?
16 A. After this?
17 Q. No, before this?
18 A. I guess I don't understand your question.
19 Q. As you reviewed the file on this case, did you come
20 across information in regard to the children having sexual
21 activity with one another?
22   MR. HOLMES: Objection, it's not relevant what this
23 witness saw in the Social Services file.
24   THE COURT: Sustained.
25 BY MR. HAUGAARD:

Page 115

1 Q. Did Thrista admit to you that she had had sexual
2 relations with any of the cousins?
3 A. Yes.
4 Q. And who was that?
5 A. Jerome Rouse.
6 Q. What was the extent or duration of that sexual
7 relationship that she had with Jerome?
8 A. The way she described it, after they had sexual relations
9 that they would just lay there and talk.
10 Q. Approximately when was this taking place?
11 A. In Donna Jordan's foster home.
12 Q. Do you know if it had taken place prior to the removal
13 from the home?
14 A. Before the removal from the home?
15 Q. Before they were removed from their mother's home and
16 placed in foster care, do you know if Thrista was sexually
17 active before that?
18 A. No, I don't know.
19 Q. Did Donovan affirm that this claimed abuse did not take
20 place?
21 A. Yes.
22 Q. What about Rosemary?
23   MR. HOLMES: Your Honor, I would ask the foundation
24 of when and where.
25   THE COURT: Sustained.

Page 116

1 BY MR. HAUGAARD:
2 Q. When did Donovan affirm to you that this claimed abuse
3 had not taken place?
4 A. I am not sure on dates or times that he --
5 Q. It followed Thrista's comment at some point?
6 A. No, not that day he never said nothing.
7 Q. But in the days or weeks following did he affirm that
8 that was accurate?
9 A. Yes.
10 Q. Do you remember how that took place?
11 A. No.
12 Q. And Rosemary's presence that one day when Thrista was in
13 your office, that was just because she was with her family
14 members, that wasn't because she was assigned to you, is that
15 correct?
16 A. Yes.
17 Q. How do you think you got along with the kids, did you
18 sense that they had a trust for you?
19 A. Not at first, but afterward, yes.
20 Q. How long do you think it took before that trust
21 developed?
22 A. Probably about five, six months.
23 Q. So they didn't really know you before this?
24 A. No.
25 Q. When this comment by Jessica took place, had there been

Page 117

1 opportunities for Jessica to reside back in her mother's home
2 at that point?
3 A. No.
4 Q. When Thrista and Donovan made comments that they made,
5 had they yet been placed back in their parents home?
6 A. Yes.
7 Q. On what kind of a basis?
8 A. Visitation, a weekend visit.
9 Q. The kids were officially in Social Service custody, is
10 that correct?
11 A. Yes.
12 Q. From your reading of the report, the timeframe in which
13 Thrista was having sexual relations with Jerome, was that
14 apparently prior to the trial?
15 A. No, I don't know what was prior to the trial.
16 Q. You don't know what the date would be?
17 A. No.
18 Q. But it was while they were in custody or in placement at
19 Donna Jordan's home, is that correct?
20 A. Yes.
21 Q. Obviously it was before Jerome was removed from the home.
22 You recall how long Jerome was in placement at Donna Jordan's
23 home?
24 A. No, I don't.
25 Q. Did you meet with Jerome during your time of supervising

Page 118

1 this family?
2 A. Yes, I visited with Jerome.
3 Q. And did he admit the sexual relationship with Thrista?
4 A. Yes.
5 Q. Did he admit sexual relationship with any of the other
6 girls?
7 A. No.
8 Q. Did Thrista and Donovan later describe for you a
9 situation where they were walking along with their cousin
10 Rosemary having a discussion about this?
11 A. No.
12 Q. What were the indicators of credibility that you found
13 attached to the kids statements?
14 A. Excuse me?
15 Q. What were the things that indicated to you that the
16 things that Thrista and Donovan were saying were accurate, what
17 made you believe them?
18 A. That the things they were saying?
19 Q. What caused you to believe they were telling the truth?
20 A. I guess what led me to believe that the children were
21 telling the truth the day in my office is because I had read
22 the case file and what had happened before I even took the
23 case, these girls were very young, and these men are big men,
24 and I would, you would think that there would have been a lot
25 of damage mentally and physically to these children.

Page 119

1 Q. Was there anything about Thrista's behavior in your
2 office that day that caused you to think that she is making
3 this up?
4 A. No.
5 Q. Did they ever report to you that their mothers had
6 badgered them about this claimed abuse?
7 A. No.
8 Q. Did you ever detect that in anything that you ever read
9 or saw or discussed?
10 A. No.
11 Q. What prompted you to eventually leave Social Services?
12 A. I left Social Services in June of '97. I had way too
13 much stress from the case, and I took a lot of that stress home
14 with me, and I decided that I needed to quit, get out of there.
15 Q. Did there also come a point in time where you felt that
16 you needed to bring this information to light?
17 A. Yes.
18 Q. And what did you do about that?
19 A. I talked to my co-workers probably every day about it.
20 There was, I felt there was something I should do, but it was
21 like my hands were tied. There was nothing I could do about
22 it. We had a meeting at the BIA one day, Michelle Tapken was
23 there, Bill Van Roe, myself, I believe Maggie Cavender, Lois
24 Weddell from the IHS, and this case came up, and I remember
25 Michelle Tapken hitting the table very hard and said that she

Page 120

1 would prosecute to the fullest anybody that was tampering with
2 federal witnesses.
3 Q. What did you take that to mean?
4 A. Anybody that even talked about the case, or even
5 suggested that there was something wrong with the case, that
6 she would prosecute them and get them for tampering with
7 federal witnesses.
8 Q. How much longer did you stay on with Social Services
9 after that?
10 A. I would say probably eight months, nine months.
11 Q. You were responsible for overseeing Jessica's return to
12 the home, is that right?
13 A. Yes.
14 Q. And Lucritia too?
15 A. Yes.
16 Q. Did you ask them questions about this claimed abuse?
17 A. No.
18 Q. Did they volunteer anything to you about it?
19 A. No.
20 Q. What was the gist of what Donovan eventually conveyed to
21 you?
22 A. Excuse me?
23 Q. What was the gist of what Donovan eventually conveyed to
24 you about the claimed abuse, what did he generally say about
25 the claimed abuse?

Page 121

1   MR. HOLMES: Objection, foundation.

2   THE COURT: Sustained.

3 BY MR. HAUGAARD:

4 Q. Did you have a discussion with Donovan at some point, or

5 did he come and speak with you about this claimed abuse?

6 A. No, he didn't come to me and talk about it.

7 Q. But he was standing there when Thrista made her comment,

8 is that correct?

9 A. Yes.

10 Q. And he didn't correct anything at that point?

11 A. No.

12 Q. And likewise, Rosemary, did she hear what Thrista said?

13 A. Yes.

14 Q. Did she make any correction to that?

15 A. No.

16 Q. Back in 1999 when we were preparing for a motion for a

17 new trial I discussed an affidavit with you that you

18 subsequently signed, I have got it, a copy of it here. In that

19 affidavit you indicate that you had had some discussions with

20 Mary Weber, and she was employed by Children's Home Society, is

21 that right?

22 A. Yes, she was.

23 Q. Did she explain to you that she had come to Marty to look

24 over the scene of what was claimed to be where the abuse had

25 taken place?

Page 122

1 A. Yes.

2 Q. Did she express doubt that the abuse could have happened?

3 A. Yes.

4 Q. In that same affidavit that you signed, that I prepared

5 and you signed, you indicated that you believed it to be in

6 August of '96 that Thrista and Donovan came to you and

7 explained the pressure they had been under to tell the story as

8 Michelle Tapken and the investigators wanted it told, is that

9 accurate?

10 A. That Michelle Tapken told them what?

11 Q. Well, did Thrista and Donovan come to you and express to

12 you they had been under pressure to go along with this story?

13 A. Yes.

14 Q. Was there a discussion within Tribal Social Services

15 about the possibility of an independent interview of the kids,

16 to hire somebody to come in to maybe speak with the kids and

17 find out if there was a problem with what they were saying?

18 A. Not that I recall.

19 Q. Well, again in the affidavit, Kathleen, I apologize for

20 this, but this is in '99 we talked about it, it indicates you

21 asked for an independent interview of the children, and your

22 supervisor agreed at first but then the interview was canceled

23 and nothing more was done, do you recall that?

24 A. No.

25 Q. Do you recall inquiring about different names that you

Page 123

1 might find as experts who could do an interview like that?

2 A. No.

3 Q. But as you received the information from the kids you

4 found it to be believable?

5 A. I don't --

6 Q. When you spoke to the kids, or they spoke to you, you

7 found them to be apparently telling the truth to you?

8 A. On what accusations, or what?

9 Q. When Thrista came to you and said it never happened, you

10 found that to be believable?

11 A. Jessica is the one that told me that, it was in the

12 report. Thrista just said that her uncles never did that, and

13 I believed for her to be telling the truth, yes.

14   MR. HAUGAARD: No further questions.

15   THE COURT: Cross.

16 CROSS EXAMINATION BY MR. HOLMES:

17 Q. Ms. Honomichl, my name is Dennis Holmes, I am an

18 Assistant United States Attorney, I have some questions for

19 you. You don't have a college education, do you?

20 A. No.

21 Q. And you received no college or technical training in the

22 field of social work, did you?

23 A. Not other than the course I took in college.

24 Q. The time you took this position in June of '95 you had no

25 training in social work other than this one course, is that

Page 124

1 correct?

2 A. No, sir.

3 Q. What other training did you have?

4 A. I took the course after I had accepted the job.

5 Q. You had two and a half years in nursing training, is that

6 correct?

7 A. Yes.

8 Q. What specific training did you have after joining Social

9 Services regarding the investigation of sexual abuse cases?

10 A. Just in sexual abuse, I had no training in that when

11 taking the job.

12 Q. And in fact, you attempted to obtain state certification

13 as a social worker, did you not?

14 A. Did I obtain it?

15 Q. You attempted to?

16 A. Yes.

17 Q. And you failed that test, didn't you?

18 A. No.

19 Q. You were never certified as a social worker through the

20 state certification process?

21 A. Not certified, no.

22 Q. It is true in fact that a portion of the examination that

23 you failed dealt with interviewing children, isn't that

24 correct?

25 A. Yes.

Page 125

1 Q. You did not become involved with this case until almost a
2 year after the trial had occurred, is that correct?
3 A. I am not sure when the trial occurred, but I became
4 involved probably in the year of '95, 1995.
5 Q. In fact, you volunteered to take over this case, is that
6 correct?
7 A. I was asked to take over the case.
8 Q. And you were friends with the Rouse family, were you not?
9 A. I knew them as growing up.
10 Q. You indicated that you formed a conclusion regarding
11 these allegations based upon your review of the file, is that
12 right?
13 A. And working with the children.
14 Q. I think your testimony on direct was that it was after
15 you had read the file you came to the conclusion this could not
16 have happened, correct?
17 A. No. After reading the file and working with the
18 children.
19 Q. Well, you read the file right after you took over the
20 case, didn't you?
21 A. Yes.
22 Q. And that is when you formed your conclusion?
23 A. No, after I worked with the children.
24 Q. You indicated you did not interview these children?
25 A. No.

Page 126

1 Q. You never interviewed them, is that correct?
2 A. No.
3 Q. And you made an effort not to discuss with them the
4 sexual abuse allegations, is that correct?
5 A. Yes.
6 Q. In fact, the only time any of these children spoke to you
7 regarding the sexual abuse was when Thrista made this statement
8 about the fact that she was saying the uncles never did that to
9 her, that's the only statement any of these children made to
10 you about the sexual abuse allegations, isn't that correct?
11 A. Jerome also made a statement.
12 Q. But as far as the children who were, who testified in
13 this case, the only one that you had any conversation with
14 regarding whether the abuse occurred was Thrista, is that
15 right?
16 A. Yes.
17 Q. And that was just this one time, correct?
18 A. Not that I remember, I talked about it before. I mean it
19 wasn't just a one time thing.
20 Q. Well, correct me, but on direct you said that there was
21 only this one occasion when Thrista, Rosemary and Donovan came
22 to your office and she said that the uncles didn't do anything,
23 right?
24 A. Yes.
25 Q. That was the only time they spoke about it?

Page 127

1 A. Yes.
2 Q. And so you formed your conclusion that none of this
3 happened based upon your review of the file and this one
4 comment by Thrista, correct?
5 A. No.
6 Q. What else did you utilize to form your conclusions?
7 A. I visited several times with their therapist, Mary Weber,
8 and the incident reports that were sent to my office.
9 Q. The only incident report that you made reference to was
10 this one where you have talked about Jessica indicating that
11 this didn't happen?
12 A. There was two, but I am not sure what the other one said.
13 There was two incident reports sent to me.
14 Q. And I think you also testified that you came to this
15 conclusion that nothing happened based upon the fact that these
16 were big men and that these children couldn't have had sex with
17 them?
18 A. I didn't come to that conclusion, I just found it awful
19 hard to believe.
20 Q. Did you review in the file the medical examinations of
21 these children?
22 A. Yes.
23 Q. And what do you remember about the medical findings?
24 A. Didn't really understand it. It was like twelve o'clock,
25 two different things like that. I don't understand that.

Page 128

1 Q. And you came to this conclusion that the abuse had not
2 occurred earlier in your involvement in this case, didn't you?
3 A. No, I never came to that conclusion.
4 Q. Well, when did you come to that conclusion?
5 A. I never came to that conclusion, it's just the reports
6 that I had.
7 Q. In fact, you let the children know this, that you didn't
8 believe the abuse occurred, did you not?
9 A. No, I did not let the children believe that.
10 Q. You told your co-workers that, didn't you?
11 A. I talked with them about it.
12 Q. Now you were personal friends with Beta Rouse, were you
13 not?
14 A. Not before the case, no.
15 Q. Well, you loaned her your car on several occasions, did
16 you not?
17 A. Yes.
18 Q. You loaned her money?
19 A. Yes.
20 Q. Did she believe that these incidents of abuse had
21 occurred?
22 A. No.
23 Q. In fact, she was not supportive of the children at all
24 regarding those allegations, was she?
25 A. She was supportive in their therapy.

Page 129

1 Q. But she consistently stated in therapy that she did not
2 believe any of this took place, didn't she?
3 A. No.
4 Q. During what period of time were the children at
5 Children's Home Society?
6 A. When I took the kids the children were already in
7 Children's Home Society.
8 Q. How long did they remain there?
9 A. I believe they were still there when I resigned.
10 Q. Which was in June of '97?
11 A. Yes.
12 Q. You indicated that you received this report from Mary
13 Weber regarding a statement made by Jessica?
14 A. Yes.
15 Q. When was that?
16 A. I am not sure of the date when she had sent that, it was
17 faxed to me.
18 Q. After you received it did you immediately fax it to the
19 U.S. Attorney's office?
20 A. Yes, I did.
21 Q. I believe you testified that you believe you did this in
22 March of 1996?
23 A. When the children came into the office, I believe that's
24 what I testified.
25 Q. No, I think, and the record would properly reflect this,

Page 130

1 my notes indicate that you testified that you received this
2 report from Mary Weber in March of 1996, does that correspond
3 with your memory?
4 A. It was probably in '96.
5 Q. About ten months after you were involved with the case?
6 A. Somewhere in there, yes.
7   MR. HOLMES: May I approach the witness, Your Honor?
8   THE COURT: You may.
9
10   (Exhibit 5 marked For identification.)
11
12 BY MR. HOLMES:
13 Q. Ms. Honomichl, I show you what has been marked as
14 Government's Exhibit No. 5, do you recognize that? You
15 recognize that as an affidavit that you signed?
16 A. Yes, that's my signature.
17   MR. HOLMES: I offer Exhibit 5.
18   MR. HAUGAARD: No objection.
19   THE COURT: 5 is received.
20 BY MR. HOLMES:
21 Q. Drawing your attention to the bottom of the first page of
22 Exhibit 5, in that paragraph you state that you received this
23 information from Mary Weber between June of '95 and November of
24 '95, is that correct?
25 A. I don't know if that is the correct dates.

Page 131

1 Q. How was this affidavit Exhibit 5 prepared?
2 A. How was it prepared? Talking with Mr. Haugaard, he would
3 ask questions and I just answered them the best I could.
4 Q. Did he bring back an affidavit after he talked to you
5 based upon your conversations with him?
6 A. Yes.
7 Q. Who typed up Exhibit 5?
8 A. I don't know who typed it up.
9 Q. You didn't?
10 A. No.
11 Q. Did you understand that you were under oath when you
12 signed Exhibit 5?
13 A. Yes.
14 Q. Were you careful in reviewing that Exhibit before you
15 signed it?
16 A. I believed the affidavit to be what we talked about.
17 Q. In fact, in that affidavit you say that this information
18 was received many months earlier than February or March of '96,
19 is that correct?
20 A. I guessed when I got it, I don't know the exact dates,
21 the date that it came in.
22 Q. Well, are you guessing today also when it came in?
23 A. I am probably not guessing, I am trying to recollect my
24 memory. I am not sure of the dates or the month. I just
25 received the reports and faxed them on.

Page 132

1 Q. Did you keep a copy of that report from Mary Weber?
2 A. Yes.
3 Q. Did you bring that with you today?
4 A. No.
5 Q. Why not?
6 A. You are not allowed to take any of those things out of
7 the case file. That would be in their file.
8 Q. You indicated that after you received this information
9 you talked to Victor Provost, is that correct?
10 A. Yes, we had discussed it.
11 Q. What did Victor Provost have to do with the supervision
12 of these children?
13 A. He was over Social Services, and he was over a lot of
14 programs at the tribe at that time.
15 Q. Is he a friend of the Rouse family?
16 A. I have no idea.
17 Q. You indicated that you had talked to Ida Ashes and Deena
18 LaPointe about it, is that correct?
19 A. Yes.
20 Q. In fact, Deena had been the social worker assigned to
21 this case before you, is that right?
22 A. Yes.
23 Q. From your dealings with the children, how did they get
24 along with Deena?
25 A. They seemed to have liked her very well.

Page 133	Page 135
1 Q. What about Donovan's feelings about Deena?	1 Donovan described how they had been walking with Rosemary and
2 A. I never talked to Donovan about his feelings about Deena.	2 she said nothing had been done to them by the uncles, and you
3 Q. Did he ever express to you that Deena had told him to	3 said they never told you that, is that correct?
4 make up things?	4 A. I am not aware of them walking or discussing it.
5 A. No.	5 Q. Drawing your attention to the second page of Exhibit 5,
6 Q. You testified that on some occasion Donovan, Rosemary and	6 the third paragraph, third full paragraph, your affidavit
7 Thrista came into your office?	7 states that Thrista and Donovan described how they had been
8 A. Yes.	8 walking with their cousin Rosemary, and she also said that
9 Q. What were the circumstances which caused them to come	9 nothing was done to her by the uncles. That statement in your
10 into your office?	10 affidavit was not true, was it?
11 A. I don't know what, why they came there, they were just	11 A. I don't recall it right offhand, but I am not saying it
12 visiting.	12 is not true. It has been several years since then.
13 Q. Were they still at the Children's Home Society at the	13 Q. You were asked by Mr. Haugaard about that statement on
14 time?	14 direct exam and you testified that it never happened, correct?
15 A. They were at Marty in the housing.	15 A. I don't remember them walking and discussing that, no.
16 Q. So they had been returned to their parents?	16 Q. When did you first talk to Mr. Haugaard about this case?
17 A. Not permanently, no, just a visit.	17 A. I don't remember when the first time was. I think he
18 Q. Explain that situation to me. When they would have	18 might have contacted me.
19 visits, how long would they be with the parents?	19 Q. In fact, you arranged to have Mr. Haugaard talk to these
20 A. It would probably be on a weekend.	20 children, did you not?
21 Q. So it's your testimony that these three children came	21 A. Did I arrange for them to talk with them?
22 into your office on a weekend?	22 Q. Yes?
23 A. They are picked up on Friday, brought home, and taken	23 A. No, I never arranged for him to talk with the children.
24 back after the weekend was over.	24 Q. You arranged to allow Dr. Underwager to interview Donovan
25 Q. Who is the mother of Thrista and Donovan?	25 and Thrista in 1996, did you not?

Page 134	Page 136
1 A. Beta is the mother of mother of Donovan, and Ursula is	1 A. Doctor who?
2 the mother of Thrista.	2 Q. Underwager.
3 Q. Who is Rosemary's mother?	3 A. I don't believe I would have the authority to do that, to
4 A. Rodrica.	4 have somebody come in and interview these children.
5 Q. It's your testimony that these three children, all who	5 Q. Were you aware they were interviewed by Dr. Underwager?
6 would have been returned to different mother's, would have	6 A. No, I don't know who they were interviewed by. Not when
7 happened to just show up at your office?	7 I was the case worker I don't recall them ever being
8 A. Yes, all three of them showed up at my office.	8 interviewed by a Dr. Underwager.
9 Q. Were their mother's with them?	9 Q. Well, the Tribe had custody over these children, correct?
10 A. No.	10 A. Yes.
11 Q. During that time, which you say took place in your	11 Q. And to do a clinical or interview of these children,
12 office, neither Donovan nor Rosemary said anything about the	12 someone would need permission from the person who had custody
13 abuse?	13 over these children, is that right?
14 A. No.	14 A. Yes.
15 Q. They never affirmed what you say Thrista said?	15 Q. Were you ever asked for permission to have these children
16 A. No.	16 interviewed by Dr. Underwager?
17 Q. They never said we weren't abused either, is that	17 A. Not that I remember, no.
18 correct?	18 Q. You also testified, I believe, that you never made an
19 A. No. They never stated that, no.	19 effort to have these children interviewed by an independent
20 Q. Have you put a date on when this took place?	20 expert or someone independent of the case, do you recall that
21 A. No, I just know the weather was nice, it would have had	21 testimony?
22 to have been probably in the summer time.	22 A. I never, I am not aware of any interviews.
23 Q. Of what year?	23 Q. But you never asked that that be done, is that correct,
24 A. I am guessing probably in '96.	24 that someone else --
25 Q. You were asked by Mr. Haugaard about whether Thrista and	25 A. Not that I remember, no.

Page 137	Page 139
1 Q. I draw your attention to the last sentence of your	1 A. Maggie Cavender.
2 affidavit, Exhibit 5. You state that I asked for an	2 Q. Who else?
3 independent interview of the children, and my supervisor agreed	3 A. She was my immediate supervisor.
4 at first, but then the interview was canceled and nothing more	4 Q. What about Mr. Frier?
5 was done. Is that a false statement?	5 A. Probably about the last two months of my employment
6 A. That could have been -- what we had talked about, that	6 there.
7 could have been on the interviewing part is where I had brought	7 Q. Did you ever tell either one of them that a lawyer named
8 up, not necessarily the Rouse case, any case, other children,	8 Steve kept calling you?
9 another family, if something like this should happen again,	9 A. I think I mentioned that to Maggie.
10 that a case worker probably should be present when they are	10 Q. What was that in reference to?
11 interviewed. Not to interfere in the line of questioning, just	11 A. He just told me who he was and it had to do with the
12 to be present.	12 Rouse case, and I told him I couldn't talk about it.
13 Q. Ms. Honomichl, you reviewed this affidavit before you	13 Q. You remember telling Karla Harmon that you better get an
14 signed it, correct?	14 attorney because you were going to be in big trouble for
15 A. Yes.	15 something you had done?
16 Q. Did you try and make an effort to make sure it was	16 A. Who?
17 accurate?	17 Q. Karla Harmon?
18 A. Yes, I did make an effort to try to make sure it was	18 A. I don't know who that is.
19 accurate.	19 Q. Did you ever make that statement, that you better get an
20 Q. And this affidavit says nothing about an interview of	20 attorney because you were going to be in big trouble for
21 children in general?	21 something that you had done?
22 A. No, it doesn't.	22 A. I don't recall that, no.
23 Q. It says I asked for an independent interview of the	23 Q. When did you become aware that these children had been
24 children, correct?	24 interviewed by Dr. Underwager?
25 A. That's what it says, yes.	25 A. I don't know that they were interviewed. The name sounds

Page 138	Page 140
1 Q. And you have testified under oath here today that you	1 familiar, Dr. Underwager, but I can't place him.
2 never did that?	2 Q. You were never told that by anybody?
3 A. I never made a request to interview these children.	3 MR. HAUGAARD: Asked and answered, Your Honor.
4 Q. So that statement in your affidavit is false?	4 THE COURT: Overruled.
5 A. That's not correct, the statement.	5 A. Can you repeat that, please?
6 Q. The statement in your affidavit is not correct?	6 BY MR. HOLMES:
7 A. No, I have never asked for the children to be interviewed	7 Q. You were never told by anybody that these children had
8 by an independent person. That would be out of my authority to	8 been interviewed by Dr. Underwager?
9 even do that.	9 A. Not that I recall, no.
10 Q. What contact were these children having with their	10 Q. Isn't it a fact, Ms. Honomichl, that you quit the
11 Grandmother Rosemary Rouse during the period of time that you	11 department of Social Services with the Tribe because of
12 were involved in the case?	12 criticism by your supervisors regarding how you were handling
13 A. What contact did they have?	13 this case?
14 Q. Yes?	14 A. No, sir.
15 A. I think Rosemary might have went with us one time for	15 Q. You were never told that you were handling the case
16 sure, maybe twice, just to visit at the Children's Home	16 inappropriately?
17 Society.	17 A. No.
18 Q. You were aware, were you not, that she did not believe	18 Q. You were never told that you were too close to the family
19 that the abuse had taken place?	19 in this case?
20 A. Yes.	20 A. I was told I was getting too involved in it, yes. I
21 Q. And she conveyed that to the children in your presence,	21 realized that myself.
22 didn't she?	22 Q. And knowing those criticisms, that is why you quit your
23 A. No.	23 employment with the Tribal Social Services, isn't that correct?
24 Q. During the time you were with Social Services who were	24 A. No, I quit the Tribal Social Services because I was too
25 your immediate supervisors?	25 stressed out over the case.

Page 141

1   MR. HOLMES: No further questions.
2   THE COURT: Redirect.
3 REDIRECT EXAMINATION BY MR. HAUGAARD:
4 Q. Kathleen, after you have had a chance to review this
5 affidavit, this Exhibit, do you believe at the time you signed
6 it, it to be accurate?
7 A. Yes.
8 Q. And if today you don't recall things the way you did two
9 and a half years ago, would you expect that probably two and a
10 half years ago your memory was better?
11 A. Yes.
12 Q. Mr. Holmes asked you about interviewing the children, I
13 believe your response was no. Would you believe that to be
14 your responsibility at all, to grill the kids about this
15 claimed abuse?
16 A. That's not my responsibility to do that.
17 Q. You also testified at first when you received the case
18 you actually did believe it to be accurate, didn't you, the
19 claimed abuse?
20 A. Yes.
21 Q. And when Thrista made the statements that she did in your
22 office, you observed the reactions of both Rosemary and Donovan
23 at that time, is that correct?
24 A. Yes.
25 Q. And they didn't indicate anything that would suggest that

Page 142

1 Thrista was --
2   MR. HOLMES: Objection, leading.
3   THE COURT: Sustained.
4 BY MR. HAUGAARD:
5 Q. Did they show any sign that Thrista's statement was
6 false?
7 A. No.
8 Q. Mr. Holmes also asked you about loaning your car or money
9 to family members, have you ever loaned your car or money to
10 people other than the Rouse family?
11 A. Yes.
12 Q. And did you in a sense see that as part of your
13 responsibilities as working with the Tribal Social Services?
14 A. No.
15 Q. But is it just part of being in the community?
16 A. Yes.
17 Q. When Thrista made the statement that she did, were the
18 kids living at the dorm at that time?
19 A. Not when I was their worker they never, ever stayed in
20 the dorm.
21 Q. Did the mothers get unsupervised visits right away?
22 A. No.
23 Q. That took some period of time before they got
24 unsupervised visits?
25 A. Yes.

Page 143

1 Q. And when the family eventually had weekend visits could
2 they come and go as they pleased with the children?
3 A. No, they were to stay home.
4 Q. But no one was there to supervise what was going on, is
5 that correct?
6 A. Not 24 hours a day, no.
7 Q. Did the children ever report to you that their family was
8 putting pressure on them to change their story?
9 A. No.
10   MR. HAUGAARD: No further questions.
11   THE COURT: Any recross?
12 RECROSS EXAMINATION BY MR. HOLMES:
13 Q. You described supervised visits. Who supervised those
14 visits?
15 A. Children's Home Society.
16 Q. Those would be situations when the mothers came up here,
17 is that correct?
18 A. Yes.
19 Q. After the children were allowed to go to Marty, those
20 visits were not supervised in any way, is that correct?
21 A. Not on a 24 hour basis. I would go down to pick them up
22 on Friday, take them home, and I would go down on Saturday just
23 to check to make sure there was no alcohol in the home when the
24 children were there.
25 Q. And when did those type of visits, those being the

Page 144

1 returns to Marty, start taking place?
2 A. Probably about a little over a year after I became the
3 case worker, and that only happened once.
4 Q. There was only one time when they were taken down to
5 Marty?
6 A. When I was their worker, yes.
7 Q. One time between June of '95 and when you left in June of
8 '97, is that correct?
9 A. Yes.
10 Q. And it just so happened that on that one visit these
11 three children just walked into your office?
12 A. On the morning that they were, that afternoon I was going
13 to take them back.
14 Q. That would have been a Sunday?
15 A. No, it would have been Monday. Monday or Tuesday.
16 Monday.
17 Q. But that happened to be the only time during your
18 supervision of the children that they were down to Marty?
19 A. As far as I can remember, yes. I don't know after that.
20 Q. And that would have been some time in the summer?
21 A. Yes.
22 Q. '96 or '97?
23 A. I would say probably in '96.
24 Q. Mr. Haugaard asked you some questions about Exhibit 5,
25 about whether your memory would have been better in 1999 when

Page 145

1 you signed it, do you recall those questions?

2 A. Yes.

3 Q. But today here you have testified that some of these

4 statements in this affidavit simply aren't true, isn't that

5 correct?

6 A. I am not saying they are not true. Like on the

7 interviewing part, the only thing I can recall about

8 interviewing was what I explained.

9 Q. As stated in the affidavit that wasn't true?

10 A. Not the way it is stated here, the way it is written.

11 Q. It's also not true that Thrista and Donovan described

12 this conversation with Rosemary while they were walking with

13 her, that never happened, did it?

14 A. I don't know if it ever, it didn't ever happen.

15 Q. You were never told that?

16 A. Not that I recall, no.

17   MR. HOLMES: Nothing further.

18 REDIRECT EXAMINATION BY MR. HAUGAARD:

19 Q. Ms. Honomichl, when you signed this you read it, is that

20 correct?

21 A. Yes.

22 Q. At that time you believed it to be accurate, is that

23 correct?

24 A. Yes.

25   MR. HAUGAARD: Nothing further.

Page 146

1   MR. HOLMES: No questions.

2   THE COURT: Ms. Honomichl, once you finished your

3 education, then did you get your registered nurse certificate?

4 A. No.

5   THE COURT: Did you complete the academic

6 requirements, or did you have some more to complete before you

7 could get that certificate?

8 A. I completed up to nursing 101.

9   THE COURT: I don't know what that means.

10 A. I didn't finish the clinical parts of it, just the first

11 one.

12   THE COURT: Thank you, you may step down. We will be

13 in recess for ten minutes.

14 (Recess at 3:08 until 3:18)

15   THE COURT: Call your next witness.

16   MR. HAUGAARD: Call Julia Gonzales.

17

18   JULIA ANN JOSEPH GONZALES,

19 called as a witness, being first duly sworn, testified and said

20 as follows:

21

22 DIRECT EXAMINATION BY MR. HAUGAARD:

23 Q. Julia, please state your name for the record?

24 A. Julia Ann Joseph Gonzales.

25 Q. Where are you employed?

Page 147

1 A. Right now Fort Randall casino.

2 Q. Were you previously employed by Tribal Social Services?

3 A. No.

4 Q. Or by the Marty Indian School?

5 A. Marty Indian School, yes.

6 Q. What were your responsibilities there?

7 A. I was a dorm parent.

8 Q. What's is your background and education?

9 A. The first I graduated from Marty, and I had two years of

10 college.

11 Q. Where did you go to college?

12 A. I had one year at Mount Marty in Yankton and a couple of

13 years down at Haskell Indian College.

14 Q. What did you study?

15 A. Accounting.

16 Q. Do you recall having conversations with me a couple of

17 years ago and preparing an affidavit in regard to information

18 that you knew to be true?

19 A. Yes.

20   MR. HAUGAARD: May I approach the witness, Your

21 Honor?

22   THE COURT: You may.

23

24   (Exhibit B marked For identification.)

25

Page 148

1   MR. HAUGAARD:

2 Q. I show you Defendant's Exhibit B, would you review that,

3 please?

4 A. Okay.

5 Q. Is that affidavit accurate?

6 A. Yes.

7 Q. So when were you employed as a dorm parent at the Marty

8 Indian?

9   MR. HOLMES: I object to the witness having the

10 Exhibit before her, she has not indicated a lack of

11 recollection, no need for her to refresh her recollection, and

12 I believe the testimony should be independent of the document

13 until the witness asserts a lack of recollection.

14   THE COURT: Sustained.

15 BY MR. HAUGAARD:

16 Q. If you would set that aside. What period of time were

17 you employed as a dorm parent at the Marty Indian School?

18 A. From 2000 to '96, I believe.

19 Q. While you were a dorm parent was Rosemary Rouse a

20 resident of the dorm?

21 A. Yes.

22 Q. When I refer to her, we are talking about little Rosemary

23 Rouse?

24 A. Yes.

25 Q. Who is her mother?

Page 149	Page 151
1 A. Rodrica Rouse.	1 Q. Did there come a point in time when she came to you and
2 Q. Did Rosemary Rouse come to you at some point while she	2 made any statements about the claimed abuse?
3 was lodged at the dorm there and speak to you about the claimed	3 A. Yes.
4 sexual abuse?	4 Q. You recall approximately when that was?
5 A. Yes.	5 A. No, I don't.
6 Q. What did she tell you?	6 Q. In your affidavit it indicates --
7 MR. HOLMES: Objection, foundation.	7 MR. HOLMES: Objection, leading and suggestive.
8 THE COURT: Sustained.	8 THE COURT: Sustained.
9 BY MR. HAUGAARD:	9 BY MR. HAUGAARD:
10 Q. What period of time was this when she spoke to you about	10 Q. Would you like to refer to the affidavit to refresh your
11 this claimed sexual abuse?	11 recollection?
12 A. Around April.	12 A. Yes.
13 Q. Of what year, do you recall?	13 Q. If you would review the last paragraph on that page.
14 A. I believe in '99.	14 A. Okay.
15 Q. What prompted her to come to you, or let me ask you this.	15 Q. When do you believe it was that Thrista came to you and
16 Did you go to her and ask her questions about this alleged	16 spoke to you about the claimed abuse?
17 sexual abuse?	17 A. In February.
18 A. No.	18 Q. Of what year?
19 Q. Did she come to you independently to speak with you?	19 A. '97.
20 A. Yes.	20 Q. What else did she tell you about the claimed, or what did
21 Q. What did she tell you?	21 she tell you about the claimed abuse?
22 A. That none of it happened.	22 A. She said she felt bad.
23 Q. Did she say more than that?	23 Q. Bad about what?
24 A. She said she, she told me she didn't know why she was	24 A. She said that she was lying.
25 going to counseling.	25 Q. She was lying about what?

Page 150	Page 152
1 Q. When did she tell you that?	1 A. About the abuse.
2 A. In April, May.	2 Q. She say the abuse had not taken place?
3 Q. What were the responsibilities you had as a dorm parent,	3 A. Yes.
4 what did they include?	4 Q. Did she talk about how the information came about?
5 A. Taking care of them, putting them to bed, showing them	5 A. She said they kept asking her questions, she said she was
6 how to wash clothes, more like a parent would do.	6 hungry, wanted to go to the bathroom, and she just after that
7 Q. Was Rosemary involved in counseling at that time?	7 started saying yes, yes, yes, whenever they would ask her a
8 A. Yes.	8 question.
9 Q. Was Thrista involved in counseling at that time?	9 Q. Did you inquire about this, or was this information she
10 A. No.	10 brought up?
11 Q. When Rosemary was involved in counseling did you have any	11 A. No, she told me that.
12 responsibilities as far as getting her to and from counseling?	12 Q. How long had you known Thrista at this time?
13 A. I took her a couple of times to Yankton.	13 A. Personally for about a year.
14 Q. During those trips to Yankton did you visit about the	14 Q. Are you related to the family?
15 claimed abuse?	15 A. Yes.
16 A. I just asked her how counseling was going, and that's	16 Q. How are you related?
17 when she told me that she didn't know why she was going.	17 A. First cousin.
18 Q. Did she say more than that?	18 Q. How long had you known Rosemary before she made these
19 A. No.	19 comments?
20 Q. Did she say that, you had mentioned before she claimed	20 A. Probably maybe a year.
21 that nothing had ever happened, when did she say that?	21 Q. As you reviewed that affidavit today, do you affirm that
22 A. Around that time.	22 affidavit, find it to be accurate?
23 Q. Did you have a conversation with Thrista Rouse as you	23 A. Yes.
24 were serving as a dorm parent?	24 MR. HAUGAARD: I offer Exhibit B, Your Honor.
25 A. Yes.	25 MR. HOLMES: Your Honor, we have already marked all

Page 153

1 of these affidavits, I have no objection to the affidavit. We
2 would ask our Exhibit which has been numbered 6 be used instead
3 of the one that has been labeled as a defense Exhibit.
4   THE COURT: Well, B has been marked also, so we will
5 receive it as B. Exhibit B is received.
6 BY MR. HAUGAARD:
7 Q. Did the girls ever say anything about the family
8 pressuring them to say these things?
9 A. No.
10 Q. Did you ever observe the family to be pressuring the
11 girls to say that the abuse did not take place?
12 A. No.
13 Q. Did you ever receive pressure yourself from the family
14 members to try to get the girls to change their stories?
15 A. No.
16 Q. And did you generally avoid discussing the alleged abuse
17 with the kids?
18 A. Yes.
19   MR. HAUGAARD: No further questions.
20   THE COURT: Cross.
21 CROSS EXAMINATION BY MR. HOLMES:
22 Q. You, Rosemary Rouse, the elder Rosemary Rouse is your
23 aunt, is that correct?
24 A. Yes.
25 Q. And two of her sons are in the courtroom today, is that

Page 154

1 right?
2 A. Yes.
3 Q. Desmond and Jessie?
4 A. Yes.
5 Q. So you are cousins to two of the defendants?
6 A. Yes.
7 Q. And you are a friend of Beta Rouse, are you not?
8 A. Yes.
9 Q. What about the other mother's, Ursula and Rodrica, you
10 are a friend of them, is that correct?
11 A. Yes.
12 Q. From your memory, when did Rosemary first come to live at
13 the Marty Indian School dorm?
14 A. In '97.
15 Q. And the statement that you have testified to occurred in
16 '99?
17 A. There that was in '97.
18 Q. You recall testifying on direct examination that she came
19 to you in April or May of 1999?
20 A. Yes, I got nervous, I am sorry.
21 Q. What about Thrista, how long was she at the dorm?
22 A. The same time Thrista was in the dorm, and Rosemary was
23 in there too.
24 Q. Do you know where they had been living before they came
25 to the dormitory?

Page 155

1 A. No.
2 Q. Were you aware of a Kathleen Honomichl testified that she
3 was the social worker of these two children?
4 A. Yes.
5 Q. And were you aware that she testified that --
6   MR. HAUGAARD: Objection, that's inaccurate, Kathleen
7 Honomichl did not testify she was the social worker as to
8 Rosemary.
9   THE COURT: Overruled.
10 BY MR. HOLMES:
11 Q. Are you aware that she has testified in this proceeding
12 that the children were never at the dormitory in Marty while
13 she was their social worker?
14 A. No.
15 Q. While the children were in the dormitory, how much
16 interaction to your knowledge did they have with their mothers?
17 A. I believe only on weekends.
18 Q. So they would routinely go home to live with their
19 mothers?
20 A. Yes.
21 Q. That would be true for most of the children at Marty, is
22 that right?
23 A. Yes.
24 Q. To your knowledge what contact did they have with the
25 Grandmother, Rosemary?

Page 156

1 A. I wouldn't know.
2 Q. Did they ever talk about that?
3 A. No.
4 Q. Were you aware that the mothers testified at the trial in
5 this case?
6 A. No.
7 Q. Were you aware that they believe that these children had
8 not been abused by the defendants?
9 A. Yes.
10 Q. And you are friend with the mothers?
11 A. Yes.
12 Q. You were aware that they were of the opinion even before
13 the trial and after the trial that these acts of abuse did not
14 occur, correct?
15 A. Yes.
16 Q. You were responsible for taking Rosemary to therapy over
17 in Yankton, is that correct?
18 A. Yes.
19 Q. I believe you testified that on one of these occasions
20 when you were coming back from counseling with her Rosemary
21 said that she didn't know why she was going to counseling?
22 A. Yes.
23 Q. But she never said in reference to the counseling
24 sessions that none of this abuse had ever happened, correct?
25 A. No.

Page 157

1 Q. He just said she didn't know why she was going to
2 counseling, that was the only thing she said, is that correct?
3 A. Yep.
4 Q. I am sorry, I didn't hear your answer.
5 A. Yes.
6 Q. So your statement in your affidavit, which says I asked
7 her how counseling was going and she said she didn't even know
8 why she was going because nothing ever happened to her, is
9 incorrect?
10 A. No, I am getting myself mixed up. No, she said that.
11 Q. But at another time?
12 A. Yes.
13 Q. So the affidavit is incorrect?
14 A. A little bit, yeah.
15 Q. Explain to me how this affidavit was prepared?
16 A. It was, I was trying to recall. I don't know, I was
17 getting them kind of mixed up.
18 Q. Well, you didn't type the affidavit up, did you?
19 A. No.
20 Q. Mr. Haugaard presented it to you, is that correct?
21 A. Yes.
22 Q. Did you review it before you signed it?
23 A. Yes, I did.
24 Q. Were you aware you were under oath when you signed it?
25 A. Yes.

Page 158

1 Q. But apparently it is not correct?
2 A. Well, she did say that, yes, but, you know, I didn't
3 really exactly know when, or what time, or anything like that.
4 Q. You have also testified that Thrista told you that the
5 investigators kept her from using the bathroom and wouldn't let
6 her eat, is that right?
7 A. Yes.
8 Q. Who specifically did she say did that?
9 A. She said a woman who was talking to her. She knows her
10 name, it is just that I don't remember the woman's name.
11 Q. So it was this woman who was interviewing her that denied
12 her anything to drink and wouldn't let her use the bathroom?
13 A. Yes.
14 Q. That's what she told you?
15 A. Yes.
16 Q. You have also testified that it was during a trip back
17 from the counselor that Thrista made, I am sorry, Rosemary made
18 the statement about she didn't know why she needed to go, is
19 that right?
20 A. Yes.
21 Q. You know who her counselor was?
22 A. I believe she was a Nun.
23 Q. Are you aware during the counseling sessions with that
24 individual that Rosemary never recanted?
25 A. No.

Page 159

1 Q. Are you aware that she always told that individual that
2 she had been abused as she testified to in this courtroom?
3 A. No.
4   MR. HAUGAARD: Objection, Your Honor, leading the
5 witness, testimony not in evidence.
6   THE COURT: Overruled, cross examination.
7 BY MR. HOLMES:
8 Q. She never told you that?
9 A. No.
10   MR. HOLMES: Nothing further.
11   THE COURT: Redirect.
12 REDIRECT EXAMINATION BY MR. HAUGAARD:
13 Q. In your affidavit you indicate that when you asked
14 Rosemary how counseling was going, she said she didn't know why
15 she was going because nothing had ever happened to her. If
16 that wasn't said at exactly the same time, was it within the
17 same general timeframe.
18 A. Yes.
19 Q. Would you ever lie for your cousins to get them out of
20 jail in this case?
21 A. No.
22   MR. HAUGAARD: No further questions.
23   MR. HOLMES: Nothing further, Your Honor.
24   THE COURT: Thank you, you may step down. Call your
25 next witness.

Page 160

1   MR. HAUGAARD: Call Victor Provost.
2
3   VICTOR W. PROVOST,
4 called as a witness, being first duly sworn, testified and said
5 as follows:
6
7 DIRECT EXAMINATION BY MR. HAUGAARD:
8 Q. Victor, please state your name for the record and spell
9 your last name?
10 A. Victor W. Provost, Senior, my last name P-R-O-V-O-S-T.
11 Q. Victor, where are you employed presently?
12 A. I am not.
13 Q. What kind of work do you do?
14 A. Right now I have a private consulting, that's what I am
15 in to now.
16 Q. What kind of things do you consult about?
17 A. Oh, anything from Tribal 638 to HUD housing, it could be
18 anything from writing organizational policies and so on and so
19 forth.
20 Q. Were you previously employed by the Yankton Sioux Tribe?
21 A. Yes.
22 Q. What was your position?
23 A. Chief executive officer.
24 Q. What does that entail generally?
25 A. I was the chief executive officer over all Tribal

Page 161

1 programs and federal programs.
2 Q. Did there come a time when you became aware of the Rouse
3 case?
4 A. Yes.
5 Q. Were you employed as the CEO for the tribe at the time
6 that Kathleen Honomichl was serving as social worker for the
7 tribe?
8 A. Yes.
9 Q. Did there come a time when Kathleen Honomichl came to you
10 to discuss the Rouse case?
11 A. Yes.
12 Q. Did she express concerns about a report that she had
13 received about one of the girls recanting her previous claims
14 of abuse?
15   MR. HOLMES: Objection, foundation.
16   THE COURT: Sustained.
17 BY MR. HAUGAARD:
18 Q. Did you have discussions with Kathleen about reports that
19 she might have received in regard to her work as social worker?
20 A. Yes, we did.
21 Q. Did she discuss the general content of those reports with
22 you?
23 A. Yes.
24 Q. Did there come a time when there was a meeting between
25 youth and Kathleen and maybe some others in regard to this

Page 162

1 report that she had received concerning the Rouse children?
2 A. Yes, but I only recall having a meeting with Kathleen.
3 There could have been others there, but I can't remember them.
4 Q. Did she express to you concerns that the report indicated
5 one of the children denied the abuse?
6   MR. HOLMES: Objection, foundation, relevancy.
7   THE COURT: Well, sustained as to foundation, not as
8 to relevance.
9 BY MR. HAUGAARD:
10 Q. Did she discuss with you the content of the report?
11 A. Yes.
12 Q. Who was the report about, was it about one of the
13 children involved in this case?
14 A. It had to do with one of the children that was, it's been
15 a few years ago, had to do with the children, or children
16 placed in a placement, I believe here around Sioux Falls.
17 Q. Do you remember approximately what month or what year
18 that would be?
19 A. Let me see. It's been such a long time ago, I would have
20 to put it approximate in the fall of '96, winter of '97.
21 Q. Did she express concerns about the content of that
22 report?
23 A. Yes.
24 Q. Did she indicate that there was a concern that the claims
25 might be false?

Page 163

1 A. Yes.
2 Q. Was there further action taken by you at that time in
3 regard to this concern about the report?
4 A. We, I took it under advisement, and the nature of it I
5 knew had to be in confidence, and I further consulted with the
6 director of the program, at that time was Maggie Cavender, and
7 asked her that since Kathleen had a good relationship with the,
8 this Ursula and Beta, that she be the one to continue this
9 working, or relationship, and then we would get back to it on a
10 later date. But from my point then I was thinking that this
11 here required, needed to be brought to somebody's attention so
12 that they could advocate this possibly.
13 Q. Are you related to the Rouse family at all?
14 A. At home we are all related, and yes, I am.
15 Q. How so?
16 A. Well, my mother and Rosemary Rouse are closely related,
17 and that relationship, my, Rosemary out there, she always
18 addresses me as nephew.
19   MR. HAUGAARD: No further questions.
20   THE COURT: Cross exam.
21 CROSS EXAMINATION BY MR. HOLMES:
22 Q. Did you ever see this document that Kathleen Honomichl
23 claims she had received?
24 A. I don't recall that document. I might have read it when
25 I was, when we had a talk over this during that time.

Page 164

1 Q. But as of today you don't recall which child that this
2 report concerned, do you?
3 A. I kind of want to say, I can't remember the child's name,
4 it sounds like Christin or something like that, that's been a
5 few years ago now for me, Christine or something like this.
6 Q. At this point in time when you had this conversation with
7 Ms. Honomichl, what was the supervisory chain of command within
8 Tribal Social Services?
9 A. Her immediate supervisor would be Maggie Cavender, and
10 then eventually it would probably get to me if they felt that
11 it needed to be shared with me.
12 Q. But apparently Ms. Honomichl went around her supervisor
13 and reported this directly to you?
14 A. I don't have no recollection of a breach of chain of
15 command. I don't recall that.
16 Q. Your only conversation regarding this was with
17 Ms. Honomichl, that's your recollection, correct?
18 A. Yes.
19 Q. And her supervisor wasn't there when she initially told
20 you about this, correct?
21 A. I don't recall, because we did have meetings off and on
22 through the year, through '96 and '97, and sometimes there were
23 more like her supervisor would be there, and most times it was,
24 had to do with case plans and this type of thing, but I didn't
25 know the specifics really on those case plans.

Page 165

1 Q. You were aware at that point in time that Ms. Honomichl
2 had a good relationship with Ursula and Beta Rouse?
3 A. Well, they did, because they were able to get a working
4 relationship where they trusted Kathleen. I know her as
5 Casper. They trusted her, and that was reciprocal, it seems
6 like she trusted them too.
7 Q. In fact, they were friends?
8 A. I don't know that.
9 Q. You directed Ms. Cavender to have Kathleen stay involved
10 with this case because of that?
11 A. Well, we consulted on it, and we came up with a consensus
12 that maybe that would be the best thing. But I felt maybe, you
13 know, since they had this good reciprocal relationship, they
14 trusted one another, it looked like the thing to do, yes.
15 Q. You were aware that neither one of these mothers believed
16 that this abuse had ever occurred, were you not?
17 A. I don't know how to put that. They had I would say
18 questions about -- are we talking about this whole case matter?
19 Q. The sexual abuse of these children, you were aware that
20 the mothers did not believe that that occurred, weren't you?
21 A. Well, I don't know specifically that. I know that they
22 did have questions about some aspects of the case, yeah.
23   MR. HOLMES: No further questions.
24   MR. HAUGAARD: Nothing further, Your Honor.
25   THE COURT: Thank you, you may step down. Call your

Page 166

1 next witness.
2   MR. HAUGAARD: Call Donovan Rouse.
3
4   DONOVAN ROUSE,
5 called as a witness, being first duly sworn, testified and said
6 as follows:
7
8 DIRECT EXAMINATION BY MR. HAUGAARD:
9 Q. Donovan, please state your name for the record and spell
10 your last name?
11 A. Donovan Rouse, R-O-U-S-E.
12 Q. Donovan, where do you live?
13 A. Marty, South Dakota.
14 Q. Who is your mother?
15 A. Beta Rouse.
16 Q. I wanted to ask you this, who are your brothers and
17 sisters?
18 A. Jerome Rouse, Lucritia Rouse, Jessica Rouse and Fury
19 Rouse.
20 Q. How old is Jerome?
21 A. He is nineteen.
22 Q. How old is Lucritia?
23 A. Thirteen.
24 Q. Jessica?
25 A. Eleven.

Page 167

1 Q. You remember being taken away from your home back in
2 1994?
3 A. Yes.
4 Q. Where were you taken?
5 A. We was taken to Donna Jordan's house.
6 Q. You remember what time of the day, or what kind of day it
7 was?
8 A. It was night time.
9 Q. What exactly took place?
10 A. Dan Hudspeth, I think, he just came and picked us up and
11 we went to the police station. We sat there for about an hour,
12 then Gene Brock came and picked us up and took us to Beresford,
13 and Roger Jordan picked is up and took us to Elk Point-
14 Jefferson.
15 Q. When you were taken who else was taken at that time?
16 A. There was -- I can't remember.
17 Q. Your sisters taken at that time?
18 A. I don't think so, I think they were taken before that.
19 Q. Did you know why you were being taken away from your
20 home?
21 A. Not at the time.
22 Q. Did you know where you were going to be taken to?
23 A. No.
24 Q. In the foster home how long did it take before you got to
25 Donna Jordan's home?

Page 168

1 A. About two hours, but I don't really remember the exact
2 time.
3 Q. Is that the first time you had ever met those people?
4 A. Yes.
5 Q. Who else lived in her home at that time?
6 A. Her, her husband, her son, his girlfriend, and her
7 daughter, adopted daughter.
8 Q. Who else was being, who else was staying in the home at
9 that time?
10 A. Me, my brother, my three younger sisters; Lucritia
11 Jessica and Fury, and Crystal and Rosemary.
12 Q. When you got there were you able to speak with them?
13 A. Well --
14 Q. When you got to the foster home were you able to speak
15 with your cousins and your sisters?
16 A. Yes.
17 Q. Did they know why they were there?
18 A. No.
19 Q. When did you come to find out why you were taken there?
20 A. When the FBI, whatever that was, came and interviewed us.
21 Q. Before they came to interview you, did Donna Jordan ask
22 you any questions?
23 A. No.
24 Q. How long was it before the FBI came to speak with you?
25 A. I don't know.

Page 169	Page 171
1 Q. How old were you at that time?	1 A. They said, well, your cousin said that you were tied in
2 A. Eight or nine.	2 the closet. And I said, well, I can't remember that far back,
3 Q. How old are you right now?	3 maybe.
4 A. Sixteen.	4 Q. Were you ever tied in the closet?
5 Q. How long total were you in Donna Jordan's home?	5 A. No.
6 A. About a year and a half maybe.	6 Q. Did you ever see your uncles abuse your sisters or your
7 Q. But it wasn't the same day that you were taken to the	7 cousins?
8 home that people began to ask questions?	8 A. Never.
9 A. No.	9 Q. Were you ever pushed up into the attic?
10 Q. Would you say it was a few days, or a week, or a month?	10 A. No.
11 A. About a month I think, about a month or two.	11 Q. Did anyone ever lock you in a closet?
12 Q. What questions were you asked?	12 A. No.
13 A. If I knew anything about my uncles touching my sisters	13 Q. Did you ever see any of your uncles tie your sisters or
14 and my cousins.	14 your cousins down?
15 Q. What did you tell them?	15 A. No.
16 A. I said no, I don't know anything about that.	16 Q. Did you talk to the other kids when you got in to custody
17 Q. What other questions did they ask at that point when you	17 down there, did you talk to them -- well, let me ask you this.
18 said no, you don't know anything about it?	18 Before this session of questions with the FBI agent, or whoever
19 A. They said, questions asked.	19 it was, did you come to understand that this was the point of
20 Q. What did they say?	20 why you were there?
21 A. They just said well, you don't have to be scared, you can	21 A. Before they came?
22 tell the truth. The sooner you cooperate then you guys will be	22 Q. Before they came?
23 able to get home sooner.	23 A. Before the first time they came?
24 Q. How long did this go on the first time that you were	24 Q. Right?
25 asked questions?	25 A. No, not before that.

Page 170	Page 172
1 A. About an hour when they asked me, or when they was	1 Q. During the interview what kind of things did they say
2 talking to me.	2 about your uncles?
3 Q. Were you with the other kids at the time?	3 A. Well, they just asked me if I ever seen them touching my
4 A. No, I was by myself, the rest of the kids were	4 sisters and my cousins, and that's just mostly what they asked.
5 downstairs.	5 They didn't really say nothing about them.
6 Q. During that period of time when they were asking you	6 Q. Did they talk to you about being safe now?
7 questions did there come a time when you changed your answers?	7 A. Being safe from what?
8 A. Yes. After a while I just started agreeing with them.	8 Q. From your uncles?
9 Q. Tell me what kind of questions they asked that you	9 A. They said you don't have to be scared of them, and you
10 disagreed with to start with?	10 are alright here, and stuff like that.
11 A. Well, do you know anything about your uncles touching	11 Q. We are talking about uncles, you look back here, do you
12 your sisters or cousins, and I said no.	12 recognize the men seated behind us?
13 Q. Then what kind of questions did they ask that you finally	13 A. Yes.
14 changed and agreed with them on?	14 Q. It's been quite a few years, but do you recognize who is
15 A. Well, it wasn't really a question, it was more like well,	15 who?
16 your cousin or your sister said this, and I just said, well, I	16 A. Um-hum.
17 can't remember that far back.	17 Q. Are all these people your uncles, or not?
18 Q. During that first session, or one of the first sessions	18 A. I know my uncle Jess, my uncle Des, and my uncle
19 when you were saying that you didn't know anything about it,	19 Garfield, but I don't know Russell at all.
20 how many times do you think you said you don't know anything	20 Q. But you know Russell is my client?
21 about it?	21 A. Yes.
22 A. Well, I can't really remember, but I remember it was more	22 Q. After this interview did you talk to the other kids about
23 than about three times, maybe about three or four. Then I just	23 what you should say?
24 wanted to get it over with, so I didn't have to talk to them.	24 A. After the interview? What we should say, just, we were
25 Q. So what things did you eventually agree with them about?	25 just sitting downstairs and just talking about what we said,

1 was just like yeah, I said that, and like yeah, we said this,
2 and we just like agreeing to what was said.
3 Q. Was it true?
4 A. No.
5 Q. Did the other kids tell you that it was not true?
6 A. Whenever we came back down to Marty, or actually after I
7 left after they interviewed us they told us we made up lies,
8 just I told them this and it was a lie, of course.
9 Q. Were you scared?
10 A. I wanted to go home. I wasn't really scared, I was just
11 wanting to go home.
12 Q. Were you afraid of your uncles?
13 A. No. Afraid that I was lying, but not afraid of my
14 uncles.
15 Q. When you were asked these questions, who all was in the
16 room with you?
17 A. Dan Hudspeth and some other FBI guy, I think, and I think
18 that was it.
19 Q. Do you recognize the other person that was in that room,
20 do you see that person in the courtroom today?
21 A. I don't really remember, I was just usually, I was mostly
22 sitting there with my head down.
23 Q. Were you, did you know these people before they came to
24 ask these questions?
25 A. No.

1 Q. Were you afraid of these men?
2 A. Well, I was afraid that they wouldn't let me go home.
3 Q. Had Donna Jordan asked you some of these questions before
4 the men came?
5   MR. HOLMES: Objection, asked and answered.
6   THE COURT: Sustained.
7 BY MR. HAUGAARD:
8 Q. Were you afraid of Donna Jordan?
9 A. Well, I was afraid for my sisters, because she slapped my
10 sister. My other sisters told me she slapped my little sister
11 Fury, and I seen her pull my little sister Fury's hair, and she
12 told me she pulled her hair, but I wasn't afraid of her really.
13 Q. So you actually saw her do some of these things. Which
14 sister did you see her touch?
15 A. I didn't see her, I just seen her pull my little sister
16 Fury's hair, but my sisters told me they seen her slap her.
17 Q. How old was Fury at that time, do you know?
18 A. She is about three or four or two, I don't know,
19 somewheres around there.
20 Q. Do you know why she pulled her hair?
21 A. Because she pee'd her pants, and she was potty training
22 her.
23 Q. Donovan, how many times did somebody come to ask you
24 questions?
25 A. Maybe once, I think.

1 Q. Did Donna Jordan ever spend time with you alone asking
2 you questions?
3 A. After the, after they came and interviewed us she did.
4 Q. What kind of questions would she ask?
5 A. She just would say did they do that, and I'd say no. She
6 would just say you don't have to be scared, you can tell the
7 truth.
8 Q. So what would you say after she had said those things?
9 A. What would I say?
10 Q. Yes.
11 A. Usually I would just say nothing, just sit there.
12 Q. Who else did you speak with about this claimed abuse?
13 A. Just Donna, the social worker, and Dan and the other guy.
14 Q. Which social worker?
15 A. Deena LaPointe.
16 Q. What did you tell Deena LaPointe?
17 A. I didn't tell her nothing, she was asking the same
18 question as Donna.
19 Q. What did you do in response, did you answer her
20 questions?
21 A. No, I was just quiet.
22 Q. Why didn't you tell her that it didn't happen?
23 A. Because if, I felt like if I didn't tell her that, if I
24 told her that it didn't happen, then I wouldn't be able to come
25 home.

1 Q. Did you ever go to counseling sessions while you were in
2 foster care?
3 A. With Ellen in Sioux City, I think.
4 Q. Ellen Kelson?
5 A. I think that's her name.
6 Q. What questions did she ask you?
7 A. I don't really remember. I just remember having visits
8 with my mom there, and she just usually sat there and wrote
9 things down.
10 Q. When you were being asked questions, did you continue to
11 go with the story that you had agreed to when you were being
12 interviewed by the men at Donna Jordan's house?
13   MR. HOLMES: Objection, leading.
14   THE COURT: Sustained.
15 BY MR. HAUGAARD:
16 Q. As people asked you questions, what did you tell them
17 after that first interview?
18 A. After that first interview I just kind of maybe, just
19 maybe kind of like.
20 Q. Did you tell them clearly that something happened?
21 A. Not at first.
22 Q. Were you -- let me ask you this. When did you find
23 yourself able to tell somebody that it didn't, this really
24 didn't happen?
25 A. Whenever we came back to the Reservation, I was just

Page 177

1 talking with my cousins and my sisters, just told them that
2 this didn't really happen. And I just wanted to come home, so
3 I just made up, made it up, and agreed with them.
4 Q. When they were asking you questions, did you add to the
5 story?
6 A. I don't think I added to the story. I might have. I
7 think I did.
8 Q. Did it seem clear to you what kind of answers they wanted
9 to hear?
10 A. Yes, pretty clear what they wanted to hear.
11 Q. Which cousins or which sisters, brothers, did you tell
12 that this didn't happen to, who did you say --
13 A. Thrista and Rosemary and my two little sisters Lucritia
14 and Jessica.
15 Q. Did they tell you anything about what they knew to be
16 true?
17 A. They said I don't know why we lied, I feel guilty, I feel
18 wrong. And I goes, like, I know, me too. I just wanted to
19 come home, that kind of thing.
20 Q. When did you think you would get to go home?
21 A. I thought we would go home, honestly I thought we would
22 just go home right after they was asking us questions, not like
23 right after, but some time after that. Like within that same
24 year I thought.
25 Q. Who else did you tell about this not being true?

Page 178

1 A. My family.
2 Q. Were you present when Thrista said that this didn't
3 happen?
4 A. One time.
5 Q. Where was that?
6 A. On, we was walking on the path behind the cemetery, and
7 we just were talking about that it wasn't true, and just that
8 we was feeling wrong, you know, and guilty.
9 Q. Who else was with you at that time?
10 A. Just me and her and Rosemary.
11 Q. Were you aware that Thrista had told Kathleen Honomichl
12 that this didn't happen?
13 A. No, I was not aware of that.
14 Q. When you finally got ready for trial, how many times did
15 people come to talk to you about the claimed abuse?
16 A. Before we went to trial? I think it was just pretty much
17 Micky, Michelle Tapken, and her and Donna is who I talked to
18 mostly.
19 Q. When you talked to them, who else was around, do you
20 know, or was there anybody else in the room when you talked to
21 them?
22 A. I think there was another girl with Micky, but I don't
23 know for sure.
24 Q. Why didn't you, or did you ever tell them that this
25 didn't take place?

Page 179

1 A. Not at that point, because I felt I wanted to go home,
2 and I was getting home sick really bad, and I felt that would
3 get me home quicker if I just told them that it happened.
4 Q. When the Judge asked you some questions about knowing the
5 difference between a truth and a lie, do you remember that?
6 A. A little bit.
7 Q. Do you remember being in Court to answer questions that
8 Ms. Tapken asked you?
9 A. Yes.
10 Q. Did you tell the truth when she asked you questions?
11 A. No.
12 Q. Why didn't you tell the truth?
13 A. I wanted to get home.
14 Q. Do you remember being asked questions about each of the
15 uncles?
16 A. Not really, because I had been trying to forget them.
17 Q. So when you said that you saw your uncles gathered around
18 Thrista poking something in to her, was that true or was that
19 false?
20 A. That was false.
21 Q. When it was, when the question was asked whether you were
22 locked in a closet or put up into the attic, was that true or
23 false?
24 A. That was false.
25 Q. Have any of these men behind us here ever abused you?

Page 180

1 A. No, never.
2 Q. Have you seen them drunk before?
3 A. Yes.
4 Q. During that time or any other time did you ever see them
5 mistreat any of your sisters, your brothers, or your cousins?
6 A. No.
7 Q. When you were in foster homes, did you try to tell
8 anybody that was in a position of authority that this didn't
9 happen?
10 A. No, because I felt what I was saying would get me home
11 faster.
12 Q. Do you remember Eva Cheney?
13 A. No, not really.
14 Q. Do you remember a lady that was supposed to be your
15 attorney at that time, dark hair?
16 A. Okay, yeah, now I remember.
17 Q. Did you speak with her very much?
18 A. No, not really.
19 Q. Did you feel that you could tell her the truth?
20 A. No, because I felt what I was saying would get me home
21 faster, so I was just saying it.
22 Q. Have any of these men, or anybody else in your family,
23 your friends or anything, has anybody tried to put pressure on
24 you to change your story from what it was back when you were
25 talking to the social workers?

Page 181

1 A. No, nobody put any pressure on me. I was kind of
2 pressured myself to tell the truth.
3 Q. Do you remember being afraid when you came into the
4 courtroom?
5 A. Yes.
6 Q. What were you afraid of?
7 A. Of lying.
8 Q. But why didn't you tell the truth then?
9 A. I wanted to go home.
10 Q. What were you told about when you could go home?
11 A. They just told me that the sooner I cooperate the sooner
12 I could go home, the sooner it will be over.
13 Q. Has your family threatened anything toward you if you
14 don't come here today and say the things you are saying?
15 A. No. I am here because I want to get my uncles out of the
16 pen, because they are in there for something they didn't do.
17 Q. Would you be willing to talk to the Judge privately about
18 this?
19 A. Yes.
20   MR. HAUGAARD: No further questions.
21   THE COURT: Cross examination.
22 CROSS EXAMINATION BY MR. HOLMES:
23 Q. Donovan, you went to live at Donna Jordan's first, is
24 that right?
25 A. Yes.

Page 182

1 Q. And you stayed there through the trial, is that correct?
2 A. Yes.
3 Q. At some point in time you were placed at another house or
4 another location, you remember that when you left Donna's?
5 A. Yes.
6 Q. Where did you go after you were at Donna's?
7 A. Children's Home.
8 Q. How long after the trial approximately do you believe
9 that occurred?
10 A. I don't know.
11 Q. A few months, a year?
12 A. About months I would say, I don't know.
13 Q. You remember how long you were at Children's Home?
14 A. No.
15 Q. Where did you go after you were at Children's Home?
16 A. Either Bonnie Conan's or the Blue Shelter.
17 Q. Where is the Blue Shelter?
18 A. It is about a mile away from Marty.
19 Q. How long were you there?
20 A. About another couple years, or about a year or something.
21 Q. When do you remember going to live at, in Marty itself?
22 A. About two or three years ago.
23 Q. Let's put it this way, do you remember what grade you
24 were in?
25 A. I was thirteen, about, I don't know, about 5th.

Page 183

1 Q. After you left Children's Home, were you going to school
2 down there at Marty?
3 A. I was going to school in Wagner.
4 Q. What grade did you go to school in Wagner?
5 A. 5th and 4th maybe. I think 4th. But 5th for sure.
6 Q. How much contact did you have with your brothers and
7 sisters when you were going to school in Wagner?
8 A. My sister Thrista and, yeah, just me and Thrista were
9 usually -- or wait. After Children's Home we went to Bonnie's,
10 and there was me, Thrista, Lucritia and Jessica, I think, were
11 there, were at that house. We pretty much saw each other every
12 day.
13 Q. Were you aware of a time when they were living in the
14 dorm at Marty?
15 A. Thrista, yes, I am aware of that.
16 Q. Where were you at when she was living in the dorm at
17 Marty?
18 A. In the shelter.
19 Q. You were still going to school in Wagner?
20 A. Yes.
21 Q. While you were going to school in Wagner how much contact
22 did you have with your mother?
23 A. Visits about monthly maybe, not even that. I only
24 remember visiting her when I was in the shelter about two
25 times.

Page 184

1 Q. When you were at Children's Home how often would your
2 mother visit?
3 A. I think she visited about three or four times while I was
4 there.
5 Q. Do you remember her being in therapy sessions with you?
6 A. Yeah.
7 Q. You were first up there was Deena LaPointe your social
8 worker for the Tribe?
9 A. When I was first in Children's Home?
10 Q. Yes.
11 A. I think so. I think when I was first up there.
12 Q. Would you agree with me, Donovan, that your memory as far
13 as what happened would have been better back when these events
14 took place than it is now?
15   MR. HAUGAARD: Objection, calls for speculation.
16   THE COURT: Overruled.
17 A. My memory would be better back then?
18 BY MR. HOLMES:
19 Q. Yes.
20 A. Well, of course.
21 Q. After Deena LaPointe was your social worker, Kathleen
22 Honomichl was your case worker, do you remember that?
23 A. Yes.
24 Q. And she brought your mom up to visit you at Children's
25 Home, correct?

Page 185

1 A. Yes.

2 Q. And you remember some time around Halloween in 1996 when

3 Kathleen took you up to be interviewed by Dr. Underwager?

4 A. Yeah.

5 Q. Tell me what you remember about how that came about?

6 A. How that came about? Well, she just asked me if I was

7 willing to talk to Dr. Underwager, and I just said yeah.

8 Q. Where were you living at at the time?

9 A. Let me think. I think maybe I was at Bonnie's maybe.

10 Q. Was that the Kathleen that came down and picked you up

11 and drove you up here to Sioux Falls to see Dr. Underwager,

12 isn't that right?

13 A. Yes.

14 Q. And you remember Mr. Haugaard being there also?

15 A. At Dr. Underwager's office, I don't think so. I don't

16 remember him there.

17 Q. When do you remember, other than the trial, seeing

18 Mr. Haugaard?

19 A. Before the trial?

20 Q. After the trial?

21 A. After the trial? I don't really think I seen him after

22 that, but then I don't know.

23 Q. Well, did your mom go with you in October of '96 when you

24 went up to be interviewed by Dr. Underwager?

25 A. Yes.

Page 186

1 Q. Talk to you about what you were going to be interviewed

2 about?

3 A. Not really. She just, she said he is just going to talk

4 about my uncles, so I just go alright then.

5 Q. Well, you knew when you talked to Dr. Underwager in

6 October of 1996 that they were in prison for thirty years,

7 didn't you?

8 A. Yes.

9 Q. Who told you that?

10 A. I don't remember.

11 Q. And you in fact had read letters that they had written to

12 your grandmother Rosemary, hadn't you?

13 A. No, I didn't read them myself personally.

14 Q. Someone told you about what they said in those letters?

15 A. Yes, my grandma told me.

16 Q. So before you went to see Dr. Underwager in October of

17 '96, your grandmother had talked to you about what these men

18 were writing from prison, correct?

19 A. Yes.

20 Q. And she made you feel very guilty about the fact they

21 were in prison?

22 A. No, she did not make me feel guilty.

23 Q. You remember telling Dr. Underwager in that interview

24 that you were told by your grandmother that they are not mad at

25 us, they just want to get out of prison?

Page 187

1 A. My grandmother had told me that they are not mad at us,

2 and they just want us to tell the truth.

3 Q. What did your mom talk to you about as far as what had

4 happened?

5 A. Just wanted me to tell the truth.

6 Q. She didn't believe that any of this had ever happened,

7 did she?

8 A. Probably not, because it didn't.

9 Q. And she told you repeatedly that she didn't believe any

10 of it had happened, correct?

11 A. No, she never told me that she didn't believe it, but I

12 knew it didn't happen to us.

13 Q. Well, when you were at Children's Home you were in

14 therapy sessions there, correct?

15 A. Correct.

16 Q. And in some of these therapy sessions your mom and

17 Kathleen Honomichl would also be there, correct?

18 A. Yeah.

19 Q. Your mom consistently said during these sessions that

20 this didn't happen, you remember that?

21 A. Yes.

22 Q. So as early as when you were at Children's Home you knew

23 that your mom did not believe these allegations, correct?

24 A. Yes.

25 Q. In fact, by October of 1996 you had read some of the

Page 188

1 interview reports in this case, hadn't you?

2 A. Maybe, I don't know. I can't remember.

3 Q. Who showed you those?

4 A. I don't know, I can't remember.

5 Q. You remember telling Dr. Underwager in this interview in

6 October of '96 that if you sit down and read the reports, they

7 don't tie together?

8 A. Yes, they don't.

9 Q. By the time you were interviewed by Dr. Underwager in

10 1996 someone in your family had shown you FBI reports, correct?

11 A. I don't think so, I don't remember.

12 Q. Do you remember seeing FBI reports about the case?

13 A. No, not really, just this stuff that I said, that I said.

14 Q. What were you given to read?

15 A. Just stuff that I had said.

16 Q. The transcript of what you had said at trial?

17 A. I don't know what a transcript is.

18 Q. Did someone give you a piece of paper where what you had

19 said had been typed up?

20 A. No, I don't think so.

21 Q. Tell me exactly what you remember reading?

22   MR. HAUGAARD: Your Honor, asked and answered, he's

23 already indicated he doesn't recall.

24   THE COURT: Sustained.

25 BY MR. HOLMES:

Page 189

1 Q. Someone showed you something to read, is that right?

2   MR. HAUGAARD: Asked and answered.

3   THE COURT: Overruled.

4 A. Maybe, I don't know though, I can't remember.

5 BY MR. HOLMES:

6 Q. Do you have an explanation why on this videotape you can

7 be heard saying if you read the reports it does not tie

8 together?

9 A. Can you repeat the question?

10 Q. Do you have any other explanation as to why you would be

11 telling Dr. Underwager in October of '96, quote, if you read

12 the reports it does not tie together, end quote.

13 A. Oh, well, if you read them, I guess they don't. Yes, I

14 remember saying that.

15 Q. How would you know that if you had not read the reports?

16 A. Well, it obviously doesn't tie together. If you,

17 probably would look at them it probably doesn't.

18 Q. But you told him you had read the reports?

19 A. Did I say those exact words?

20 Q. You remember also saying that Donna Jordan at trial had

21 lied about people jumping on the car during the course of the

22 trial?

23 A. Yes, she lied that my uncle, he is not exactly my uncle,

24 but he is a real close friend of the family, she said he was

25 jumping on the van and hollering, but he wasn't, he was just

Page 190

1 whistling and saying hey, high, and saying that.

2 Q. What caused you to believe in October of '96 that Donna

3 Jordan had lied about that?

4 A. Well, she was lying about a bunch of other things, so I

5 goes, well, that's another lie.

6 Q. How did you know that Donna Jordan had described to

7 anybody someone had jumped on the vehicle?

8 A. In my eye he was just jumping on the van, I guess.

9 Q. Someone had told you what Donna Jordan had testified to

10 at trial, isn't that right?

11 A. No, I don't think so.

12 Q. Or had you read that portion of the transcript?

13 A. I don't know, I don't think so.

14 Q. But someone, something caused you to say to

15 Dr. Underwager that Donna lied when she testified at trial

16 about that man jumping on the car.

17 A. Well, after the trial she told us that, did you see that

18 guy jumping on the van. And we was just like what guy? And

19 she said that guy with the beard. We goes oh, yeah.

20 Q. What had you been told by members of your family about

21 what had happened at the trial between the time that the trial

22 took place and when you talked to Dr. Underwager in October of

23 '96?

24 A. What did my family tell me?

25 Q. Yes?

Page 191

1 A. They just, they didn't really tell me all that much, they

2 just told me that they were looking for us just to see us.

3 Q. Who had spoken to you, that being members of your family,

4 about what had happened at the trial?

5 A. Just my aunt and my mom, they said we were looking for

6 you guys and they must have took you guys out the back door.

7 Q. You remember telling Dr. Underwager in October of '96

8 that at the time of the trial they sat you in a room until they

9 got the answer they wanted?

10 A. They didn't sit me in a room, they just kept asking me

11 the same question. Questions like did they do this, you don't

12 have to be scared, you can tell the truth.

13 Q. I am talking about here in the courthouse during the

14 trial you told Dr. Underwager that you were, they sat you in a

15 room until they got the answer they wanted, was that true?

16   MR. HAUGAARD: Objection, Your Honor, there is no

17 foundation for the discussion on the tape, it is not in

18 evidence.

19   THE COURT: It was provided to me as something to

20 review for your motion, overruled.

21 A. That I was sat in, I was sat in a room by myself. I was

22 in a room, but there was other people in there, but nobody was

23 talking.

24 BY MR. HOLMES:

25 Q. So what you told Dr. Underwager wasn't true about what

Page 192

1 happened here in the courthouse, was it?

2 A. That little portion.

3 Q. Do you remember also telling Dr. Underwager that Eva

4 Cheney said to you if the boys go to prison we are going to

5 party?

6 A. Yes, I remember that.

7 Q. And that never happened, did it?

8 A. It did.

9 Q. Here in the courthouse?

10 A. It was in her office, I think. I don't know where her

11 office is, but it's what she said.

12 Q. When?

13 A. When ever I was in her office, I don't know the exact

14 time and date.

15 Q. Was that before or after the trial?

16 A. That was before I testified.

17 Q. According to you was Ms. Cheney talking to you in her

18 office?

19 A. She was not talking to me, but I was there and I heard

20 her say that.

21 Q. To who?

22 A. I think it was Micky Tapken, Michelle.

23 Q. You never told Dr. Underwager that, did you?

24 A. Well, he never asked, and I forgot about it, because I

25 have been trying to forget most things.

Page 193

1 Q. Donovan, your mother took you to see Dr. Underwager,
2 correct?
3 A. Correct.
4 Q. And this was to help your uncles out, correct?
5 A. Yes.
6 Q. Was there any reason for you to lie to Dr. Underwager?
7 A. No, but I was confused at the time.
8 Q. Why?
9 A. Because I was still believing that, or not believing, but
10 still, I still had in my mind that I was, that that happened,
11 and then I was just realizing that it was a lie, and I was just
12 confused.
13 Q. Wasn't until October of '96 when you talked to
14 Dr. Underwager that you started thinking that maybe this wasn't
15 true, isn't that correct?
16   MR. HAUGAARD: Objection, he's already testified as
17 to recanting earlier.
18   THE COURT: As to what?
19   MR. HAUGAARD: As to having indicated to others that
20 this didn't happen much earlier.
21   THE COURT: Overruled.
22 BY MR. HOLMES:
23 Q. Isn't it true -- you have just said it wasn't until
24 October of '96 when you were talking to Dr. Underwager that you
25 started to have doubts about whether this had happened?

Page 194

1 A. It didn't happen, and you are confusing me, I am sorry.
2 Q. Well, you were in therapy at Children's Home, correct?
3 A. Yes.
4 Q. And you were consistently telling the workers there all
5 through this period of time that this abuse had occurred?
6 A. Yes, but I still wanted to go home.
7 Q. And it wasn't until you talked to Dr. Underwager that now
8 you started having doubts, correct?
9 A. No, it was when I was talking to my cousins. Actually,
10 no, wait, wait. It was whenever they was interviewing us, I
11 knew I was lying the first time they interviewed us, but then I
12 just went along with it.
13 Q. Okay, let's talk about that for a minute. You have
14 testified here persistently that the reason you lied was
15 because you wanted to go home?
16 A. Yes.
17 Q. You felt that telling investigators that you had been
18 abused in this home, and that you had seen your brothers and
19 sisters abused in this home, and your cousins abused, that that
20 would cause people to put you back in that same home?
21 A. That's what they said, they told me the sooner I
22 cooperate the sooner I will be able to go home.
23 Q. Who is they?
24 A. The people who interviewed us.
25 Q. No, tell me who is they that told you this?

Page 195

1 A. Dan Hudspeth and the other guy, whoever he is.
2 Q. The FBI agent?
3 A. Yes.
4 Q. It's your testimony that they were the ones that started
5 this by saying as soon as you lie, you will get to go home?
6 A. Cooperate.
7 Q. Why did that mean lie?
8 A. Because it just seemed like that's what they wanted to
9 hear, and I would be able to go home sooner.
10 Q. But did you understand what you were saying?
11 A. Yes, I did.
12 Q. What caused you to believe that by saying you had been
13 abused you would be put back in that same place where you had
14 been abused?
15   MR. HAUGAARD: Asked and answered.
16   THE COURT: Overruled.
17 A. Can you repeat the question?
18 BY MR. HOLMES:
19 Q. What caused you to believe that by telling these people
20 that you had been abused that they would then place you back in
21 the same home where you had been, you just said at that home I
22 was abused?
23 A. Yes, but my uncles were not there if I was to say that,
24 then they would be out of the house and I would be able to go
25 home.

Page 196

1 Q. So I am clear here, you remember that it was Kathleen
2 Honomichl and your mom that brought you up here in October of
3 '96 to talk to Dr. Underwager?
4 A. Yes.
5 Q. And they brought Thrista up here too, correct?
6 A. Yes.
7 Q. You two rode up here to together, correct?
8 A. Yes.
9 Q. Where was Thrista living at that time?
10 A. I don't know the exact times where we were living. I
11 think I was maybe in the shelter. I don't know actually.
12 Q. My question, Donovan --
13 A. Yes, and I don't know where she was, obviously, because I
14 can't remember where I was.
15 Q. Well, do you know where they picked her up?
16 A. No, because I cannot remember.
17 Q. Who was running the camera that day?
18 A. It was running itself. On a post and he just had it
19 recording.
20 Q. Mr. Haugaard there?
21 A. Maybe, I don't know.
22 Q. You remember telling Dr. Underwager that the FBI made us
23 sit there for hours?
24 A. Yes.
25 Q. That wasn't true, was it?

Page 197

1 A. No, but they did have us sitting there asking us the same
2 questions.
3 Q. Well, you testified here today that the interview was for
4 about an hour, you remember that?
5 A. Yeah.
6 Q. What you told Dr. Underwager wasn't true?
7 A. About what?
8 Q. How long the FBI had interviewed you?
9 A. Well, it felt like hours.
10 Q. You were trying to make this as bad as it could be,
11 weren't you, when you talked to Dr. Underwager?
12   MR. HAUGAARD: Objection, Your Honor, argumentative.
13   THE COURT: Overruled.
14 A. I was trying to make it as bad as it could be?
15 BY MR. HOLMES:
16 Q. You wanted to make these FBI guys sound like evil people,
17 didn't you?
18 A. Well, I believe they were at the time.
19 Q. So you were telling Dr. Underwager something that wasn't
20 true to help show that they were bad people, correct?
21 A. Correct.
22 Q. And you are doing the same thing here today, correct?
23 A. About who?
24 Q. The FBI?
25 A. I am not exaggerating anything.

Page 198

1 Q. You want to show they are bad people, don't you?
2 A. They are.
3 Q. Why do you believe that?
4 A. Because they messed up my family.
5 Q. They caused your uncles to go to prison, correct?
6 A. Yes.
7 Q. Now after this interview with Dr. Underwager in October
8 of '96, how many other times did you learn from your
9 grandmother or somebody else what your uncles were writing or
10 saying in phone calls from prison?
11 A. Just about a couple of times.
12 Q. Tell me about that?
13 A. What they had said?
14 Q. No, how you learned about that?
15 A. My family just told me that just to tell the truth, they
16 said just to tell the truth, and that they are not mad or
17 anything, just to tell the truth.
18 Q. And who is telling you what your uncles had said?
19 A. My grandma, my aunty Urs.
20 Q. Your aunt Ursula?
21 A. Ursula, yes.
22 Q. Did they show you these letters?
23 A. Well, I didn't really look at them.
24 Q. So they were there?
25 A. Yes.

Page 199

1 Q. The letters were right in front of you?
2 A. Um-hum.
3 Q. You ever talk to your uncles on the phone?
4 A. Yes.
5 Q. How often did that occur?
6 A. Well, I only talked to them about maybe three or four
7 times.
8 Q. When?
9 A. Since I moved back in with my mom.
10 Q. How long have you been with your mom?
11 A. About three years.
12 Q. Your mom was having you talk to your uncles over the
13 phone?
14 A. No, she was not having me, I was talking to them because
15 I wanted to.
16 Q. And did that make you feel guilty that they were in
17 prison?
18 A. Yes, because they were in there because of a lie, and I
19 was the one who was lying.
20 Q. Well, you talked to Dr. Underwager a second time in
21 January of 1999, correct?
22 A. Yes.
23 Q. Tell me how that came about?
24 A. I don't remember.
25 Q. Well, Mr. Haugaard was there that time, wasn't he?

Page 200

1 A. Yeah, I think so.
2 Q. He was running the camera, correct?
3 A. I don't know, maybe.
4 Q. And Jessica was there, correct?
5 A. Yes.
6 Q. Lucritia?
7 A. Yes.
8 Q. Thrista?
9 A. Yes.
10 Q. Who brought you all up to see Dr. Underwager on that
11 occasion?
12 A. I don't know, I think it was either my grandma or my mom
13 and them.
14 Q. So this is your mom, who didn't believe that any of this
15 had ever happened, and your grandma, who didn't believe that
16 any of this had ever happened, were driving you up to see
17 Dr. Underwager, correct?
18 A. Correct, because it didn't happen.
19 Q. In this interview with Dr. Underwager you again tried to
20 make the FBI look really bad, didn't you?
21 A. Maybe.
22 Q. And you lied to him about what had taken place, didn't
23 you?
24 A. I don't know, maybe.
25 Q. Well, you told him that they made you sit in a room for

Page 201

1 over an hour without water and wouldn't give us food?
2   MR. HAUGAARD: Objection, asked and answered.
3   THE COURT: Overruled.
4 BY MR. HOLMES:
5 Q. You remember telling Dr. Underwager that in January of
6 1999?
7 A. Yes.
8 Q. That wasn't true, was it?
9 A. Yes, it was, because I was thirsty and I was hungry.
10 Q. You also told him that the FBI interviewed you fifty
11 times?
12 A. Did I say that?
13 Q. Yeah.
14 A. I don't remember.
15 Q. Was that true?
16 A. I don't think so, but then I don't know.
17 Q. You also indicated that you were being offered money,
18 remember that?
19 A. No.
20 Q. Would that be true?
21 A. I don't know, because I don't remember.
22 Q. And you remember Dr. Underwager was telling you things
23 like he knew these guys didn't do it, you remember that?
24 A. Yes, because they didn't?
25 Q. And he was telling you he was going to get this case on

Page 202

1 Nightline, the TV program, you remember that?
2 A. Yes.
3 Q. How did that make you feel?
4 A. Made me feel like I didn't feel like going on TV.
5   THE COURT: We are going to recess. We will commence
6 again at 9:00 in the morning.
7 (Evening recess at five o'clock p.m.)
8 (9:00 a.m., 9-6-01)
9   THE COURT: There was a procedural matter I wanted to
10 take up. I have been thinking about the Children's Home
11 records, I can see why you wanted them. But on the other hand,
12 I can't imagine why you didn't try to get them a long time ago,
13 to be blunt about it. Aside from you wanting them, I would
14 like to see them too. Has there been any communication before
15 you dropped that subpoena off yesterday with Children's Home?
16 Apparently not.
17   MR. HAUGAARD: No.
18   THE COURT: Do you have consents from the minors as
19 well as from their parents that have been provided to
20 Children's Home.
21   MR. HAUGAARD: I have a release I could have signed
22 today and get it sent out there somehow. Just a matter of
23 manpower, Your Honor.
24   THE COURT: Well, consents from the minors as well as
25 their parents. If they are in some sort of guardianship, from

Page 203

1 the guardian, should all be provided to Children's Home so that
2 they have, they should be advised these things are being
3 requested so that if they are going to make a question about
4 it, which sometimes institutions do with regard to minors'
5 records, they have an opportunity to do so. But after hearing
6 some of the testimony I would like to have those records
7 available. So if you accomplish that, I would like to know
8 ultimately what Children's Home's response is, because being
9 slapped with a subpoena they should have the courtesy of not
10 only receiving those consents, but likewise, you know, when
11 they can reasonably produce the records, and then we can
12 provide a subpoena. Alright, proceed with the testimony.
13   MR. WILKA: Your Honor, if I may, I would like the
14 Court's indulgence. If it is permissible could Dr. Bruck sit
15 in the front row so she may, if she finds it necessary, to pass
16 a note up to defense counsel.
17   THE COURT: Certainly. There is nothing sacred about
18 the front row, anyway.
19   MR. WILKA: Also there have been passed a number of
20 notes from the defendants asking the Court, I am not sure if I
21 am using the correct terminology, but a separation policy by,
22 of the defendants while they are incarcerated at the prison.
23 These are brothers that haven't seen each other for eight
24 years, and they just want to know if this Court is against them
25 seeing each other or being housed together. If in the opinion

Page 204

1 of the people who run it, the chief of security of the South
2 Dakota State Penitentiary, that that would be okay, would this
3 Court be opposed to that?
4   THE COURT: Are they going to testify?
5   MR. WILKA: I don't anticipate that.
6   THE COURT: Well, I am all for brothers being able to
7 see each other and be able to talk to each other, and I
8 understand that. On the other hand, if they are going to
9 testify they are not going to have any contact with each other.
10   MR. WILKA: They aren't going to testify, Judge.
11   THE COURT: Then it's up to the people at the
12 penitentiary, because if it is okay with them, it is alright
13 with me that they see each other.
14   MR. WILKA: I did speak with the deputy warden last
15 night, so I will visit with him again today.
16   THE COURT: You realize from the representations you
17 have made then they are not going to testify.
18   MR. WILKA: Yes. It would be in a void, people who
19 have been incarcerated for eight years and now the recantation.
20   MR. HOLMES: Your Honor, I wasn't finished with
21 cross.
22   THE COURT: That's right, excuse me.
23 BY MR. HOLMES:
24 Q. Donovan, I just have a few more questions. You remember
25 telling Dr. Underwager in 1999 that you were brain washed by

Page 205

1 the FBI?

2 A. Yes.

3 Q. And you remember Dr. Underwager at that time talking to

4 you about experiments that were being done in the United States

5 military, give soldiers training on how they could resist

6 questioning such as you had went through?

7 A. Yes.

8 Q. He told you that that training never worked?

9   MR. HAUGAARD: Objection, Your Honor, based on

10 hearsay.

11   THE COURT: Overruled.

12 BY MR. HOLMES:

13 Q. You remember him telling you that?

14 A. No, actually I don't remember him telling me that.

15 Q. You were interviewed by Dan Hudspeth and a FBI agent down

16 in Donna Jordan's house, is that right?

17 A. Yes.

18 Q. That was about a week after you were taken to Donna

19 Jordan's residence?

20 A. No, about a month or two.

21 Q. And were you interviewed at all after that?

22 A. No, I can't remember. Probably, most likely.

23 Q. And then you were brought up here for the trial, you

24 remember that, don't you?

25 A. Yes.

Page 206

1 Q. So you were telling Dr. Underwager in 1999 that based

2 upon those one or two contacts with the FBI that you felt they

3 brain washed you?

4 A. At the time, yes.

5 Q. Well, do you today believe that the FBI brain washed you?

6   MR. HAUGAARD: I object based on the technicality of

7 such a question, I don't think the witness understands the

8 details of that.

9   THE COURT: Overruled.

10 A. Do I understand that if I was brain washed?

11 BY MR. HOLMES:

12 Q. Do you believe today that the FBI brain washed you?

13 A. Well, no.

14 Q. You remember telling Dr. Underwager that you were forced

15 to say that these guys touched you?

16 A. Do I remember telling Dr. Underwager that?

17 Q. Yes, that the prosecutor said here is what you got to

18 say, you have to say they touched you in the wrong way and say

19 you were molested by your uncles?

20 A. Yeah, I remember saying that.

21 Q. Did the prosecutor tell you that?

22 A. Myself, yeah.

23 Q. When?

24 A. When I was in her office.

25 Q. Before or after the trial?

Page 207

1 A. Before.

2 Q. Isn't it a fact, Donovan, that you never admitted that

3 you had been touched by your uncles until you were in therapy

4 at Children's Home?

5 A. Yes.

6 Q. So you never told, you were never told by anybody that

7 you had to say that the uncles touched you, correct?

8 A. No, correct.

9 Q. The first time that came out from you was when you were

10 in therapy at Children's Home?

11 A. Yes, I was tired of therapy and I wanted to go home.

12 Q. In those therapy sessions you started talking about your

13 uncles, correct?

14 A. Maybe.

15   MR. HOLMES: May I approach the witness, Your Honor?

16   THE COURT: You may.

17

18   (Exhibit 3 marked For identification.)

19

20 BY MR. HOLMES:

21 Q. Donovan, I have handed you a document that has been

22 marked as Government's Exhibit 3. Do you recognize your

23 signature?

24 A. Yes.

25 Q. Is that an affidavit that you signed?

Page 208

1 A. Yes.

2   MR. HOLMES: We would offer Exhibit 3.

3   MR. HAUGAARD: No objection, Your Honor.

4   THE COURT: Exhibit 3 will be received.

5 A. Read what, what did you say?

6 BY MR. HOLMES:

7 Q. Just a second. Can you tell me what you remember about

8 how this affidavit was typed up and given to you for your

9 signature?

10 A. Yes, I wrote some of it, most of this down. Actually I

11 wrote all this down and then Steve typed it up for me.

12 Q. This happened -- well, you signed it in May of '99, is

13 that right?

14 A. Yes.

15   MR. HAUGAARD: Objection, that's incorrect, it is

16 dated.

17 A. No, ninth month.

18   MR. HOLMES: May of '99.

19   MR. HAUGAARD: September of '99.

20   THE COURT: We are looking at a different document,

21 mine is the 9th of September, '99.

22   MR. HOLMES: I have two affidavits, Your Honor. May

23 I approach again, Your Honor?

24   THE COURT: You may.

25

Page 209

1   (Exhibit 9 marked For identification.)

2

3   BY MR. HOLMES:

4   Q. Now before you is what has been marked as Government's

5   Exhibit No. 9, is that another affidavit that you signed?

6   A. Yes.

7   Q. Is your signature on that document?

8   A. Yes.

9   MR. HOLMES: We offer Exhibit 9.

10   MR. HAUGAARD: No objection, Your Honor.

11   THE COURT: Exhibit 9 is received.

12   BY MR. HOLMES:

13   Q. How long have you been talking to Mr. Haugaard before

14   Exhibit 9 was typed up for your signature?

15   A. I don't remember.

16   Q. Let's do it this way. You remember Mr. Haugaard being

17   involved when you were interviewed by Dr. Underwager in January

18   of 1999?

19   A. Maybe, I don't know.

20   Q. Well, didn't those interviews take place in his office?

21   A. Oh, yeah.

22   Q. He talked to you about what you were going to be asked by

23   Dr. Underwager?

24   A. No, I pretty much knew what was, what he was going to

25   ask, talk about.

Page 210

1   Q. How did you know that?

2   A. I didn't know exactly, I just kind of figured.

3   Q. The other Exhibit, Exhibit 3, tell us what you remember

4   about how that was typed up and given to you for your

5   signature?

6   MR. HAUGAARD: Asked and answered, Your Honor.

7   THE COURT: Overruled.

8   Q. The same way as the last one.

9   BY MR. HOLMES:

10   Q. Mr. Haugaard typed it up and gave it to you?

11   A. Yes.

12   Q. Yesterday afternoon when you were seated in the hallway

13   of this courtroom, or courthouse, who handed you those

14   affidavits to read before you testified?

15   A. I don't know. It was one of the lawyers, it was just

16   this affidavit right here, the Exhibit 9.

17   Q. And that happened after Kathleen Honomichl testified,

18   didn't it?

19   A. Yeah, I think so.

20   Q. So one of the lawyers ran out and handed you this

21   affidavit to read before you came on the witness stand, is that

22   right?

23   A. Yes.

24   MR. HOLMES: No further questions.

25   THE COURT: Redirect.

Page 211

1   REDIRECT EXAMINATION BY MR. HAUGAARD:

2   Q. Donovan, let's go back to those affidavits. You

3   indicated on cross examination from Mr. Holmes that at least

4   one of these you had written these things down and passed that

5   information along to me for typing, is that correct?

6   A. Yes.

7   Q. Donovan, did I tell you what you had to say in these

8   affidavits?

9   A. No.

10   Q. Are these things that happened to you and that you wanted

11   to make known, the things that are down in the affidavits?

12   A. Did these things happen to me.

13   Q. The things you said in the affidavit, is it true?

14   A. Yes, these things I said are true.

15   Q. When Mr. Holmes was talking about brain washing, do you

16   know all the technical features of brain washing?

17   A. No.

18   Q. So when you say that, what do you mean?

19   A. Just that I was, I just kind of figured what I had to

20   say, said it.

21   Q. You figured that from what, the questions?

22   A. Yeah.

23   Q. When you were called on to testify, why did you repeat

24   those things?

25   A. Repeat what things?

Page 212

1   Q. The things that you had been asked by the investigators?

2   A. I don't understand that question.

3   Q. Let me back up a little bit more then. When you think

4   back on the interviews, did you feel like you could just get up

5   and leave whenever you wanted to?

6   A. No.

7   Q. Did it seem like you needed to cooperate with what their

8   questions were to be able to get finished with the interview?

9   A. Yeah.

10   Q. And what did you think was going to happen if you

11   cooperated with their questions?

12   A. That I would go home.

13   Q. At that time how old were you?

14   A. Eight or nine when they first questioned us.

15   Q. Do you remember what grade you were in before you were

16   taken away from your home?

17   A. No, I don't really remember.

18   Q. What grade were you in when you were at Donna Jordan's?

19   A. I don't remember that either.

20   Q. When you went back to Marty do you remember what grade

21   you were in then when you stayed at the Blue Shelter?

22   A. I went to Wagner and I was in 5th.

23   Q. What is your birth date?

24   A. November 15th, '84.

25   Q. As an eight year old were you scared of the people that

Page 213

1 were asking you questions?

2 A. As an eight year old, yes.

3 Q. For clarification, did Kathleen Honomichl bring you to

4 Sioux Falls to see Dr. Underwager?

5 A. No. Now that I think back on it, I don't think she did.

6 I think it was my grandma borrowed a van from the Tribe, or my

7 mom, or one of them.

8 Q. And your mom and Ursula came along probably?

9 A. Yes.

10 Q. When you had visits with your mom, did she pressure you

11 to say anything different than what you had said at trial?

12 A. No.

13 Q. She ask you questions about this stuff?

14 A. She just asked me if it was true, and asked me to tell

15 the truth. She just asked me to tell the truth.

16 Q. When you were first taken in to custody you said you

17 denied that anything happened about three or four times, is

18 that true?

19 A. Yes.

20 Q. The first time they asked you questions did you

21 eventually change and go along with the questions?

22 A. The first time, yeah.

23 Q. But during that interview you denied any abuse up to that

24 point?

25 A. Yeah, up, yeah.

Page 214

1 Q. When you were being asked questions, did there come a

2 time when you started to just add to the story?

3 A. Yeah, I think so, yeah.

4 Q. What was the reason for doing that?

5 A. Thought that is what they wanted to hear.

6 Q. Were most of the questions -- well, tell me what some of

7 the questions were like, if you recall?

8 A. They were like just, well, just say that you were tied up

9 in the closet. And I said I don't know, I can't remember that

10 far back, because I didn't want to get in trouble.

11 Q. Did they ask you those questions again?

12 A. Yes.

13 Q. And again?

14 A. Um-hum.

15 Q. And eventually did you agree that you had been tied up in

16 the closet?

17 A. Yes.

18 Q. Did you eventually agree that you had been put up in the

19 attic?

20 A. Yes.

21 Q. Is that something you made up, or was that a question

22 they asked?

23 A. That was a question they asked.

24 Q. When you went along with their questions did that seem to

25 make them happy?

Page 215

1 A. Yes.

2 Q. And have you had a chance now to read these two

3 affidavits as you have been sitting there?

4 A. Yes.

5 Q. Do you still agree that all those things are accurate?

6 A. Um-hum.

7 Q. You have to say yes or no.

8 A. Yes.

9 Q. There came a point in time during your testimony at

10 trial, you remember being in here?

11 A. Yeah.

12 Q. You remember testifying and Ms. Tapken asking you

13 questions, you remember that?

14 A. Yes.

15 Q. Do you remember when there came a point where you were

16 really upset and she asked do you need to take a little break

17 or can we go on?

18 A. Yes.

19 Q. Were you about to cry at that point?

20 A. Yeah.

21 Q. Why was that?

22 A. Because I was lying, and I knew it, I was just feeling

23 guilty for lying.

24 Q. Did you have any idea what was really going to happen to

25 your uncles?

Page 216

1 A. Yeah.

2 Q. Did you know how long they might be in prison?

3 A. No, not how long.

4 Q. Had you ever been up in that attic before?

5 A. Yes, by myself.

6 Q. Why did you go up to the attic?

7 A. Just to see what was up there.

8 Q. You knew there was an attic up there?

9 A. Um-hum, yes.

10 Q. You ever seen mice up there?

11 A. Yeah.

12 Q. What did you tell me about mice the other day?

13 A. That there is usually mice in houses on the Reservation.

14 Q. And specially what time of year?

15 A. About this time when it starts getting cold.

16 Q. But all throughout the year you can probably find mice?

17 A. Um-hum, pretty much.

18 Q. When you were being interviewed tell me who was in the

19 room, if you recall?

20 A. Interviewed by who?

21 Q. When you were down at Donna Jordan's, how many people do

22 you remember being in the room?

23 A. I just remember those two, those two FBI, Dan and that.

24 Q. Sometimes when you were being asked questions did Donna

25 Jordan ask questions?

Page 217

1 A. I don't know, I think she was in the other room.
2 Q. When the investigators weren't there did she sometimes
3 ask questions of you or the other kids?
4 A. Yeah.
5 Q. Do you remember who it was that first asked you any
6 questions about all this?
7 A. It was Dan when he came to interview us.
8 Q. And you denied that anything happened?
9 A. Um-hum, yes.
10 Q. Before you went in to have him ask questions of you, did
11 you already know what kind of questions were going to be asked?
12 A. Before he asked me, no.
13 Q. Was that the first time you heard about these claims of
14 abuse?
15 A. Yeah, yes.
16 Q. You remember about how old you were when you finally got
17 back to Marty around your mother's home?
18 A. About thirteen. Thirteen or fourteen.
19 Q. You remember what grade you were in?
20 A. Sixth.
21 Q. What grade are you in now?
22 A. I am in seventh.
23 Q. Taking you a while to get through school?
24 A. Yeah.
25   MR. HAUGAARD: No other questions.

Page 218

1   THE COURT: Recross.
2 RECROSS EXAMINATION BY MR. HOLMES:
3 Q. Donovan, you say you were interviewed first by someone
4 about a month after you got to Donna Jordan's?
5 A. About a month or two, yeah.
6 Q. You don't remember when you were interviewed after that?
7 A. No.
8 Q. Isn't it a fact you were only interviewed at Donna
9 Jordan's one time?
10 A. Maybe.
11 Q. Well, no one talked to you, that being Dan Hudspeth or
12 Bill Van Roe, they only talked to you once at Donna Jordan's,
13 isn't that correct?
14   MR. HAUGAARD: Objection, asked and answered.
15   THE COURT: Overruled.
16 A. Maybe.
17 BY MR. HOLMES:
18 Q. That is not what you said in your affidavit, is it,
19 Exhibit 9? You said Hudspeth and some other man were there at
20 the same time, and then in the third paragraph you say the
21 third week, about a week later Dan Hudspeth and the other man
22 came back. Isn't that what you said in your affidavit?
23 A. Yes, that's what I said.
24 Q. Also in your affidavit on the second page, second
25 paragraph, you state many things were promised by the adults,

Page 219

1 but the adults didn't do what they promised. The promises
2 including being able to go home, and they also promised to give
3 us some clothes. Who do you claim made those promises to you?
4 A. Dan Hudspeth and that other guy.
5 Q. At the time of this one interview?
6 A. Yes.
7 Q. They were promising to buy you clothes?
8 A. No, I don't remember that part.
9 Q. Well, what are you talking about in your sworn affidavit
10 there when you say you were promised to give you some clothes?
11 A. I don't know.
12 Q. So that is not accurate?
13 A. That one little part, I don't remember saying that.
14 Q. After you testified here yesterday, who talked to you
15 about whether Ms. Honomichl drove you up to see Dr. Underwager?
16 A. Just my mom.
17 Q. But you testified here you remembered Kathleen Honomichl
18 driving you up here in October of '96 for this interview with
19 Dr. Underwager, correct?
20 A. Correct.
21 Q. And last night your mom got ahold of you and told you
22 that you should change your testimony, didn't she?
23   MR. HAUGAARD: Objection, Your Honor, form of the
24 question.
25   THE COURT: Overruled.

Page 220

1 A. Well, she didn't get ahold of me, and no, I just, she
2 just remember, just told me, and I said oh, yeah, now I
3 remember, and I just remembered.
4 BY MR. HOLMES:
5 Q. She wanted to correct your testimony, correct?
6   MR. HAUGAARD: Objection, Your Honor.
7   THE COURT: Overruled.
8 A. I don't know how she could correct my testimony when she
9 didn't even know what I was talking about.
10 BY MR. HOLMES:
11 Q. Why was she talking to you about whether Kathleen
12 Honomichl had driven you up here to see Dr. Underwager?
13 A. I guess it was just something we was talking about.
14 Q. Because she knew that Kathleen Honomichl had testified
15 that that never happened, didn't she?
16 A. I guess.
17 Q. You know how she knew that?
18   MR. HAUGAARD: Objection, Your Honor.
19   THE COURT: Overruled.
20 A. No, I do not know how she knows that.
21   MR. HOLMES: Nothing further.
22   THE COURT: Redirect.
23 REDIRECT EXAMINATION BY MR. HAUGAARD:
24 Q. Donovan, were there times when Kathleen has driven you
25 other places?

Page 221

1 A. Yes.

2 Q. So if you got confused as an eight or ten or twelve year
3 old, whatever you were at the time, it could be because you
4 have been in her car before?

5 A. Yes.

6 Q. While you were in foster care did anybody promise to get
7 you certain things, clothes or toys or anything?

8 A. I don't remember.

9 Q. Did they promise that you would get to go home as soon as
10 you tell the truth?

11 A. Yes.

12 Q. And did that mean to you that you just had to go with
13 this lie?

14 A. Yes.

15 Q. Mr. Holmes got down to details as far as how many times
16 you were interviewed. Do you remember seeing these men,
17 Mr. Hudspeth, and Mr. Van Roe more than once?

18 A. Yes.

19 Q. Could it be that they interviewed someone else?

20   MR. HOLMES: I object as leading and suggestive.

21   THE COURT: Overruled.

22 A. I don't know, maybe.

23 BY MR. HAUGAARD:

24 Q. You saw them on more than one occasion, is that right?

25 A. Um-hum.

Page 222

1 Q. Did you see Micky Tapken more than once?

2 A. I don't remember.

3 Q. You saw her around the time of trial?

4 A. Yes.

5 Q. And were there many times that Donna Jordan would ask you
6 or the other kids questions?

7 A. Yes.

8 Q. So did it seem to you like this was a subject that was
9 being discussed a lot?

10 A. Pretty much.

11 Q. Was it clear to you what kind of an answer you were
12 supposed to give?

13 A. Yes.

14 Q. Even if that was not true?

15 A. Yes.

16 Q. Donovan, we could go through piece by piece all the
17 things that were said at trial, but those allegations of abuse
18 that you claim, or you testified to at the time of trial, did
19 any of those things ever happen?

20 A. No.

21 Q. Did your uncles ever do anything harmful to you?

22 A. No.

23 Q. Would you still like to be able to talk to the Judge
24 privately?

25 A. Yes.

Page 223

1 Q. Is there anything else you would like to tell the Judge?

2 A. Just that it didn't happen, and it never would happen.

3 Q. If it would happen, what would you do?

4 A. I don't know, because it never would.

5 Q. But if were you around your uncles again, say that things
6 all get straightened out and they are living back at Marty and
7 they ever touched you or touched one of the girls, what would
8 you do?

9 A. I don't know.

10 Q. Would you lie for them?

11 A. Probably not.

12 Q. Are you lying now?

13 A. No.

14 Q. Has your mom or anybody else forced you to come in here
15 and say these things?

16 A. No.

17 Q. What has this made you feel like over the past eight
18 years as you have been growing up?

19 A. Just feel wrong.

20 Q. How often do you think about it?

21 A. I try not to think about it. I try not to.

22 Q. When you do, what does it make you feel like?

23 A. Makes me feel real like I have lied and guilty, so just
24 bad.

25   MR. HAUGAARD: No further questions.

Page 224

1   THE COURT: Any additional cross?

2   MR. HOLMES: No, Your Honor.

3   THE COURT: I have some questions for you Donovan.

4 You are in the 6th grade starting this fall, is that right?

5 A. No, I am in 7th grade, and I am not going back to school.

6   THE COURT: Why aren't you going back to school?

7 A. Because I will probably go to Job Corps.

8   THE COURT: Why is that?

9 A. I don't know, just because I got to get off the
10 Reservation.

11   THE COURT: Why do you feel you have to get off the
12 Reservation?

13 A. Because it is boring there.

14   THE COURT: You find school boring?

15 A. No.

16   THE COURT: Then if you go to the Job Corps, though,
17 you wouldn't be going to school, would you?

18 A. It is kind of like school.

19   THE COURT: Beg pardon?

20 A. It is kind of like school, because they help you get your
21 GED or whatever.

22   THE COURT: Where would you go to Job Corps?

23 A. Probably Montana.

24   THE COURT: Have you applied for that?

25 A. Not yet.

Page 225

1   THE COURT: Does your mother know about that?
2 A. Um-hum.
3   THE COURT: Is she supporting you in that?
4 A. Yes.
5   THE COURT: Now last year when you were in the 6th
6 grade, then you went to school in Wagner, is that right, or did
7 you go to school at Marty?
8 A. I didn't go to school last year, the year before that I
9 was in Wagner.
10   THE COURT: What did you do last year?
11 A. Nothing.
12   THE COURT: Didn't your mother require you to go to
13 school?
14 A. Yeah, but I didn't listen.
15   THE COURT: Did anybody from the school come out and
16 say you are supposed to go to school?
17 A. No, because I was sixteen and nobody really cared.
18   THE COURT: Let's see, and then in November of this
19 year you will be seventeen, is that right?
20 A. Yes.
21   THE COURT: When you went to school, were there some
22 subjects that were easier for you and some subjects that were
23 more difficult?
24 A. Yeah.
25   THE COURT: What were the subjects that were easier

Page 226

1 for you?
2 A. Math and science.
3   THE COURT: What were the subjects that were more
4 difficult for you?
5 A. English and social studies and language arts.
6   THE COURT: With regard to English, was it the
7 grammar, or what was it that was more difficult for you?
8 A. I don't know, I just didn't pay attention in that class.
9   THE COURT: With regard to reading, do you have any
10 problem reading?
11 A. No.
12   THE COURT: By going to Job Corps do you hope to
13 ultimately get your GED that way?
14 A. Yes.
15   THE COURT: When you were in school in the 6th grade
16 the year before last, did you get in any trouble in school?
17 A. In 6th grade?
18   THE COURT: That was the last year you went to
19 school, wasn't it?
20 A. 7th, no, that was the year before.
21   THE COURT: So if you went back to school this fall
22 you would be in the 8th grade, is that right?
23 A. No, because I didn't pass.
24   THE COURT: What was the reason you didn't pass?
25 A. Because I didn't go to school.

Page 227

1   THE COURT: So the year before last when you were in
2 school you weren't going to school enough to pass, is that
3 right?
4 A. Yes.
5   THE COURT: Did they prevent you from coming to
6 school this past year, or were you going to have to repeat a
7 grade if you did come to school?
8 A. They prevented my cousin from coming back this year
9 because he is just a month younger than me, and they just told
10 him it would be better, they told him that he better just get a
11 GED and go to Job Corps.
12   THE COURT: They never told you that, you assumed the
13 same would apply to you?
14 A. Yes.
15   THE COURT: Of course, you were getting older and was
16 it a problem going back to school when you were going to be
17 older than the other kids in your class?
18 A. Yes.
19   THE COURT: It really wasn't the fact that the school
20 work would be difficult for you, because it really wouldn't be,
21 would it?
22 A. No.
23   THE COURT: Did any of these people that have been
24 talked about, Donna Jordan, or Dan Hudspeth, or the FBI guy, or
25 Micky Tapken, did any of them ever tell you to lie, or words to

Page 228

1 that effect?
2 A. Tell me to lie?
3   THE COURT: Right, or words to that effect?
4 A. No, they just, I just kind of figured that if what I
5 said, that if I said that then I would be able to go home.
6   THE COURT: Do the Court's questions give rise to
7 questions by either side?
8   MR. HOLMES: Not from the government.
9   MR. HAUGAARD: Not from the defense.
10   THE COURT: Thank you, you may step down, call your
11 next witness.
12   MR. HAUGAARD: Your Honor, we still would like to
13 make that available, the kids could individually speak with the
14 Court if you choose.
15   THE COURT: I just can't do that, because, I just
16 can't. I mean, you know, whatever they have to say they are on
17 the stand, and that's what we have the hearing for, that's why
18 I am having it.
19
20
21
22
23
24
25

Page 229

1   INDEX TO WITNESS

2   MAGGIE BRUCK

3   DIRECT EXAMINATION BY MR. WILKA   7
     CROSS EXAMINATION BY MR. SEILER   31
4   REDIRECT EXAMINATION BY MR. WILKA   79
     RECROSS EXAMINATION BY MR. SEILER   89
5

6   KATHLEEN HONOMICHL

7   DIRECT EXAMINATION BY MR. HAUGAARD   102
     CROSS EXAMINATION BY MR. HOLMES   123
8   REDIRECT EXAMINATION BY MR. HAUGAARD 141
     RECROSS EXAMINATION BY MR. HOLMES   143
9   REDIRECT EXAMINATION BY MR. HAUGAARD 145

10

11   JULIA ANN JOSEPH GONZALES

12   DIRECT EXAMINATION BY MR. HAUGAARD   146
     CROSS EXAMINATION BY MR. HOLMES   153
13   REDIRECT EXAMINATION BY MR. HAUGAARD 159

14   VICTOR W. PROVOST

15   DIRECT EXAMINATION BY MR. HAUGAARD   160
     CROSS EXAMINATION BY MR. HOLMES   163
16

17   DONOVAN ROUSE

18   DIRECT EXAMINATION BY MR. HAUGAARD   166
     REDIRECT EXAMINATION BY MR. HAUGAARD 211
19   RECROSS EXAMINATION BY MR. HOLMES   218
     REDIRECT EXAMINATION BY MR. HAUGAARD 220
20

21

22

23

24

25

Page 230

1   INDEX TO DEFENDANT EXHIBITS
     Exhibit A Marked   10
2   A Offered   11

3   A Received   11
     Exhibit B Marked   147
4   B Offered   152

5   B Received   153

6

7

8

9

10   INDEX TO GOVERNMENT EXHIBITS
     Exhibit 3 Marked   207
11   3 Offered   208

12   3 Received   208
     Exhibit 5 Marked   130
13   5 Offered   130

14   5 Received   130
     Exhibit 9 Marked   209
15   9 Offered   209

16   9 Received   209

17

18

19

20

21

22

23

24

25

Page 229

```
 1        UNITED STATES DISTRICT COURT
 2          DISTRICT OF SOUTH DAKOTA
 3            SOUTHERN DIVISION
 4    * * * * * * * * * * * * * * * * * * *
 4                                         *
      UNITED STATES OF AMERICA,            *
 5                                         *
          Plaintiff,      *     Volume II
 6                                         *
        -vs-             *      CR. 94-40015
 7                        *     MOTION FOR NEW TRIAL
      DESMOND ROUSE, JESSIE ROUSE          *
 8    GARFIELD FEATHER, RUSSELL            *
      HUBBELING,                           *
 9                                         *
10          Defendants.    *
11    * * * * * * * * * * * * * * * * * *
12
13    BEFORE:      The Honorable Lawrence L. Piersol
                   Chief United States District Judge
14                 For the District of South Dakota
                   Sioux Falls, South Dakota
15
16
17    PROCEEDINGS:    The above-entitled matter came on for
                      hearing on the 5th day of September, 2001
18                    commencing at the hour of 9:00 a.m. in the
                      courtroom of the Federal Building, Sioux
19                    Falls, South Dakota.
      Proceedings recorded by mechanical stenography, transcript
20    produced by computer.
21
22
23
24
25
```

Page 230

```
 1   APPEARANCES:
 2         Mr. Randy Seiler
           Ms. Michelle Tapken
 3         Mr. Dennis Holmes
           Assistant United States Attorneys
 4         Pierre, South Dakota
           Sioux Falls, South Dakota
 5
              Attorneys for the United States;
 6
 7         Mr. John Wilka
           Attorney at Law
 8         Sioux Falls, South Dakota
 9            Attorney for Desmond Rouse;
10
           Mr. Steven Binger
11         Attorney at Law
           Sioux Falls, South Dakota
12
13            Attorney for Jessie Rouse;
14         Mr. David Carter
           Attorney at Law
15         Sioux Falls, South Dakota
16            Attorney for Garfield Feather;
17
           Mr. Steve Haugaard
18         Attorney at Law
           Sioux Falls, South Dakota
19
              Attorney for Russell Hubbeling.
20
21
22
23
24
25
```

Page 231

```
 1        THE COURT:  Call your next witness.
 2
 3            THRISTA ROUSE,
 4   called as a witness, being first duly sworn, testified and said
 5   as follows:
 6
 7   DIRECT EXAMINATION BY MR. HAUGAARD:
 8   Q.  Thrista, please state your name and spell your last name?
 9   A.  Thrista Rouse, R-O-U-S-E.
10   Q.  How old are you, Thrista?
11   A.  I am sixteen.
12   Q.  What is your birth date?
13   A.  5-21-85.
14   Q.  Thrista, tell me about, tell me who your mother is?
15   A.  Who my mother is?
16   Q.  Yes, who is your mom?
17   A.  Ursula Rouse.
18   Q.  Do you have brothers and sisters?
19   A.  I have one sister.
20   Q.  What is her name?
21   A.  Alexis.
22   Q.  You are how old right now?
23   A.  Sixteen.
24   Q.  When you were taken away from your home how old were you
25   then?
```

Page 232

```
 1   A.  Seven.
 2   Q.  You remember being taken away from home?
 3   A.  Yep.
 4   Q.  Tell me what you remember about that particular
 5   situation, just the very time it happened, what took place?
 6   A.  At my grandma's.
 7   Q.  You were at your grandma's house?
 8   A.  Yeah.
 9   Q.  You were staying there?
10   A.  Yeah.
11   Q.  What took place, what time of the day was it, what time
12   of the year was it?
13   A.  I don't know.
14   Q.  Was it in the morning, or night?
15   A.  In the daytime.
16   Q.  Do you remember who came?
17   A.  The FBI.
18   Q.  How did you know it was the FBI?
19   A.  They had FBI on the back of their jackets.
20   Q.  How many people were there?
21   A.  About four or five.
22   Q.  How many kids were there at the time at the house?
23   A.  I don't know, I can't remember.
24   Q.  Can you name off some of the people that were there, some
25   of the kids?
```

Page 233

1 A. No, because I can't remember.
2 Q. Who were the adults who were at home at the time?
3 A. My mom, my grandma, my uncle Jess, my aunty Donata.
4 Q. When the people came, what did they say to you or to the
5 adults?
6 A. I don't know, they didn't talk to me, they talked to the
7 adults.
8 Q. Did you figure out that you were being taken away from
9 them?
10 A. Yeah.
11 Q. What did you do when you figured that out?
12 A. I ran to my uncle Jess.
13 Q. What did you do?
14 A. Told him not to let them take me.
15 Q. Were you afraid of your uncle Jess?
16 A. No.
17 Q. Is he sitting here today?
18 A. Yes.
19 Q. Did he ever do anything to you?
20 A. No.
21 Q. Tell us where you went when you were taken away?
22 A. To the Brock's, Jim Brock's.
23 Q. Did you know them? At that time did you know Brocks?
24 A. No.
25 Q. How old were you at that time?

Page 234

1 A. Seven.
2 Q. How long did you stay at the Brock's?
3 A. A day.
4 Q. Then where did you go after that?
5 A. Elk Point.
6 Q. To what house?
7 A. Donna Jordan's.
8 Q. Were you scared?
9 A. No.
10 Q. Why not?
11 A. I don't know.
12 Q. Were you with your cousins?
13 A. Yep.
14 Q. Did you know why you were being taken away when the FBI
15 came?
16 A. No.
17 Q. Did you find out when you got to Jean Brock's?
18 A. No, I found out when I got to Donna Jordan's.
19 Q. How did you find out there?
20 A. Donna started asking me questions.
21 Q. What questions did she ask?
22 A. Like --
23 Q. Go ahead and state some of the questions that she asked,
24 the things that she said to you. Thrista, was it hard for you
25 to come here today?

Page 235

1 A. Yes.
2 Q. Was it hard for you to come here last time you were in
3 trial?
4 A. Yes.
5 Q. Why was it hard for you to come here and testify at the
6 trial?
7 A. Because I knew I was lying.
8 Q. Why did you lie?
9 A. Because I was young.
10 Q. What did you think would happen if you lied?
11 A. I would get to go home.
12 Q. How many questions do you suppose Donna Jordan asked
13 you -- well, let me ask you this.
14 Was it the first day that you were there that you found out
15 what kind of questions she was going to be asking?
16 A. Yes.
17 Q. How long do you suppose she spent asking you questions?
18 I know it is seven or eight years ago, but did it seem like a
19 long time?
20 A. Hours.
21 Q. Maybe it wasn't hours, but it seemed like hours?
22 A. I don't know, I was the last one she talked to.
23 Q. Did she talk to each one of the kids?
24 A. Yes.
25 Q. Was anybody else there with her when she was asking

Page 236

1 questions?
2 A. Yep. No. not the first day, second day.
3 Q. So the first day she was there by herself asking
4 questions? You have to say yes?
5 A. Yes.
6 Q. As you recall, was it the next day that somebody started
7 asking more questions?
8 A. Yep, yes.
9 Q. You didn't write down the dates that you went any place,
10 did you?
11 A. Nope.
12 Q. If you think of it as one day and the next day, you might
13 be right, might be wrong as far as the timeframe, is that
14 right?
15 A. Yes.
16 Q. But it seemed to you that it was early on that you were
17 asked a lot of questions?
18 A. Yep.
19 Q. Based on the questions she asked you, did you figure out
20 who had said what?
21 A. Yeah.
22 Q. How did you figure that out?
23 A. Because they was asking me those questions.
24 Q. What kind of questions exactly do you remember now, what
25 names did she say had said certain things? Is it hard for you

Page 237

1 to answer any of these questions today?
2 A. Yes.
3 Q. Why is that?
4 A. Because it is.
5 Q. When Donna asked you these questions, did she say things
6 about what other people had already said?
7 A. Probably.
8 Q. Because it was the kind of questions that she asked that
9 you figured out what was going on?
10 A. Yes.
11 Q. Did you at first say no, that is not true?
12 A. Yes.
13 Q. How many times do you think you said no, that's not true?
14 A. A lot, until she said you don't have to lie no more,
15 because the other cousins already told the truth.
16 Q. The things that you testified to at trial, or actually
17 you didn't testify, but the things you answered yes to at trial
18 about being abused or seeing that your uncles abused others,
19 was that true?
20 A. No.
21 Q. Have you ever seen your uncles abuse anybody -- well?
22 A. No.
23 Q. Let me ask you this. When you were living there in the
24 home, it wasn't uncommon for your uncles to have a party, was
25 it?

Page 238

1 A. No.
2 Q. And they might rough around with each other, is that
3 true?
4 A. I don't know.
5 Q. Did you ever see them hurt any of the kids?
6 A. No.
7 Q. Did you ever hear any of the other kids say that they had
8 been hurt by the uncles?
9 A. No.
10 Q. Did your uncle Jess ever touch you?
11 A. No.
12 Q. Did your uncle Desmond ever touch you in any wrong way?
13 A. No.
14 Q. Did your uncle Garfield ever touch you in any wrong way?
15 A. No.
16 Q. You recognize Russ Hubbeling?
17 A. No.
18 Q. If I tell you this is Russ Hubbeling back here, do you
19 think that makes sense, you believe that? Did you know Russ
20 back then?
21 A. No.
22 Q. Did you ever see Russ pick up Echo or Fury and try to
23 have sex with them?
24 A. No.
25 Q. Russ ever try to have sex with you?

Page 239

1 A. No.
2 Q. Did people ask you questions along that line? When you
3 were at the foster home, did Donna Jordan or anybody else ask
4 you questions like that?
5 A. Like what?
6 Q. Like did you see Russ touch the little girls?
7 A. Yeah, they did.
8 Q. Did there come a time when you might have lied about
9 these things and made up some things?
10 A. Yes.
11 Q. Why would you do that?
12 A. Because I was young.
13 Q. What did you think that would accomplish?
14 A. I would be able to go home, that's all I wanted to do.
15 Q. Do you remember, was it a long time before you got to see
16 your mom again? You have to say yes or no, Thrista.
17 A. Yes.
18 Q. When they asked the questions, could you tell by the
19 sound of their voice what kind of answer they wanted?
20 A. Yes.
21 Q. How many times do you think you told Donna Jordan that it
22 didn't happen?
23 A. A lot.
24 Q. By the time the other people came to ask you questions,
25 did you tell them it didn't happen?

Page 240

1 A. Yep, yes.
2 Q. Do you think you told them that once, or twice, or more
3 than that?
4 A. More than that.
5 Q. After a while did you agree with what they were asking?
6 A. Yes.
7 Q. What was your reason for doing that?
8 A. Doing what?
9 Q. To agree with them? Did you want the interviews to stop?
10 A. Yes.
11 Q. Did you think that would make the interviews stop?
12 A. No.
13 Q. If you agreed with them did you think that would help?
14 A. Yes.
15 Q. When you were being asked questions did you feel like you
16 couldn't get up and leave the room?
17 A. Yeah.
18 Q. Were there times when you wanted to get up and leave the
19 room?
20 A. Yes.
21 Q. Did you ask if you could do that?
22 A. No.
23 Q. Were you afraid of what they would tell you?
24 A. Yes.
25 Q. During the time you were at Donna Jordan's did she ask

Page 241

1 you, did she have times when she would sit with you alone and
2 ask you these questions over?
3 A. Sometimes.
4 Q. Did you eventually have meetings with Micky Tapken and
5 did she ask you the same questions?
6 A. Yes.
7 Q. How many times do you think you met with her before you
8 actually came into the courtroom, or came into the Judge's
9 office to testify?
10 A. About twice.
11 Q. What did she tell you?
12 A. Wouldn't tell me nothing.
13 Q. Did she ask you questions?
14 A. Yes.
15 Q. Did you know how you were supposed to answer the
16 questions?
17 A. No.
18 Q. Did you tell the truth when you answered her questions?
19 A. No.
20 Q. What did you think it was going to take for you to be
21 able to go home to your mother?
22 A. I didn't think I was going to go home.
23 Q. When you were with your cousins in the foster home did
24 you talk about these things that the interviewers were asking
25 you?

Page 242

1 A. No.
2 Q. Did you ever tell any of your cousins that these things
3 didn't happen?
4 A. I told my cousin Derrick.
5 Q. Did you ever tell Jerome?
6 A. No.
7 Q. Or Moses?
8 A. No.
9 Q. Do you remember being in the Judge's office to answer
10 questions?
11 A. Yes.
12 Q. Were you afraid to tell the truth?
13 A. Yes.
14 Q. Why were you afraid to tell the truth?
15 A. Because they would never listen to me anyway.
16 Q. Were you afraid to come into the courtroom?
17 A. Yes.
18 Q. Why?
19 A. Because I knew I was lying.
20 Q. Were you afraid to face your uncles at that time?
21 A. Yes.
22 Q. Are you afraid of them right now?
23 A. No.
24 Q. Was it hard for you to remember the story that you were
25 supposed to tell at the trial?

Page 243

1 A. I didn't have to tell a story, I just had to answer yes
2 or no.
3 Q. Did that make it a lot easier?
4 A. Yes.
5 Q. Thrista, did your mom pressure you in to coming in here
6 today?
7 A. No, I pressured myself.
8 Q. Why?
9 A. Because they aren't true.
10 Q. How old were you when this took place, you are sixteen
11 now?
12 A. Seven.
13 Q. At that time did you know how serious all this was?
14 A. No.
15 Q. Did you have any idea what was going to happen to your
16 uncles?
17 A. Yeah.
18 Q. Did you know how long they might go to prison?
19 A. No.
20 Q. Even if somebody would have told you thirty years back
21 then, did you know what thirty years was when you were seven,
22 eight, nine years old?
23 A. No.
24 Q. When did you first decide, besides the first day when you
25 denied anything took place, when is the next time that you

Page 244

1 remember telling somebody that this wasn't true, your cousins
2 or?
3 A. I was telling my cousins.
4 Q. How soon after this do you think it was that you told
5 your cousins?
6 A. What?
7 Q. How soon do you think it was before you told your cousins
8 that this didn't happen?
9 A. I don't know.
10 Q. Do you remember what grade you were in before you were
11 taken away?
12 A. Fourth, I think.
13 Q. Do you remember what grade you were in when you were at
14 Donna's house?
15 A. I was in fifth grade then.
16 Q. When you were at Donna's house were there counseling
17 sessions that she would take you to?
18 A. Yes.
19 Q. Where did you go to counseling?
20 A. In Jefferson.
21 Q. Who was the counselor?
22 A. I don't know. I know she had black hair.
23 Q. Was it Ellen?
24 A. I don't know, she had black hair, though.
25 Q. Did she ask you the same kinds of questions?

Page 245

1 A. Sometimes.
2 Q. Would you be alone during those times, or would there be
3 other kids in the room?
4 A. Yeah, we was all in the same room.
5 Q. When you were being interviewed, I don't know if it was
6 by Donna or Ellen or the FBI, did they show you a picture of a
7 rope, do you remember that?
8 A. Yeah.
9 Q. Did you know anything about a rope before that?
10 A. No.
11 Q. Did anybody ever tie you up in the house?
12 A. No. I wouldn't be here if they did.
13 Q. If anybody did that to your cousins would you be here?
14 A. No.
15 Q. How many times did you get to see your mom while you were
16 in foster care?
17 A. I can only remember one time that I seen her, there was
18 people around listening and watching us.
19 Q. Did your mom ever put pressure on you in those sessions
20 to change your story?
21 A. No.
22 Q. Have they told you to come here today and make up a new
23 lie?
24 A. No. I told myself to come here today.
25 Q. Is it because you want the Judge to hear the truth this

Page 246

1 time?
2 A. Yes, and this time I am not seven years old.
3 Q. I want to get in to something I told you I was going to
4 ask you about, and it is not pleasant for you, but you know it
5 is important.
6 Before you were taken out of your home did you ever have sex
7 with one of your cousins?
8 A. Yes.
9 Q. Which one?
10 A. Jerome and Moses.
11 Q. You remember about how old they were at the time?
12 A. No.
13 Q. They were a little bit older, though?
14 A. Yeah, they were older than me.
15 Q. Where did that take place?
16 A. In Marty.
17 Q. Where at in Marty?
18 A. Places.
19 Q. Was it sometimes -- did you say places?
20 A. Um-hum.
21 Q. Was it sometimes in the house?
22 A. No.
23 Q. Usually outside?
24 A. Yep.
25 Q. Did you just go out in the field with them?

Page 247

1 A. Yep.
2 Q. When you were in foster care at Donna Jordan's, Moses or
3 Jerome got in trouble for something there, what was that?
4 A. The same thing.
5 THE COURT: I can't hear you, I am sorry, what?
6 A. The same thing.
7 Q. Were you having sex with him there?
8 A. Yes.
9 Q. Did they take Jerome out of the home at that point?
10 A. Yes.
11 Q. Did you get caught by somebody?
12 A. No, I told.
13 Q. Who did you tell?
14 A. Donna.
15 Q. When that happened to you, you went to somebody and told
16 about it, right?
17 A. Yeah.
18 Q. Was it because you were mad at Jerome, maybe?
19 A. No.
20 Q. You just didn't want him to do it?
21 A. Yes.
22 Q. If your uncles had been doing that to you, who would you
23 have told?
24 A. I would have told the FBI when they came to my house.
25 Q. Would you have told your mom?

Page 248

1 A. Yeah, and my grandma.
2 Q. Some of these reports said that your uncles were doing
3 these things to your grandma and your mom?
4 A. Yeah.
5 Q. Was that true?
6 A. No.
7 Q. You know if anybody has ever molested your cousin
8 Rosemary?
9 A. I don't know. I know she was real quiet.
10 Q. Did your uncles ever do anything to her?
11 A. No. Her mom's boyfriends did.
12 Q. Did there come a time when you were able to talk to
13 Rosemary about this stuff?
14 A. Yeah.
15 Q. Your cousin Rosemary. What did she say took place?
16 MR. HOLMES: Objection, foundation.
17 THE COURT: Sustained.
18 BY MR. HAUGAARD:
19 Q. When did you talk to her about this?
20 A. I talked to her. I don't know when, but I know I talked
21 to her.
22 Q. Where were you at when you talked to her about this
23 stuff?
24 A. We was walking around in Marty.
25 Q. This was after you were placed back in the dorm at Marty,

Page 249

1 is that right?
2 A. Yeah.
3 Q. What did she say?
4 A. Nothing, she won't say nothing, she is just quiet. I try
5 to talk to her, she will start crying.
6 Q. What did you say to her?
7 A. Huh?
8 Q. What did you say to her?
9 A. I just asked her if anything happened to her, and she
10 won't say nothing to me.
11 Q. Has she told you whether anything happened to her now?
12 A. No, she won't.
13 Q. Did you tell the investigators that Jessie and Desmond
14 had been sexually abusing Ebony and Tabetha?
15 A. No.
16 Q. Do you remember them asking you questions about that?
17 A. No.
18 Q. Were there a lot of questions asked?
19 A. Yes.
20 Q. And did you agree with some of them?
21 A. Yeah.
22 Q. Did you make up some lies?
23 A. A lot of lies, yes, I did.
24 Q. Why did you do that?
25 A. Because I was young, and I wanted to go home.

Page 250

1 Q. Garfield ever tie you up on the bed?
2 A. No.
3 Q. Anybody ever tie you up on the bed?
4 A. No.
5 Q. When you think back on it seven years later, how long do
6 you think you answered no, or denied the questions, how long do
7 you think you did that before you finally went along with the
8 questions?
9 A. I don't know how long it was, but I know I said no when
10 they first asked me.
11 Q. Could you tell that those people asking you questions
12 controlled where you were going to be at the time?
13 A. Yes.
14 Q. Were you afraid of Donna Jordan?
15 A. When I first got there.
16 Q. Did you ever see her mistreat anyone there?
17 A. Yes.
18 Q. Can you tell us about that?
19 A. She had. She mistreated all of us, she was mean.
20 Q. What did she do that was mean?
21 A. Like whenever we caught head lice at her house she made
22 us take a bath in rubbing alcohol, and that burned.
23 Q. What else did she do that was mean?
24 A. She just would say that our family never feed us, she
25 never feed us.

Page 251

1 Q. Say that again?
2 A. She said that my family never used to feed us, she never
3 used to feed us. She said our family never used to feed us,
4 she hardly never used to feed us.
5 Q. Did you ever see her mistreat any of the little girls?
6 A. Yeah, Fury.
7 Q. What did she do to Fury?
8 A. Spank her.
9 Q. What?
10 A. She would spank her.
11 Q. Why would she spank her?
12 A. I don't know. Ask Jessica and them, they know.
13 Q. She ever grab anybody by the hair?
14 A. What?
15 Q. Did she ever grab anybody by the hair?
16 A. Yeah, Fury.
17 Q. What did she do then?
18 A. Grabbed her by the hair and spanked her.
19 Q. You remember what Fury was doing that caused her to do
20 that?
21 A. No, or --
22 Q. How old was Fury at the time?
23 A. She was still a baby.
24 Q. How old would you think she is at that time?
25 A. Two.

Page 252

1 Q. When you were interviewed by Dr. Underwager, do you
2 remember that?
3 A. Yes.
4 Q. Did anyone tell you to lie?
5 A. No.
6 Q. Did anyone tell you what kind of a story you had to say
7 to get your uncles out of prison?
8 A. No.
9 Q. When the Judge was asking you questions in his office
10 about knowing the difference between a truth and a lie, why
11 didn't you tell him the truth at that time?
12 A. Probably because I lied.
13 Q. Did you feel like you had to go with that story?
14 A. Yeah.
15 Q. Did there come a time when you -- let me ask you this.
16 Was Kathleen Honomichl the case worker for you for a while?
17 A. Yeah.
18 Q. Did there come a time when you came to her and told her
19 that this didn't happen?
20 A. Yes.
21 Q. Why did you go to her?
22 A. She was our social worker.
23 Q. Did you trust her?
24 A. Yeah.
25 Q. Why did you trust her more than Donna Jordan?

Page 253

1 A. Because she was nice to us. Nicer than Deena LaPointe,
2 too.
3 Q. Did you think you had to stick with your story with
4 Deena?
5 A. Yes.
6 Q. Did Kathleen ask you a bunch of questions to get you to
7 say these things?
8 A. No.
9 Q. When you went to her, do you remember what time of the
10 year that was?
11 A. No.
12 Q. You remember what grade you were in at that time?
13 A. I was up here in Sioux Falls at the CHS when I left from
14 Jordan's, that's where I went is up here.
15 Q. Children's Home Society?
16 A. Yes.
17 Q. Why didn't you tell somebody there that this didn't
18 happen, or did you?
19 A. No.
20 Q. Why didn't you tell them what really happened?
21 A. Because I forgot all about it.
22 Q. You didn't forget all about it, but why didn't you tell
23 them?
24 A. Because I didn't want to.
25 Q. The case worker at the Children's Home Society, were

Page 254

1 there any Indian case workers that you knew?
2 A. No.
3 Q. Before you saw Dr. Underwager had you already told other
4 people that this didn't happen?
5 A. No.
6 Q. You had seen Kathleen Honomichl about it before that,
7 hadn't you?
8 A. No. I can't remember if --
9 Q. You are how old right now, sixteen?
10 A. Yes.
11 Q. The first time you saw him was probably five years ago,
12 so you were eleven or so. Did he tell you what to say?
13 A. No. I never talked to him.
14 Q. Well, when you answered some questions for him, did you
15 tell him the truth?
16 A. No.
17 Q. Would you want a drink of water?
18 A. No.
19 Q. You just want this to be done, right?
20 A. Yes.
21 Q. Do you remember what grade you were in when you were,
22 maybe you already answered this, when you were at Children's
23 Home Society, or didn't they have a grade?
24 A. Yeah, they did, I was still in fifth because I didn't
25 finish in Jefferson. I don't remember.

Page 255

1 Q. It was during that time when you went to Kathleen
2 Honomichl and told her that this didn't happen?
3 A. Yes.
4 Q. Do you remember who Dr. Underwager is?
5 A. Yeah, kind of.
6 Q. Do you remember him being a big guy?
7 A. Yeah.
8 Q. Fat guy. After while your moms came to know that you
9 were saying this wasn't true, is that right?
10 A. Yeah.
11 Q. Had they been asking you a bunch of questions to get you
12 to that point?
13 A. No.
14 Q. You knew that your grandma was sad about this whole deal,
15 right?
16 A. Yes.
17 Q. You were sad about it too, weren't you?
18 A. Yeah.
19 Q. And as you sit here today, if you would look at the Judge
20 and tell him the absolute truth -- go ahead and look at him --
21 did your uncles molest you or your cousins?
22 A. My cousins -- what?
23 Q. Did your uncles ever touch you or rape you?
24 A. No. I wouldn't be here trying to get them out of prison
25 if they did. I wouldn't even bother coming back here.

Page 256

1 Q. Did your uncles ever touch your cousins?
2 A. No.
3 Q. But you did have sex with your cousins Moses and Jerome?
4 A. Yeah.
5 Q. Do you have anything else you want to say to the Judge?
6 A. No, I just said it.
7 Q. Are you at all afraid of your uncles?
8 A. No.
9 Q. When you ran to Jess when they came to take you away, was
10 it because you knew he would protect you?
11 A. Yes.
12 MR. HAUGAARD: No other questions.
13 THE COURT: Cross.
14 CROSS EXAMINATION BY MR. HOLMES:
15 Q. Thrista, what is your date of birth?
16 A. 5-21-85.
17 Q. You went to live with Donna Jordan after you were removed
18 from your home, is that right?
19 A. Yes.
20 Q. And you stayed there through the trial, do you remember
21 that?
22 A. Yeah, yes.
23 Q. After the trial how long did you stay at Donna Jordan's
24 until you went to Children's Home?
25 A. I can't remember. I know we moved there after Jerome

Page 257

1 moved out of the house, I moved there to CHS.
2 Q. How long were you at Children's Home?
3 A. I think for two years.
4 Q. And then where did you go?
5 A. I went to the shelter by Marty, and then after the
6 shelter I moved with Mike and Julia, and Mike and Julia put me
7 in a dorm, I went with my aunt Julia.
8 Q. That is Julia Joseph?
9 A. Yes.
10 Q. She is the one that put you in the dorm?
11 A. Yes.
12 Q. She is the one that arranged to have you moved from the
13 shelter to the dorm?
14 A. No, from the shelter I moved with my aunty Julia, then I
15 went to the dorm.
16 Q. So there was a period of time when you just lived with
17 her?
18 A. No, because I moved from the shelter, and then I got in
19 to school with my aunty Julia, and she moved me into the dorm
20 and I stayed in the dorm that whole year.
21 Q. Then where did you go to live?
22 A. My aunty Julia.
23   THE COURT: Where?
24 A. My aunty Julia's.
25 Q. After that?

Page 258

1 A. I got to go on home visits.
2 Q. Where was your mother living at that time?
3 A. With my grandma.
4 Q. Rosemary?
5 A. Yeah.
6 Q. Did you eventually go back to live with your mother?
7 A. Yes.
8 Q. How long was that after you were living in the dorm at
9 Marty that you went back to live with your mother full time?
10 A. About a year.
11 Q. Where did your mother live?
12 A. Where does she live?
13 Q. Yes?
14 A. She lives with my grandma.
15 Q. After you went, left the dorm, you went back to live in
16 your grandmother Rosemary's house, is that right?
17 A. Yes.
18 Q. And you have been there ever since?
19 A. Yes.
20 Q. Who else lives in that house?
21 A. My aunty Donata, and my aunty Sonja, and me, and my
22 grandma, and my mom, and my sister, and my cousin Josh.
23 Q. After you got out of Children's Home, have you seen
24 letters that your uncles had written to your grandma Rosemary?
25 A. No.

Page 259

1 Q. Has anyone talked about those letters?
2 A. No.
3 Q. Have you ever talked to your uncles on the phone?
4 A. Yeah.
5 Q. How often have you done that?
6 A. Whenever they called.
7 Q. And how often does that occur?
8 A. I don't know, whenever they get to make phone calls, I
9 guess.
10 Q. So it happens a lot?
11   MR. HAUGAARD: Objection, foundation.
12   THE COURT: Overruled.
13 A. No, it doesn't happen a lot.
14 BY MR. HOLMES:
15 Q. That started as soon as you got out of Children's Home,
16 didn't it?
17 A. No. No, it didn't.
18 Q. When did you start talking to your uncles on the phone?
19 A. When I got to come home.
20 Q. As soon as you got to Rosemary's house?
21 A. Yeah.
22   MR. HAUGAARD: Objection, foundation, there is not a
23 timeframe?
24   THE COURT: Overruled, the chronology has been
25 established, go ahead.

Page 260

1 BY MR. HOLMES:
2 Q. I think you were asked by Mr. Haugaard about whether at
3 the time all this happened you knew how serious this matter
4 was, you remember that question?
5 A. Yeah.
6 Q. I think he told you that no one ever said to you that
7 they would get thirty years in prison?
8 A. No.
9 Q. Is that right, no one ever told you that?
10 A. No, they told me they were going to jail.
11 Q. Who told you that they were going to get thirty years?
12 A. Probably as I got older I figured it out.
13 Q. Well, someone in your family told you that, didn't they?
14 A. No.
15 Q. Did that make you feel guilty?
16 A. No.
17 Q. Your grandmother Rosemary never believed that this
18 happened --
19   MR. HAUGAARD: Objection, Your Honor, foundation.
20   THE COURT: Overruled.
21 BY MR. HOLMES:
22 Q. Did she?
23 A. Yeah.
24 Q. She has told you that, hasn't she?
25 A. No. She probably tells my mom and them that, but she

Page 261

1 never tells me that.
2 Q. Your mom has told you she doesn't believe this happened?
3 A. No.
4 Q. What has she told you?
5 A. She never told me that. I know that this never happened,
6 or else I wouldn't even be here.
7 Q. What have you talked to your uncles about on the phone?
8 A. About how I am doing and stuff like that.
9 Q. Have they talked to you about this case?
10 A. No.
11 Q. Do you remember when you first talked to Dr. Underwager?
12 A. Do I remember?
13 Q. Yes.
14 A. Some of it, kind of, sort of.
15 Q. Who brought you up to see Dr. Underwager?
16 A. Donna, I think.
17 Q. Donna Jordan?
18 A. Yeah, I think so.
19 Q. Who else saw Dr. Underwager?
20 A. My other cousins, Jessica and Lucritia and Rosemary, Fury
21 and them.
22 Q. You think Donna Jordan took you up to see him?
23 A. I don't remember, but I know I remember seeing a big guy,
24 it was at a hospital, and he was looking at us.
25 Q. Well, do you remember the time it was just you and

Page 262

1 Donovan?
2   MR. HAUGAARD: Objection, I believe the witness is
3 confused.
4   THE COURT: Sustained.
5 BY MR. HOLMES:
6 Q. You remember the time that just you and Donovan were
7 interviewed by Dr. Underwager.
8 A. No.
9 Q. And it's your testimony here that you never told anybody
10 that this didn't happen until you talked to Dr. Underwager,
11 correct?
12 A. Um-hum, yes.
13   MR. HAUGAARD: Objection, Your Honor, I believe the
14 witness is confused as to the identity.
15   THE COURT: Overruled.
16 BY MR. HOLMES:
17 Q. He was the first person that you ever said --
18 A. No, I never told him that.
19 Q. You remember telling Dr. Underwager that Donna Jordan
20 treated you nice?
21 A. No.
22   MR. HAUGAARD: Objection, Your Honor, she's already
23 testified that she does not remember.
24   THE COURT: An objection can be asked and answered, I
25 don't want a narrative telling the witness what to say.

Page 263

1 Overruled.
2 BY MR. HOLMES:
3 Q. You remember telling him that?
4 A. No.
5 Q. And didn't you in fact send Donna Jordan letters when you
6 were at the Children's Home Society?
7 A. No, I never even wrote to her, never spoke to her since
8 the last time I seen her when we moved to CHS.
9 Q. You never sent her letters saying that you would like to
10 have her come and visit you?
11 A. No.
12 Q. I think you testified that you were not afraid of your
13 uncles, is that right?
14 A. Yep.
15 Q. You remember telling Mary Weber up at Children's Home
16 that you were afraid your uncles would come and get you there?
17 A. No.
18 Q. When you were at Children's Home, do you remember being
19 in therapy there?
20 A. Yeah, kind of.
21 Q. Do you remember your mom coming to some of those
22 sessions?
23 A. Yes.
24 Q. Do you know who brought your mom to those sessions?
25 A. Casper.

Page 264

1 Q. Kathleen Honomichl?
2 A. Yeah, Casper.
3 Q. They call her Casper, is that right?
4 A. I do, yeah.
5 Q. She is a friend of the family?
6 A. No, she is just a social worker.
7 Q. You remember in one of these therapy sessions at
8 Children's Home your mom apologizing to you because she said
9 she walked in while you were being abused?
10 A. No.
11 Q. You remember your mom saying that?
12 A. No.
13 Q. I think you testified that the only person that you
14 talked to as far as your cousins that you told that it didn't
15 happen, the only person that you told it didn't happen to was
16 your cousin Derrick, is that right?
17 A. Yes.
18 Q. You didn't tell anyone else?
19 A. He was the first one I told.
20 Q. You testified that the day that you were taken from the
21 home you believe that it was the people from the FBI that did
22 this?
23 A. Yes.
24 Q. And they had FBI printed on their jackets?
25 A. Yes.

Page 265

1 Q. And it's your testimony that those were the individuals
2 who took you out of the house and took you to the foster home?
3 A. No, there was social workers there too.
4 Q. And the first day you were there Donna Jordan interviewed
5 each one of you children separately, that's your testimony?
6 A. Yep.
7 Q. And Rosemary has never talked to you about this, has she?
8 A. No.
9 Q. I think Mr. Haugaard was asking you some questions about
10 Donna Jordan mistreating the children, and you answered ask
11 Jessica and them, they know, you remember that answer?
12 A. Yeah.
13 Q. Have you and the other children talked about this?
14 A. About what?
15 Q. Well, what Donna Jordan did?
16 A. Maybe. Yeah, we did.
17 Q. When?
18 A. Whenever we were around each other.
19 Q. Were the grown-up's present then too?
20 A. No.
21   MR. HAUGAARD: Your Honor, the witness has indicated
22 she would like to go to the bathroom.
23   THE COURT: Very well, we will take a fifteen minute
24 recess.
25 (Recess at 11:05 until 11:20.)

Page 266

1   THE COURT: You may proceed.
2 BY MR. HOLMES:
3 Q. Thrista, I think you told Mr. Haugaard that you spoke to
4 Ms. Honomichl about this, you remember that testimony?
5 A. Um-hum, yes.
6 Q. And that your memory is you were still at CHS when that
7 happened?
8 A. I don't know.
9 Q. Was there anyone else present when you told her for the
10 first time that this didn't happen?
11 A. No, just me and her.
12 Q. I think you testified that you lied when you talked to
13 Dr. Underwager, is that right?
14   MR. HAUGAARD: Objection.
15   THE COURT: The basis of the objection?
16   MR. HAUGAARD: Misstatement of the testimony, I
17 believe.
18   THE COURT: Overruled.
19 BY MR. HOLMES:
20 Q. Is that right?
21 A. What?
22 Q. Did you lie to Dr. Underwager when you talked to him?
23 A. When?
24 Q. I think you said in response to Mr. Haugaard's question I
25 didn't tell him the truth?

Page 267

1 A. When, the last time we went to court?
2 Q. No, when you talked to Dr. Underwager?
3 A. Yeah.
4   MR. HAUGAARD: May I voir dire the witness for the
5 purposes of an objection?
6   THE COURT: No, this is cross examination. What is
7 the objection.
8   MR. HAUGAARD: The objection is I believe the witness
9 is confused, and Mr. Holmes has not laid a foundation as to who
10 he is talking about specifically that the witness will
11 understand.
12   THE COURT: The witness is confused is not an
13 objection, as to their not being a foundation, there that is,
14 of course, an objection. I think it is clear when this witness
15 was talking to Dr. Underwager, so I am going to overrule the
16 objection. Ask the question again, though.
17 BY MR. HOLMES:
18 Q. I believe you stated in response to Mr. Haugaard's
19 questions in referring to talking to Dr. Underwager, you said I
20 didn't tell him the truth?
21   MR. HAUGAARD: Objection, foundation.
22   THE COURT: Overruled.
23 BY MR. HOLMES:
24 Q. You remember that response to Mr. Haugaard's question?
25   MR. HAUGAARD: Your Honor, may we approach the bench?

Page 268

1   THE COURT: You may.
2 (Bench conference.)
3   MR. HAUGAARD: It is clear she thinks we are talking
4 about Dr. Kaplan, she is confused as to the doctors.
5   THE COURT: I don't think so. The fact the witness
6 is confused, you are sending a signal, I have already said
7 that's not an objection, foundation is. I think she knows who
8 Underwager is.
9   MR. HAUGAARD: The foundation objection would be to
10 put a timeframe on it when she talked to Dr. Underwager so she
11 understands who she is talking to.
12   THE COURT: So we don't have any question about that,
13 I think she knows who Underwager is, let's establish for sure
14 who it is.
15 (End of bench conference.)
16 BY MR. HOLMES:
17 Q. Thrista, you remember being interviewed by someone where
18 you were being videotaped?
19 A. Yeah.
20 Q. That was Dr. Underwager?
21 A. When I was being videotaped by Dr. Underwager?
22 Q. While you were talking to Dr. Underwager?
23 A. No.
24 Q. Who do you remember talking to when you were videotaped?
25 A. I don't remember it being videotaped.

Page 269

1 Q. You remember a time when you went up to Mr. Haugaard's
2 office and spoke to an elderly gentleman?
3 A. Oh, yeah, yeah.
4 Q. Do you remember telling that gentleman that people made
5 us sign papers to give them money?
6 A. No.
7 Q. Was that true?
8 A. I don't remember saying that.
9 Q. Would that have been true, do you remember anyone making
10 you sign papers to get money?
11 A. Yeah, Donna.
12 Q. When?
13 A. After we had court.
14 Q. What kind of papers?
15 A. I don't know, all I know it was a paper.
16 Q. Did someone promise you money to testify?
17 A. No.
18 Q. Who took you up to talk to that elderly gentleman when
19 you were videotaped?
20 A. Steve.
21 Q. Steve Haugaard. Do you remember talking to that same
22 elderly gentleman back in 1996?
23 A. No.
24 Q. You don't remember being videotaped when you talked to
25 him then?

Page 270

1 A. No.
2 Q. You don't remember that?
3 A. I don't remember that.
4 Q. Do you remember who first interviewed you after you were
5 taken from your home?
6 A. Yeah.
7 Q. Who was that?
8 A. Donna.
9 Q. Who talked to you next about it?
10 A. Dan Hudspeth, or whatever his name was.
11 Q. Was anyone else there?
12 A. Yeah, a guy in a cowboy hat.
13 Q. You remember talking to anyone else?
14 A. Nope.
15 Q. Those were the only people that interviewed you?
16 A. Yes.
17 Q. Do you remember about a week after you went to live at
18 Donna Jordan's going to see Dr. Kaplan?
19 A. Yeah.
20 Q. When you talked to Dr. Kaplan it was just you and him,
21 wasn't it?
22 A. I don't remember talking to him, I remember him looking
23 at us.
24 Q. You remember telling him that your uncle Jessie hurt me
25 there when you pointed to your private parts?

Page 271

1   MR. HAUGAARD: Objection, asked and answered.
2   THE COURT: Overruled.
3 A. No.
4   MR. HOLMES: You don't remember telling Dr. Kaplan
5 that. Nothing further.
6   THE COURT: Redirect.
7 REDIRECT EXAMINATION BY MR. HAUGAARD:
8 Q. Do you remember when you went to Dr. Kaplan who took you
9 there?
10 A. Donna.
11 Q. Was that examination good?
12 A. I don't know.
13 Q. Did he look at everything on your body?
14 A. Yeah.
15 Q. Did you want to be there?
16 A. No.
17 Q. When you were at court did you have to sign some papers
18 so Donna could get paid for bringing you there?
19 A. Yes.
20 Q. Did you get any of the money?
21 A. No, we got to go out to eat.
22 Q. Did you ever sign a release for Mr. Holmes to look at
23 your records from Children's Home Society?
24 A. To who?
25 Q. To let Mr. Holmes here, did you ever authorize him to go

Page 272

1 look at your records at Children's Home Society?
2 A. No.
3 Q. Or any other therapy sessions that you attended, have you
4 ever signed a release for him to look at any records?
5 A. No.
6 Q. When you were in these different counseling sessions did
7 you just go along with the story that had developed?
8 A. Yes.
9 Q. Was that story true?
10 A. No.
11 Q. When you were first taken out of the home was Tabetha
12 with you?
13 A. I don't remember of her being at this place. I guess she
14 was.
15 Q. When you think back on this for the past eight years, do
16 a lot of these things kind of blur together?
17 A. Yes.
18 Q. You remember Dr. Underwager as being the guy that was in
19 Sioux Falls here and you told him what did or did not happen?
20 A. Yeah.
21 Q. Did you tell him the truth?
22 A. Yes.
23 Q. Did he pressure you to tell, pressure you to say certain
24 things?
25 A. No.

Page 273

1 Q. Why did you want to do that?

2 A. To get my uncles out.

3 Q. Were you concerned about the fact that you had lied when

4 you were at trial?

5 A. When I was where?

6 Q. When you were here before at the trial?

7 A. Yeah.

8 Q. Did your mom or anyone else in your family put pressure

9 on you to lie?

10 A. No.

11 Q. Do you know who Cheryl Fridel is?

12 A. No.

13 Q. If your mom said that she walked in on you while you were

14 being abused by your uncles, is that true?

15 A. No.

16 Q. Did your uncle Jessie ever touch you?

17 A. No.

18 Q. Your uncle Desmond ever touch you?

19 A. No.

20 Q. Your uncle Garfield ever touch you?

21 A. No.

22 Q. Your uncle Russ ever touch you?

23 A. No.

24 Q. Is Russ even your uncle?

25 A. Huh-uh.

Page 274

1 Q. Did you ever see them, any of those four ever do anything

2 to anybody?

3 A. No.

4   MR. HAUGAARD: No further questions.

5   MR. HOLMES: No recross.

6   THE COURT: I have some questions, Thrista. Are you

7 going to school this fall?

8 A. Yeah.

9   THE COURT: Where are you going to school?

10 A. I am not going to school, I am going to Job Corps.

11   THE COURT: Where is that?

12 A. In Montana.

13   THE COURT: Did you go to school last year?

14 A. Yeah.

15   THE COURT: Where did you go?

16 A. Wagner.

17   THE COURT: What grade were you in.

18 A. Seventh.

19   THE COURT: What is the reason you have decided to go

20 to Job Corps in Montana?

21 A. They told me I had to get my GED, because I am too old to

22 be in seventh grade.

23   THE COURT: When you have gone to school has your

24 attendance been a problem?

25 A. Yeah.

Page 275

1   THE COURT: Is that the main problem with school?

2 A. Yeah.

3   THE COURT: In school are there some courses that you

4 like better than others?

5 A. Yeah.

6   THE COURT: Which ones do you like better?

7 A. I like math and science better than English and reading.

8   THE COURT: Why is that?

9 A. They are easier for me.

10   THE COURT: Are you able to read alright, though?

11 A. Yeah.

12   THE COURT: So when you are in school, when you are

13 actually in school, did you have much trouble with the course

14 work?

15 A. Sometimes.

16   THE COURT: When you had trouble with the course work

17 was it because you had missed a lot of classes?

18 A. Yeah, I missed some days of school.

19   THE COURT: What was the reason you missed school?

20 A. I don't know, because I didn't want to go.

21   THE COURT: Beg pardon?

22 A. Because I didn't want to go.

23   THE COURT: And nobody made you go?

24 A. Yeah, my mom did, but I just always went away from school

25 with my friends.

Page 276

1   THE COURT: At one point in your questioning you said

2 that your uncles had never molested Rosemary, but that maybe

3 one of your mother's boyfriends might have. How would you know

4 that one way or the other?

5 A. I don't know, because she has a problem, don't want to

6 say it.

7   THE COURT: How would you know, you are not around

8 all the time, how do you know that your uncles didn't ever

9 molest Rosemary?

10 A. I don't know.

11   THE COURT: I want to ask you a question. The entire

12 time you have been in court now you have not looked at your

13 uncles, why is that?

14 A. I don't know.

15   THE COURT: Thank you. Do the Court's questions give

16 rise to questions by either side?

17   MR. CARTER: Your Honor, I didn't hear the last

18 question.

19

20 (Whereupon, the requested portion of the Record was read by the

21 Reporter.)

22

23   MR. HOLMES: The government has no further questions.

24 REDIRECT EXAMINATION BY MR. HAUGAARD:

25 Q. Thrista, would you be glad to come over here and sit with

Page 277

1 your uncles?
2 A. Yes, and hug them.
3 Q. Has this whole thing just been so embarrassing you didn't
4 want to look at anybody?
5 A. What?
6 Q. Has this whole thing been so embarrassing that you didn't
7 want to look at anybody?
8 A. Yes.
9 Q. Can you tell the Judge, there is no reason I didn't look
10 at them?
11   THE COURT: Why don't you, I don't want an
12 instruction, ask a question.
13 Q. You feel you can look at them and have no problem doing
14 that?
15 A. Yeah.
16   MR. HAUGAARD: No further questions.
17   MR. HOLMES: No further questions.
18   THE COURT: You may step down.
19   THE COURT: Call your next witness.
20
21   LUCRITIA ROUSE,
22 called as a witness, being first duly sworn, testified and said
23 as follows:
24
25 DIRECT EXAMINATION BY MR. HAUGAARD:

Page 278

1 Q. Lucritia, please state your name for the record?
2 A. Lucritia Mae Rouse.
3 Q. Spell your first name?
4 A. L-U-C-R-I-T-I-A.
5 Q. How old are you?
6 A. Fifteen.
7 Q. What's your birth date?
8 A. October 8, 1987.
9 Q. Who is your mother?
10 A. Beta.
11 Q. Who are your brothers and sisters, Donovan and Jerome and
12 Jessica?
13 A. Jessica, Donovan, Ebony, Jerome, Fury.
14 Q. Do you remember being taken away from your family a long
15 time ago?
16 A. A little bit.
17 Q. Do you remember what happened that day?
18 A. Not really.
19 Q. Can you remember what it looked like as far as who was
20 there?
21 A. Cops, and bunch of other people, Jean, and I don't know
22 who else was there.
23 Q. Jean Brock you mean? You have to say yes or no?
24 A. Yes.
25 Q. Were you living, or what house was that, that you were at

Page 279

1 that day?
2 A. My grandma's.
3 Q. Were you living there at that time?
4 A. Yeah.
5 Q. Do you remember who else was living there at that time?
6 A. No.
7 Q. Do you remember which other kids were there that day?
8 A. Thrista, Moses, Donovan, Jerome, Derrick, Jessica and
9 Echo and Fury, and that's it.
10 Q. Do you remember your uncles that lived in that area at
11 that time?
12 A. Yeah.
13 Q. Do you recognize them now?
14 A. Yes.
15 Q. Would you have recognized them if somebody hadn't pointed
16 them out?
17 A. No.
18 Q. Do you know which uncles are which?
19 A. Yeah.
20 Q. Who is the one on the end down there?
21 A. Russell.
22 Q. Who is next to him?
23 A. Jessie.
24 Q. Next to him?
25 A. Desmond and Russ.

Page 280

1 Q. Is Russ your uncle?
2 A. Yes.
3 Q. Do you remember Russ from before?
4 A. No.
5 Q. Do you remember Desmond from before?
6 A. Yes.
7 Q. Do you remember Jessie from before?
8 A. Yes.
9 Q. Do you remember Garfield from before?
10 A. Yes.
11 Q. How old were you at that time?
12 A. I was six, I think.
13 Q. What grade were you in then?
14 A. I don't know.
15 Q. Were you even in school then?
16 A. No.
17 Q. Where did you go when you were taken away?
18 A. Went to foster care called CHS.
19 Q. Did you go any place before that?
20 A. Donna.
21 Q. Do you remember Donna's last name?
22 A. Jordan.
23 Q. Do you remember how long you were there?
24 A. No.
25 Q. Do you remember who was around when you got there?

Page 281

1 A. Donna and her husband.
2 Q. Who was her husband?
3 A. I forgot his name.
4 Q. Anybody else around?
5 A. No.
6 Q. When you got there did you know why you were there?
7 A. No.
8 Q. When did you find out why you were there?
9 A. I don't know.
10 Q. Did anybody ask you questions about what was going on at
11 your grandma's house?
12 A. Yeah.
13 Q. Who asked you those questions?
14 A. Micky.
15 Q. Did Donna ever ask you those questions?
16 A. Yeah.
17 Q. When you got there the first few days do you remember did
18 Donna ask you those questions?
19 A. Yes.
20 Q. Did she ask you a lot of questions?
21 A. No.
22 Q. Were you afraid?
23 A. Yes.
24 Q. Did you want to be there?
25 A. No.

Page 282

1 Q. Do you remember were you by yourself when she asked
2 questions?
3 A. No.
4 Q. Who was with you?
5 A. Thrista, Jessica, Donovan and Jerome.
6 Q. While you were there in her home, did she talk a lot
7 about this?
8 A. Not really.
9 Q. Did she ask questions every once in a while about it?
10 A. Yeah.
11 Q. Did she ask you if your uncles had touched you in the
12 wrong places?
13 A. Yeah.
14 Q. What did you tell her?
15 A. I said no, if my uncles did touch me I wouldn't be in
16 there.
17 Q. Did any of these uncles that are here today, or anybody
18 else, ever touch you in the wrong places?
19 A. No.
20 Q. Did Donna keep asking those same kind of questions?
21 A. A little bit.
22 Q. After a while did you go along with the questions?
23 A. Yeah.
24 Q. Were they true?
25 A. No.

Page 283

1 Q. Why did you change and start going along with the
2 questions?
3 A. Because we didn't know better.
4 Q. When you did start going along with the questions, did
5 that make Donna happy?
6 A. Yes.
7 Q. Did you talk to any of the other kids about what you
8 should say?
9 A. No.
10 Q. But you could tell what kind of answers you needed to
11 give?
12   MR. HOLMES: Objection, leading.
13   THE COURT: Sustained.
14 BY MR. HAUGAARD:
15 Q. Do you remember when you told somebody else that this
16 stuff didn't really happen?
17 A. No.
18 Q. But at first you told Donna that it didn't happen, right?
19 A. Yeah.
20 Q. Did you tell her that a lot of times?
21 A. Yes.
22 Q. When you stayed with Donna, do you remember, did you go
23 to school right away that year?
24 A. No.
25 Q. When you were with Donna did there ever come a time when

Page 284

1 you started school?
2 A. Yeah.
3 Q. Did you go to school in Jefferson?
4 A. Yes.
5 Q. Was that first grade?
6 A. Yeah.
7 Q. After that did you get moved to Sioux Falls?
8 A. Yes.
9 Q. Where did you stay?
10 A. The Children's Home Society.
11 Q. Do you recognize Ms. Tapken here in the courtroom?
12 A. Yes.
13 Q. Did you ever tell her that this didn't happen?
14 A. Yes.
15 Q. Did that make her happy?
16 A. Yes.
17 Q. What kind of questions did she ask, or did she ask you
18 questions?
19 A. Like what did your uncles touch you in the wrong spot, and did
20 your mom ever leave you in a room with them alone, that's about
21 it.
22 Q. What did you tell her?
23 A. I said no.
24 Q. Did you change after a while and say something else?
25 A. Yes.

Page 285

1 Q. Who else asked you questions about this stuff?
2 A. Micky.
3 Q. Besides Micky and Donna, anybody else?
4 A. No.
5 Q. Do you know, were there men sitting in the room when they
6 were asking questions?
7 A. Yes.
8 Q. Do you know who those men were?
9 A. No.
10 Q. Did you want to go back to your mom?
11 A. Yes.
12 Q. What did you think it was going to take for you to be
13 able to go home to your mother?
14 A. To lie.
15 Q. Were you afraid of Donna Jordan?
16 A. Yes.
17 Q. Why?
18 A. Because of what she did to us when we were in foster care
19 with her.
20 Q. What things did she do to you?
21 A. My little sister, when she didn't want to eat she --
22 Q. She used to do what to your little sister?
23 A. Stuff her face with food and put food in her hair.
24 Q. Some of the food got in her hair?
25 A. Yeah.

Page 286

1 Q. What did she do with your sister?
2 A. We went down there and picked her up and put her in the
3 crib, and when we started going to school we came home and we
4 had head lice and the only way she said to get rid of it was
5 with alcohol, and she put us in the bathtub with alcohol.
6 Q. You could tell what you needed to tell Donna when she
7 asked questions, is that right?
8   MR. HOLMES: Objection, leading and suggestive.
9   THE COURT: Sustained.
10 BY MR. HAUGAARD:
11 Q. You were afraid of Donna?
12 A. Yes.
13 Q. After a while did you answer her questions the way she
14 wanted you to answer?
15 A. Yes.
16 Q. Did you just want to go home to your mom?
17 A. Yes.
18 Q. Did the people asking you questions tell you that after
19 you tell this story then you can go home?
20   MR. HOLMES: Objection, leading and suggestive.
21   THE COURT: Sustained.
22 BY MR. HAUGAARD:
23 Q. What did the people tell you about answering the
24 questions?
25 A. I don't remember.

Page 287

1 Q. What did they tell you it was, what did you think it was
2 going to take for you to be able to go home?
3 A. To lie.
4 Q. Did anybody tell you directly to lie?
5 A. I don't know. I don't remember.
6 Q. Did they ask a lot of questions, though?
7 A. Yes.
8 Q. Could you tell what the answer was supposed to be?
9 A. Yes.
10 Q. Did you lie to get them to quit asking questions?
11 A. Yes.
12   MR. HOLMES: Objection, leading and suggestive.
13   THE COURT: Sustained, the answer is stricken.
14 BY MR. HAUGAARD:
15 Q. Are you afraid to be here today?
16 A. Yes.
17 Q. Are you afraid of your uncles?
18 A. No.
19 Q. Were you afraid of your uncles seven years ago when you
20 were at this trial?
21 A. No.
22 Q. Why were you afraid to be in the courtroom then?
23 A. Because there was too much people.
24 Q. Why are you afraid today?
25 A. Because all these people.

Page 288

1 Q. Did they ask you questions about your uncle Desmond
2 throwing a knife at you?
3   MR. HOLMES: Objection, foundation.
4   THE COURT: Sustained.
5 BY MR. HAUGAARD:
6 Q. Did Donna Jordan ask you questions about a knife being
7 thrown at you?
8 A. No.
9 Q. Did Micky Tapken ask you questions like that?
10 A. No.
11 Q. Do you remember who did?
12 A. No.
13 Q. Has your uncle Desmond ever thrown a knife at you?
14 A. No.
15 Q. How did you cut your head?
16 A. Me and my sister were playing in the car, and my grandma
17 was driving and I jumped up and hit my head on the mirror.
18 Q. Do you remember coming here to the courthouse for the
19 trial?
20 A. Yes.
21 Q. At that time were you still in school down at Jefferson?
22 A. Yes.
23 Q. Were you going to a counselor that summer?
24 A. Yes.
25 Q. Do you remember her name?

Page 289

1 A. No.
2 Q. Did she talk a lot about this same sort of stuff?
3 A. Yes.
4 Q. Were you sometimes by yourself, or was it always with the
5 other kids?
6 A. By ourselves.
7 Q. Sometimes did you get together in a bigger group and
8 talk?
9 A. Yeah.
10 Q. Do you remember being taken to the doctor?
11 A. Yes.
12 Q. What did he do when you were at the doctor's office?
13 A. Looked inside of me.
14 Q. Did you want him to do that?
15 A. No.
16 Q. When you went to that counselor, do you remember telling
17 her that your uncles tied up your grandma?
18 A. No.
19 Q. Did they ever do that?
20 A. No.
21 Q. Do you remember telling the counselor that your uncles
22 tied up Beta and Ursula?
23 A. No.
24 Q. Did they ever do that?
25 A. No.

Page 290

1 Q. Do you remember telling the counselor that your uncles
2 did the same thing to your grandma that they did to you?
3 A. No.
4 Q. Did they ever do that?
5 A. No.
6 Q. Did they ever do anything to you?
7 A. No.
8 Q. When you think back on those counseling sessions, do you
9 remember telling that counselor that you saw your uncles doing
10 things to Beta and Ursula?
11 A. No.
12 Q. If they would have done that, would you remember it?
13 A. Yes.
14 Q. Would that scare you?
15 A. Yes.
16 Q. If your uncles had touched you, would you be here today
17 to testify?
18 A. No.
19 Q. Do you remember telling the counselor that you saw your
20 uncles touch your mom's private spot?
21 A. No.
22 Q. Did you ever see that?
23 A. No.
24 Q. Do you remember telling the counselor that you were
25 standing outside and you looked in the window and you were able

Page 291

1 to see that?
2 A. No.
3 Q. So you didn't stand outside the window and see anything?
4 A. No.
5 Q. You look in any of your windows on any of your houses?
6 A. No.
7 Q. Why?
8 A. Because, I don't remember.
9 Q. Are they tall or short?
10 A. They are tall.
11 Q. Even as much as you have grown now can you look through
12 the windows?
13 A. No.
14 Q. At the trial I asked you a question. I said do you like
15 being here today, and you said yeah. Did you like being there
16 at the trial?
17 A. No.
18 Q. Did you really miss your mom at that time?
19 A. Yes.
20 Q. When Donna Jordan talked to you, did she tell you that
21 your uncles had done bad things to you?
22   MR. HOLMES: Objection, leading and suggestive.
23   THE COURT: Sustained.
24 BY MR. HAUGAARD:
25 Q. Do you remember some of the things that Donna told you?

Page 292

1 A. No.
2 Q. Would you just as soon forget all of it?
3 A. Yes.
4 Q. When you think about your uncles, which one do you
5 remember best?
6 A. Uncle Des and Jess.
7 Q. Because they were around the most?
8 A. Yes.
9 Q. What do you think about uncle Jess when you look at him?
10 A. He is nice. I don't want him to be in prison, because he
11 didn't do anything to me.
12 Q. When you look at your uncle Desmond what do you think?
13 A. He is nice.
14 Q. Did they ever touch you?
15 A. No.
16 Q. Did you ever see them touch anybody else?
17 A. No.
18 Q. Did you just want to go home?
19 A. Yes.
20 Q. So the things you said when you came to this building a
21 long time ago, seven years ago, were you telling the truth or
22 were you telling lies?
23 A. Telling lies.
24 Q. Do you remember who it was that you told that this didn't
25 happen?

Page 293

1 A. I don't remember.

2 Q. Did you talk to your cousins about it after a while?

3 A. No.

4 Q. Did you talk to Thrista or Donovan about it after a

5 while?

6 A. Thrista.

7 Q. What did you tell her then?

8 A. That our uncles didn't do this to us, and we thought we

9 were going to go home if we lied, we would go home and we would

10 go free.

11 Q. You remember where you were at when you talked to her

12 about that?

13 A. At Donna's house.

14 Q. That was before the trial?

15 A. Yes.

16 Q. Has anyone threatened you or pressured you to come here

17 today to testify?

18 A. No.

19 Q. Do you want to be here?

20 A. Yes.

21 Q. Why do you want to be here?

22 A. So my uncles could get out.

23 Q. When I asked you these questions about whether your

24 uncles touched you, is that the truth, that they did not touch

25 you?

Page 294

1 A. Yes.

2 Q. Lucritia, is there anything else you would like to tell

3 the Judge?

4 A. Yes, if my uncles, if they did touch us, then I wouldn't

5 be here, and I wouldn't want them to get out of prison, I

6 wouldn't want to see them.

7   MR. HAUGAARD: No further questions.

8   THE COURT: Cross examination.

9 CROSS EXAMINATION BY MR. HOLMES:

10 Q. Lucritia, that last answer you gave, did you talk to your

11 brothers and cousins about saying that?

12 A. No.

13 Q. You talk to anyone else about saying that?

14 A. No.

15 Q. After you left Donna Jordan's house, where did you go to

16 live?

17 A. I went to CHS.

18 Q. And you remember how long you were at CHS?

19 A. No.

20 Q. Did you see your mother when you were at CHS?

21 A. Yes.

22 Q. That is Beta?

23 A. Yes.

24 Q. Donovan is your brother, is that right?

25 A. Yes.

Page 295

1 Q. Did your mom come up and go to some of these counseling

2 sessions with you at CHS?

3 A. No.

4 Q. She never sat in with you?

5 A. No.

6 Q. Where did you go after you left CHS?

7 A. The Brown's.

8 Q. Pardon?

9 A. The Brown's.

10 Q. How long were you at the Brown's?

11 A. For a year.

12 Q. That was another foster home?

13 A. Yes.

14 Q. Where did you go after the Brown's?

15 A. To Stafford's.

16 Q. The Stafford's?

17 A. Yes.

18 Q. That was another foster home, correct?

19 A. Yes.

20 Q. After that where did you go?

21 A. We went to, I don't remember.

22 Q. Where are you living now?

23 A. Marty.

24 Q. With whom?

25 A. My mom.

Page 296

1 Q. And you live at your grandmother Rosemary's?

2 A. No.

3 Q. Where do you live?

4 A. With my mom, she has her own house.

5 Q. Who else lives there?

6 A. Just us girls; me, Jessica and Tabetha.

7 Q. Where is that from your grandmother's house?

8 A. A while.

9 Q. How far away?

10 A. I don't know.

11 Q. And you can you walk there?

12 A. Yeah.

13 Q. Do you go over and see your grandmother?

14 A. Yeah.

15 Q. Did you talk to your uncles about this?

16 A. No.

17 Q. You talk to them on the phone?

18 A. Yeah.

19 Q. How often does that happen?

20 A. Once in a while.

21 Q. Where are you when you talk to them on the phone; are you

22 at your mom's house or your grandmother's house?

23 A. Grandma's.

24 Q. Grandmother doesn't believe any of this ever happened,

25 does she?

Page 297

1 A. No.
2 Q. Neither does your mother, does she?
3 A. No.
4 Q. And they both told you that, isn't that right?
5 A. No.
6 Q. Have you ever seen letters that your uncles have written
7 your grandmother from prison?
8 A. Yes.
9 Q. And where were you when you saw those letters?
10 A. At my grandma's house.
11   MR. HAUGAARD: Objection, foundation, Your Honor.
12   THE COURT: Overruled.
13 BY MR. HOLMES:
14 Q. How many of those letters have you seen?
15 A. About two.
16 Q. Have those letters made you feel bad?
17 A. Yes.
18 Q. Has your grandmother and mother made you feel bad about
19 your uncles being in prison?
20 A. No.
21 Q. Do you remember a time when Mr. Haugaard brought you up
22 here to see Dr. Underwager and you were videotaped?
23 A. No.
24 Q. Do you remember you and Jessica playing around with the
25 video camera?

Page 298

1 A. No.
2 Q. Well, do you remember being interviewed in 1999,
3 somewhere around there, a couple of years ago, by an elderly
4 heavy set man, a fat man?
5 A. No.
6 Q. Don't remember that at all. Do you remember
7 Dr. Underwager?
8 A. No.
9   MR. HAUGAARD: Objection, asked and answered.
10   THE COURT: Overruled.
11 BY MR. HOLMES:
12 Q. You don't remember him?
13 A. No.
14 Q. And you don't remember this interview?
15 A. No.
16 Q. The lady seated next to me, how many times did you talk
17 to her?
18 A. A couple of times.
19 Q. But you remember her name?
20 A. Yes.
21 Q. What is her name?
22 A. Micky.
23 Q. What is her last name?
24 A. I don't know.
25 Q. I think in response to one of Mr. Haugaard's questions

Page 299

1 you referred to this lady as Mrs. Tapken?
2 A. No.
3 Q. Did anybody tell you that's what her name was?
4 A. No.
5 Q. Well, did you ever tell anybody that the lawyer said lie
6 for us and we will buy you toys, clothes and stuff?
7 A. Yes.
8 Q. Who did she tell that to?
9 A. I meant no. Micky told that to us, and Donna.
10 Q. It's your testimony that both Micky and Donna said lie
11 for us and we will buy you toys, clothes and stuff?
12 A. Yes.
13 Q. When did Donna tell you that?
14 A. Before we went to court.
15 Q. Where were you when she said that?
16 A. In a room.
17 Q. In this building?
18 A. No.
19 Q. At Donna's house?
20 A. Yes.
21 Q. Who else was there?
22 A. Micky was.
23 Q. Micky was at Donna's house?
24 A. Yes.
25 Q. Who else was there?

Page 300

1 A. Them two.
2 Q. Pardon?
3 A. Just them two.
4 Q. None of the other children?
5 A. No.
6 Q. Donna is not a lawyer, is she?
7 A. No.
8 Q. You said that Micky said that to you. When did she say
9 that to you?
10 A. Before court started.
11 Q. Here in this courthouse?
12 A. Yes.
13 Q. What did she tell you?
14 A. That if you lie for us, we will buy you toys and clothes.
15 Q. What did you understand it to mean when she said,
16 according to you, if you lie for us?
17 A. When we went in that room she was sitting by us holding
18 our hands and said, I don't know --
19 Q. Do you remember saying in response to one of
20 Mr. Haugaard's questions that you told Micky that it didn't
21 happen and that made her happy?
22 A. No.
23 Q. Do you remember telling anybody that you were told that
24 there was a hundred dollars in the basement that you could
25 have?

Page 301

1 A. No.
2 Q. Did you ever tell Dr. Underwager that?
3 A. No.
4 Q. When do you first remember meeting this man,
5 Mr. Haugaard?
6 A. When I was little in the courtroom.
7 Q. After you were in the courtroom when is the next time
8 that you saw him?
9 A. I don't know, I can't remember.
10 Q. Did he ever pick you up and take you places?
11 A. No.
12 Q. Did your mom ever take you to see him?
13 A. No.
14 Q. You ever remember coming to Sioux Falls to see him?
15 A. Yes.
16 Q. When?
17 A. When we came here and we were little.
18 Q. Well, was that before or after you went home to live with
19 your mom?
20 A. Before.
21 Q. Do you remember after you went to Donna's being talked to
22 by anybody else?
23 A. No.
24 Q. Was it just Donna and then later Micky?
25 A. Yes.

Page 302

1 Q. No one else talked to you about this?
2 A. No.
3 Q. You do remember going to see the doctor after you were at
4 Donna's, don't you?
5 A. Yes.
6 Q. And that doctor checked you out?
7 A. Yes.
8 Q. Do you remember telling that doctor to check your peach
9 because it hurt, because that's where my uncles hurt me?
10 A. No.
11   MR. HOLMES: No further questions.
12   THE COURT: Redirect.
13 REDIRECT EXAMINATION BY MR. HAUGAARD:
14 Q. Lucritia, was it a long time before you got to see your
15 mom?
16 A. Yes.
17 Q. What is it that makes you feel bad about your uncles
18 being in prison?
19 A. Lying.
20 Q. Who lying?
21 A. When I was little.
22 Q. When you were little you lied?
23 A. Yes.
24 Q. You lied about your uncles?
25 A. Yes.

Page 303

1 Q. The counselor talked to you about this stuff too?
2   MR. HOLMES: Objection, outside the scope of cross.
3   THE COURT: I have to look at my notes on that one.
4 Overruled.
5 BY MR. HAUGAARD:
6 Q. Did you tell Ellen Kelson about this claimed abuse?
7 A. No.
8 Q. You remember Ellen Kelson, the counselor?
9 A. No.
10 Q. When you were at Donna Jordan's home did she take you to
11 a counselor sometimes?
12 A. Sometimes.
13 Q. Did you have to talk about this stuff there?
14 A. Yeah.
15 Q. Does this scare you being here today?
16 A. No.
17 Q. Why not?
18 A. Because I am telling the truth.
19   MR. HAUGAARD: No further questions.
20   MR. HOLMES: Nothing further, Your Honor.
21   THE COURT: I would like to ask Lucritia, you are
22 thirteen now, is that right?
23 A. Yes.
24   THE COURT: What day of October is your birthday?
25 A. Eighth.

Page 304

1   THE COURT: Are you going to school this fall?
2 A. Yes.
3   THE COURT: Where are you going?
4 A. Wagner.
5   THE COURT: What grade are you in?
6 A. Eighth.
7   THE COURT: How is school going for you?
8 A. Good.
9   THE COURT: Did you go to Wagner school last year?
10 A. Yes.
11   THE COURT: You were in the seventh grade?
12 A. Yes.
13   THE COURT: How did school go for you then?
14 A. Good.
15   THE COURT: Are there some classes you like better
16 than others?
17 A. Yes.
18   THE COURT: Which ones do you like best?
19 A. Science and math.
20   THE COURT: Which ones do you like the least?
21 A. English and social studies.
22   THE COURT: Why is it you like science and math the
23 best?
24 A. Because it is more funner.
25   THE COURT: Then English and social studies, what is

Page 305

1 the reason you don't like those?

2 A. English is boring.

3   THE COURT: Alright. Do you plan on then going on

4 after the eighth grade. Now in Wagner are you in high school

5 in the eighth grade, or is that middle school?

6 A. That's high school.

7   THE COURT: So this is your first year of high school

8 then, is that right?

9 A. Yes.

10   THE COURT: You plan on going ahead there and

11 finishing high school at Wagner?

12 A. Yes.

13   THE COURT: What do you hope to do after that?

14 A. Be a cop.

15   THE COURT: Do you plan on going to college to be a

16 cop?

17 A. Yes.

18   THE COURT: Where do you hope to go to college?

19 A. Probably Colorado.

20   THE COURT: You have any school in mind out there?

21 A. No.

22   THE COURT: You just would like to be in Colorado?

23 A. Yes.

24   THE COURT: Have you been there before?

25 A. No.

Page 306

1   THE COURT: It sound like a nice place to you and

2 that's why you would like to be there?

3 A. Yes.

4   THE COURT: Lucritia, you spelled your name, first

5 name, and I didn't write it down, would you spell your first

6 name again.

7 A. L-U-C-R-I-T-I-A.

8   THE COURT: Your mother's name again is what?

9 A. Beta.

10   THE COURT: B-E-T-A, isn't it?

11 A. Yes.

12   THE COURT: Has your mother talked to you about your

13 testimony here today?

14 A. Yes.

15   THE COURT: What did she say?

16 A. You go to court and see our uncles.

17   THE COURT: Did she talk about your testimony?

18 A. No.

19   THE COURT: Did your grandmother talk to you about

20 your testimony here today?

21 A. No.

22   THE COURT: When you walked from your mother's house

23 to your grandmother's house, how long does it take you to walk

24 from one house to the other?

25 A. Five minutes.

Page 307

1   THE COURT: Thank you. Do the Court's questions give

2 rise to questions by either side?

3   MR. HOLMES: Not from the government.

4 REDIRECT EXAMINATION BY MR. HAUGAARD:

5 Q. Lucritia, does your grandmother live in what they call

6 West Housing?

7 A. Yes.

8 Q. And your mother lives in East Housing?

9 A. Yes.

10 Q. So that's on the other side of the school, right?

11 A. Yes.

12   MR. HAUGAARD: No further questions.

13   MR. HOLMES: Nothing further.

14   THE COURT: Thank you, you may step down. We will be

15 in recess until 1:45. We went long, of course, obviously,

16 because I wanted to finish up the witness if we could. We will

17 be in recess until 1:45.

18 (Recess at 12:40 until 1:45)

19   THE COURT: Call your next witness.

20   MR. WILKA: Your Honor, over the noon hour we did

21 obtain authorized release for information and records for the

22 Children's Society, and we have that along with an Order

23 previously drafted by Mr. Haugaard.

24   THE COURT: Children's Home Society doesn't have it,

25 has anybody talked to them?

Page 308

1   MR. WILKA: That is where the children were staying,

2 at CHS.

3   THE COURT: I know, but with regard to there is a

4 request coming and so on, has anybody talked to the Children's

5 Home Society.

6   MR. WILKA: That, too, will be forthcoming.

7

8   ROSEMARY ROUSE,

9 called as a witness, being first duly sworn, testified and said

10 as follows:

11

12 DIRECT EXAMINATION BY MR. HAUGAARD:

13 Q. Rosemary, please state your name and spell your last

14 name?

15 A. Rosemary Rouse, R-O-U-S-E.

16 Q. How old are you, Rosemary?

17 A. Eighteen.

18 Q. What is your birth date?

19 A. March 7, '88.

20 Q. Are you nervous? Do you want to be here today?

21 A. Yes.

22 Q. Why is it you want to be here today?

23 A. For my uncles.

24 Q. What about your uncles? Rosemary, who is your mom?

25 A. Rodrica.

Page 309

1   THE COURT: I am sorry, you have to speak up, what

2 was your mother's name?

3 A. Rodrica.

4 Q. Do you live with your mother now?

5 A. Yes.

6 Q. Where is that at?

7 A. Marty.

8 Q. In Marty, South Dakota?

9 A. Yes.

10 Q. Who are your brothers and sisters?

11 A. Heather, Derrick, Wilbert and Verdell.

12 Q. You remember years ago when you were placed in a foster

13 home, do you remember that?

14 A. A little bit.

15 Q. Do you remember being taken away from your grandma's

16 house?

17 A. Yes.

18 Q. Where did you go to live after that?

19 A. The Brock's.

20 Q. Is that Jean Brock?

21 A. Yes.

22 Q. How long did you live with her?

23 A. I think a couple months.

24 Q. Then where did you go?

25 A. Donna Jordan's.

Page 310

1 Q. When you got to Donna Jordan's, were your cousins there?

2 A. Yes.

3 Q. Were you taken there at the same time?

4 A. No, we were all separated.

5 Q. Do you remember how long you stayed at Donna Jordan's

6 house?

7 A. No.

8 Q. Did you stay there for a school year?

9 A. Yeah.

10 Q. Did you leave during the summer, or can you remember?

11 A. No.

12 Q. Were you there as long as the other kids were there?

13 A. Yes.

14 Q. Did they leave the same time you did, or did they leave

15 later?

16 A. Later.

17 Q. When you left Donna Jordan's where were you taken to

18 stay?

19 A. With my aunt Julia.

20 Q. Did you stay with Jean Brock for a while?

21 A. Yes.

22 Q. You remember how long you stayed with Jean Brock?

23 A. No.

24 Q. Did you go to school in Delmont for a while?

25 A. Yes.

Page 311

1 Q. Is that where Jean Brock lives?

2 A. Yes.

3 Q. When you were at Donna Jordan's home did you get asked a

4 lot of questions?

5 A. Yes.

6 Q. By who?

7 A. By her.

8 Q. How often would she ask you questions?

9 A. Like every other day.

10 Q. Do you know why you were taken from Donna Jordan's home

11 to Jean Brock's home?

12 A. No.

13 Q. Were you afraid of Donna Jordan?

14 A. A little bit.

15 Q. Why?

16 A. Because of what she did to Fury.

17 Q. What did she do to Fury?

18 A. He grabbed her by her hair and threw her down, down the

19 steps.

20 Q. Why did she do that?

21 A. Because she peed her pants.

22 Q. Because Fury peed her pants?

23 A. Yeah.

24 Q. How old was Fury then?

25 A. One.

Page 312

1 Q. Was she walking at that time?

2 A. Yeah.

3 Q. Did other people ask you questions about your uncles

4 besides Donna?

5 A. Yes.

6 Q. Do you remember who?

7 A. I don't know their names.

8 Q. Men, or women, or who?

9 A. Men.

10 Q. How many?

11 A. Two.

12 Q. Did they ask you a lot of questions?

13 A. Yes.

14 Q. Did they ask you the same questions a lot of times?

15 A. Yes.

16 Q. Do you recognize the men who are in the courtroom here

17 today behind us?

18 A. Yes.

19 Q. Who is the person seated down at the end with the white

20 shirt on?

21 A. My uncle Garfield.

22 Q. Who is sitting with the orange?

23 A. Uncle Jessie.

24 Q. With the white shirt and the long hair?

25 A. Desmond.

Page 313

1 Q. Is the other guy, who is this?
2 A. My uncle Russell.
3 Q. Have you talked to any of these guys on the telephone?
4 A. Yes.
5 Q. Have any of them told you to lie for them?
6 A. No.
7 Q. Did any of these guys ever touch you in a bad way?
8 A. No.
9 Q. They ever touch your private parts?
10 A. No.
11 Q. Did you ever see them touch any of your cousins in any
12 wrong way?
13 A. No.
14 Q. Are you afraid of your uncles today?
15 A. No.
16 Q. Were you afraid of your uncles back at the time of the
17 trial about seven years ago?
18 A. A little bit.
19 Q. Why was that?
20 A. I thought they would be mad at me.
21 Q. Mad at you for what?
22 A. For lying.
23 Q. Who is the first one of your family that you ever told
24 that this didn't happen?
25 A. My brother.

Page 314

1 Q. Which brother?
2 A. Derrick.
3 THE COURT: I am sorry, I couldn't hear you, you will
4 have to speak up.
5 A. Derrick.
6 Q. Where was Derrick when you told him that?
7 A. What?
8 Q. Where was Derrick living when you told him that?
9 A. The Brock's.
10 Q. Did you tell him that when you got moved back to the
11 Brock's?
12 A. Yes.
13 Q. When you came to trial before you were how old?
14 A. Five, six.
15 Q. Were you in school at that time, do you remember?
16 A. I don't remember.
17 Q. Where is the first place you went to school?
18 A. Elk Point.
19 Q. You think it was at Elk Point. Do you remember how long
20 you went to school there?
21 A. No.
22 Q. Did the bus pick you up?
23 A. Yes.
24 Q. When you went to school at Delmont what grade were you in
25 then?

Page 315

1 A. I can't remember.
2 Q. How long did you stay at Delmont with the Brock's?
3 A. Like a couple months.
4 Q. Where did you go after you lived at the Brock's?
5 A. To stay with my aunt Julia.
6 Q. Is that Julia Joseph?
7 A. Yes.
8 Q. How long did you stay there, if you remember?
9 A. I can't remember.
10 Q. Who else have you told that this didn't happen?
11 A. Thrista and Donovan.
12 Q. When did you tell Thrista and Donovan? Where were you
13 living when you told them that?
14 A. With my grandma -- no, my aunt Ursula's house.
15 Q. At whose house?
16 A. Ursula.
17 THE COURT: Whose house?
18 A. Ursula.
19 Q. Did your grandma or your aunts tell you that you had to
20 change your story?
21 A. No.
22 Q. Why do you want to be here today?
23 A. To get me uncles out.
24 Q. Why do you want them out?
25 A. Because they didn't do anything.

Page 316

1 Q. When you look at them today are you afraid of them?
2 A. No.
3 Q. Has anybody promised you that they would be nice to you
4 if you would just say these things today?
5 A. No.
6 Q. Is there anything else that you want to tell the Judge
7 today?
8 A. No.
9 Q. Are you telling the truth today?
10 A. Yes.
11 Q. Would you be willing to go and talk to him alone?
12 A. Yes.
13 MR. HAUGAARD: No further questions.
14 THE COURT: Cross examination.
15 CROSS EXAMINATION BY MR. HOLMES:
16 Q. Rosemary, where do you live now?
17 A. With my mother.
18 Q. And where is her house?
19 A. Marty.
20 Q. And what part of Marty is that in?
21 A. In the new housing.
22 Q. Pardon?
23 A. In the new housing.
24 Q. Where is that from your grandmother's house? How far
25 away is it from your grandmother's house?

Page 317

1 A. Not far.
2 Q. How long does it take you to walk there?
3 A. Like ten minutes.
4 Q. How far are you away from your aunt Beta's house?
5 A. Five minutes.
6 Q. Do you spend time at your grandmother's house?
7 A. Yes.
8 Q. How often?
9 A. Most of the time.
10 Q. When you aren't in school you are usually at your
11 grandmother's house?
12 A. I am at my house.
13 Q. When you spoke to your uncles on the phone were you at
14 your house or your grandmother's house?
15 A. Grandmother's.
16 Q. How often did you talk to them on the phone?
17 A. Not very often.
18 Q. Were there several of the children over there that talked
19 to your uncles on the phone at the same time?
20 A. Yes.
21 Q. Who else do you remember talking to the uncles on the
22 phone at the same time you did?
23 A. All of us.
24 Q. Pardon?
25 A. All of us.

Page 318

1 Q. Well, can you give us the names?
2 A. Lucritia, Jessica, Jessica, Thrista, Donovan, Echo, Fury.
3 Q. Did your mother bring you over to your grandmother's
4 house so you could talk to your uncles on the phone?
5 A. I was already there.
6 Q. What about the other children?
7 A. They was already there too.
8 Q. Did you ever see letters that your uncles had written
9 from prison?
10 A. No, but I seen pictures.
11 Q. Who showed you those?
12 A. My grandma.
13 Q. Your grandma doesn't believe any of this ever happened,
14 does she?
15 A. No, it didn't.
16 Q. She doesn't believe that, does she?
17 A. No.
18 Q. She has told you that, correct?
19 A. Yes.
20 Q. And your mother has told you the same thing, correct?
21 A. Yes.
22 Q. And so have your aunts, isn't that right?
23 A. Yes.
24 Q. In fact, all your family members have told you that they
25 don't believe any of this happened, isn't that right?

Page 319

1 A. Yes.
2 Q. And they have told you that since the day you left the
3 Brock's, isn't that right?
4   MR. HAUGAARD: Objection, foundation.
5   THE COURT: Overruled.
6 A. Yes.
7 BY MR. HOLMES:
8 Q. They have all been telling you that, that they don't
9 believe you or what the other children said, isn't that right?
10 A. Yes.
11 Q. When you left the Brock's, you went to live with your
12 aunt Julia, is that right?
13 A. Yes.
14 Q. That is Julia Joseph?
15 A. Yes.
16 Q. Who else lived at aunt Julia's at the same time you did?
17 A. All Julia's kids.
18 Q. I am sorry?
19 A. All my aunty Julia's kids.
20 Q. What are their names?
21 A. Nupa, Waumbli, Hokshila and Wakia.
22 Q. Thrista ever live there?
23 A. Yes.
24 Q. Did she live there at the same time you did?
25 A. Yes.

Page 320

1 Q. Aunt Julia told you that she didn't believe any of this
2 happened, didn't she?
3   MR. HAUGAARD: Objection, foundation.
4   THE COURT: Overruled.
5 BY MR. HOLMES:
6 Q. Isn't that right?
7 A. Yes.
8 Q. Now when you were staying at your aunt Julia's, you
9 remember going to counseling sessions with Sister Michaeleen in
10 Yankton?
11 A. No.
12 Q. You remember going to Yankton to see a lady?
13 A. No.
14   MR. HAUGAARD: Objection, beyond the scope.
15   THE COURT: Just a minute, I have to take a look on
16 that one. Counselor in Yankton was not covered in direct. The
17 different living arrangements post-trial were, as was the,
18 between the post-trial recantation for the first time. Without
19 my knowing further where this is going, sustained.
20   MR. HOLMES: Your Honor, I make reference to the
21 Court to the affidavit of Julia Joseph which is Exhibit 6.
22   THE COURT: That isn't in evidence.
23   MR. HOLMES: In her testimony.
24   THE COURT: Wait a minute, I don't have it.
25   MR. HOLMES: It's been submitted to the Court

Page 321

1 previously, I can submit it now.

2   THE COURT: No, it hasn't, I don't have Exhibit 6.

3   MR. HOLMES: Not in this proceeding, it was filed by

4 counsel with their motion for new trial.

5   THE COURT: Oh, yes, but not in this proceedings

6 since I don't have it before me.

7   MR. HOLMES: But she was asked about it while she

8 testified that she took this girl to these counseling sessions.

9   THE COURT: Who was that?

10   MR. HOLMES: Julia Joseph.

11   THE COURT: In the affidavit?

12   MR. HOLMES: While she was on the stand on cross.

13   THE COURT: Wait a minute. Yes, she was. Objection

14 is overruled.

15 BY MR. HOLMES:

16 Q. You remember your aunt Julia taking you to see a lady in

17 Yankton?

18 A. Didn't you already ask me that question?

19 Q. Yes.

20 A. I said no.

21 Q. You don't remember that?

22 A. No.

23 Q. You don't remember going to see someone there between

24 1994 and 1997?

25   MR. HAUGAARD: Objection, asked and answered.

Page 322

1   THE COURT: Overruled.

2 A. No.

3 BY MR. HOLMES:

4 Q. You remember seeing a Nun in counseling sections, a lady?

5 A. No.

6   MR. HOLMES: Your Honor, for the record, the

7 affidavit of Julia Joseph I believe was admitted as defense

8 Exhibit B rather than the Government's Exhibit No.

9   THE COURT: You are right, it was. That's right, you

10 had 6 and you wanted to put that in, but the defense had

11 already marked Exhibit B and that is admitted.

12   MR. HOLMES: May I approach the witness.

13   THE COURT: You may.

14

15   (Exhibit 8 marked For identification.)

16

17 BY MR. HOLMES:

18 Q. Rosemary, I put a document in front of you that has been

19 marked as Exhibit 8. Is your signature on that document?

20 A. Yes.

21 Q. Do you remember signing that affidavit?

22 A. Yes.

23   MR. HOLMES: I would offer Exhibit 8.

24   MR. HAUGAARD: No objection.

25   THE COURT: Exhibit 8 is received.

Page 323

1 BY MR. HOLMES:

2 Q. You remember where you were when you signed this?

3 A. At my house.

4 Q. Was Mr. Haugaard there?

5 A. Yes.

6 Q. Had you talked to Mr. Haugaard about this before the day

7 you signed the document?

8 A. No.

9 Q. He just brought it there for you to sign, is that right?

10 A. No, he typed it.

11 Q. But you hadn't talked to him before, had you?

12 A. No.

13 Q. Correct?

14 A. Yes.

15 Q. So he just had this typed and he brought it to you to

16 sign, is that right?

17 A. Yeah, I was there when he typed it.

18 Q. Rosemary, do you remember after you were first at Donna

19 Jordan's house going to see a doctor?

20 A. Yes.

21 Q. Do you remember telling that doctor that I have a bruise

22 where my uncle Garfield put it in my private spot?

23 A. No.

24 Q. You don't remember telling the doctor that?

25 A. No.

Page 324

1 Q. You remember the doctor asking you if he did that to you

2 anywhere else, and you said yes, my butt?

3 A. No.

4   MR. HOLMES: No further questions.

5   THE COURT: Redirect.

6 REDIRECT EXAMINATION BY MR. HAUGAARD:

7 Q. Rosemary, did Garfield do any of those things to you?

8 A. No.

9 Q. Did any of your uncles do those kinds of things to you?

10 A. No.

11 Q. You remember that day that I was out to see you at your

12 house?

13 A. Yes.

14 Q. When Mr. Holmes was asking you about this affidavit?

15 A. Yes.

16 Q. Do you remember we talked?

17 A. Yes.

18 Q. And do you remember that I typed that while I was there?

19 A. Yes.

20 Q. Is it still true today, what it says on that paper?

21 A. Yes.

22 Q. Was it a long time before you got to see your mom?

23 A. Yes.

24 Q. Did you see Derrick before you saw your mom?

25 A. Yes.

Page 325

1 Q. Did you tell Derrick this didn't happen when you saw him?

2 A. Yes.

3   MR. HAUGAARD: No further questions.

4   MR. HOLMES: Nothing further.

5   THE COURT: I have some questions for you. You are

6 thirteen, are you going to school this fall?

7 A. Yes.

8   THE COURT: Where are you going to school?

9 A. Wagner.

10   THE COURT: What grade are you in?

11 A. Sixth.

12   THE COURT: Did you go to school last year?

13 A. No.

14   THE COURT: How come?

15 A. I don't know.

16   THE COURT: Beg pardon?

17 A. I don't know.

18   THE COURT: Did you go to school the year before

19 that?

20 A. Yes.

21   THE COURT: You were in the fifth grade then, is that

22 right?

23 A. No, I was, supposed to be in eighth, but I am in sixth.

24   THE COURT: Well, are you repeating the sixth grade

25 this year then?

Page 326

1 A. Yes.

2   THE COURT: Why is that?

3 A. Because I missed too many days.

4   THE COURT: When you are in school, though, are there

5 some courses that you like better than others?

6 A. Yes.

7   THE COURT: Which ones do you like better?

8 A. Science and math.

9   THE COURT: Which ones don't you like as well?

10 A. English.

11   THE COURT: Why is that?

12 A. The teacher.

13   THE COURT: What?

14 A. The teacher.

15   THE COURT: Can you read alright, though?

16 A. A little bit.

17   THE COURT: Beg pardon?

18 A. Yeah, a little bit.

19   THE COURT: Has your trouble with school been not

20 that you can't do the work if you are there, but that you miss

21 a lot of days and then you get behind, is that your main

22 problem?

23 A. Yes.

24   THE COURT: Is there a time when you go to school

25 pretty regularly then are you able to do the work alright?

Page 327

1 A. Yes.

2   THE COURT: Do you plan on going ahead and going

3 through, finishing grade school and going through high school?

4 A. Yes.

5   THE COURT: What do you hope to do after that?

6 A. College.

7   THE COURT: Thank you. Do the Court's questions give

8 rise to questions by either party?

9   MR. HOLMES: Not from the government.

10   MR. HAUGAARD: Nothing from the defense, Your Honor.

11   THE COURT: Call your next witness.

12

13   DERRICK WESTON,

14 called as a witness, being first duly sworn, testified and said

15 as follows:

16

17 DIRECT EXAMINATION BY MR. HAUGAARD:

18 Q. Please state your name for the record and spell your last

19 name?

20 A. Derrick Weston, W-E-S-T-O-N.

21 Q. Who is your mother?

22 A. Rodrica Rouse.

23 Q. Do you have any brothers or sisters?

24 A. I have two sisters and two brothers.

25 Q. Who are your sisters?

Page 328

1 A. Rosemary Rouse and Heather Rouse.

2 Q. Did there come a time -- tell me, how old are you right

3 now?

4 A. I am 21, about to be 22.

5 Q. What is your birth date, Derrick?

6 A. Tomorrow.

7 Q. Tomorrow is your birthday?

8 A. Yes.

9 Q. What year?

10 A. '79.

11 Q. Several years ago were you, or tell me, when you lived in

12 Marty several years ago who did you live with?

13 A. I lived with my grandma Rosemary.

14 Q. Did there come a time when you were taken out of her

15 custody and placed elsewhere?

16 A. Yeah.

17 Q. When was that, how old were you?

18 A. I was fifteen.

19 Q. You remember what year that was?

20 A. '95 or '96.

21 Q. '94?

22 A. '94.

23 Q. Do you remember what time of the year it was?

24 A. It was getting, I know it was like the second semester of

25 school.

1 Q. Where were you going to school?

2 A. In Marty.

3 Q. Had your sister been taken out of the home before that?

4 A. I believe she had been.

5 Q. Is that your sister Rosemary?

6 A. Yes, that is.

7 Q. Do you know why you were taken away from the custody of

8 your grandmother?

9 A. Not until I was placed in foster care.

10 Q. Where were you at in foster care?

11 A. At Jean Brock's in Delmont.

12 Q. What did you find out about the reason for being taken

13 out of the home?

14 A. Probably a couple of days after I got sent to the home.

15 Q. Who told you anything?

16 A. Jean Brock was the one who told me what was going on and

17 what the charges was.

18 Q. What did she tell you?

19 A. She told me that my uncles had been charged with child

20 molesting, and that the house was not safe for me so I had to

21 get out of the house.

22 Q. Did you ever see anything like that happen at that house?

23 A. No.

24 Q. Ever see anything like that happen any place around your

25 uncles?

1 A. No.

2 Q. Had anybody ever molested you or touched you in the wrong

3 way?

4 A. No.

5 Q. Did there come a time -- let me ask you this. Do you

6 remember what month it was that you were taken to Jean Brock's?

7 A. Probably in October or November.

8 Q. Let me get off the subject for just a second and back up.

9 Did you graduate from high school?

10 A. No, I have not. I have a GED.

11 Q. What is your plan for the years to come?

12 A. Just to keep on going to school and make ready for my

13 family I created.

14 Q. You are not married, are you?

15 A. No.

16 Q. Do you live with someone?

17 A. Yes, I live with my girlfriend.

18 Q. Do you have children?

19 A. Yeah, we have two kids.

20 Q. How old are they?

21 A. One is two years and one is three months.

22 Q. How do you provide for your family?

23 A. By working from the TERO office down there, they supply

24 part time jobs.

25 Q. Back seven or eight years ago when you were taken out of

1 your grandma's home and placed in foster care, how long were

2 you in foster care before you returned to your family?

3 A. Four years.

4 Q. Where did you live those four years?

5 A. In Jean Brock's residence.

6 Q. That was the only place you were placed?

7 A. Yes.

8 Q. Did there come a time when Rosemary was taken out of the

9 house, out of your grandma's house?

10 A. Yeah, there was, but that was before I got there.

11 Q. Did there come a time when Rosemary was placed at Jean

12 Brock's house?

13 A. Yeah, there was.

14 Q. Do you remember approximately when that was?

15 A. That was approximately, I don't remember when it was, but

16 I know it was about a month after the trial had ended.

17 Q. Was it during the summer?

18 A. Yeah, it was.

19 Q. And when you saw her when you were living at Jean Brock's

20 house, what did she tell you?

21 A. I had asked her if any of this was true and if the uncles

22 had done anything like this to her, she told me no, they

23 didn't. And that she was just scared.

24 Q. What was she scared of?

25 A. Being told what to say and how to, she was just young, we

1 just left it at that.

2 Q. How much younger is she than you?

3 A. She is seven years younger.

4 Q. Did you ever see any of your uncles, or anyone else in

5 that home, your grandma Rosemary's home, or any of the other

6 homes in Marty for that matter, did you see anyone abuse your

7 cousins?

8 A. No, I haven't.

9 Q. Or your brothers or sisters?

10 A. No.

11 Q. There was a report that supposedly you were locked in a

12 closet at some point at grandma Rosemary's, did that ever

13 happen?

14 A. No, not that I am aware.

15   MR. HAUGAARD: No further questions, thank you, Your

16 Honor.

17   THE COURT: Cross examination.

18 CROSS EXAMINATION BY MR. HOLMES:

19 Q. Derrick?

20 A. Yes.

21 Q. Did you like your uncles?

22 A. Yeah, they are good guys, raised me.

23 Q. You didn't want to see them in jail, did you?

24 A. I didn't even know that they was going to jail.

25 Q. You were upset when you knew they were in jail, weren't

Page 333

1 you?

2 A. I felt bad, and I was hurt.

3 Q. In fact, before the trial you told Jessica and Lucritia

4 not to tell anybody about this, didn't you?

5   MR. HAUGAARD: Objection, foundation.

6   THE COURT: Overruled. Answer the question.

7 A. No.

8 BY MR. HOLMES:

9 Q. You don't remember talking to them and telling them don't

10 say anything about this, they will take you away?

11 A. No.

12 Q. And you were a lot older than these other kids, weren't

13 you?

14 A. Yes.

15 Q. You were fourteen, and Rosemary at the time was seven,

16 six?

17 A. Yes.

18 Q. And you told her you were upset that your uncles were in

19 jail?

20 A. I never got to talk to her.

21 Q. Well --

22 A. Until after.

23 Q. When she got to Jean Brock's you told her that, didn't

24 you?

25 A. When she got to Jean Brock's?

Page 334

1 Q. Yes.

2 A. No.

3 Q. Well, you were upset, weren't you?

4 A. I was, you know, hurt, but I wasn't mad like I was going

5 to do anything or say anything.

6 Q. After she supposedly told you this at Jean Brock's what

7 did you do?

8 A. What could I do?

9 Q. What did you do?

10 A. Nothing.

11 Q. Tell Jean Brock about it?

12 A. I let her know.

13 Q. How?

14 A. Just by letting her know what I had talked about.

15 Q. You told Jean Brock that?

16 A. Yeah.

17 Q. You tell anybody else?

18 A. Yeah, I told the Judge Julie Weddell, that's why she let

19 me go home.

20 Q. That's why Julie Weddell let you go home with your mom?

21 A. Pretty much.

22   MR. HOLMES: No further questions.

23   MR. HAUGAARD: No questions, Your Honor, thank you.

24   THE COURT: Thank you, you may step down. Call your

25 next witness.

Page 335

1

2   JESSICA ROUSE,

3 called as a witness, being first duly sworn, testified and said

4 as follows:

5

6 DIRECT EXAMINATION BY MR. HAUGAARD:

7 Q. Jessica, please state your name?

8 A. Jessica Rouse.

9 Q. Spell your last name?

10 A. R-O-U-S-E.

11 Q. You see your uncles here in the courtroom today?

12 A. Yes.

13 Q. You recognize who they are?

14 A. Yeah.

15 Q. Can you name each one of them, who is the one down on the

16 end?

17 A. Garfield.

18 Q. In the orange?

19 A. Jessie.

20 Q. In the white?

21 A. Desmond.

22 Q. Right behind me here?

23 A. Russell.

24 Q. Are you afraid of them today?

25 A. No.

Page 336

1 Q. A long time ago were you afraid of them?

2 A. No.

3 Q. What is your birth date, Jessica?

4 A. June 20th.

5 Q. What year?

6 A. '89.

7 Q. So you are twelve right now?

8 A. Yep.

9 Q. Who is your mother?

10 A. Beta Rouse.

11 Q. Who are your brothers and sisters?

12 A. Jerome, Donovan, Lucritia, Fury and Ebony.

13 Q. You remember several years ago when you were taken away

14 from your mother's home?

15 A. A little bit.

16 Q. How old were you at that time?

17 A. Three and a half.

18 Q. Do you remember the day that that happened?

19 A. No.

20 Q. Do you remember where you were taken?

21 A. To Jean Brock's.

22 Q. How long did you stay at Jean Brock's?

23 A. For about a couple months.

24 Q. Where did you go after that?

25 A. To the Donna Jordan's.

Page 337

1 Q. How long did you stay at Donna Jordan's?
2 A. A year.
3 Q. Who were the kids that were living with Donna Jordan at
4 that time when you first got there?
5 A. Sonja, Leland, Larry and Lisa.
6 Q. Were those Donna Jordan's kids?
7 A. No.
8 Q. They were other kids that were there?
9 A. Yes.
10 Q. Which of your family went there with you?
11 A. Rosemary, Donovan, Jerome and Lucritia and Fury and Echo.
12 Q. Can you spell her name?
13 A. E-C-H-O.
14 Q. Did you know why you were being taken away from your
15 home?
16 A. No.
17 Q. When did you find out?
18 A. The day before we went to Court, or the day we went to
19 Court.
20 Q. When you were at Donna Jordan's house did she ask you
21 questions?
22 A. I can't remember.
23 Q. Were you afraid of Donna Jordan?
24 A. Yeah.
25 Q. Why were you afraid of her?

Page 338

1 A. Because she used to hit us.
2 Q. Why would she hit you?
3 A. Like if we didn't do what she told us to, she would just
4 get mad and she will hit us or something.
5 Q. And do what?
6 A. And hit us.
7 Q. Did you ever see her do anything to the other kids?
8 A. Yeah.
9 Q. What did you see?
10 A. She pulled my little sister by her hair.
11 Q. Which sister?
12 A. Fury.
13 Q. Why did she do that?
14 A. Because she was chewing with her mouth open.
15 Q. Did you ever see her do anything else?
16 A. No.
17 Q. Did she do bad things to you?
18 A. No.
19 Q. You mentioned that she would slap you, how would she slap
20 you?
21   MR. HOLMES: Objection, leading, misstatement of the
22 response by the witness.
23   THE COURT: Sustained.
24 BY MR. HAUGAARD:
25 Q. Did she ever hit you?

Page 339

1 A. Yeah.
2 Q. Did it seem like you were there for a long time?
3 A. Yeah.
4 Q. Did you want to go home?
5 A. Yeah.
6 Q. Did you think you would be able to go home?
7 A. No.
8 Q. Why? Why didn't you think you would be able to go home?
9 A. Because we were there for a while.
10 Q. Did people ask you questions when you were away from your
11 home?
12 A. No.
13 Q. Did anyone ever ask if your uncles did bad things to you?
14 A. Yeah.
15 Q. Who was that?
16 A. Those people at Children's Home.
17 Q. Do you remember when you came here to the courthouse to
18 testify?
19 A. Not really.
20 Q. Did you go to the Children's Home after that?
21 A. Yeah.
22 Q. Were you living at Donna Jordan's when you, at the time
23 the trial took place?
24 A. Yes.
25 Q. When you lived in Marty, whose house did you live in?

Page 340

1 A. My grandma's.
2 Q. Who else lived there at that time, do you remember?
3 A. My mom, my aunty Sonja.
4   THE COURT: Your aunty what?
5 A. My aunty Sonja. My aunty Ursula, and my uncles and my
6 grandma.
7 Q. When you lived there, you are twelve today, you were
8 about five then, four or five. When you lived there did your
9 uncles, any of your uncles here touch you in a wrong way?
10 A. No.
11 Q. When I say in a wrong way, do you know what I mean by
12 that?
13 A. Yes.
14 Q. When I say that, I mean did they ever touch you in your
15 private parts?
16 A. No.
17 Q. Do you remember going into the Judge's office that is
18 back here, do you remember going in there and the Judge asking
19 you some questions?
20 A. No.
21 Q. When you think back on what happened that day at trial,
22 do you remember what was said?
23 A. No.
24 Q. At the trial Mr. Binger, this guy right over here in the
25 Gray suit, he asked you a question, he said do Alan and Donna

Page 341

1 talk to you lots of times about your uncles? And you said

2 yeah.

3   MR. HOLMES: I object to references to the

4 transcript, this witness said she doesn't remember being in the

5 courtroom.

6   THE COURT: Sustained.

7 BY MR. HAUGAARD:

8 Q. When people first asked you questions about your uncles,

9 did you know what they were talking about?

10 A. A little bit.

11 Q. Had your uncles ever touched you in a wrong way at that

12 time?

13 A. No.

14 Q. Did you try to tell the people that this didn't happen?

15 A. Yeah.

16 Q. Do you remember being at the Children's Home Society?

17 A. Yeah.

18 Q. Did you have counselors there that talked to you about

19 this?

20 A. Yeah.

21 Q. Did you tell one of them that this didn't happen?

22 A. Yeah.

23 Q. Do you remember which counselor it was?

24 A. Norma.

25 Q. You know what Norma's last name is?

Page 342

1   MR. HOLMES: Objection.

2   THE COURT: Overruled.

3 BY MR. HAUGAARD:

4 Q. Do you know what Norma's last name is?

5 A. No.

6 Q. Did you think you would get to go home after the trial?

7 A. Yeah.

8 Q. Why was that?

9 A. Because I was told so.

10 Q. Who told you that?

11 A. Micky.

12 Q. Do you remember who Micky is?

13 A. The lady right there.

14 Q. She the lady sitting next to Mr. Holmes here?

15 A. Yes.

16 Q. Jessica, are you telling the truth today?

17 A. Yes.

18 Q. Did any of your uncles touch you in a wrong way?

19 A. No.

20 Q. Are you willing to speak with the Judge alone and tell

21 him these things, or talk to him alone?

22 A. Yeah.

23 Q. Did any of your aunts, or uncles, or mom, or grandma tell

24 you that you had to come here today to say these things?

25 A. No.

Page 343

1 Q. Why do you want to be here?

2 A. Because I want my uncles to come home.

3 Q. Why is that?

4 A. Because they didn't do nothing.

5   MR. HAUGAARD: No further questions.

6   THE COURT: Cross.

7 CROSS EXAMINATION BY MR. HOLMES:

8 Q. Jessica, have you talked to your uncles on the phone?

9 A. Yes.

10 Q. Where were you when you spoke to them on the phone?

11 A. At my grandma's.

12 Q. Who else was there?

13 A. My mom and my grandma.

14 Q. Were any of the other children there?

15 A. Yes.

16 Q. Who took you over to your grandma's that time?

17 A. My mom.

18 Q. You live with your mom now, right?

19 A. Yes.

20 Q. Who else lives with you?

21 A. With who?

22 Q. You and your mom, who else lives with you in the same

23 house?

24 A. My three sisters and my brother Donovan.

25 Q. Your mom has told you that she doesn't believe any of

Page 344

1 this happened, hasn't she?

2 A. No.

3 Q. Has your grandmother told you that?

4 A. Yes.

5 Q. Has your grandmother told you that she doesn't believe

6 this happened?

7 A. Yes.

8 Q. In fact, you have told other people that your grandmother

9 Rosemary cries a lot and says that she misses your uncles a

10 lot?

11 A. Yes.

12 Q. After you left Children's Home where did you go to live?

13 A. To Brown's.

14 Q. How long did you stay there?

15 A. For about a year.

16 Q. And then where did you go?

17 A. To Terry and Bob Stafford's.

18 Q. From there where did you go?

19 A. Home.

20 Q. How long have you been living with your mother?

21 A. Three or four years.

22 Q. I think maybe one of the other children may have told us

23 this, but how far is your mom's home from your grandmother

24 Rosemary's house?

25 A. About two blocks or so.

Page 345

1 Q. You go over there a lot?

2 A. Yeah.

3 Q. Do you remember a time about two years ago when you came

4 up here to Sioux Falls and talked to Dr. Underwager?

5   MR. HAUGAARD: Objection, beyond the scope.

6   THE COURT: I think it is appropriate examination.

7 It is beyond the scope of the direct examination that took

8 place here, but due to the fact that you submitted the

9 Underwager videos for the Court to review as a part of the

10 submission for this motion I consider it to be allowable

11 examination, so I am going to overrule the objection for that

12 reason.

13 BY MR. HOLMES:

14 Q. Jessica, do you remember when that happened?

15 A. A little bit.

16 Q. You remember there was a camera on that you and Lucritia

17 played with after you talked to this man?

18 A. Yeah.

19 Q. Do you remember who drove you, or who drove the car that

20 you rode in when you came up here to talk to that man?

21 A. No.

22 Q. Did you and some of the other children come up together?

23 A. Yeah.

24 Q. Did you see Mr. Haugaard there that day?

25 A. Yeah.

Page 346

1 Q. Had you met him before that?

2 A. No.

3 Q. You remember telling Dr. Underwager that you didn't

4 remember what happened?

5 A. No.

6 Q. You remember Dr. Underwager, while he talked to you,

7 telling you that he was trying to be helpful to the family?

8 A. No.

9 Q. Do you remember him telling you that we all know it did

10 not happen?

11 A. A little.

12 Q. You remember him saying that to you, that we all know

13 this did not happen, you remember that?

14 A. No.

15 Q. Do you remember him telling you that we all would like

16 your uncles to come home from prison?

17 A. No.

18 Q. Other than these times that you have spoken to your

19 uncles on the phone at your grandmother's house, have you had

20 any other contact with them?

21 A. No.

22 Q. Have you been shown letters that they have written from

23 prison?

24 A. Yeah.

25 Q. Who has shown you those letters?

Page 347

1 A. My sister.

2 Q. Which sister?

3 A. Lucritia.

4 Q. You know where she got the letters from?

5 A. From my uncle Jess.

6 Q. So uncle Jess has written letters to Lucritia that you

7 have seen?

8 A. Yeah.

9 Q. Have you read those letters?

10 A. No.

11 Q. How many of those letters do you know about that Lucritia

12 has received from your uncle Jess?

13   MR. HAUGAARD: Objection, beyond the cope.

14   THE COURT: Overruled.

15 A. One.

16 BY MR. HOLMES:

17 Q. Do you remember when you were talking to Dr. Underwager

18 asking him at the end of the interview are you a Priest or

19 something like that?

20 A. No.

21 Q. Did you think he was a Priest?

22 A. No.

23 Q. In 1999 do you remember where you were going to school

24 at, two years ago?

25 A. Wagner.

Page 348

1 Q. Do you remember a lady by the name of Cheryl Fridel?

2 A. Yeah.

3 Q. What do you remember about Ms. Fridel?

4 A. Like what?

5 Q. Was she a teacher, or a counselor, or what did she do at

6 the school?

7 A. She was a counselor.

8 Q. Did you ever talk to Ms. Fridel?

9 A. Yeah.

10 Q. How often?

11   MR. HAUGAARD: Objection, beyond the scope.

12   THE COURT: Overruled.

13 A. Not too often.

14 BY MR. HOLMES:

15 Q. Did you like her?

16 A. Yeah.

17 Q. Do you remember talking to her at some time before

18 Christmas in 1999 and telling her that you were afraid for

19 Christmas because you thought your uncles were coming home from

20 prison?

21 A. No.

22 Q. Did you tell her that your uncles were in prison because

23 someone said they did a bad thing to you and your sister?

24 A. No.

25 Q. Did you tell her that your grandmother Rosemary misses

Page 349

1 your uncles very much?

2 A. Yeah.

3 Q. A few days later did Cheryl Fridel talk to you and tell

4 you that she had found out that your uncles were not coming

5 home for Christmas?

6 A. No.

7 Q. You don't remember that?

8 A. No.

9 Q. Did you tell them that, tell her, Cheryl Fridel, that

10 your uncles had done bad things to you?

11 A. Did I tell her?

12 Q. Yes?

13 A. No.

14 Q. Did you tell her that your cousin Rosemary had told you

15 and Lucritia to lie to the social worker this last summer and

16 to say that this didn't happen?

17 A. No.

18 Q. Jessica, do you remember after you went to live at Donna

19 Jordan's a time when you went to see a doctor?

20 A. No.

21 Q. Do you ever remember telling a doctor that an uncle Jess

22 hurt you and touched your private parts?

23   MR. HAUGAARD: Objection, asked and answered.

24   THE COURT: Overruled.

25 BY MR. HOLMES:

Page 350

1 Q. You remember telling the doctor that?

2 A. No.

3   MR. HOLMES: No further questions.

4   THE COURT: Redirect.

5 REDIRECT EXAMINATION BY MR. HAUGAARD:

6 Q. Jessica, you know your mom and grandma don't believe this

7 happened, right?

8 A. Yes.

9 Q. And you know -- well, you tell me, did this happen, the

10 things that they say your uncles did to you, did it ever

11 happen?

12 A. No.

13 Q. If you told the counselor that, is that true that it

14 happened?

15 A. No.

16 Q. Do you remember this Ms. Fridel, Cheryl Fridel?

17 A. Yes.

18 Q. Did she talk to you once in a while about this stuff?

19 A. Yeah.

20 Q. Did you tell her that it did not happen?

21 A. Yeah.

22 Q. Did you tell her that it did happen?

23 A. No.

24 Q. Has any of the family put any pressure on you, or your

25 uncles when you talked to them, have they put any pressure on

Page 351

1 you to lie today?

2 A. No.

3 Q. Are you at all afraid of your uncles?

4 A. No.

5 Q. If they tried to touch you, or if anybody else tried to

6 touch you in a wrong way, what would you do?

7 A. Like what?

8 Q. If somebody tried to touch you in a bad way like they say

9 your uncles did, would you tell somebody?

10 A. Yeah.

11   MR. HAUGAARD: No further questions.

12   MR. HOLMES: Nothing further, Your Honor.

13   THE COURT: I have a question. If somebody tried to

14 touch you in a bad way then who would you tell?

15 A. My mom.

16   THE COURT: Your mother didn't believe that this

17 happened, so would you tell her now?

18 A. I don't know.

19   THE COURT: What year will you be in school now?

20 A. Sixth.

21   THE COURT: Did you go to school last year?

22 A. Yeah.

23   THE COURT: Have you missed any grades?

24 A. No.

25   THE COURT: In other words, you are in the sixth

Page 352

1 grade starting now?

2 A. No, I flunked.

3   THE COURT: Beg pardon?

4 A. I flunked.

5   THE COURT: Which year.

6 A. Sixth.

7   THE COURT: So you are repeating sixth grade this

8 year?

9 A. Yes.

10   THE COURT: What was the reason that you flunked.

11 A. I missed too much school.

12   THE COURT: If you would have been able to go to

13 school all the time would you have passed do you think?

14 A. No.

15   THE COURT: Why not?

16 A. My grades were bad.

17   THE COURT: Yes, but what I am trying to find out is

18 were your grades bad because you missed school, or because even

19 if you would have been to school you think your grades wouldn't

20 have been good?

21 A. I don't know.

22   THE COURT: Are any of your courses, are some courses

23 easier for you than other ones?

24 A. Yes.

25   THE COURT: Which ones are the ones that are easiest

Page 353

1 for you?

2 A. Math and English.

3 THE COURT: Are those the ones you like the best?

4 A. Yes.

5 THE COURT: Which ones don't you care for so much?

6 A. Social studies and science.

7 THE COURT: What is the reason you don't like those

8 as much?

9 A. Because they are confusing.

10 THE COURT: Thank you. Do the Court's questions give

11 rise to questions by either side?

12 MR. HOLMES: Not from the government.

13 REDIRECT EXAMINATION BY MR. HAUGAARD:

14 Q. Jessica, do you trust your mom?

15 A. Yes.

16 Q. Do you feel safe with your mom?

17 A. Yes.

18 Q. Do you think she would believe you if you said somebody

19 touched you in the wrong way?

20 A. Yes.

21 MR. HAUGAARD: No further questions.

22 MR. HOLMES: Nothing further, Your Honor.

23 THE COURT: Thank you, you may step down. Call your

24 next witness.

25 MR. HAUGAARD: Can we just have a moment, Your Honor?

Page 354

1 THE COURT: Certainly.

2 (Whereupon, an off the record discussion was held.)

3 THE COURT: Take a fifteen minute recess.

4 (Recess at 3:15 until 3:30)

5 MR. WILKA: We would recall Maggie Bruck.

6 THE COURT: Very well.

7

8 MAGGIE BRUCK,

9 called as a witness, being previously duly sworn, testified and

10 said as follows:

11

12 REDIRECT EXAMINATION BY MR. WILKA:

13 Q. Good afternoon, Dr. Bruck?

14 A. Good afternoon.

15 Q. When you first testified you had testified about some

16 materials that you had reviewed, do you recall that?

17 A. Yes.

18 Q. When you had first testified, were you aware of the

19 existence of two 1996 taped interviews conducted by Dr. Ralph

20 Underwager of Thrista and Donovan Rouse?

21 A. I was not.

22 Q. When were you made aware of that?

23 A. About 24 hours ago.

24 Q. In the intervening 24 hours have you had an opportunity

25 to review the 1996 interviews by Dr. Ralph Underwager of

Page 355

1 Donovan and Thrista Rouse?

2 A. I watched all of Donovan's, and I have seen the first

3 half of Thrista's twice, and all but the last maybe seven

4 minutes of her's.

5 Q. You are aware that there are some 1999 taped interviews?

6 A. That's correct.

7 Q. Is it, to you, is it more important to you to review, of

8 Donovan and Thrista, the 1996 or the 1999 interviews?

9 A. '96.

10 Q. Why is that?

11 A. Well, it was within the ballpark of the alleged

12 recantations, and one always wants the earliest records of the

13 testimony that one can get, because those are the most

14 reliable.

15 Q. And why is that?

16 A. Well, as we make errors in terms of memory, I mean we

17 naturally forget things over a period of time, we forget

18 conversations, we forget parts of interviews, and we forget

19 details, and asking people in 2001 about interviews or

20 conversations that took place five or six years ago, specially

21 for children, is a very, very difficult task. I didn't know

22 that there was actually quite an early record of these children

23 on videotape, and I was, I wanted to see what they looked like,

24 because I was concerned that from the description of

25 Dr. Underwager's interviewing techniques as expressed by one of

Page 356

1 the government's witnesses that in fact maybe the children were

2 led in these interviews, and I wanted to know, you know, what

3 did they look like, how much leading did it take them to get to

4 the point. And I just was, I wanted to see, I was concerned

5 that perhaps these were not, that these were in fact statements

6 that might have arisen from very suggestive interviews, that

7 maybe it was the first time that there had been claims of

8 recantation, and the '99 tapes wouldn't really have given me

9 that information, because already three of four years would

10 have lapsed since the alleged allegations of recantations.

11 Q. Would it be a fair statement -- you have been in Court

12 when the children have testified?

13 A. I have.

14 Q. Would it be a fair statement to say that we have seen

15 examples of how a person, specially children's memories can

16 fade over time?

17 A. These are very natural processes that happen to all of

18 us.

19 Q. And the government witness you were talking about is

20 Mindy Mitnick, is that correct?

21 A. That's correct.

22 Q. Are you referring to the March 19, 2001 critique she did

23 of Dr. Underwager's interviews?

24 A. That's correct.

25 Q. When you reviewed these interviews, what part of an

Page 357

1 interview, when you look at the whole interview from the
2 beginning to the end, if you had to pick out a part that you
3 could only see, would you rather see --
4   MR. SEILER: I object, Your Honor.
5   THE COURT: How do you know, she hasn't seen all of
6 it.
7   MR. WILKA: I am saying of an interview, just asking
8 generally.
9 A. The most important part is, the first interview, is the
10 beginning of the interview to see how much work it takes to get
11 the child in to making statements, and how much prompting they
12 need. That is the important part. But I was able to,
13 specially with Donovan, to really see how this traced through
14 the whole interview. And with Thrista, I got to most of it,
15 but she just was so talkative that it was, I just didn't have
16 time to get right to the end.
17 BY MR. WILKA:
18 Q. I believe it was the government that had asked you a
19 question that there is no such thing as a perfect interview, do
20 you recall that?
21 A. I recall the question.
22 Q. Is there such a thing as a perfect interview?
23 A. I guess we could put one together, but in real life it is
24 very hard.
25 Q. When you reviewed the 1996, of your 1996 review, did you

Page 358

1 see what you consider to be a pattern of suggestibility by
2 Dr. Underwager with either Donovan or Thrista?
3 A. I did not.
4 Q. Let's talk about the Donovan interview real quick. What
5 did you see as far as Dr. Underwager's interaction with
6 Donovan?
7 A. Let me state right off, there is a concern I have about
8 that interview, and that is that I see the beginning part as
9 they are kind of setting the tapes up and doing a little bit of
10 talking and writing things down, then the next thing I here is,
11 and, let's see, I took these notes. Sorry about this. Okay,
12 here it is. So then the next thing I hear, so you were telling
13 me about being in a room for a long time, I didn't hear that,
14 so of course one's very first suspicion is what is missing, how
15 much is missing, what went on before, I would state that for
16 the record.
17 Q. That's fair. After that?
18 A. After that what I see is a very spontaneous child who
19 goes on for actually minutes at a time with very, very little
20 prompting. This is quite unusual. You know, I wrote down, I
21 mainly paid attention to what Dr. Underwager was saying rather
22 than to what the child was saying except to notice the child
23 was being spontaneous. What I, I mean I was quite actually
24 surprised by how gentle, and patient, and non-pressurizing he
25 was of these children. That's the, actually follows the rule

Page 359

1 that very few interviewers follow, I don't know if he's aware
2 of it, but it is called the five second rule. You ask a
3 question, the child answers, then when they are finished
4 talking you wait for five seconds to ask the next question. So
5 there is this feeling of there is plenty of time, anything you
6 want to say, and he does that a lot. But his questions are
7 these kinds of questions. Tell me who ever told you about the
8 abuse? Tell me anything else you remember? Tell me about the
9 day they came to take you? He asks sometimes for clarifying
10 questions where he, I just wrote these things down, you said
11 was it Rosemary who he took, sometimes he does ask children to
12 repeat things they have already said because he doesn't
13 understand them or to get back on track. He doesn't question
14 this child long because this child is on a roll, and there is
15 so much that is coming out that it would really be
16 inappropriate to stop him and to start to challenge him, and I
17 think that's what happened, and he is not taking notes, so, I
18 mean I don't know, there certainly was an issue that he didn't
19 challenge these children. But certainly these two had so much
20 to say. And he asked questions about tell me everything about
21 the people who asked questions? Was there anybody else? Is
22 there anything else you can remember? What is that about? And
23 Donovan says something about being mad, and he says, well, tell
24 me about feeling mad. Just very gentle, open-ended questions.
25 He asked him what do you want to have happen now? And is there

Page 360

1 anything else? And that, those are the kind of questions I
2 wrote down in that interview. It probably wasn't I would guess
3 a standard forensic interview.
4   MR. SEILER: We object to this testimony, she is
5 guessing.
6 A. No, I am saying it was not a standard.
7   THE COURT: There is an objection outstanding. When
8 there is an objection made you don't say anything because I
9 rule on it. The objection is?
10   MR. SEILER: Speculative, has no factual basis for
11 her testimony, and based only on a review of some of the tapes.
12   THE COURT: She saw some of the tapes, I understand
13 that, but on the basis of what she did see she can testify.
14 Overruled.
15 A. This one tape does not follow a traditional standardized
16 interview form, it doesn't have a lot of warm up, but this kid
17 didn't need a lot of warming up. One of the things I know from
18 training interviewers, and watching interviewers, and being an
19 interviewer, is that once you have some experience you don't
20 want to spend ten minutes warming up a kid when you know they
21 are ready to go, you just really go on. There is not a lot of
22 warming up here, I know this child was bubbling over. I didn't
23 see any ground rules whereby Dr. Underwager said now I want you
24 to only tell me everything that you remember, and don't guess,
25 and, you know, just tell me those kinds of things. He didn't

Page 361

1 do that in this interview, which is part of the standardized
2 interview, but he certainly did better than most people I have
3 seen in terms of opening it up and letting the child say things
4 in his own words, and following those statements up with just
5 more general statements of is there anything else you can tell
6 me, and then asking more specific questions about tell me about
7 the people who asked you questions, what kinds of questions did
8 they ask you? That's all I have to say about it. I looked
9 very carefully to see if, when I look at interviews for
10 suggestiveness, I am not interested in is there a leading
11 question, are there three leading questions. I am interested
12 in the structure of the interview in terms of are there themes
13 that are repeated again and again, are children kind of pushed
14 off in to a certain direction, are they ignored and so on.
15 This is as best, I think this was a pretty good one. I mean,
16 but you know, sometimes you are pretty good because you have a
17 really easy kid to interview, and I think Donovan might have
18 been one of those easy kids.
19 BY MR. WILKA:
20 Q. With regard to the, all but the seven minutes of the
21 Thrista interview did Dr. Underwager, did you have concerns
22 with how he structured that interview?
23 A. Well, as Dr. Mitnick notes, properly noted, it is a
24 little bit unusual and bizarre to talk about oneself as much as
25 he does at the beginning. He talks about his grandson being

Page 362

1 killed, which, you know, is not really a good way to set off an
2 interview about someone else. He talks about eating and
3 cucumbers and gardening, you know, it is really not
4 appropriate. But this, as far as I can see, is the only time
5 it happens at the beginning of the interview, and it is not
6 spreckled throughout about, oh, these other kinds of personal
7 things. Once he gets down to business, they are down to
8 business.
9 Q. When he made the comment about his grandson dying, was
10 that in the context of the cucumbers, or warm up, or food, or
11 anything like that?
12 A. Yes, she, he started to talk to her about food, what food
13 do you like to eat, or what did you eat coming up here, and she
14 said pizza, and he talked about his grandson was killed and he
15 loved pizza.
16 Q. And then did they move back in to Thrista?
17 A. No, then what do you like to eat.
18 Q. Then after that did the warm up continue, or did they get
19 down to business, or what?
20 A. I don't know how long it went on for, but then there is a
21 silence, and he transitions and says well, what do you remember
22 about the time that you were taken away.
23 Q. During that part of the interview that you saw, did he
24 attempt to push Thrista in any particular direction, or framed
25 questions that would suggest her answers that you noted?

Page 363

1 A. Well, I am, I have to tell you that I don't have a
2 transcript in front of me, and so if I did I might be able to
3 find -- this was, this was a fairly long interview. It was 31
4 minutes, but it felt like 47 hours actually, and I actually
5 stopped at 26 and then skidded through to the end to 31. So in
6 that full time I am sure that there must, I am not sure, there
7 could be.
8 Q. Did you note any?
9 A. I didn't. I am just looking through my notes. I didn't
10 note anything that was repeated where she, he didn't like the
11 answer so he kept on going, I didn't notice that -- again with
12 her, he asked her a lot of very open ended questions. Do you
13 remember anyone doing this to you, what were they asking you.
14 He says here, tell me if you don't remember, it's okay. Did
15 you tell them, the foster mother that nothing happened? Is
16 there anything else you want to talk to me about? Usually in
17 most interviews with children, forensic interviews and normal
18 interviews, by the time you get to the end and ask that
19 question, by the, I want to go home I have told you everything.
20 This child really wants to talk, she is pouring her guts out to
21 this man at the end for the last five to six to seven minutes,
22 and I didn't really spend a lot of time listening to what she
23 was saying, because in order to do this you have to get an
24 enhancer to pipe up the sound, but I got tidbits, and talked
25 about crying and things that had happened to her. So she felt

Page 364

1 comfortable with him in that she was not the one who stopped
2 that interview, just kept going and going and going, and at the
3 very end he said now, this was something that he was criticized
4 for, and I absolutely would agree with this criticism except
5 for the statement occurs at the very end of the interview, at
6 26 minutes, not at two minutes at the beginning. And he says
7 the reason I am here today is to help you do what you want to
8 do. This is interpreted I think in here as a biasing statement
9 putting forth his bias, but it really doesn't come out until
10 the very end where he said, well, you told me all this now. I
11 am here to help you see where we can go. Then he starts to ask
12 her about what is it like for you now where you are living, can
13 you look at a TV, you have a nice smile, and tell me what you
14 are doing now, and it goes on for another five minutes. There
15 are things throughout the interview that he asks that are, I
16 have a few things noted down here, but as I said, you know, we
17 all make mistakes, and I just found him to be extremely patient
18 and thoughtful, and he listened to this child throughout this
19 interview. And when anybody gets a transcript of it, I think
20 that you will see that this child offers a tremendous amount of
21 information. She certainly looks very different on that tape
22 than she did in the courtroom just in terms of her
23 verbalizations. She is still the same kind of uncomfortable,
24 mumbling child, but she is very talkative on this tape.
25 Q. Were the wide range and bubbly conversation she had with

Page 365

1 Dr. Underwager, and did they --

2 A. It wasn't a bubbly conversation.

3 Q. That was Donovan, excuse me. With Thrista did the

4 statements contain statements that you would consider to be

5 recantation of a disclosure of sexual abuse?

6 A. Well, all I want to say is that there was a lot of

7 spontaneity. She would talk for sentences at a time, and

8 certainly I have written down here she told her mom it didn't

9 happen. She said spontaneously, he asked her something else,

10 and it came around she made it up in counseling. I begged, she

11 said I begged my mom, I said I wanted to go to Court again and

12 tell them whatever happened. So I think that there are several

13 places throughout this where she keeps coming back to what

14 happened.

15 Q. In those several places that you have noted were there

16 types of questions that you would interpret to be suggesting an

17 answer, or pushing to a particular statement?

18 A. No. I think that by and large the questions he asked her

19 were either very open ended such as, well, is there anything

20 else you want to talk about, or tell me what happened, or he

21 directs her toward a period of time or a location. There are

22 comments in this report that some of the questions are leading.

23 What I found out when I listened really carefully was in fact

24 these were not leading questions, but they were repetitions of

25 things that she had just said. That, you know, I think he is

Page 366

1 either asking for clarification because she mumbles a lot, and

2 sometimes it is just to proceed with the interview, because

3 that is sometimes what we do, is just repeat what other people

4 say.

5 Q. If I did not ask, back to the Donovan 1996 interview that

6 you reviewed, did Donovan make statements that you would

7 consider to be recantations of earlier disclosures?

8 A. You know, I can tell you, but your most accurate answer

9 is going to be to look at transcripts. I really went through

10 this not so much for individual, for listening to what the

11 children were saying, but I want to hear what Dr. Underwager

12 was saying, because I was concerned given this report that

13 maybe the recantations were planted, or maybe began in this '96

14 interview.

15 Q. From your review of those do you have an opinion as to

16 whether they were planted, or began in that '96 interview?

17   MR. SEILER: I object as to foundation, and also

18 credibility determination, and invading the province of the

19 Court.

20   THE COURT: I can't hear you.

21   MR. SEILER: Calls for a credibility determination.

22   THE COURT: I am going to sustain it on that basis,

23 but also on the basis of form because it is a compound

24 question.

25 BY MR. WILKA:

Page 367

1 Q. You are not here to say whether or not the recantations

2 are true or not, are you?

3 A. No.

4 Q. You are not here to say whether the initial disclosures

5 are true or not?

6 A. No, I am not.

7 Q. Based upon that, do you have an opinion with the Donovan

8 tape as to, whether true or not, the recantation heard in the

9 Donovan tape was planted by the questioning of Dr. Underwager?

10   MR. SEILER: I object. One, it can be answered yes

11 or no. And two, inadequate foundation.

12   THE COURT: Before you get on with the rest of it,

13 that just asked if you have an opinion, you can say yes I have

14 an opinion, not what the opinion is, then we get on to the next

15 one.

16 BY MR. WILKA:

17 Q. Do you have an opinion?

18 A. I have an opinion for the Thrista tape, not for the

19 Donovan tape.

20 Q. For the Thrista tape do you have an opinion?

21 A. Yes, I do.

22 Q. What is that opinion?

23   MR. SEILER: Objection, Your Honor. When Mrs. Bruck

24 originally testified she basically indicated she only testifies

25 based upon her understanding of the literature and does not

Page 368

1 exhibit or express her personal opinions, it is only based upon

2 what she's read and what she's done, or what she's read, and

3 that in her literature search for recantation issues she went

4 on about how she was unable to find anything, so I think there

5 is an inadequate basis for her to express her opinion, and

6 inadequate foundation for it.

7   THE COURT: Let me see that other report, the

8 government report, because it isn't in evidence yet, because I

9 anticipate with regard to that, that this opinion in part is to

10 try and poison the well with regard to that which is fair game,

11 but there has to be enough foundation, so I want to see the

12 report of the government witness.

13   MR. SEILER: This is my copy, it is highlighted.

14   MR. WILKA: I have a unmarked copy, Your Honor.

15   MR. SEILER: Can we mark it and introduce it.

16   THE COURT: Your marked up one?

17   MR. SEILER: My original is back at the office. I do

18 intend to have it marked and offered in evidence, Your Honor.

19   THE COURT: We will just put it in evidence tomorrow

20 then. Would you read the question back again, please, to me?

21

22   (Whereupon, the requested portion of the Record was

23   read by the Reporter.)

24

25   THE COURT: I am going to allow the answer. I do

Page 369

1 have to say that given the distinction between clinical and
2 academic comment in psychology upon this I consider the
3 foundation to be limited, but I want to hear this expert's
4 opinion on this, although I think the foundation is limited.
5 Go ahead, you may answer.
6 A. It's my scientific opinion based on a review of the
7 questions that when Thrista first started talking about
8 recantation, that there was no major suggestive structure to
9 elicit those responses from her.
10 BY MR. WILKA:
11 Q. What else, is there anything else that you would base
12 that opinion upon, aside from just a review of the questions?
13 A. No. Well, I mean, you know, I have to know a little bit
14 about what she says to see do the questions follow.
15 Q. You stated you didn't have an opinion with regard to
16 Donovan, would that be -- why don't you have such an opinion?
17 A. I don't know what happened before, all I know is
18 Dr. Underwager said you were just telling me about, I don't
19 know what happened before you were just telling me about.
20 Q. After that, you know, aside from that, do you find
21 suggestive -- frames of questions that would suggest an answer
22 for Donovan to report a recantation?
23   MR. SEILER: I object again on foundation, form of
24 the question, and asked and answered in that she didn't have an
25 opinion with respect to Donovan and had an opportunity to

Page 370

1 explain why.
2   THE COURT: Sustained as to form, and as to stated by
3 the witness she didn't have an opinion as to Donovan. You are
4 now asking why didn't she have an opinion which is the negative
5 side of it, but also sustained as to form, I don't understand
6 the question.
7   MR. WILKA: We will take another run at it.
8 BY MR. WILKA:
9 Q. In -- just in these two interviews, and I want to focus,
10 draw your attention to the initial parts of the interviews, and
11 that is what my question is limited to where Dr. Mitnick states
12 that Dr. Underwager does not adopt the neutral attitude toward
13 these interviews. Now, based upon your review, do you agree
14 with that?
15 A. Where does she say this?
16 Q. Paragraph three, first sentence.
17 A. Does not question where he got the idea he was brain
18 washed. Okay, I am sorry, going back to the very beginning?
19 Q. Yes?
20 A. Does not adopt a neutral, okay. Well --
21   MR. SEILER: I object to this, too, Your Honor. I
22 think it is improper collateral impeachment in a sense. One,
23 the report is not in evidence yet; and two, Ms. Mitnick has not
24 testified, it is kind of a preemptive skewed missile strike at
25 an attempt to discredit this report without giving Ms. Mitnick

Page 371

1 the benefit to be here and testify. I mean maybe we won't
2 offer it and maybe she won't testify. We would object on those
3 grounds.
4   THE COURT: Come on, she is going to testify, don't
5 give me that, isn't she?
6   MR. SEILER: Our current plan is to have her testify,
7 yes.
8   THE COURT: So don't forget about that part of it.
9 Now, counsel, though, you are asking about two interviews. Are
10 we talking about Donovan and Thrista?
11   MR. WILKA: Actually what I am doing is I had asked
12 her if she agrees with the first sentence of the third
13 paragraph of Dr. Mitnick's report, but, Your Honor, I will
14 withdraw it.
15   THE COURT: Because Donovan and Thrista were worked
16 in to that too, so let's start over again.
17   MR. WILKA: I withdraw the question, and I have
18 nothing further.
19   THE COURT: With regard then to this limited area
20 covered on this recalling, cross examination.
21 RECROSS EXAMINATION BY MR. SEILER:
22 Q. You testified on direct examination previously, I guess
23 yesterday morning, that you had had an opportunity to at least
24 have seen this Mitnick report and your response was quote her
25 report seems to be fair. You recall that testimony?

Page 372

1 A. I also said --
2 Q. You recall that testimony, Ma'am?
3 A. Yes, but that's not what I said. I said that if the
4 videotapes actually show what she said, then it is a fair
5 testimony.
6 Q. And you are saying the videotapes do not say what she
7 says?
8 A. The two that I looked at, I looked at because I was
9 concerned that her, I looked at the two videotapes because I
10 said if her statements are, line up with the videotapes, I
11 would think this was fair. And you in fact did ask me
12 questions about suggestibility and recantation, and because of
13 those I wanted to make sure that I got the record straight, or
14 that I would in fact provide testimony to the Court as a whole,
15 regardless of who I was testifying for, that these early tapes
16 that I did not know about the degree to which they had
17 suggestive interviewing properties to them. I didn't want it
18 to go on record that even, though, that I agreed with this
19 report for those two very important tapes.
20 Q. So after you sat here for two days, had an opportunity to
21 visit with defense counsel, you now want to change your
22 testimony and say that the report doesn't seem to be fair any
23 more?
24   MR. WILKA: Objection, argumentative.
25   THE COURT: It's cross examination, overruled.

Page 373

1 A. Well, first of all, I didn't know there were the two
2 tapes until toward the end of Donovan's cross examination
3 yesterday. So that is number one.
4 BY MR. SEILER:
5 Q. You didn't know about the tapes when you testified
6 yesterday morning?
7 A. I didn't know about the two '96 tapes.
8 Q. You knew about the Mitnick review of the tapes, didn't
9 you?
10 A. I knew about the Mitnick review, but I thought they were
11 a review of the '99 tapes.
12 Q. We talked about this report, she breaks it down by the
13 '96 interview and the '99 interviews?
14 A. Does she say '96 and '99 in them?
15 Q. She talks about -- well, Donovan number one interview and
16 Donovan number two interview?
17 A. That's right. I was told --
18 Q. Your response was you didn't know about the tapes, you
19 knew about the tapes?
20 A. I knew about the '99 tapes, and I thought, I said at that
21 point I wasn't going to review those tapes because they were so
22 late in the process that if the interviews were terrible, there
23 was a lot more to look at before the interviews.
24 Q. Plus you wanted to stay away from getting on board with
25 Dr. Underwager, didn't you?

Page 374

1 A. Not at all. In fact, I was very surprised to see how he
2 handled these children. Why would I want to get on board with
3 him?
4 Q. Do you understand how this process works, Ma'am?
5   MR. WILKA: Objection, argumentative, Your Honor.
6   THE COURT: Sustained, ask your next question.
7 BY MR. SEILER:
8 Q. So you are here now testifying in support of
9 Dr. Underwager's work?
10 A. I am here to testify that the two interviews that he
11 conducted with these two children did not contain unduly
12 suggestive influences in them.
13 Q. In your opinion such as it is?
14 A. Okay.
15 Q. Didn't you also say yesterday morning that it appeared
16 from your review of the Mitnick information that Dr. Underwager
17 was quote breaking common standards with respect to the
18 interviewing of those children?
19   MR. WILKA: I am going to object to this, it is
20 beyond the scope of the limited recall, because we were talking
21 about the '96 interviews only.
22   THE COURT: Overruled.
23 A. Can you repeat the question?
24
25   (Whereupon, the requested portion of the Record was

Page 375

1   read by the Reporter.)
2
3 A. I also appended to that. If in fact this lined up with
4 what was on the tapes, and when I saw the tapes I didn't feel
5 that there was a huge travesty of breaking standards that it
6 would make these tapes unreliable pieces of information or
7 testimony.
8 BY MR. SEILER:
9 Q. You are changing your testimony from yesterday then?
10   MR. WILKA: Objection, argumentative.
11   THE COURT: Overruled.
12 A. I am not changing MY testimony from yesterday.
13 BY MR. SEILER:
14 Q. You have previously written in a book entitled Expert
15 Witnesses In Child Abuse Cases that an expressed disdain about
16 paid advocates for one side becoming, or trained experimental
17 psychologist for one side becoming paid advocates for one side --
18 Is it true that after two days here you have now become an
19 advocate and lost your impartiality as an expert?
20 A. Absolutely wrong.
21 Q. Absolutely wrong?
22 A. Yes. I deny that.
23 Q. And in this same little article you wrote on your first
24 two experiences testifying as an expert witness, you said it is
25 important to look at the big picture, didn't you?

Page 376

1 A. I don't know.
2 Q. And you were criticizing the prosecutor for singling out
3 individual little lines in works, and you said that they had to
4 look at the bigger picture, the big picture and not single out
5 little individual stuff, you remember that?
6 A. I was talking about --
7 Q. Do you remember that, Ma'am?
8   MR. WILKA: Your Honor, I would ask that the witness
9 be allowed to answer the question before another one is fired
10 at her.
11   THE COURT: The witness can go ahead and answer the
12 question.
13 A. I was talking about interpretation of journal articles
14 where prosecutors or defense attorneys would put the article in
15 front of you and ask you to look at a line and to make comment
16 about the line. My point was it was important to read the
17 whole article and to put a series, I was talking about science
18 in general, that it was important to do a survey of the
19 literature so you wouldn't rely on one piece, but you could see
20 how the whole thing was coming together, that's what I meant by
21 the big picture.
22 Q. Isn't that what you have done with your testimony now,
23 you didn't even watch the entire Thrista tape, you only looked
24 at a portion of it and you singled out individual aspects of
25 what Dr. Underwager did without looking at the totality of the,

Page 377

1 all of the interviews that he did?

2 A. Well, I wanted to -- that's absolutely wrong. That is

3 absolutely wrong.

4 Q. And you are denying that you became an advocate, but for

5 the last two days in fact you requested permission to allow you

6 to move up to the front row right behind defense counsel so you

7 could continue to pass notes to them to assist them in

8 examining witnesses, isn't that true?

9 A. I didn't do that as an advocate.

10 Q. Isn't that true?

11   MR. WILKA: I would ask once again the witness be

12 allowed to answer her question, then I would just request that

13 counsel have the courtesy to remain seated without advancing

14 upon the witness.

15   THE COURT: Well, I will deal with those in order.

16 The first one is we are not in a rush here to the extent that

17 you should interrupt the witness, and don't, because you have

18 been.

19   MR. SEILER: I apologize, Your Honor.

20   THE COURT: Secondly, though, just for the record,

21 counsel did stand up, but he is about thirty feet from the

22 witness, so I don't consider that he was advancing in a

23 threatening manner, and if he were I stop counsel, I won't let

24 them do that, but he wasn't. So with regard to the first one,

25 sustained. So whether you like the answer or not, don't come

Page 378

1 back, you know, and before the witness has been able to answer,

2 because you don't like it then you can work over the next one

3 with your next question.

4 A. If I were an advocate I wouldn't have looked at those

5 tapes, I looked at those tapes very carefully because I was

6 concerned in fact that there was suggestive interviewing in

7 those tapes. I didn't look at those tapes to whitewash anyone,

8 I was surprised that they were there, I wanted to make sure

9 that they hadn't been hidden from me for whatever reason, and I

10 wanted to be sure that I was being honestly and accurately told

11 what was going on in this case. It was for no other reason

12 than that.

13 Q. I think the question related to the fact about whether

14 you became an advocate because for the last two days you have

15 been sitting behind defense table, in fact requested permission

16 to move into the front pew so that you could continue feed them

17 information as they examined their witnesses?

18 A. Well, I was giving them questions about how to question

19 children. I think that people in the courtroom actually lose

20 sense of the kind of language you use with children. I think

21 that you are not developmental psychologists, so you don't

22 really understand children's sense of time or the kinds of

23 things that they do know and don't know, and that is what I was

24 doing. I was sitting there listening to the kids and trying to

25 see, understand what they were trying to say.

Page 379

1 Q. How many interviews then have you done in your career of

2 children who are alleged to have been sexually abused?

3 A. I have done thousands of interviews with normal children

4 who were talking about their life, when things happened, what

5 happened to them.

6 Q. How many interviews, forensic interviews of sexually

7 abused children have you done as a psychologist?

8 A. I have done none.

9 Q. Zero?

10 A. Zero.

11 Q. And you heard Donovan testify yesterday that he lied to

12 Dr. Underwager, didn't you?

13 A. Did Donovan say that? I don't know. When we got to that

14 part of the testimony all I heard was that there was a '96

15 interview, my ears were ringing. He lied to Dr. Underwager?

16 Q. So Donovan admitted --

17 A. Wait a minute. I didn't hear that, or I don't remember

18 hearing that.

19 Q. Assume that in his testimony Donovan admitted that he

20 lied to Dr. Underwager, wouldn't that impact your opinion in

21 terms of whether he had made truthful or untruthful statements

22 to Dr. Underwager in this interview on the tapes?

23 A. No, I didn't look at this tape to determine whether or

24 not he made truthful or untruthful statements. I looked at

25 this tape to see how Dr. Underwager was treating and

Page 380

1 questioning these children. And I know it would be an exercise

2 to look at the consistency between the responses in '96 and '99

3 and now, but that was not what I was doing, I just wanted to

4 see what Dr. Underwager was saying to these children, that's

5 it.

6 Q. That's it?

7 A. That's my area of expertise.

8 Q. But you do admit in response to a question just recently

9 that there really are some unusual and bizarre, I think you

10 said, aspects to the manner in which he interacted with the

11 children, isn't that correct?

12 A. Well, I thought that the beginning of the tape with

13 Thrista was a little bit unusual, but somehow or other it

14 didn't slow her down, or maybe it did, but, maybe it slowed her

15 down, maybe she is very verbal instead of just verbal.

16 Q. And Underwager in his examination of the children on the

17 tape becomes an advocate for the defense position in terms of

18 making statements like our job is to now do what you want to

19 do, our job is to get your uncles out of jail, do you remember

20 those statements?

21 A. At the very end, at the very end.

22 Q. Doesn't that, isn't that an indication that he is an

23 advocate for one position versus the other?

24 A. Well, it doesn't come out at the beginning, and it is

25 after the children, I can't remember which one it is, has made

Page 381

1 their major statement and has gone on for a bit, and I almost
2 looked at it, I am not -- well, it wasn't, it has a lot of
3 interpretations, but he didn't say it adamantly, you know,
4 horses to the cavalry, it could be seen as almost a supportive
5 statement. You know, you said what you have had to say and now
6 where are we going to go. But if he had said that at the very
7 beginning of the videotape, I would have been very, very
8 concerned about the reliability of that testimony.
9 Q. So you don't believe Underwager was an advocate during
10 the time that he was interviewing the children on the '96 tape?
11   MR. WILKA: That's just been asked and answered, Your
12 Honor.
13   THE COURT: Overruled.
14   THE WITNESS: Do I answer now?
15   THE COURT: Yes.
16 A. I didn't see it coming out in any overriding way. He
17 simply sat there and asked the children about things that
18 happened. He didn't say that was bad, tell me more. Well,
19 there was one time where he did say, well, there was something
20 he said, but it was just a repetition of what the children had
21 said, made the comment about foster homes not being a great
22 place to be, better to be home with mom and dad. You know, as
23 you said, they are not perfect interviews, but when you look at
24 how much these children actually say in the first third, or the
25 first, you know, five or ten minutes before any, he says

Page 382

1 anything else, most of the information you want is there.
2 Q. If the converse were true and you were looking at an
3 interview of an FBI agent and the FBI agent or social worker
4 had made statements to a child in this type of forensic
5 interview about I am here to help you put your uncle in jail,
6 you would be criticizing the dickens out of him?
7 A. Absolutely not. If I saw this tape, if it were sent to
8 me by a defense attorney to come and to, and they told me that
9 this was an FBI agent who was interviewing this child, and they
10 wanted me to see if it was suggestive, I would send this back
11 and tell them to get themselves another tact for this case. I
12 talked about this yesterday how there are many, many tapes that
13 I send back, this would be one of them.
14 Q. That you would send back and wash your hands of it, say I
15 don't want anything to do with it?
16 A. I don't say I wouldn't want anything to do with it, my
17 job is to say that I don't, I cannot be useful to you in terms
18 of talking about the suggestive techniques or the suggestive
19 atmosphere, because I don't, it is not overwhelming.
20 Suggestibility runs on a continuum. Some interviews are highly
21 suggestive, some are not suggestive at all, and some are, you
22 know, everyone always asks a leading question or reveals a like
23 or a dislike, and usually what, when those things happen, you
24 want to look and see how the child responds to those in any
25 unusual way, and then it becomes a concern. It is not a

Page 383

1 perfect, there are things in this interview, but there are real
2 traits in this interview in terms of his patience with the
3 children, and his ability to give them really a lot of room to
4 say things in their own words, which is a problem that most
5 interviewers or adults have when speaking to children, is you
6 don't give them the space.
7 Q. Your opinion and analysis has to be impacted by the fact
8 that you don't know and have no idea what was said to these
9 children before they turned on the video camera, either by
10 family members, by friends, by lawyers, or by Dr. Underwager?
11 A. That's true with any videotape that I look at, that's
12 absolutely true.
13 Q. And the reason that's specially true in this particular
14 case is because when the videotape is turned on there is no
15 lead in, there is no discussion of ground rules, or anything
16 else like that, that is suggested in the literature by folks
17 who write extensively in this field, isn't that correct?
18 A. No, but the transition with Thrista seems to be a natural
19 transition and not one that really jolts her. But, you know, I
20 must agree with you that I don't know what happened before
21 these children came in there. They could have had a long car
22 ride where they had been rehearsed and rehearsed, and all of
23 those things. But all I wanted to do was I wanted to look to
24 see how he talked to those children. And all those factors
25 that you bring up are real possibilities.

Page 384

1 Q. And the longer the length of time, the more time that has
2 elapsed from the actual event until the interview, the more
3 vulnerable individuals are to false memories, isn't that
4 correct?
5 A. I don't want to call them false memories, because false
6 memory, I think that there is more of a chance of memory loss
7 or memory distortion, which could be the result of just natural
8 processes. We also get these things over time, which most of
9 us know because of conversations we have with people where our
10 memories don't jibe. Then there are the more directed changes
11 which could result from suggestive interviews, suggestions in
12 the community, and that the weaker the memory is for the
13 original event and the later the suggestions occur, the easier
14 it is going to be to accept this information. You are right
15 about that, but there are, I just want to make the point that
16 the longer the delay between an event and the interview, the
17 more chance there is for, let's just call it reporting error,
18 recall error, and not give it a card, could be false memory,
19 could be forgetting, or confabulation, or whatever. That's why
20 I wanted to look at the '96 one instead of the '99 one, because
21 I felt the '99 one would be much more prone to those kinds of
22 errors. Not that the '96 one isn't prone, could be.
23 Q. So the possibility is that the '99 tape then is even more
24 susceptible to the memory loss, the false impressions, the
25 false reporting?

Page 385

1 A. Exactly, that's why I really didn't want to look at it,
2 because I felt that, you know, whatever the children said,
3 there could be multiple explanations for what was on that tape,
4 and I only had a limited amount of time to work on this case,
5 and I really didn't feel that that was an important part at
6 that point.
7 Q. Ms. Bruck, in a matter of this importance --
8 A. I am sorry, the matter what?
9 Q. In a matter of this importance, you said that this was
10 not a forensic interview, I mean when you are interviewing
11 children for purposes of recantation or for Court, a forensic
12 interview with the ground rules, with seriousness, with
13 non-laughing, with the non-advocacy position, that's the way to
14 approach this, not in the unusual and bizarre manner that
15 Underwager did?
16   MR. WILKA: Object to the form of the question, Your
17 Honor.
18   THE COURT: Overruled.
19 A. I felt the two interviews that I saw -- Dr. Mitnick could
20 be totally correct about the four other interviews in '99, but
21 the two that I saw, I didn't see a lot of joking and a lot of
22 laughter. Dr. Underwager does have this sort of unusual laugh
23 that comes out once in a while, but I felt that this was a very
24 serious interview, actually. It wasn't forensic, but in that I
25 didn't see him sit in front of a protocol. I felt, but he

Page 386

1 certainly did follow many, many of the rules. And we know
2 there are no standard forensic protocols, it is not like we
3 have to follow one thing or another. He certainly did not lay
4 out ground rules, and he did tell the children once in a while,
5 you know, if you don't remember, tell me you don't remember.
6 He never asked them to guess. But I agree with you, that, you
7 know, it is too bad it is not perfect. I don't know why, I
8 don't know under what circumstances they were done, or what,
9 how he was told to proceed, but certainly these two were not,
10 would not bear the characteristics of the descriptions that I
11 read here. And the reason I wanted to look at them was because
12 if they had -- I don't know what I would have done, to tell you
13 the truth.
14 Q. Well, you have, you seemed upset when I was questioning
15 you about my perception that you have now become an advocate
16 for the defense, you have lost your impartial ability, you lost
17 your objectivity, and you are now feeding information to the
18 defense, and you are denying that. So assuming that to be true
19 for the moment, Dr. Underwager did a lot of things wrong,
20 didn't he, and why don't you list those things for the Court
21 then?
22 A. Okay, that I found in this interview. Well, do you want
23 me to go through each of these points and to comment on them,
24 or just pick up the ones I thought were most salient, or what?
25 Q. You were giving your opinion in response to questions

Page 387

1 about counsel regarding the tape, and you said he did some
2 things right, you talked about those, what did he do wrong?
3 A. I am glad to be your witness now, so if there is anything
4 you want to ask me, I am very glad to be your witness. If you
5 could help me along it would be easier. So at the beginning he
6 shares personal information with children.
7 Q. I want your opinion.
8 A. You want me to look through my notes and see what I
9 picked out? Okay.
10   THE COURT: So it is clear on the record, while the
11 witness is looking at her notes, the tapes were filed, the
12 Court has reviewed them all.
13   MR. SEILER: So they are in evidence for purposes of
14 this hearing, Your Honor, and will be considered part of the
15 record of this hearing?
16   THE COURT: Yes, they were submitted for it, and I
17 looked at them when I decided whether to have this hearing or
18 not, they are part of the record in this case. The Court does
19 not have a transcript, but I have pretty detailed notes as to
20 what was said in each of the interviews.
21   MR. SEILER: In the interest of moving this along,
22 Your Honor, she's looked through her notes, I would ask the
23 record to reflect for a minute or two now, and is unable to
24 find anything, so we will just, no further questions.
25   THE COURT: Well, maybe you are not, but I am

Page 388

1 interested in, because I have watched all the tapes. Of course
2 Dr. Underwager testified here before. He has some unusual
3 mannerisms as you had mentioned. One of the things I wanted to
4 ask you about was I noticed when Thrista was being interviewed
5 by him, I made the comment --
6 A. Is this the '96 one, because I didn't see the '99 one.
7   THE COURT: This is '96. That she didn't look at
8 him, and then she turned all the way away from him later on
9 during the interview, and he asked her to turn back to him
10 even.
11 A. That was at the very end where he said could you turn
12 around and look at the camera and smile. I notice that you
13 notice things like that. That you notice whether she looked
14 at, you asked her whether, why she wasn't looking at her
15 uncles. He was here, and she was sort of catercorner so they
16 were right opposite each other. I didn't note that. She is
17 not a child who makes eye contact.
18   THE COURT: But she turned away from him, not eye
19 contact, she turned her body away from him, and the interviewer
20 asked her to turn back, is that a typical interviewing conduct
21 with a child, to ask them to turn back?
22 A. I was surprised, I was wondering whether someone had
23 asked him to ask her.
24   THE COURT: I don't know if anybody else was there.
25 A. Now that you mention it, it was quite at the end, it was

Page 389

1 about, because I wrote it down, about 26 minutes in to it he
2 said could you turn around.
3   THE COURT: You don't attach anything to that one way
4 or the other?
5 A. Well, I would never like to make a child aware that there
6 is a camera going on, so I would never do anything like that,
7 I would never suggest anything like that. I didn't make
8 anything of it. You know, then he said you have such a nice
9 smile, he got a smile out of her for the first time, that was
10 all I paid attention to.
11   THE COURT: If you were an academician.
12 A. I am.
13   THE COURT: I was starting to say, if were you an
14 academician that was critiqueing Dr. Underwager, who is a
15 clinician, I guess.
16 A. Yes.
17   THE COURT: What would you tell him that he should do
18 that he didn't do in the interview and a half that you watched?
19 A. The major thing that I would coach him to do is have a
20 much more standard warm up with the children that includes much
21 less of him. A little of him, I think that is very nice for
22 children to know that you are a person, or that you like dogs
23 or you like cats. I hate it when interviewers go on about
24 their families and stuff like that, I think that is really
25 beyond the bounds.

Page 390

1   THE COURT: Like he did?
2 A. I thought that was inappropriate. But, you know, talk
3 about I have a garden, you have a garden? She didn't have a
4 garden, so what is the next topic, she likes pizza. He really
5 doesn't have those kinds of boundaries between himself and this
6 child, obviously, so that's the first thing. The second thing
7 is that there is a lot of debate about how do you start
8 interviews, you know why you are here. He could have asked her
9 that. I think he probably should have asked her do you know
10 why you are here, how did you get here, who did you talk to
11 before you came here, what were they talking to you about. I
12 think I would ask that. A lot of that is recommended for the
13 beginning of the interviews. I really ask that at the end of
14 the interview. I think that kind of stops any freedom all of
15 the sudden, you know, I think you should try to get the child
16 in to it as quickly as possible. He didn't do that for any of
17 these, and I certainly would have hoped that at some point he
18 would have asked these children something that you know there
19 are people that are concerned, you have given lots of different
20 kinds of answers, you have said this to these people, you have
21 said this to these people.
22   THE COURT: Of course he didn't remind them of that.
23 A. No, he didn't. You know, I don't know, but in order to
24 make this interview perfect, I certainly would have asked the
25 children those things. Would have asked them at the very end

Page 391

1 of the interview after they had really kind of given their
2 whole story, because it just kept coming out, was really no
3 place to stop. And so I think that he could have had a larger
4 veneer of objectivity had he asked them much more about the
5 recantations, about what was going on in their homes, and then
6 in order to begin the interview, I mean certainly with Thrista
7 he gets right in to it, she doesn't seem to mind, but if there
8 was a child that did mind, how would I, what is generally
9 recommended, was generally recommended is I want to ask you
10 some questions now about what happened whenever. And then
11 there is the grand rules, and you know, sometimes I am going to
12 ask you about things you don't know because it was a long time
13 ago. And if you don't remember, you should tell me you don't
14 remember. And if you don't know, tell me you don't know. I
15 only want you to remember things you saw and you heard. If
16 there are some things that people told you about, you should
17 tell me. He is very good about asking the kids who told you
18 what. These are quite difficult questions for most people,
19 they are called Swiss moderator questions, that is did you
20 really see it, did you hear it and see it, did you hear it.
21 What he is trying to do is separate what happened and who told
22 them what kinds of things. I mean he does that here
23 successfully because it is centered around recantation. So you
24 ask those kind of things, most people don't ask those kind of
25 questions.

Page 392

1   THE COURT: But remember I was asking you if you as
2 an academician were critiqueing him what else should he do?
3 A. I would have him change his act at the beginning about
4 warm up, I would have him do a short thing with the ground
5 rules, and then at the end I certainly would have asked about
6 alternative hypotheses, and also about potential sources of
7 coercion.
8   THE COURT: Asking about the potential sources of
9 coercion, you would have asked who brought you here and how
10 long did it take you to get her, would you ask that sort of
11 thing?
12 A. I didn't come prepared to make up the interview.
13   THE COURT: It is over three and a half hours from
14 where they live to get here.
15 A. Right. How did you get here, who were you with, what did
16 you talk about in the car.
17   THE COURT: Would you ask if you were over at the
18 lawyer's office before you were brought here?
19 A. Yes.
20   THE COURT: You would ask probably who have you been
21 living with?
22 A. Who do you, I think at some point he does say to them
23 what is life like with you now, where are you.
24   THE COURT: I am not asking -- who are you living
25 with, wouldn't you ask that when there is an issue with regard

Page 393

1 to coercion?
2 A. Are we going to specifically talk about this child, or
3 these kinds of interviews in general?
4   THE COURT: Talking about Dr. Underwager's
5 interviews.
6 A. With these children, yes, I would have asked who they are
7 living with, what is going on in their homes, what kinds of
8 things they talk about at home, absolutely.
9   THE COURT: Wouldn't you have some point asked in the
10 interview, since Dr. Underwager knew full well what they
11 testified to, as did the children, about why did you testify as
12 you did?
13 A. Well, these children, the two of them were so vocal in
14 terms of telling what happened, that the question would have
15 been redundant.
16   THE COURT: Not if you asked it before they had
17 talked for half an hour maybe.
18 A. No, but I would never ask those questions first, because
19 I think they are ones that inhibit, and you should do, you
20 should do the most you can at the beginning to get the
21 spontaneity and the spontaneous statements out, and when that
22 is finished, and this is usually recommended in lots of
23 protocols also, draw the line, you know, you say okay, and now
24 you can do more probing, and you can ask, you can start to go
25 in to these other fields. But I certainly wouldn't ask those

Page 394

1 questions at the beginning, because I just think that they set
2 up an atmosphere that maybe, I mean maybe up want to set up
3 that atmosphere, hey, we really don't believe you are telling
4 the truth, there are some people that don't and some who do,
5 convince me. Tell me what happened. I don't think that's a
6 great way to interview children. All the standardized
7 interviews are built around the precept it is real important to
8 make the child feel comfortable and to be in a supportive
9 environment where whatever they say is okay, and that at
10 different times you can challenge, but you don't start at that
11 level.
12   THE COURT: You mentioned ground rules, and what
13 ground rules at the beginning should have been stated?
14 A. Right, I think, I mentioned they are very short, you
15 know, I want you to tell me as much as you remember. If there
16 is something you don't remember, say you don't remember. If
17 there is something you don't know, tell me you don't know. And
18 only tell me things that actually happened, don't tell me
19 things that someone told you happened. Now in this one it is a
20 little bit different, because really what he wants to know is
21 what other people told these children, right, but he never --
22 well, he does ask those two questions, he asks questions what
23 did other people tell you.
24   THE COURT: Those aren't ground rules, though.
25 A. No, no, that's fine. And these kind of interviews, I

Page 395

1 mean you want to know what these children remember about what
2 other people were telling them. But at the beginning there
3 could have been some kind of way of, you know, and I don't see,
4 I don't like this lie-truth dimension. I think that, and from
5 what I know about the scientific literature, it is antithetical
6 to what is going on in the interviews with these children,
7 because they don't think, they are not there to tell a lie. In
8 the courtroom today you heard these children sobbing about
9 lying. Now I don't know if they are telling the truth or not,
10 but at the time that these children made their statements, they
11 did not make them -- okay, let me start again.
12 Suppose they are false allegations, okay, just suppose. They
13 did not make those statements to be consciously deceptive, they
14 made those statements to please. And it is a very different
15 concept, their lie has always negative aspects to it. I think
16 this is a real problem in terms of setting up interviews for
17 children so they understand that it is not that we, I mean we
18 don't want you to lie, but we want you to tell us what happened
19 to you. If you don't remember, then tell us you don't
20 remember. I guess you can say don't make it up. But I really
21 think that the use of the word lie is antithetical, and also it
22 is detrimental to a lot of interviews, because these kids don't
23 think they are lying, so they say it anyway. They say this
24 isn't a lie, this is what they want to hear, so you are not
25 really instructing them the right way. So that is what is in

Page 396

1 the ground rules, and a lot of people want this, we call it the
2 truth/lie mantra. They want this removed from instructions to
3 children at the beginning of these interviews, because there is
4 very little correlation between children's knowledge of truth
5 and lie, and their suggestibility, and their understanding of
6 suggestibility.
7   THE COURT: Of course you are aware before a child is
8 even allowed to testify the Court makes inquiry as to whether
9 or not they understand what a lie is, and what the truth is?
10 A. Absolutely, one day we will make a change in the American
11 justice system in that one too.
12   THE COURT: Alright, thank you. Do the Court's
13 questions give rise to questions by either side?
14   MR. WILKA: No, Your Honor.
15   MR. HOLMES: No, Your Honor.
16   THE COURT: Thank you, you may step down. Any other
17 witnesses?
18   MR. WILKA: We are out of witnesses, Your Honor. We
19 do have the matter of Jerome Rouse, we understand that hasn't
20 been, there hasn't been time to get him out.
21   THE COURT: Because he didn't get a subpoena in time.
22   MR. WILKA: Correct, but with that, at this point we
23 would rest.
24   THE COURT: Alright. In terms of time, I am
25 concerned about this because I understand that the defendants

Page 397

1 wanted to have a family visit of some sort, but the question
2 has been put to me whether we go beyond five o'clock tonight
3 because apparently if we did that would not facilitate what
4 ever kind of visit they can have while in jail, is that
5 correct?
6   MR. CARTER: I have made some contacts with people at
7 the penitentiary, and I believe Mr. Wilka has too, to try to
8 get some visits done. Being in and out of Court it is my
9 understanding they were going to try to accommodate that. I
10 didn't know what timeframe to tell them, but I would hope that
11 even if we did go later than five o'clock they could maybe
12 still do that tonight. I am hopeful that we can get back and
13 talk to some people who may have more answers at this point
14 than they did at three o'clock when I last faxed the list.
15 There was a list of information that the state penitentiary
16 needed of the people that were going to be coming in, names,
17 Social Security Number and a number of questions like that, and
18 I faxed that to the penitentiary when we were on our last
19 break, and so hopefully there are some people up there that
20 have received that and are carrying forward on that end, but it
21 is, that's the details such as I know them.
22   THE COURT: Well, the defense case took two days, and
23 I am not critical of that, just observing that fact. We had
24 three set aside for this, and the government is entitled to
25 what ever time it takes to put on their case. About how long

Page 398

1 is that going to take do you anticipate, recognizing you don't
2 know how long the cross examination will go?
3   MR. HOLMES: I would think a day and a half at least.
4 I think we have a lot of witnesses that are very short, but
5 then there are two experts.
6   THE COURT: I take it your experts are probably here.
7   MR. HOLMES: One is here, one is arriving this
8 evening.
9   THE COURT: Well, it looks to me like we going
10 another hour or so tonight isn't going to change the course of
11 things very much in terms of when we get done, and I would like
12 to have the defendants have a family visit, frankly, if it is
13 possible. We could go tomorrow, and all day tomorrow, and see
14 how much of your case we get in, and what we don't get in, I
15 have to, on Sunday I am going to Washington and I am in a long
16 range planning meeting for the federal courts then, and I am
17 after that giving a speech and I can't cancel that, so I get
18 back here on Tuesday, so we could, assuming we are not done
19 tomorrow, we could finish up on Wednesday afternoon. And if we
20 did that, that would give us time enough then for Jerome Rouse
21 to be brought here, and the government could finish up what
22 ever witnesses it didn't get in. If that is a schedule that
23 will work for everybody.
24   MR. SEILER: I have a three day jury trial with Judge
25 Kornmann starting Tuesday in Pierre.

Page 399

1   THE COURT: Well.
2   MR. SEILER: We would try to make, we could probably
3 work around those dates, though, with respect to our schedules.
4   THE COURT: Well, Mr. Holmes is capable counsel, too,
5 I imagine that he can handle what ever else isn't done on
6 Tuesday. I recognize you have a division of labor, but if you
7 are taking the experts and both experts are here, you can do
8 both of those tomorrow it seems to me.
9   MS. TAPKEN: I will be gone, but Mr. Holmes can
10 certainly handle everything for me.
11   THE COURT: It's your authority to delegate to him.
12   MS. TAPKEN: I will take advantage of that.
13   THE COURT: Can the defense all be here participating
14 Wednesday afternoon.
15   MR. WILKA: Yes, Your Honor, we will make it work.
16   THE COURT: Let me make sure there isn't something
17 that isn't on this schedule, make sure it is fine with me,
18 because I have things in the morning. I am sure I am free in
19 the afternoon, I will be right back. From 10:30 on on
20 Wednesday morning, so we could start at 10:30, because I have
21 something at 9:00 and something at 10:00. The one at 10:00
22 should be done by 10:30, so we could start at 10:30 to finish
23 up. By the way, I haven't reneged on my authorization that
24 Dr. Bruck can sit behind you in case there is any question, I
25 notice she is sitting back there now. We will be in recess

Page 400

1 until 9:00 tomorrow morning.
2 (Recess at 5:00 p.m. until 9:00 a.m., 9-7-01)
3   THE COURT: The government may proceed.
4   MR. HOLMES: United States calls Cheryl Fridel.
5
6   CHERYL FRIDEL,
7 called as a witness, being first duly sworn, testified and said
8 as follows:
9
10 DIRECT EXAMINATION BY MR. HOLMES:
11 Q. Good morning.
12 A. Good morning.
13 Q. Would you please tell us your full name and spell your
14 last name for the record?
15 A. My name is Sherry Fridel, F-R-I-D-E-L.
16 Q. Ms. Fridel, during the school year 1999-2000 where were
17 you employed?
18 A. 1999-2000, I actually was at the Wagner school until
19 March of 2000.
20 Q. Could you, I am sorry, what position did you hold at the
21 Wagner school?
22 A. Family service coordinator.
23 Q. Can you briefly tell us what your educational background
24 was at that time?
25 A. Sure. I am, I graduated from the University of South

Page 401

1 Dakota with a Bachelors in social work, and I am also a
2 licensed social worker in the State of South Dakota.
3 Q. What had been your professional experience up to that
4 point in time, where have you worked and what had you done?
5 A. Prior to coming to Wagner I was the assistant program
6 supervisor at the Children's Inn here in Sioux Falls, before
7 that the shelter for abused and neglected children as well as
8 the abused women's shelter.
9 Q. Can you describe to the Court what your duties were there
10 at the school in Wagner?
11 A. It was a brand new position, so my duties kind of evolved
12 as my position went through the school year, but the basic
13 understanding was that it was my job to kind of be the middle
14 person from the families to the school. What I did was I
15 assisted the children in school with situations that they maybe
16 struggle with in school, home work assignments, peer problems,
17 and I also did home visits and worked with the families in
18 their homes.
19 Q. Going into the fall of 1999, were you aware of children
20 from the Rouse family being involved there, enrolled there at
21 Wagner?
22 A. I knew there were some Rouse children that attended
23 Wagner school, that was about all I knew.
24 Q. At some point in time did you have some contact primarily
25 with Jessica Rouse?

Page 402

1 A. I did.
2 Q. Were there any of the other Rouse children that you
3 eventually had some contact with?
4 A. Yes, there were.
5 Q. Who were those children?
6 A. Actually Lucritia would stop in my office sometimes, and
7 Fury would stop in as well.
8 Q. The fall of '99 did you have any knowledge of the
9 criminal case where those children had been witnesses?
10 A. I had not, no knowledge at all.
11 Q. Had you had any contact with anyone from law enforcement
12 or the Department of Social Services regarding that case up to
13 that point in time?
14 A. No, I did not.
15 Q. Tell us what you remember about your involvement with
16 Jessica and how that developed during the fall of '99?
17 A. How our relationship started?
18 Q. Yes?
19 A. Part of what I did for my job was, since I was new and
20 there were several children in the Wagner school, and it was my
21 responsibility to kind of serve all the children the best of my
22 ability, what I would do is go in the hallways in between
23 classes and meet the kids and find out how their day was going.
24 A lot of times one of the big things with me was they give me a
25 high five or hug, it was their choice. So lots of times I

Page 403

1 would be walking down the hallway and little kids would stop me
2 and high five. I remember on one occasion, I never actually
3 met Jessica personally, but in hallway she was high fiving,
4 boom, boom, boom, kind of in a row, and after that I remember
5 she saying, because I would speak with a lot of her little
6 friends, so when I go in the classroom to remove one of the
7 kids, a lot of times the kids would say take me, please take
8 me. One time Jessica came up and said I would like to talk to
9 you. I said okay, I will stop down and get you some time. So
10 that's how we started conversing individually.
11 Q. Were there occasions when she would just talk to you
12 about various things that were going on with her in school?
13 A. Absolutely. A lot of times that happened in the hallway,
14 you know, a lot of times it wasn't necessarily in my office, in
15 the hallway, how are you today, general chit-chat.
16 Q. Describe to the Court what contact you had with Lucritia
17 during that same period of time?
18 A. With Lucritia during that same period of time would be
19 basically just like Jessica, in the hallway I would see her.
20 Lucritia wasn't quite as forthcoming as Jessica was, but there
21 would be times when she would, my assessment would be that she
22 was just a little bit more standoffish, but there would be
23 times she would be with Jessica and Fury and a couple other
24 friends and give me a high five. Ms. Fridel, can we stop down
25 to your office and get a pencil, or things like that, so

Page 404

1 sometimes I would chat with her in the hallway.
2 Q. Do you recall a specific occasion in the end of November
3 of 1999 when you spoke with Jessica and she indicated to you
4 that she was afraid --
5 MR. WILKA: Objection, leading.
6 THE COURT: Sustained.
7 BY MR. HOLMES:
8 Q. Did you speak to Jessica some time around the end of
9 November?
10 A. Yes, I did.
11 Q. Did she talk to you at all about being afraid of
12 Christmas?
13 A. Yes, she did.
14 Q. Tell the Court how that conversation came about as you
15 recall?
16 MR. WILKA: Objection, hearsay, and also asking the
17 witness to comment on the mental state of another.
18 THE COURT: Overruled.
19 A. Actually what happened was prior to Christmas time, it
20 was kind of a regular thing that I did at the Children's Inn as
21 well as in Wagner, I would touch base with all the kids that I
22 had worked with to talk to them about Christmas. From my
23 experiences, Christmas is a tough time for individuals that I
24 work with, and I wanted to make sure that there was going to
25 be, it was going to be safe, there was going to be food in the

Page 405

1 house, different things like that. So pretty standard I talked
2 to lots of the children, and Jessica happened to be one of
3 them. When I asked her about Christmas and what she had
4 planned for Christmas, and different things like that, she told
5 me that she was afraid for Christmas. And I asked her why, and
6 she said because my uncles are coming home. And I said okay, I
7 had no knowledge as to what that meant at that point. We
8 continued talking about what she was going to do over Christmas
9 and whether or not she was going to get Christmas presents and
10 what their standard tradition is for Christmas. And then I
11 asked where are your uncles, and she told me they were in
12 prison. I believe at that point we chatted a little bit more
13 about why she was so afraid. I am trying to remember if it was
14 right then or if I met her again, but we didn't talk in detail
15 a lot about it at that point. And after that conversation was
16 over, I went in to my principal's office and I said I need to
17 know what is going on, because Jessica is extremely afraid for
18 Christmas time, and I told her that I would find out whether or
19 not her uncles were going to be home, and I would let her know
20 from there. At that point is when we --
21   MR. WILKA: At this point I object as the
22 non-responsive nature of the answer, we are going far afield
23 from the question.
24   THE COURT: The question has been answered, ask your
25 next question.

Page 406

1 BY MR. HOLMES:
2 Q. Did you generate a report that was later submitted to the
3 FBI regarding this conversation with Jessica?
4 A. Yes, I did.
5 Q. Are you a mandatory reporter under the child abuse
6 statute?
7 A. Yes, I am.
8 Q. Was that the purpose behind generating this report?
9 A. Absolutely.
10   MR. HOLMES: May I approach the witness, Your Honor?
11   THE COURT: You may.
12
13   (Exhibit 19 marked For identification.)
14
15 BY MR. HOLMES:
16 Q. Ms. Fridel, I have handed you a document marked as
17 Government's Exhibit 19, do you recognize that?
18 A. Yes, I do.
19 Q. Is that the report that you generated following this
20 conversation with Jessica?
21 A. Yes, it is.
22 Q. And to your memory does it fairly and accurately set
23 forth what was said during your meeting with her on the 30th of
24 November?
25 A. Yes, it does.

Page 407

1   MR. HOLMES: We would offer Exhibit 19.
2   THE COURT: Being no objection, Exhibit 19 is
3 received.
4 BY MR. HOLMES:
5 Q. When you review Exhibit 19 --
6   MR. HAUGAARD: Your Honor, may we have a moment to
7 consult?
8   THE COURT: Yes.
9   MR. WILKA: For the record, we will object as
10 hearsay, Your Honor.
11   THE COURT: Overruled.
12 BY MR. HOLMES:
13 Q. Does the report refresh your recollection as to some of
14 the specifics that were discussed in that conversation?
15 A. Yes, it does.
16 Q. And was there some discussion in that conversation with
17 Jessica about if she had been touched by someone?
18 A. Yes, there was.
19 Q. What do you recall now, after reviewing Exhibit 19, was
20 discussed in that regard?
21 A. Jessica stated to me in that conversation that her uncle
22 had touched her in her private parts.
23 Q. And was there some further discussion regarding why the
24 individuals were in prison and what she was afraid of?
25   MR. WILKA: Excuse me, I object to the previous

Page 408

1 question and answer. It was asked that if this report
2 accurately reflected the conversations, and no where in there
3 is there that Jessica telling her that her uncle touched her in
4 her private spot.
5   THE COURT: What about the part that says Jessica
6 explained that her uncle had touched her in her private parts.
7   MR. WILKA: Where is that?
8   THE COURT: Third line down. Objection overruled,
9 ask your next question.
10 BY MR. HOLMES:
11 Q. Did she also say that she was afraid that when their
12 uncles came home they would be mad at her and her sister for
13 telling?
14 A. Yes, she did.
15 Q. Did she talk at all about her sister and her having to
16 tell a social worker that someone had made stories about her
17 uncle?
18 A. Yes, she did.
19 Q. Do you recall any more specifics about that than are in
20 your report?
21 A. I do.
22 Q. What do you remember about that?
23 A. I remember her telling me that she was afraid because her
24 mother and her grandmother cried a lot, and they missed mom's
25 brothers and grandmother's sons a lot, and they wanted them to

Page 409

1 come home from prison, and so they told them to tell the social
2 worker that what happened to them was not true.
3   MR. WILKA: I object as to hearsay to that last
4 statement, Your Honor.
5   THE COURT: Overruled. I should say under the
6 circumstances of the statement that, even if hearsay, which it
7 is, that I find that, given the circumstances of the statement
8 in this setting, that I find it credible and subject to
9 exception of the hearsay rule.
10   MR. HOLMES: We would also offer it as a prior
11 inconsistent statement, because I specifically asked Jessica
12 about these questions when she was on the stand yesterday, so
13 we would also submit it on that basis.
14   THE COURT: That's true also. Go ahead.
15 BY MR. HOLMES:
16 Q. Did you learn from her where she had this belief, or the
17 origin of her belief that her uncles were coming home for
18 Christmas?
19 A. Are you still referring to the November 30th
20 conversation?
21 Q. Yes.
22 A. Can you repeat the question one more time?
23 Q. Well, maybe I need to rephrase it because it was somewhat
24 confusing. She was telling you she was afraid her uncles were
25 going to come home for Christmas, is that correct?

Page 410

1 A. That's correct.
2 Q. Did you come to any understanding as to how she had that
3 belief that they were going to come home, did she tell you
4 someone had told her, or do you recall in any way the source
5 that she explained for that belief?
6 A. I don't believe that during the November 30th
7 conversation that during that conversation anything was
8 mentioned as to that. I don't believe that happened until a
9 little later of a conversation.
10 Q. Ms. Fridel, is there anything else that is significant
11 that you recall regarding that November 30th conversation with
12 Jessica?
13 A. I don't believe so.
14 Q. What did you do then after talking to her on that day?
15 A. After I spoke with Jessica and during that conversation I
16 told her that I would indeed find out if I could whether or not
17 her uncles were going to be home for Christmas. As soon as
18 Jessica left my office that is when I went to Ms. Rehwaldt's
19 office and said I need a little background, I need to know what
20 is going on here, can you tell me? And at that point
21 Ms. Rehwaldt gave me a very brief history of what she knew, and
22 I made a phone call to the FBI at that point.
23 Q. Did you eventually receive information that the uncles
24 would not be coming home for Christmas?
25 A. I did.

Page 411

1 Q. After that did you have another conversation with
2 Jessica?
3 A. I did.
4 Q. Can you explain to the Court the circumstances which led
5 up to that conversation?
6 A. The circumstances that led up to that was that in the
7 November 30th conversation I had told Jessica that I would
8 follow up on that and try and find out whether or not they
9 would indeed be coming home. I did that, I called the FBI and
10 found out that no, they would not be home for Christmas, and at
11 that point then I met with Jessica again so I could tell her
12 that they would not be at home for Christmas.
13 Q. Did that take place at the school also?
14 A. It did.
15 Q. What do you remember about that meeting with Jessica?
16 A. I remember that she came in to my office and I gave her
17 the news that they would not be coming home for Christmas, and
18 I remember Jessica responding in a positive way, and I
19 explained to her how I knew that they wouldn't be coming home
20 for Christmas.
21 Q. Did she tell you that she was still afraid of her uncles?
22   MR. WILKA: Objection, leading.
23   THE COURT: Sustained.
24 BY MR. HOLMES:
25 Q. What else did she tell you in that conversation?

Page 412

1   MR. WILKA: Objection, hearsay.
2   THE COURT: Yes, it is, and I am going to receive it
3 again because coming up in this setting I consider it, albeit
4 hearsay, and I consider that it is hearsay, but I consider it
5 to be a significant indicia of reliability, and I will accept
6 the hearsay.
7 A. In that conversation, after I informed her that her
8 uncles would not be coming home, I asked her if that made her
9 feel better, and she said that it did. She then shared with me
10 that she does not want them to come home. She said she was
11 still afraid of them. Then at that point I asked her if she
12 felt that she could tell me a little bit about what, about the
13 way her uncles hurt her.
14 BY MR. HOLMES:
15 Q. Did she proceed to tell you?
16   MR. WILKA: Your Honor, I object at this point as to
17 hearsay. That is far removed, and not only is it hearsay, it
18 is not relevant to what this person's duty was at the time. It
19 is, it doesn't fit under any exception to the hearsay.
20   THE COURT: Yes, it does, and I consider, number one,
21 it is relevant to her duties, specifically relevant to her
22 duties; and secondly, it is relevant with regard to this
23 proceedings, because Jessica, of course, has since said that
24 nothing of the sort happened, and further having come up in
25 this sort of a setting, which is completely removed from law

Page 413

1 enforcement, I consider that it is sufficient indicia of
2 reliability that the Court will receive the testimony even
3 though it is hearsay, although it is contrary to Jessica's
4 previous testimony here in Court. Overruled. Proceed.
5 BY MR. HOLMES:
6 Q. What did she tell you about how her uncles had hurt her?
7 A. She explained that when the adults that were in her house
8 were partying, Beta would tell Jessica to go into the back
9 room, and then once she was in bed uncle Desmond would come
10 into the room and crawl in to bed with her. She said she then
11 said that he would touch me down there. She also said that he
12 made her touch him down there. Then I inquired as to what down
13 there meant, and she said it meant private parts. She also
14 shared with me that her cousin Rosemary will never talk about
15 this, and she is one person that told Jessica as well as
16 Lucritia to lie to the social worker this last summer. Then I
17 asked her if anyone else told her that she shouldn't tell the
18 truth, and she said that her mom also told her to lie. She
19 said that her mom explained to her that her uncles did the same
20 thing to Rosemary that they did to her and Lucritia, that's why
21 Rosemary pooped her pants. Then I just explained to Jessica
22 that I would try and help her stay safe, and we are going to
23 work on different ways to go do that, and then we removed
24 ourselves from that and worked on probably some pictures of a
25 story that we were reading about ways to stay safe.

Page 414

1 Q. Were you aware at that time that there had been an
2 incident where Rosemary had had an accident in her clothing in
3 school?
4 A. Yes, I was.
5 Q. That occurred earlier in the school year?
6 A. Yes, it did.
7 Q. This second conversation that we are discussing here with
8 Jessica, when did that occur?
9 A. On December 6th. So it was almost a week after.
10 Q. Did you once again prepare a report that you submitted to
11 the FBI?
12 A. I did.
13   MR. HOLMES: May I approach the witness, Your Honor?
14   THE COURT: You may.
15
16   (Exhibit 20 marked For identification.)
17
18 BY MR. HOLMES:
19 Q. Ms. Fridel, I have handed you what has been marked as
20 Government's Exhibit 20, is this the report you generated
21 regarding your conversation with Jessica Rouse on December 6th,
22 1999?
23 A. It is.
24 Q. In fact, you referred to that in your testimony here this
25 morning to refresh your recollection?

Page 415

1 A. Yes.
2   MR. HOLMES: I would offer Exhibit 20.
3   MR. WILKA: No objection.
4   THE COURT: Exhibit 20 is received.
5   MR. HOLMES: No further questions.
6   THE COURT: Cross examination.
7   MR. WILKA: Thank you, Your Honor.
8 CROSS EXAMINATION BY MR. WILKA:
9 Q. Good morning, Ms. Fridel, my name is John Wilka, and I
10 will be asking you a few questions. You stated that you worked
11 at the Wagner school during the 1999 and 2000 school year?
12 A. I worked there as well as the year prior to that.
13 Q. You left in March of 2000?
14 A. That is correct.
15 Q. Where did you become employed in March of 2000?
16 A. At the March of Dimes in Sioux Falls.
17 Q. Were we on the same committee last year?
18 A. I don't know.
19 Q. Why did you leave the employ of the Wagner school?
20 A. Personal reasons.
21 Q. What were those?
22   MR. HOLMES: Objection, relevancy.
23   THE COURT: If it had to do with work performance,
24 you can ask about that. So objection is overruled to that
25 extent.

Page 416

1 BY MR. WILKA:
2 Q. What were those?
3 A. What were the reasons I left the Wagner school?
4 Q. Yes.
5 A. It had absolutely nothing to do with work performance.
6 It was a personal decision I made that I needed to leave Wagner
7 and relocate to a different town. I resigned from my position.
8 Q. There were -- you did not feel that you could any longer
9 professionally perform your duties in the Wagner School
10 District?
11 A. I did not feel that it was to the best of my interest to
12 stay in the Wagner School District at that point.
13 Q. Why is that?
14   MR. HOLMES: Objection, relevancy.
15   THE COURT: Well --
16   MR. HOLMES: May we approach, Your Honor?
17   THE COURT: Yes, you may.
18 (Bench Conference.)
19   MR. HOLMES: Your Honor, we would move that the
20 personal reasons in Wagner, what defense counsel wants to do is
21 place on the record the witness's husband was in effect
22 involved in something in Wagner and in connection with a
23 criminal case involving him, and it has nothing to do with this
24 witness. I think this has gone as far as it should.
25   THE COURT: So nothing that had to do with this

Page 417

1 witness, it was this witness's husband. It was in State Court,
2 not Federal Court?
3   MR. HOLMES: Yes.
4   THE COURT: I don't remember it, what was it?
5   MR. CARTER: He was the ex Augie football player.
6   MR. HOLMES: It was a intercollegiate matter.
7   THE COURT: Well, I can understand that. I don't
8 think it has any relevance to this proceedings.
9   MR. WILKA: I would still rely on the witness is
10 predisposed to aggravation.
11   THE COURT: I would think the contrary.
12 (End Bench Conference.)
13   MR. WILKA: I withdraw the question.
14   THE COURT: Very well.
15 BY MR. WILKA:
16 Q. Ms. Fridel, you did not hear Jessica testify yesterday,
17 did you?
18 A. I did not.
19 Q. You are not here to tell the Court whether or not what
20 Jessica told you in November and December of '99 is true or
21 not, are you?
22 A. I am here to tell the Court what I documented in November
23 and December of 1999.
24 Q. Because you don't know whether her statements in '99 or
25 in 2001 are true, do you?

Page 418

1 A. I believe what Jessica said to me in November of '99 and
2 December of '99.
3 Q. You believe them, so you disbelieve the statements that
4 she makes that none of this ever happened then?
5 A. I disbelieve that statement.
6 Q. That is from these two conversations with her?
7 A. Correct.
8 Q. If you look at Exhibit 19, please. Just please take a
9 second to review that, details of incident, let me know when
10 you are done?
11 A. I am completed.
12 Q. In any of your career have you ever done work with
13 sexually abused children?
14 A. I have.
15 Q. Do you believe it is possible for a false allegation of
16 sexual abuse to be made?
17 A. That is possible.
18 Q. Do you believe that it is possible that a false
19 allegation of sexual abuse may be made due to suggestion to
20 small children or a child?
21 A. That is possible.
22 Q. Is it not true that when Jessica came up to you as it
23 states in the report, she stated that her uncles are in prison
24 because someone said they did a bad thing to her. Is that in
25 there?

Page 419

1 A. I am just reviewing.
2 Q. Be the second sentence, Ma'am.
3 A. That is in there, correct.
4 Q. So from the, would you agree with me that the plain
5 reading of that sentence indicates that Jessica learned of the
6 sexual abuse because someone told her that she had been abused?
7 A. That would not be my interpretation of that statement.
8 Q. So the interpretation of the statement because someone
9 said they did a bad thing to her means that someone did not say
10 that they did a bad thing to her?
11 A. Can you rephrase that question, please?
12 Q. Well, obviously her uncles are in prison because someone
13 said they did a bad thing to her.
14 A. Correct.
15 Q. Did you ask her who the someone was?
16 A. I don't recall asking her that specific question, no.
17 Q. So it would be a fair statement to say you did not ask
18 whether an FBI agent told her that someone had did a bad thing
19 to her?
20 A. I didn't ask that specific question. I could elaborate
21 on that a tad if you would like me to.
22 Q. I would like to know who told her, if she reported to
23 you, who told her someone had did something bad to her?
24 A. When she was talking to me about the incidents that I
25 have reported, Jessica stated to me that someone said that her

Page 420

1 uncles did a bad thing to her. She never specifically stated
2 to me that anyone told her that. The way our conversation was
3 at that point was Jessica was somewhat withdrawn in our
4 conversation at that point, didn't want to give me details of a
5 very difficult experience in her life. That was my
6 interpretation of that.
7 Q. That was your interpretation. So her uncles are in
8 prison because someone said they did a bad thing to her is
9 different than that she was told that somebody did a bad thing
10 to her?
11 A. I would call those two things different.
12 Q. And so in your interpretation is there an operative
13 difference between the word something was said to me and
14 something was told to me?
15 A. In an operative way as in my documentation, yes, there
16 is.
17 Q. Could you tell me the difference between the word said
18 and told then in your operative definition?
19 A. In my documentation I can. When I wrote someone said
20 that they did a bad thing to her, I was under the impression
21 that what had happened was bad, and somebody said that after
22 she had talked about it that it was a bad thing to talk about
23 it. As opposed to somebody told me that it was bad. My
24 interpretation was Jessica already knew it was a bad thing
25 because of the way she felt about it.

Page 421

1 Q. Now you stated that she was withdrawn, but earlier in
2 your direct did you not say that she was a talkative child?
3 A. They were in two different situations, sir. She was very
4 talkative in the hallway, and at that moment when this topic
5 came up, children tend to, at least in my experience, somewhat
6 withdraw.
7 Q. When we look at -- you got a case history of what had
8 occurred in this matter at some point?
9 A. You mean up to this point today?
10 Q. No.
11 A. Or in this situation at school?
12 Q. No, I believe you stated on direct examination that you
13 had received some information about what had happened with the
14 children.
15 A. The only thing, the only information that I received was
16 after my November 30th meeting, I walked in to my principals
17 office, Ms. Rehwaldt, and I said I need some history, I am
18 confused. And she said all I can tell you is that Jessica's
19 uncles are in prison currently for sexually abusing the
20 children, that is all.
21 Q. So it was just a statement made to you by the principal,
22 you did not receive the FBI 302 reports or the social worker
23 reports?
24 A. On November 30th, sir, I hadn't even spoken at that time
25 with the FBI. So no, I did not receive those.

Page 422

1 Q. At the, about by the December 6th had you received any
2 pieces of paper?
3 A. Absolutely not.
4 Q. So when Jessica was talking about the abuse that she had
5 received, it was Beta would tell Jessica to go into the back
6 room and then uncle Des would come in and touch her and make
7 her touch him, correct?
8 A. She would say uncle Desmond, I remember that. I don't
9 remember ever referring to him as Des. And I don't believe
10 touch her, touch him, we talked about private parts and down
11 there.
12 Q. I apologize, but just summarizing, we are like in the
13 same room, right?
14 A. Correct.
15 Q. On the same page, we are together here. Are you aware
16 that those are completely different allegations than Jessica
17 made at the trial?
18 A. Here? I am absolutely not aware, I didn't hear Jessica
19 testify.
20 Q. I am talking about the trial in '94?
21 A. I know nothing about that trial.
22 Q. You did not observe Jessica's demeanor on the witness
23 stand yesterday, did you, because you weren't here?
24 A. Correct, I did not.
25 Q. So you did not hear Jessica say that she missed her

Page 423

1 uncles, did you?
2 A. I did not hear that.
3 Q. You didn't hear her say that the foster parent had been
4 abusive to her, did you?
5 A. I didn't hear anything that she said.
6 Q. You didn't hear her say that she was not pressured to
7 lie, did you?
8   MR. HOLMES: I object, the witness has already made
9 it clear she did not hear Jessica's testimony, and this is
10 simply argument.
11   THE COURT: Sustained.
12   MR. WILKA: That's all I have.
13   THE COURT: Redirect.
14   MR. HOLMES: No redirect --
15   MR. WILKA: Your Honor, other counsel may have
16 questions, at the outset we had reserved cross examination.
17   THE COURT: That's true.
18 CROSS EXAMINATION BY MR. HAUGAARD:
19 Q. Ms. Fridel, you expressed earlier a quote unquote belief
20 in the accuracy of her statements, is that correct?
21 A. Are you asking me whether or not I believed what she said
22 to me?
23 Q. Well, just a little while ago you said you believed that
24 she was telling the truth?
25 A. I absolutely did believe that.

Page 424

1 Q. If you had more information in regard to a rather
2 threatening foster home situation where, as you said in your
3 earlier report, that someone said that they did bad things to
4 her, if you were aware of the fact that the foster home setting
5 and a foster parent had repeatedly asked questions and
6 discussed this sort of thing, and told this child that someone,
7 these uncles had done bad things to her, would that affect how
8 you might receive that information from her?
9 A. I don't know that I can fairly answer that question,
10 because at the time when I had this conversation with Jessica I
11 didn't even give that a remote thought.
12 Q. I understand that, I am just saying if you had additional
13 information, do you think that might affect the way you would
14 have received information as far as whether you believe it or
15 questioned it?
16 A. It may have, it may have not.
17   MR. HAUGAARD: No further questions.
18 CROSS EXAMINATION BY MR. BINGER:
19 Q. My name is Steve Binger, I am the attorney for Jessie
20 Rouse. You had two conversations with Jessica, is that
21 correct?
22 A. Relevant to this case I had two conversations with
23 Jessica. I spoke with Jessica on several different occasions.
24 Q. That's what I meant, about the case.
25 A. Okay.

Page 425

1 Q. November 30 and December 6th?

2 A. That's correct.

3 Q. So you have the first conversation, and then you

4 generated a written report to the FBI?

5 A. Yes. I put it on a report to the FBI after speaking with

6 Ms. Rehwaldt, there were several different report forms that I

7 generated on my own computer.

8 Q. You do it on that very day you think?

9 A. Absolutely I did it on that day.

10 Q. Well, if you look at Exhibit 19, it says you reported to

11 Bill Van Roe on December 6th?

12 A. That is correct.

13 Q. Am I right in concluding from that you didn't generate a

14 report on it until a week later?

15 A. I generated the report for myself on November 30th of

16 1999. My direct reporting source in my position at the Wagner

17 school was my principal Ms. Rehwaldt. At that point on

18 November 30th, 1999, I did make a mandated report to

19 Ms. Rehwaldt. Then after reporting to her she asked me to

20 report further. I made a phone call, and I believe left a

21 message for Mr. Van Roe. We did not connect that day.

22 Q. Did you talk to him on December 6th?

23 A. I did.

24 Q. And then after talking to him you went back and

25 interviewed Jessica some more? Here is my question. Before

Page 426

1 you talked to her the second time had you spoken to Bill Van

2 Roe?

3 A. To be quite honest with you, I can't remember if it was

4 Bill Van Roe or Matt Miller that I spoke to. What I can

5 remember is what I documented, and that was that I spoke to the

6 FBI and found out that her uncles were not going to be home for

7 Christmas. That is what I can remember, is what I have written

8 down.

9 Q. Well, when you interviewed her the second time, was that

10 on your own initiative, or was that done on the initiative of

11 anybody else?

12 A. Well, on November 30th I told her that I would find out

13 whether her uncles were coming home for Christmas, and so I

14 like to follow up with what I say I am going to do, that's

15 exactly what I did. When I had that answer, I provided that

16 answer to Jessica. So it was on my own initiative, because I

17 promised her I would find out an answer, and I did.

18 Q. Did the FBI tell you simply that they weren't coming home

19 from prison, or did they also tell you some things, some

20 relevant facts concerning the case?

21 A. The only thing they mentioned to me on my first telephone

22 conversation with the FBI was that they will not be home at

23 Christmas time. I said thank you, that's all I needed,

24 goodbye.

25 Q. Your report makes some reference to a Desmond Rouse. Is

Page 427

1 there any mention in either one of your reports about Jessie

2 Rouse, a person by that name?

3 A. Not specific Jessie Rouse. There was mention of uncles

4 in the plural sense, and if he is an uncle. Then how ever you

5 interpret that I guess, but not his name specifically.

6 Q. She brought up the names to you, right? You didn't know

7 the names of the uncles?

8 A. I had no idea.

9 Q. So all you knew is what she told you?

10 A. That's correct.

11 Q. In the body of either one of these reports Jessie is not

12 named at all?

13 A. That's correct.

14 Q. She never mentioned his name to you, not even once?

15 A. That is not necessarily correct.

16 Q. Well, by reading your report there would be no reason to

17 believe she ever mentioned him by name, wouldn't that be fair?

18 A. That would be fair for you by reading these reports.

19 However, I don't know if you know how you document when you are

20 a social worker, but it is absolutely impossible to write down

21 every word that was mentioned and every name that was

22 mentioned. So you do the best of your ability the relevant

23 facts of your conversation. Jessie was not in my view.

24 Q. Jessie was not in either one of your reports?

25 A. In my reports his name is not mentioned specifically.

Page 428

1 Q. But his name isn't mentioned in the upper part of your

2 report where you refer to the alleged perpetrator, Desmond,

3 isn't it?

4 A. That's correct.

5 Q. Who gave you that information?

6 A. Jessica would have said that.

7 Q. How do you know that? You just told me you couldn't

8 remember everything that was said?

9 A. I can tell you that when I had conversations with Jessica

10 we talked about uncles in the plural sense. More than Desmond,

11 and Jessie were mentioned in our conversations. We talked

12 about lots of different family members. Not necessarily about

13 abuse. I talk to these children about lots of different

14 things, sir.

15 Q. Your report doesn't say anything about, I mean it gives a

16 specific example of Desmond crawling in to bed with her, but

17 doesn't have any specific examples of any conduct by Jessie?

18 A. That is correct.

19 Q. Can you sit there today and tell me for sure that you

20 didn't hear Jessie's name from the FBI instead of Jessica?

21 A. I can tell you that for sure, and I can also tell you

22 that I heard Jessie's name from Ms. Rehwaldt as well.

23 Q. So maybe that's how you came to put it on here, because

24 it was told you by someone within the school, right?

25 A. That is correct. You will notice that it says alleged

Page 429

1 perpetrators.

2 Q. Yes, I do notice that. But I am just referring to the

3 fact that you made no specific note of Jessica telling you

4 anything about Jessie, and that is true, isn't it?

5 A. That part is absolutely correct.

6   MR. BINGER: That's all I have.

7   THE COURT: Mr. Carter.

8 CROSS EXAMINATION BY MR. CARTER:

9 Q. Ms. Fridel, my name is Dave Carter, I am representing

10 Garfield Feather. Just a couple of questions here. How many

11 telephone conversations did you have with the FBI regarding

12 this matter?

13 A. Conversations. I believe what happened was I called the

14 FBI and on different occasions we were playing phone tag, I

15 left a message, I got a return phone call, got a message as

16 well, returned phone call from my end again. So how many

17 conversations I had with the FBI, to the best of my

18 recollection it would be two phone conversations. One was when

19 they said, when I found out the information that her uncles

20 would not be home for Christmas, and the other one was a

21 conversation as in the reports, the actual report that I was

22 giving.

23 Q. So as I would understand it, the first conversation you

24 said was just limited to the matter of the uncles are not

25 coming home, is that correct?

Page 430

1 A. That is very correct.

2 Q. What was the substance then of the second conversation?

3 A. The substance of the second conversation was exactly what

4 I have on my report.

5 Q. So you were basically at that point reporting this

6 information to them?

7 A. Correct.

8 Q. Did they say anything back to you that you were

9 incorporating somehow in your knowledge base from which you are

10 testifying today?

11 A. Can you explain to me a little further about what you

12 mean by that?

13 Q. Well, what did they tell you in this conversation?

14 A. They actually told me that they would like to come to

15 Wagner and talk to me.

16 Q. Is that all they said?

17 A. Yes, that is all they said in that phone conversation.

18 Q. So that is the second conversation, the sum and substance

19 of all that they said, they wanted to come and visit you in

20 Wagner?

21 A. I gave that information over the phone, and they set up

22 an appointment with me to come to the school and talk to me.

23 Q. Then was there a subsequent time when they did come and

24 interview you?

25 A. Sure, there was.

Page 431

1 Q. When was that?

2 A. I cannot tell you the exact date of that interview.

3 Q. So you didn't keep any detailed notes of that occasion

4 then?

5 A. The only detailed notes, the only thing that was talked

6 about in that interview was exactly what is on my report here.

7 Q. My question was did you keep any notes of that in-person

8 interview with the FBI?

9 A. That in-person interview would have been recorded in the

10 file that is currently in the Wagner school.

11 Q. You haven't reviewed any of that before coming here

12 today?

13 A. The only thing that would be in their file would be in a

14 little file box that says spoke with the FBI, reported the

15 incident of the 12-6 conversation with Jessica. I don't feel

16 like there was really anything I needed to review.

17 Q. This recording that you referred to, was that an actual

18 tape recording, or was that just the written thing that you put

19 into the document in the file?

20 A. I don't believe I said anything about a recording. I

21 wrote down in a follow-up box that I spoke with the FBI about

22 the incident that I have documented on 12-6.

23 Q. When did you first become aware of the fact that this

24 proceeding, this new trial proceeding was under way?

25 A. I cannot tell you an exact time, but I can tell you that

Page 432

1 it was after I left the Wagner school. So that would have been

2 in March, after March of 2000.

3 Q. Were you still in the Wagner school when the FBI came to

4 personally interview you?

5 A. Yes, I was.

6 Q. You recall the date of that interview?

7 A. I do not.

8 Q. How long did this interview last?

9 A. To the best of my knowledge, 45 minutes maybe.

10 Q. Who participated?

11 A. Bill Van Roe and Matt Miller.

12 Q. And that was not taped then as I understand?

13 A. It was taped. It was tape recorded, but I don't think I

14 referred earlier to a recording of that. When I said record, I

15 meant on my forms, that is what I was referring to.

16 Q. So that was something that the FBI then brought their

17 tape to record the conversation?

18 A. Yes, they did.

19 Q. And have you ever listened to or seen a copy of that

20 tape?

21 A. I know I have never seen a copy of it. I don't believe I

22 have ever listened to it. I remember what I said, I don't need

23 to listen to that tape.

24 Q. So it's your testimony that you remember things without

25 having to go back and refresh your memory from files and

Page 437

1   MICHAELEEN MUHOVICH,
2 called as a witness, being first duly sworn, testified and said
3 as follows:
4
5 DIRECT EXAMINATION BY MR. HOLMES:
6 Q. Please state your full name for the record, and spell
7 both your first name and last name?
8 A. M-I-C-H-A-E-L-E-E-N, Muhovich, M-U-H-O-V-I-C-H.
9 Q. Ma'am, can you briefly detail to the Court what your
10 educational background is?
11 A. Yes, I have a Doctorate in Clinical Psychology from
12 St. Louis University.
13 Q. What has been your professional experience since
14 receiving your Doctorate?
15 A. I spent about a year and a half at Benedictine Family
16 Services, about two to three years at the Human Services
17 Center, and since 1994 have been a member of the staff of
18 Heartland Psychological Services.
19 Q. And are you a member of any Catholic Order?
20 A. I didn't hear you, please?
21 Q. Are you a member of any Catholic Order?
22 A. Yes, I am a Benedictine Sister from Sacred Heart
23 Monastery in Yankton.
24 Q. Can you generally describe what work you did at Heartland
25 Psychological Services in Yankton beginning in '94?

Page 438

1 A. You mean with Rosemary?
2 Q. Yes.
3 A. She was referred to our agency for staffing as a
4 consequence of having experienced sexual abuse.
5 Q. That is Rosemary Rouse, correct?
6 A. Correct.
7 Q. Before we talk about her specifically, what type of work
8 were you doing at that facility at that time in general?
9 A. I saw adults and adolescent children, I worked over a
10 number of different kind of areas. I consider myself a
11 generalist.
12 Q. Rosemary was referred to you by whom, if you recall?
13 A. The Tribe.
14 Q. Tribal Social Services?
15 A. Correct.
16 Q. During what period of time did you see Rosemary?
17 A. I saw her first in October of 1994 until September of
18 1997.
19 Q. Doctor, what do you recall about where she was living
20 during that period of time and who was transporting her to the
21 counseling sessions?
22 A. She was living with foster parents Arden and Jean Brock,
23 I believe they lived in Armour, and they brought her to the
24 sessions, or else one of the Tribal social workers brought her
25 to the sessions.

Page 439

1 Q. How frequently did you see her between '94 and '97?
2 A. For the first couple of years I saw her on almost a
3 weekly basis, and then toward 1997 I saw her maybe every other
4 week to maybe once a month until she ended in September.
5 Q. Can you give us a general idea of what a standard
6 counseling session with Rosemary would have involved during
7 that period of time?
8 A. Initially when I would work with anyone who has
9 experienced sexual abuse the important thing to develop rapport
10 and a relationship and a safe and trusting environment. So as
11 a matter of when I started or when I ended, the environment was
12 always that I wanted her to feel safe and trusted, and then we
13 would talk about the issues for which she was brought to
14 therapy.
15 Q. Generally how long would these sessions last?
16 A. About an hour.
17 Q. During your experience with her, did she detail to you in
18 these sessions the abuse that she had incurred?
19 A. Yes, she did.
20   MR. HAUGAARD: For the record I would like to
21 register an objection with regard to the ongoing hearsay which
22 will be presented.
23   THE COURT: You have the objection, but of course as
24 you understand it is overruled.
25 BY MR. HOLMES:

Page 440

1 Q. Did she describe to you in detail what her uncles did to
2 her and what she had seen them do to her cousins?
3 A. Yes.
4 Q. And did she describe acts of sexual abuse both to her and
5 her cousins?
6 A. Yes.
7 Q. During any of these counseling sessions that you had with
8 her between 1994 and 1997 did she ever recant those statements
9 regarding sexual abuse by her uncles?
10 A. No, she did not.
11 Q. Did she ever say they did not happen?
12 A. No, she did not.
13   MR. HOLMES: No further questions.
14   THE COURT: Cross.
15 CROSS EXAMINATION BY MR. WILKA:
16 Q. Can I call you Sister?
17 A. Sure.
18 Q. I have to, I am a Catholic kid.
19 A. That's fine.
20 Q. Rosemary was referred to you, I believe you stated she
21 was referred to you for therapy as a consequence of being
22 sexually abused, correct?
23 A. Correct.
24 Q. And so your function was to provide a safe environment
25 where she could work through events and heal for things that

Page 441

1 had already occurred, correct?

2 A. That's correct.

3 Q. And so your job as a, as her, working with her, was not

4 to determine if abuse had occurred, because for your purposes

5 it had already been established the abuse had occurred,

6 correct?

7 A. Correct.

8 Q. Your job was not to inquire into the disclosure process

9 by which Rosemary may have said that her uncles did a bad thing

10 to her, correct?

11 A. No. What I would do is, in order for her to work through

12 those things, I would have to have some idea of what had

13 happened to her. So part of the therapy in order to help her

14 work through that would be to disclose to me what happened so

15 that I could help her work through that.

16 Q. Yes, to tell you, you know, how the abuse occurred,

17 correct?

18 A. Correct.

19 Q. Let me rephrase that. Your job was not to go in to, for

20 instance, whether or not, or when certain interviews with

21 previous social workers or investigators took place, was it?

22 A. That was not my job.

23 Q. So you didn't, for instance, inquire as to whether she

24 first made a disclosure to Jean Brock or Donna Jordan, did you?

25 A. Actually I did attempt to get the record from the Tribe,

Page 442

1 but I was told that there were no documents in her file.

2 Q. Really? Who told you that?

3 A. The social worker to whom I asked for the records.

4 Q. Did you, and who did you ask, who is the social worker

5 that you talked to?

6 A. Dana Wanahooka, I am sure I am not pronouncing that

7 correctly.

8 Q. That's close enough.

9   MR. WILKA: May I have a moment, Your Honor?

10   THE COURT: Yes.

11 BY MR. WILKA:

12 Q. Did you generate any written reports of your therapy?

13 A. Many.

14 Q. Did you bring those with you today?

15 A. No.

16 Q. Are they at your office in Yankton?

17 A. Yes.

18 Q. Did you ever provide copies of those reports to the

19 United States Attorney's Office?

20 A. No, I did not.

21 Q. Did you ever provide copies of those reports to any law

22 enforcement agencies?

23 A. No, I did not.

24 Q. Did you ever discuss the substance of those reports with

25 the United States Attorney's Office?

Page 443

1 A. Not other than that Rosemary had talked about the abuse

2 and that she had never recanted.

3 Q. So you were specifically asked by the United States

4 Attorney's Office if Rosemary had ever recanted?

5 A. Correct.

6 Q. Were you ever specifically asked by the FBI if Rosemary

7 had ever recanted?

8 A. I don't believe so.

9 Q. Were you ever interviewed by the FBI with regard to this

10 case?

11 A. We had a discussion.

12 Q. When was that?

13 A. I think maybe in March.

14 Q. March of what year, Ma'am?

15 A. Of this year.

16 Q. Sister, I am sorry.

17 A. Of this year.

18 Q. Who was present from the FBI at that discussion?

19 A. Mr. Matt Miller.

20 Q. Did Matt Miller, do you know, make a recording of that

21 discussion?

22 A. No.

23 Q. Do you know if Matt Miller ever made a report, which is,

24 I believe they call them 302's, of that?

25 A. I do not know.

Page 444

1 Q. Did you take any notes during that discussion?

2 A. I did.

3 Q. Did you make any reports of that?

4 A. I did.

5 Q. Would that be part of your general file on Rosemary Rouse

6 that you keep?

7 A. Correct.

8 Q. When is -- Rosemary left your care in 1997?

9 A. Correct.

10 Q. Between 1997 and March of 2001 did you generate any

11 reports regarding Rosemary Rouse?

12 A. The affidavit.

13 Q. And the affidavit you made in this case, did you type

14 that?

15 A. No.

16 Q. Who typed that?

17 A. I presume the office of, that it came from.

18 Q. The United States Attorney's Office?

19 A. Yes.

20 Q. Were you present when they typed it?

21 A. No.

22 Q. How many conversations did you have with them around the

23 time that they typed this affidavit?

24 A. They sent me a copy to look at to make certain that what

25 they wanted me to attest to was correct. I read through it, I

Page 445	Page 447
1 made some corrections, I sent it back. They sent a corrected	1 A. No, I did not.
2 copy.	2 Q. Did you test the accuracy of the allegations against any
3 Q. And then you signed that and sent that back to them?	3 foster home reports?
4 A. Yes.	4 A. No, I did not.
5 Q. Aside from that affidavit was there anything in your --	5 Q. Did you test the accuracy of the allegations against
6 when in 1997 did Rosemary leave your care?	6 other therapists' reports?
7 A. September.	7 A. No, I did not.
8 Q. In between September of 1997 and March of 2001, aside	8 Q. Did you test the accuracy of the allegations against
9 from the affidavit, were there any entries in your file	9 family reports?
10 regarding Rosemary Rouse?	10 A. No, I did not.
11 A. Between what dates, please?	11 Q. So is it fair to say that as you began your counseling
12 Q. September of 1997 and March of 2001, aside from the	12 with Rosemary you presumed the information you received from
13 affidavit, were there any entries in your file regarding	13 others, other than Rosemary, you presumed that to be true as to
14 Rosemary Rouse?	14 the alleged abuse?
15 A. I don't remember.	15 A. I was told that she reported to the authorities, and that
16 Q. And so approximately -- when you made this affidavit,	16 had been reported to social services, and I took that to be the
17 would it be a fair statement that you reviewed the materials	17 truth.
18 between 1994 and 1997 and used that information to make the	18 Q. So that is the presumption you entered in to counseling
19 affidavit that you submitted for this matter?	19 with?
20 A. Yes.	20 A. Correct.
21 Q. So have you had any contact with Rosemary Rouse for the	21 Q. Do you have any idea how long the interview took when you
22 approximately three and a half years between 1997 and -- well,	22 spoke with FBI Agent Matt Miller?
23 between 1997 and today have you had any contact with her?	23 A. What are you talking about?
24 A. No, I have not.	24 Q. When you spoke with Matt Miller in approximately March of
25 MR. WILKA: That's all I have, Your Honor. Thank	25 this year, do you have any idea how long that interview took

Page 446	Page 448
1 you, sister.	1 place?
2 CROSS EXAMINATION BY MR. HAUGAARD:	2 A. It was about an hour.
3 Q. When you first began to meet with Rosemary, how soon	3 Q. And did you observe him make notes?
4 thereafter did you ask for reports from the Tribal Social	4 A. No, I did not.
5 Services?	5 Q. Do you know whether he made notes later?
6 A. What kind of reports?	6 A. No, I do not.
7 Q. Any kind of information to give you background on the	7 Q. Do you know if he tape recorded the session?
8 case?	8 A. No, I do not.
9 A. I couldn't say for sure, maybe -- I couldn't say for	9 Q. As he was speaking with you did he provide information to
10 sure.	10 you about the case itself?
11 Q. When you first met with her what information did you	11 A. Only that there was to be a hearing to determine whether
12 have?	12 a new trial would be held.
13 A. That she had been sexually abused by her uncles, that	13 Q. Did he explain what the basis of that hearing might have
14 they were in prison, and I believe around that time that there	14 been?
15 were attempts to have a new trial.	15 A. I believe that some of the children had withdrawn their
16 Q. When you first met with her?	16 testimony.
17 A. Around about that time.	17 Q. So apparently you had somewhat of a back and forth
18 Q. You began meeting with her back in October of '94, is	18 conversation with Mr. Miller about this case?
19 that correct?	19 A. One or two phone calls.
20 A. Yes.	20 Q. Well, what I am saying is in this interview in March of
21 Q. You don't know when you asked social services for	21 this year you didn't simply answer questions for one hour, did
22 additional reports?	22 you?
23 A. I am sorry, I do not.	23 A. No.
24 Q. Did you test the accuracy of the allegations against any	24 Q. You had a conversation with Mr. Miller about his
25 FBI reports?	25 understanding of the case and your understanding of the case?

Page 449	Page 451
1 A. I wouldn't call it a conversation, he talked, I talked.	1 BY MR. CARTER:
2 Q. Did you make other attempts to obtain reports about this	2 Q. If it weren't for the fact the abuse occurred she
3 case other than the one contact with Tribal Social Services?	3 wouldn't have been there, isn't that correct?
4 A. I did try to contact the counseling center that Rosemary	4 A. Correct.
5 initially went to after she was removed from the home, but I	5 Q. That was your premise?
6 got no reply.	6 A. Correct.
7 Q. So did you pursue it after that?	7 Q. When it comes to that, then you have these meetings and
8 A. No, I did not.	8 these sessions with her, did you ever have any conversations
9 Q. You received no reports from them?	9 with Julia Joseph, or Julia Joseph about this case?
10 A. No, I did not.	10 A. Let's see, around maybe July or August of 1997 I believe
11 Q. Did you make any efforts to contact the family to discuss	11 she was the family placement person who took Rosemary in to her
12 this case with them?	12 care after she was taken from the Brock's.
13 A. Rosemary's mother came to the sessions on occasion.	13 Q. Did you ever make any statement to Julia Joseph to the
14 Q. Did you take opportunity to speak with her about the	14 effect that you didn't even know why Rosemary was there?
15 details of the allegations?	15 A. I never did.
16 A. I took opportunity to see what her attitude was about	16 Q. Your role in this was basically as being a counselor, as
17 what Rosemary had disclosed.	17 I would understand, as opposed to determining where the kids
18 Q. Did your contact with Rosemary end then in September of	18 would reside, is that a fair statement?
19 '97?	19 A. Yes.
20 A. Correct.	20 Q. In these, in the times that you have worked then, were
21 Q. It tapered off over the course of that last six months or	21 working, it was basically Rosemary you worked with, isn't that
22 a year, something like that?	22 correct?
23 A. Probably the last six months.	23 A. That's correct.
24 MR. HAUGAARD: No further questions.	24 Q. Did you find Rosemary to be a naturally talkative child?
25 MR. BINGER: I have no questions.	25 A. No, she was not.

Page 450	Page 452
1 CROSS EXAMINATION BY MR. CARTER:	1 Q. So there really was not a lot said by her in many of
2 Q. Sister, MY name is David Carter, I represent Garfield	2 these sessions, would that be true?
3 Feather. I have a couple of questions for you. You had, I was	3 A. Initially she was very uncomfortable about talking about
4 trying to understand I guess your testimony regarding the	4 the abuse, and as I said earlier, part of my job was to provide
5 social worker. Is it possible that the name you were thinking	5 her with opportunity to trust me so that when the time came
6 of was Honomichl?	6 that she was ready to talk about the abuse she would feel safe
7 A. No, it was not.	7 in doing so.
8 Q. It was not Honomichl, okay. Again, you answered some	8 Q. Could it be that one of the reasons she was uncomfortable
9 questions and I think earlier on from some of the other	9 about talking about it was that it didn't occur?
10 attorneys here about as I understand it when you got involved	10 A. I suppose it could be.
11 with this you were basically doing a counselor role to be	11 Q. You never pursued that?
12 supportive and you basically presumed that the allegations	12 A. I didn't need to.
13 against these uncles were true, is that a fair statement?	13 Q. You didn't need to. As to the interview that you had
14 A. Because they had been imprisoned, yes, I thought that was	14 with the FBI, did you ever see a copy of any written report of
15 probably true.	15 that interview?
16 Q. So when Rosemary came to you, the reason she was there	16 A. No, I did not.
17 was premised, was it not, on the fact that the abuse occurred?	17 MR. CARTER: I have no further questions. I would
18 A. That's correct.	18 again like to ask we be provided a copy of that interview from
19 Q. So would it not then be natural for her as part of this	19 the FBI records if possible.
20 therapy session to, as long as she is going along with this and	20 THE COURT: Well, this isn't ongoing discovery, but
21 participating in it, is that sort of the underlying premise,	21 what is the government's response?
22 isn't it, that it occurred, otherwise she wouldn't be there?	22 MR. HOLMES: Your Honor, there was no request for
23 MR. HOLMES: Objection, compound question.	23 disclosure made by counsel prior to this hearing. But
24 THE COURT: Overruled.	24 regarding this witness, there are no witness statements that
25 A. I am sorry, would you say the question again?	25 were generated from that interview. The only thing that was

Page 453

1　generated is the affidavit which has been submitted to the
2　Court and Counsel.
3　　THE COURT: Very well, any redirect?
4　　MR. HOLMES: Yes, Your Honor.
5　REDIRECT EXAMINATION BY MR. HOLMES:
6　Q. Doctor, you said that there were times when the mother
7　was present during some of these counseling sessions and you
8　had some discussions with her. What do you recall her attitude
9　to be regarding these allegations?
10　A. Rosemary's mother did not believe that the children had
11　been sexually molested. She felt that the children had been
12　molesting each other, and that when they were caught they were
13　afraid of being spanked and therefore blamed the uncles.
14　　MR. HOLMES: No further questions.
15　　MR. WILKA: I have no questions.
16　RECROSS EXAMINATION BY MR. HAUGAARD:
17　Q. In a therapeutic session such as you are engaged in with
18　Rosemary over a long period of time, don't you believe it would
19　be vitally important for you to test the accuracy, the
20　truthfulness of the allegations to ensure that you are not
21　counseling someone in a false direction?
22　　MR. HOLMES: Objection, outside the scope of
23　redirect.
24　　THE COURT: Sustained.
25　　MR. HAUGAARD: No further questions.

Page 454

1　　MR. BINGER: Nothing.
2　　MR. CARTER: Nothing else.
3　　THE COURT: Thank you, you may step down Sister, or
4　Doctor. I am a little bit of a loss as to which title to use,
5　but thank you. Call your next witness.

Page 455

INDEX TO WITNESS

THRISTA ROUSE

DIRECT EXAMINATION BY MR. HAUGAARD 231
CROSS EXAMINATION BY MR. HOLMES 256
REDIRECT EXAMINATION BY MR. HAUGAARD 271
REDIRECT EXAMINATION BY MR. HAUGAARD 276

LUCRITIA ROUSE

DIRECT EXAMINATION BY MR. HAUGAARD 277
CROSS EXAMINATION BY MR. HOLMES 294
REDIRECT EXAMINATION BY MR. HAUGAARD 302
REDIRECT EXAMINATION BY MR. HAUGAARD 307

ROSEMARY ROUSE

DIRECT EXAMINATION BY MR. HAUGAARD 308
CROSS EXAMINATION BY MR. HOLMES 316
REDIRECT EXAMINATION BY MR. HAUGAARD 324

DERRICK WESTON

DIRECT EXAMINATION BY MR. HAUGAARD 327
CROSS EXAMINATION BY MR. HOLMES 332

JESSICA ROUSE

DIRECT EXAMINATION BY MR. HAUGAARD 335
CROSS EXAMINATION BY MR. HOLMES 343
REDIRECT EXAMINATION BY MR. HAUGAARD 350
REDIRECT EXAMINATION BY MR. HAUGAARD 353

MAGGIE BRUCK

REDIRECT EXAMINATION BY MR. WILKA 354
RECROSS EXAMINATION BY MR. SEILER 371

Page 456

CHERYL FRIDEL

DIRECT EXAMINATION BY MR. HOLMES 400
CROSS EXAMINATION BY MR. WILKA 415
CROSS EXAMINATION BY MR. HAUGAARD 423
CROSS EXAMINATION BY MR. BINGER 424
CROSS EXAMINATION BY MR. CARTER 429

MICHAELEEN MUHOVICH

DIRECT EXAMINATION BY MR. HOLMES 437
CROSS EXAMINATION BY MR. WILKA 440
CROSS EXAMINATION BY MR. HAUGAARD 446
CROSS EXAMINATION BY MR. CARTER 450
REDIRECT EXAMINATION BY MR. HOLMES 453
RECROSS EXAMINATION BY MR. HAUGAARD 453

INDEX TO GOVERNMENT EXHIBITS

Exhibit 8 Marked 322
　　8 Offered 322
　　8 Received 322

Exhibit 19 Marked 406
　　19 Offered 407
　　19 Received 407

Exhibit 20 Marked 414
　　20 Offered 415
　　20 Received 415

MISCELLANEOUS INDEX
Movant Rests 396

Page 455

```
 1        UNITED STATES DISTRICT COURT
 2        DISTRICT OF SOUTH DAKOTA
 3           SOUTHERN DIVISION
   . . . . . . . . . . . . . . . . . .
 4                              *
   UNITED STATES OF AMERICA,     *
 5                              *
         Plaintiff,     Volume III
 6                              *
      -vs-              *   CR. 94-40015
 7                     *  MOTION FOR NEW TRIAL
   DESMOND ROUSE, JESSIE ROUSE   *
 8  GARFIELD FEATHER, RUSSELL    *
   HUBBELING,                    *
 9                              *
10         Defendants.  *
11  . . . . . . . . . . . . . . . . . .
12
13 BEFORE:        The Honorable Lawrence L. Piersol
                  Chief United States District Judge
14                For the District of South Dakota
                  Sioux Falls, South Dakota
15
16
   PROCEEDINGS:   The above-entitled matter came on for
17                hearing on the 5th day of September, 2001
                  commencing at the hour of 9:00 a.m. in the
18                courtroom of the Federal Building, Sioux
                  Falls, South Dakota.
19
   Proceedings recorded by mechanical stenography, transcript
20 produced by computer.
21
22
23
24
25
```

Page 456

```
 1 APPEARANCES:
 2    Mr. Randy Seiler
      Ms. Michelle Tapken
 3    Mr. Dennis Holmes
      Assistant United States Attorneys
 4    Pierre, South Dakota
      Sioux Falls, South Dakota
 5
         Attorneys for the United States;
 6
 7    Mr. John Wilka
      Attorney at Law
 8    Sioux Falls, South Dakota
 9       Attorney for Desmond Rouse;
10
      Mr. Steven Binger
11    Attorney at Law
      Sioux Falls, South Dakota
12
         Attorney for Jessie Rouse;
13
14    Mr. David Carter
      Attorney at Law
15    Sioux Falls, South Dakota
16       Attorney for Garfield Feather;
17
      Mr. Steve Haugaard
18    Attorney at Law
      Sioux Falls, South Dakota
19
         Attorney for Russell Hubbeling.
20
21
22
23
24
25
```

Page 457

```
 1  (Recess from 10:50 until 11:00)
 2       THE COURT:  Call your next witness.
 3       MR. HOLMES:  Before we proceed, I would like the
 4  record to reflect I provided counsel a copy of the tape
 5  recorded interview with Cheryl Fridel that occurred on December
 6  10th, 1999 between her and the FBI agents.
 7       THE COURT:  Very well.  Call your next witness.
 8       MR. SEILER:  Dr. David Corwin.
 9
10           DR. DAVID CORWIN,
11  called as a witness, being first duly sworn, testified and said
12  as follows:
13
14  DIRECT EXAMINATION BY MR. SEILER:
15  Q.  Would you introduce yourself to the Court, please?
16  A.  My name is David Corwin.
17  Q.  How do you spell your last name?
18  A.  C-O-R-W-I-N.
19  Q.  Where do you currently live?
20  A.  I live in the Salt Lake City Utah region.
21  Q.  Are you currently employed in private practice, or with
22  any agency or organization?
23  A.  I am employed by the University of Utah School of
24  Medicine.
25  Q.  In what capacity?
```

Page 458

```
 1  A.  Professor of pediatrics, and specifically I am the
 2  medical director of Primary Children's Center for Safe and
 3  Healthy Families at Primary Children's Medical Center.
 4  Q.  As the medical director for the Primary Children's Center
 5  for Safe and Healthy families what are your responsibilities
 6  and what do you do?
 7  A.  I do a variety of things.  I am ultimately responsible
 8  for the quality of the work that we do clinically in the
 9  medical diagnosis and evaluation of suspected child abuse in
10  the hospital and outpatient settings.  I am also responsible
11  for program development, for liaison to the community in a
12  variety of ways for the development of research efforts within
13  the department.  Supervision of the physicians who work for us,
14  and work with the hospital management with the hospital
15  employees that are involved.
16  Q.  What is the primary focus and goal of the children's
17  center in terms of its operation?
18  A.  The goals are to try to do the best to prevent, identify,
19  treat and educate about child abuse and neglect, and to promote
20  healthy families.  In my previous answer I left off the one
21  function that I am responsible for that I am doing here today,
22  and that is I also have duties directly for providing clinical
23  service in terms of evaluating children in our treatment
24  program who may benefit from psychotropic medication because of
25  my credentials as a child psychiatrist, but I am also, I head
```

Page 459

1 up our forensic evaluation teams that review and consult on
2 legal matters related to child abuse and neglect.
3 Q. Let's talk a little bit about your educational
4 background, Doctor. Would you briefly summarize for the Court,
5 please, your education?
6 A. Sure. I received a Bachelor of Science degree from the
7 University of Michigan, basically premed, major in zoology;
8 medical degree from Michigan State college of Human Medicine.
9 I trained in a psychiatry and medicine internship and did a
10 psychiatry residency at Sepulveda at the UCLA-VA Medical
11 Center. Did a fellowship in child psychology at the UCLA
12 Neuropsychiatric Institute. I finished my training in child
13 psychology in December of 1981, became board certified in
14 psychiatry in 1981, board certified in child psychiatry in
15 1982, and board certified in forensic psychiatry in 1998. It
16 was during my training in child psychiatry that I was offered
17 the opportunity to focus on the problem of child sexual abuse
18 and to serve as co-director of the family support program,
19 which was a relatively new effort in the child psychiatry
20 outpatient department, which worked with sexually abused
21 children and their families. That was when I really began the
22 major part of my focus on child abuse, child sexual abuse.
23 Q. Are you licensed as a doctor in any states?
24 A. Yes, I am licensed in California, Ohio and Utah.
25 Q. In addition to your position with the Primary Children's

Page 460

1 Center for Safe and Healthy Families, would you just again
2 briefly for the Court summarize your professional background
3 and work experience?
4 A. Well, after finishing my training in child psychiatry at
5 UCLA I entered private practice. I was in private practice
6 first in Southern California, then about a year later I moved
7 to Northern California to a community called Orinda which is in
8 the east San Francisco Bay area. I continued in practice up
9 until 1990 when I joined the department of psychiatry at
10 Washington University in St. Louis, and I worked there in a
11 variety of capacities first as director of the inpatient unit
12 at St. Louis Children's Hospital. I established the Washington
13 University Center for Child and Family Development. I worked
14 for a year as medical director of Hawthorn Children's
15 Psychiatric Hospital, which was the state hospital for the
16 eastern part of Missouri for children and adolescents as part
17 of an affiliation between that state hospital and our
18 department of psychiatry and the introduction of our training
19 programs for residents and fellows in to that hospital. Then
20 in 1994 I moved to University of Cincinnati and Cincinnati
21 Children's Hospital where I worked in the childhood trust,
22 which was a joint effort of the children's hospital, concerned
23 citizens in the community, and the department of psychiatry.
24 In the childhood trust I became the director of child forensic
25 psychiatry, I established the forensic training institute

Page 461

1 within the childhood trust. And then in 1999 I accepted my
2 present position at the University of Utah, and because I am
3 employed within the department of pediatrics I am a professor
4 of pediatrics, even though my training is psychiatry, child
5 psychiatry, forensic psychiatry.
6 Q. Have you also been involved in publishing a number of
7 articles in your field throughout the course of your career?
8 A. Yes, I have. I have published a number of articles and
9 various other book reviews, commentaries, things mostly
10 focusing on child abuse, child sexual abuse, in that range. I
11 think there is twenty.
12   MR. SEILER: May I approach the witness?
13   THE COURT: You may.
14
15   (Exhibit 21 marked For identification.)
16
17 BY MR. SEILER:
18 Q. I show you what's been marked as Government Exhibit 21
19 and ask you if you can identify that for me?
20 A. It is my Vita in the University of Utah School of
21 Medicine format.
22 Q. Does your curriculum vitae more fully set forth your
23 background, your experience, your education, training,
24 publications, and other educational and professional
25 experiences?

Page 462

1 A. Yes, it does.
2   MR. SEILER: Your Honor, we offer Government Exhibit
3 21.
4   MR. WILKA: No objection.
5   THE COURT: Exhibit 21 is received. Just for my own
6 information, because I was looking through the one previously
7 that had been supplied with the government's witness list,
8 docket number 463 here that was filed in January of 2001, and
9 must be that the format of, maybe this one is updated, because
10 the one we got before had not been updated with regard to
11 articles since 1998, I don't think, and this other one has 262
12 listings, the first one had 247, is that the difference?
13   THE WITNESS: Right, I updated it for the purpose of
14 what is called RPT retention and review by the University this
15 summer, so this version is current through the end of August.
16   THE COURT: This version being Exhibit 21?
17   THE WITNESS: University of Utah format, yes, Exhibit
18 21.
19   THE COURT: Exhibit 21 is received.
20 BY MR. SEILER:
21 Q. Now, Doctor, you are working in both the academic field
22 and the practice or clinical field, is that correct?
23 A. Correct. I am a professor of pediatrics and teach, and I
24 am involved in the supervision and guidance of residents, and
25 medical students, and other professionals who have interest or

Page 463

1 concern about child abuse and neglect, but I am also involved
2 clinically as a child psychiatrist in terms of evaluating
3 children in our treatment program who have a history of child
4 abuse, and I am involved in doing forensic evaluations, so that
5 is the clinical side of my work.
6 Q. I want to talk a little bit about that clinical
7 experience and forensic experience. Would you again briefly
8 outline for the Court some of the experiences that you have
9 been involved in in terms of have you represented and testified
10 for both the prosecution and the defense previously?
11 A. Yes, I have.
12 Q. Again in terms of the clinical and forensic side of your
13 professional background, what do you do in those areas?
14 A. Well, I am generally asked to look at cases involving
15 either suspected or known instances of abuse, and to look at a
16 variety of issues ranging and dependent upon the forum in which
17 I am being asked to look at it, and those forums range from
18 juvenile court to family court, sometimes criminal court,
19 administrative hearings, some military tribunals.
20 Q. Have you testified in court previously?
21 A. Yes, I have.
22 Q. As an expert witness?
23 A. Yes.
24 Q. Do you know in approximately how many different
25 jurisdictions or states?

Page 464

1 A. It is many. I think, I was going across the weather map
2 in USA Today yesterday trying to remember, I think it is 27 or
3 28 states, and the District of Columbia. I have also worked in
4 Panama for the U.S. Army when they were still there. And I
5 have worked on cases in Canada as well. Though I have not
6 testified in Canada, I have worked on the cases and submitted
7 reports and the cases have been settled.
8 Q. You said submitted reports. Some of these instances you
9 have been retained by the plaintiff, some by the defendant, in
10 some cases the prosecution, some cases the defense, and in
11 other cases you were actually retained by the Court?
12 A. Correct. Court appointed in many of the situations,
13 particularly in the family law matters it is my preference to
14 be court appointed.
15 Q. As part of your academic qualifications and your teaching
16 responsibilities do you also stay current with the updated
17 literature in this area?
18 A. I do my best, although it is, has changed over these last
19 20, 25 years from a trickle to a torrent, and so I do my best
20 at this point.
21 Q. Do you have any experience in cases involving
22 recantation?
23 A. Yes, I do.
24 Q. Again would you briefly summarize that experience, and
25 what capacity?

Page 465

1 A. I have in the course of doing my evaluations, and in
2 treatment cases, and in the course of my career I have worked
3 with a number of cases in which there have been recantations,
4 and so that is my clinical experience. I am also involved in
5 various efforts like multi-disciplinary teams reviewing cases.
6 I did that first at UCLA, then I did it at Oakland Children's
7 Hospital when I was in private practice, I continued that. I
8 chaired the child abuse committee at St. Louis Children's, and
9 I am involved in those efforts at Primary Children's Medical
10 Center in Salt Lake City. So I have been familiar, both
11 directly in cases I have worked on, I have secondarily been
12 present and party to consultations reviewing case history and
13 cases that are being evaluated, and I followed the literature
14 on that topic, and I have testified with regard to recantation.
15 Q. Based on the totality of that experience, as you say a
16 review of the literature, your actual clinical involvement, and
17 consultation in this area, are there factors that have been
18 identified, Doctor, both in the literature and in your own
19 experience in working with child sexual abuse that impact or
20 affect the issue of recantation in children?
21 A. Yes.
22 Q. And do you have knowledge of those factors?
23 A. Yes.
24 Q. Again, is there literature in this area that talks
25 generally and identifies again factors that impact the issue of

Page 466

1 recantation?
2 A. Yes.
3 Q. We have heard testimony within the last couple of days
4 that efforts have been made to conduct a search in this area
5 about whether family or societal pressures may impact
6 recantation in some form, and that person was unable to find
7 any. Did you have an opportunity to review the literature in
8 this area to see if you could identify some?
9 A. Yes.
10 Q. Did you do that?
11 A. Yes, I did.
12 Q. Were you able to identify a number of articles that
13 address these issues, again that is the issue of recantation in
14 children who have been sexually abused?
15 A. Yes.
16 Q. When we talk about the factors, is your opinion in part
17 based upon the identification of these factors currently in the
18 literature?
19 A. Yes. My opinion about what these factors are, to be
20 clear about what that opinion relates to.
21 Q. What are some of the articles that you have reviewed with
22 respect to the issue of recantation by children who have
23 previously been sexually abused?
24 A. Well, they follow two or possibly three categories. The
25 first are theoretical and clinical articles that are based on

Page 467

1 observations of cases, and consultation. There are several
2 articles like that. They go in to greater depth about the
3 dynamics, what is happening around the recantations, more
4 descriptions, they are more descriptive. The second class of
5 articles are those that are research studies which, along with
6 other facts and things that they were looking at, they included
7 information about recantation, and there is eight that I
8 reviewed in that category. Then there is a third category
9 which I would call scholarly reviews of that entire literature,
10 and consensus guideline documents, and there is two in that
11 category. Perhaps those would be two separate categories,
12 scholarly review and then consensus guidelines.
13 Q. When you talk about consensus guidelines, what does that
14 mean?
15 A. Well, consensus development guidelines is the process of
16 trying to look at a whole body of literature and knowledge
17 about a particular area of practice, and then to begin to
18 articulate what is known and what is seen as best practice for
19 that particular area. And then to begin drafting descriptions
20 of that and submit it for review of the large body of
21 clinicians and researchers who are knowledgeable about that
22 area. And then go through an iterative process of refining
23 that, including the holding usually of public meetings, forums
24 at professional society meetings where those are discussed and
25 different viewpoints are heard. And then finally after all

Page 468

1 that process is gone through and the document has been revised
2 numerous times, it is submitted to the authoritative governing
3 body of the organization, and approved or not approved. And I
4 have first hand familiarity with this process, because I was
5 the person who developed that process for the American
6 Professional society on the Abuse of Children, I chaired the
7 guidelines committees for that organization after it was
8 founded. And then I also contributed to the development of the
9 current practice parameters for the American Academy of Child
10 and Adolescent Psychiatry of which I am a member.
11 Q. Again these consensus guidelines then are basically the
12 work of the field generally, and do they identify factors again
13 that are present in the area of recantation?
14 A. Right, and specifically what I am referring to in that is
15 the practice parameters addressing forensic evaluation of
16 children and adolescents who may have been physically or
17 sexually abused, which was published in 1997 in the Journal of
18 the American Academy of Child and Adolescent Psychiatry, that
19 does have a section that addresses recantation, both addresses
20 it in a text prose and it addresses it in an outline format.
21 Q. Again the literature that you reviewed I asked you to
22 submit to us so we could make copies for the Court and counsel,
23 is that correct?
24 A. That's correct.
25   MR. SEILER: Your Honor, with the Court's permission,

Page 469

1 I will just leave copies of the articles that he has referred
2 and consulted with respect to his testimony, I have copies for
3 defense counsel also.
4   THE COURT: Yes, thank you.
5 BY MR. SEILER:
6 Q. In the literature that you reviewed, Doctor, is there any
7 mention of recantation rates with respect to cases in which
8 there have been a high degree of physical evidence, including
9 medical evidence?
10 A. Yes. A couple of the studies did a sub group analysis of
11 those cases that had independent high levels of corroboration,
12 like sexually transmitted diseases or physical findings, and
13 one of the studies also used confessions and court convictions.
14 So there have been studies that attempt to look at just the
15 highest independently, highest probable independently
16 corroborated cases. Shall I say what they found?
17 Q. Yes, sir, what did they find?
18 A. What they found is a higher rate --
19   MR. WILKA: Objection, foundation.
20   THE COURT: Overruled.
21 A. What they found was a higher rate of recantation in those
22 subgroups. And I think probably the best discussion of that
23 that I have seen is the discussion in the scholarly review of
24 all of that literature by Tom Lyon who is a law professor from
25 the University of Southern California and also is a

Page 470

1 psychologist trained at Stanford. But he discusses that whole
2 literature and noted that fact, which seems counter intuitive,
3 but then pointed out that the most likely reason for the higher
4 rates of recantation in the most certain of child sexual abuse
5 cases has to do with the fact that if a child is tentative, or
6 recants during investigation, or pre-investigation process, or
7 time, that case of child sexual abuse or possible, probable,
8 will not be categorized as a case. It will not be
9 substantiated, probably will not be prosecuted, and so it is
10 only that group of children are only found in the literature
11 among those cases that have independent corroboration, the rest
12 of them are not included.
13 Q. Is there generally a recantation rate that was arrived at
14 or mentioned in the literature with respect to these kinds of
15 cases where there is a high degree of corroboration or medical
16 evidence?
17 A. The two that were limited to medical evidence, that
18 focused primarily upon that, that is Gordon and Jaudes 1996
19 publication.
20 Q. How do you spell Jaudes?
21 A. I am hoping I am pronouncing it right. It is
22 J-A-U-D-E-S.
23 Q. Okay.
24 A. It listed for the fourteen cases among their larger
25 sample the cases that had sexually transmitted diseases, and

Page 471

1 they were comparing interviews done at the emergency room when
2 the physical exam was done to a later investigative interview,
3 21 percent of those children who were with sexually transmitted
4 diseases recanted, did not reaffirm the, their description of
5 the sexual abuse at the later investigative interview. The
6 other study that includes analysis of the subgroup was Elliott
7 and Briere, published in 1994, and that was based on a large
8 series of cases seen out at the UCLA Harbor Medical Center, and
9 they looked at 118 cases with external evidence of abuse, and
10 those children were seen between '92 and '93, subgroup of 399
11 seen in that clinic, and they had a 17 percent rate of
12 recantation.
13 Q. You also reviewed articles by Dr. Summit and Sorenson and
14 Snow with respect to a process that children go through in
15 terms of the disclosure of sexual abuse?
16 A. Yes.
17 Q. Does recantation play a factor, is recantation mentioned
18 in their literature and research regarding this process that
19 children go through?
20 A. Yes.
21 Q. What were the findings generally with respect to
22 recantation?
23   MR. WILKA: I will object to foundation on that one,
24 Your Honor.
25   THE COURT: What basis?

Page 472

1   MR. WILKA: On Summit and Snow. I mean -- well, I
2 will leave it for cross examination. I withdraw it.
3   THE COURT: Alright, go ahead.
4 A. Summit's article is the earliest in this series, 1983,
5 published in Child Abuse and Neglect, and he addressed
6 recantation as one of the elements of what the article is
7 entitled The Child Sexual Abuse Accommodation Syndrome. And it
8 was based on his experience in serving as a consultant to a
9 variety of treatment, private, non-profit organizations in the
10 community of Los Angeles, and a large number of cases, I think
11 in excess 3,000 he once testified in a deposition. That he had
12 observed this phenomena, and he talked about principally three
13 different factors that he had observed in these case reviews
14 and consultations. One of those factors being a desire to
15 preserve the family. Another factor being the consequences of
16 disclosure, all of the things that happen once a disclosure is
17 made from the investigations to being removal from the homes,
18 and adverse consequences to both the child and family members,
19 others. Then he also addressed direct pressure from the mother
20 to recant. He was looking primarily at intra-familial child
21 sexual abuse at that time. So he was focused in that in his
22 discussion of recantation.
23 BY R. SEILER:
24 Q. That was Dr. Summit?
25 A. That is Dr. Summit, 1983. Sorenson and Snow published in

Page 473

1 1991 in Child Welfare, they had a series of cases which they
2 had direct clinical experience or forensic experience with over
3 a period of years, and I think the years on that one were '85
4 to mid 1989. There were what they called a high probability
5 subgroup of 630 consecutive cases, 116 cases that had some form
6 of independent corroboration. And they looked at these 116
7 what they called high probability cases, and they identified a
8 number of factors which are included in I think it is table, or
9 figure 5 from that article. Pressure from the perpetrator
10 being one; pressure from the family being the second; negative
11 personal consequences to the child being the third; videotaping
12 being the fourth; retelling the parents being fifth; judicial
13 proceedings being the sixth; and investigatory efforts by
14 police or CPS being the last category or type of reason for
15 recantation that they identified in the cases that they had.
16 And it was I think 22 percent of that 116 cases, 93 percent of
17 which reaffirmed.
18   THE COURT: I didn't understand the 93 percent
19 reaffirming.
20   THE WITNESS: Of the 22 percent who recanted of the
21 116, 93 percent of the 22 percent reaffirmed over time.
22 BY MR. SEILER:
23 Q. And again with respect to the literature you reviewed, is
24 there any information or indication that family support plays
25 any sort of role with respect to the issue of recantation by

Page 474

1 children who have been sexually abused?
2 A. Yes. It is often noted in the discussion and in some of
3 the reasons given for recantation, but there is one article
4 that had the methodology that allowed that to be looked at, and
5 that was Elliott and Briere's series of cases from the Harbor
6 UCLA Medical Center, and they specifically in their article on
7 page 271 in the last sentence or so from the first paragraph on
8 that page noted that finally, children with nonsupportive
9 mothers were more likely to recant their original disclosure of
10 abuse, 15.4 percent versus 3.3 percent. And then they have the
11 statistical information that supported it. And to be removed
12 from their mother's custody following the evaluation, 31
13 percent versus 3.2 percent.
14   THE COURT: That seems to be the one article I don't
15 have, let me look again.
16   THE WITNESS: It is entitled Evaluations of Older
17 Children: Disclosures and Symptomatology.
18   MR. WILKA: If I may, that was in the literature
19 provided by Dr. Bruck.
20   MR. SEILER: There was some duplication, Your Honor,
21 I think three articles that had been in the information
22 provided by Dr. Bruck, and we did not copy those three.
23   THE COURT: Alright, thank you. I have it now. Page
24 what?
25   THE WITNESS: It is on page 271. It is at the top,

Page 475

1 the first paragraph showing on that page, and the last sentence
2 in that paragraph.
3   THE COURT: Finally, children with nonsupportive
4 mother's?
5   THE WITNESS: Correct, and continuing on to the end
6 of that paragraph.
7   THE COURT: Thank you.
8 BY MR. SEILER:
9 Q. Are there articles again that you reviewed in preparation
10 for your testimony here this morning, Dr. Corwin, which we have
11 not mentioned?
12 A. Well, as I did state there are eight which have data. We
13 have, I didn't mention them by author, I talked about them as a
14 group. They have all been provided.
15 Q. Would you just briefly identify for purposes of the
16 record the eight by author then or title?
17 A. The first, this is in order of descending frequency of
18 recantation noted. I ranked them in that order just for my own
19 review. First one is Gonzalez Waterman, Kelly, McCord and
20 Oliveri, 1993. The next is Sorenson and Snow, 1991. The next
21 is Gordon and Jaudes, 1996. Then Elliott and Briere, 1994.
22 Gries, Goh and Cavanaugh, 1996 is number five. Number six is
23 Dybee and Mowbrey, and I did not have a copy of that one with
24 me. I saw it cited in the Lyon critique. Number seven is
25 Jones and McGraw, 1987. Number eight is Bradley and Wood,

Page 476

1 1996. Those are the empirical articles. Then of the other
2 references or articles cited which had explanations for the
3 recantation or factors, the first cited, and I don't have this
4 with me is Sgroi, 1982, that was out of a handbook. We have
5 already talked about Summit, 1983. Rieser, 1991. Sorenson and
6 Snow, 1991. Again Gonzales, Waterman, Kelly, McCord, they
7 cited some of the reasons. Then finally the AACAP Practice
8 Parameters, which I believe have been copied. And then the
9 last, the same being Tom Lyons scholarly review entitled
10 Scientific Support for Expert Testimony on Child Sexual Abuse
11 Accommodation Syndrome in the version that I have dated
12 January, 1998, and it is to be published in November of this
13 year in a book.
14 Q. All of these articles that we have been discussing
15 basically address the issue of recantation and the various
16 factors that may impact recantation or talk about issues with
17 respect to recantation?
18 A. Yes.
19 Q. Taking the totality of those articles and the information
20 that are contained therein, Doctor, and again based upon your
21 own personal experience as a clinician and being involved as
22 the medical director, I want to talk specifically about the
23 factors, and identify the factors that impact recantation in
24 children who have been sexually abused. Were you able to
25 identify factors, and what are those factors?

Page 477

1 A. Yes, I have taken each of the articles and extracted the
2 various factors that they cite in the articles, and then I
3 grouped them together into logical categories. And they really
4 break down in to three major groups. With a fourth that is not
5 really a group, but I will describe that as I get to it. The
6 first category is direct pressure from parents or family
7 members or perpetrators, or other influence from those
8 individuals. And that is cited in all six of the publications
9 that go in to detail about factors contributing to recantation.
10 That is the most commonly, most frequently cited explanation,
11 or factor.
12 Q. Most frequently cited factor for why children recant?
13 A. Yes.
14 Q. Again that is direct pressure from family members, the
15 perpetrators?
16 A. Or other influence related to the family and the accused.
17 The second category being consequences of disclosure. And that
18 includes the investigation, removal, the Court proceedings, and
19 the other kinds of adverse consequences to children and
20 families that go along with disclosures of child sexual abuse.
21 Q. For example, children being removed by social services
22 from the home and being placed in foster care or some other
23 group care facility?
24 A. Correct.
25 Q. That would fall under this general factor?

Page 478

1 A. Correct, yes. Consequences of disclosure. I would, I
2 categorize these first two as external influences. So these
3 are things happening around the child. And the third category
4 I am describing as psychological or internal, and that has to
5 do with the various emotions and reactions and feelings the
6 children have about these situations. Those can include guilt,
7 shame, denial, fear, avoidance, and other internal motivations
8 and influences upon them. And I have seen that as well as the
9 others, I have seen that directly in cases that I have worked
10 on.
11   MR. WILKA: I object to that last part as
12 non-responsive, they are asking about the literature, Your
13 Honor.
14   THE COURT: I am going to allow the comment to stand,
15 however. Go ahead.
16 A. And then although the bulk of this literature addresses
17 situations in which abuse is probable or the substantiated
18 physical findings, et cetera, the broader look at the whole
19 phenomena such as is done in the Guidelines of the Practice
20 Parameters from the American Academy of Child and Adolescent
21 Psychiatry includes, among things to be considered in the
22 context of a recantation, the fact that perhaps the abuse did
23 not occur. That another factor is the motivation to set the
24 record straight.
25 BY MR. SEILER:

Page 479

1 Q. Again are there other factors, this is the first group
2 you are talking about?
3 A. This is, these are the articles that are more
4 descriptive, include descriptions of factors they have seen
5 operating with regard to recantation, and which is a subgroup
6 of six, six articles which I have already cited for the Court.
7 And there are more fine points within those major categories,
8 but those are the major categories, and the fine points are
9 included in the articles.
10 Q. I was under the impression that you talked about three
11 different general areas or categories with respect to the
12 literature and recantation, and this was the first?
13 A. What is this that you are referring to?
14 Q. Let's go on. From your own involvement and experience as
15 a clinician, and being involved in forensic interviews, and
16 working with children who have been sexually abused, does your
17 own experience also bear this out in terms of these factors?
18 A. Yes. I have seen each of these categories and variations
19 upon them in cases that I have direct clinical experience with.
20 Q. So your own experience would corroborate or reaffirm
21 basically the factors that are contained in the literature?
22 A. Yes, what I just described is consistent with my clinical
23 and forensic experience in working with cases of child sexual
24 abuse.
25 Q. Where, for example, would continuing or ongoing contact

Page 480

1 with the defendant or the abuser in the form of like telephone
2 calls or letters fall within these factors that we previously
3 discussed?
4 A. Well, it certainly could fall within the first one.
5 Q. Direct pressure from family members?
6 A. Or influence.
7   MR. WILKA: I object to that last question as
8 leading, Your Honor.
9   THE COURT: The interjection was leading, sustained.
10 BY MR. SEILER:
11 Q. The question, I think, Dr. Corwin, which of the factors
12 would information like direct contact with the abuser through
13 telephone calls or letters fall, under which factor?
14 A. It would fall under the first directly, and could fall
15 indirectly under the third in terms of it could move the child
16 to feel some of those emotions that have been associated with
17 recantation.
18 Q. Are there any other factors we have not discussed that
19 may impact upon the issue of recantation of children who have
20 been sexually abused?
21 A. Those are the major categories, we have talked about
22 them.
23 Q. I want you to assume, Dr. Corwin, the following facts for
24 purposes of the next question. Assume that the children who
25 have recanted have had direct contact with the people who have

Page 481

1 abused them via telephone calls from prison, via being told
2 about letters from prison, and also receiving letters from the
3 abusers. What role would that play in terms of a child's
4 recantation?
5 A. Well, it would fall primarily under the first category,
6 parental and family pressure. And it could also be related to
7 the induction of some of the third category, those related to
8 the internal feelings of the child, guilt, shame, sense of
9 responsibility, loyalty, other internal feelings.
10 Q. Again I want you to assume that the children who have
11 been sexually abused have been returned to a nonsupportive
12 family including a mother and a grandmother who are
13 nonsupportive, who testified at the trial, and who believe that
14 the abuse did not occur. What impact would that have on
15 children as far as recantation is concerned?
16 A. It is within the first category, and it would be very
17 difficult in my opinion as a clinician, child psychiatrist, for
18 most children to maintain an allegation of sexual abuse in the
19 context of an unsupportive family.
20   MR. WILKA: I object to foundation for that last
21 part, and also non-responsive to the question.
22   THE COURT: Overruled.
23 BY MR. SEILER:
24 Q. Were you done with the answer, Doctor?
25 A. Yes.

Page 482

1 Q. Again I want to go one step further, and I want you to
2 assume that the child or the children may actually have been
3 told that they need to lie or change their testimony, their
4 trial testimony where they outlined the abuse. What impact
5 would that have upon the child as far as their ability to
6 maintain the recantation?
7 A. Again it is within the first category, and it is a notch
8 considerable higher than the previous question. Again, given
9 that children are dependent upon their families when they are
10 in the care of their families, it would be a very unusual child
11 who could withstand that and not recant.
12 Q. Again assume this fact, that the abused child had actual
13 knowledge of a thirty year prison sentence, and that they had
14 been told by family, trusted family members, like a grandmother
15 or a mother, that the abusers had been sentenced to thirty
16 years in prison. What would be the likely impact upon the
17 child as far as recantation?
18 A. Well, it would depend upon the child's feeling probably
19 toward that individual or individuals, and it would depend upon
20 their relationships with those around them, and the attitudes
21 of that family. But, you know, I would think that that could
22 be a factor that would cause a child to think boy, I hate to
23 feel responsible for this, and I can change all this through
24 recanting. I think there is, children tend to have a sense
25 that they are the center of the universe, the sense of

Page 483

1 omnipotence, and they tend to take on more sense of
2 responsibility than is their rightful share, so that also
3 contributes to their vulnerability to feeling responsible.
4   MR. WILKA: I object to that last part as
5 non-responsive and move to strike, Your Honor.
6   THE COURT: Overruled.
7 BY MR. SEILER:
8 Q. Doctor, for purposes of the next question again I want
9 you to assume that, the following facts, that the children had
10 previously been in foster care or group home settings during
11 the trial, and following that the process of returning the
12 child to the home had to be done in, including visits by mother
13 and grandmothers who were nonsupportive, and that therapy that
14 they had previously been involved in had been terminated.
15 Again what would be the impact on the child as far as the issue
16 of recantation, being returned from a group home, foster home
17 setting, and being taken from therapy and placed in that
18 setting?
19 A. If the family, I think this is in your hypothetical, if
20 the family is unsupportive, and in the group home and the
21 therapy they were being supported, then that would be a
22 substantial shift in the environment around them, and it would
23 be likely to precipitate recantation.
24 Q. What is the impact of no supportive or ongoing therapy,
25 or working with professional counselors with respect to the

Page 484

1 issue of recantation?
2   MR. WILKA: Object to foundation as to time, Your
3 Honor.
4   THE COURT: I think the question is more general than
5 that, I don't think it is case specific at this point.
6 Overruled.
7 A. Resonating throughout the literature addressing
8 recantation is this observation that for children to maintain
9 and to continue to describe having been sexually abused they
10 need to have support from outside, and that without the support
11 they often can't do that.
12 BY MR. SEILER:
13 Q. Without the support are they more likely to recant?
14 A. Yes, that's what I meant by can't do that. But they are
15 more likely to recant.
16 Q. I want you to assume for purposes of the next question
17 the following facts. That the children have been returned to a
18 location different from the one they had been placed in in
19 foster care or group home care, that that location is more
20 isolated, and that when returned to that location the children
21 were not and have not been attending school on a regular basis.
22 What would be again your opinion with respect to the impact on
23 recantation under those facts?
24   MR. WILKA: May I voir dire the witness on this one,
25 Your Honor?

Page 485

1   THE COURT: You may.
2   MR. WILKA: Do you know of any studies that have
3 addressed the issue about any rates of recantation where
4 children have been isolated and aren't going to school?
5 A. Not specifically.
6   MR. WILKA: Generally?
7 A. It is inferentially through the issue of family support,
8 and so, but not specifically.
9   MR. WILKA: So there are no percentages, nothing
10 subject to any review as to what recantation rates would be
11 among children who have been returned to an isolated place and
12 are not going to school, would that be a fair statement?
13 A. That's a fair statement.
14   MR. WILKA: I object to foundation, Your Honor.
15   THE COURT: Overruled.
16 BY MR. SEILER:
17 Q. You may answer the question.
18 A. Could I have the question restated?
19   THE COURT: You can either have it read back or
20 restated.
21
22   (Whereupon, the requested portion of the Record was
23   read by the Reporter.)
24
25 A. Well, that set of facts, which in general just increases

Page 486

1 the dependence of that child upon that group family group,
2 because they have less contacts with outside groups or
3 individuals, like therapists, or school, or classmates, or
4 teachers, or others, makes the attitudes and the influence of
5 that family group more powerful. And so depending upon what
6 the attitudes of that family group are, it would have more
7 influence over those children in that situation.
8 Q. My last question with respect to hypothetical. Assume
9 there have been a group of children that have been sexually
10 abused and that there are five of them, and they have all been
11 returned to this location, and have continuing ongoing contact
12 with each other and with the nonsupportive family. Again with
13 respect to the group of children, what would be the impact with
14 respect to an individual child within that group of five being
15 able to resist the pressure of recantation once one recanted?
16 A. Well, what you have in that hypothetical scenario is you
17 add to the influence of a family, the parents and others, you
18 add peer pressure within the group of children, and that is a
19 very powerful influence over children as well. So again that
20 would just increase the tendency or the pressure upon the child
21 to recant if the majority of that group were in favor of
22 recantation, and if the majority of that group were against
23 recantation, it could potentially support the child in not
24 recanting against the pressures around the children, the parent
25 and family.

Page 487

1   MR. WILKA: May I voir dire the witness for a
2 foundation objection, Your Honor?
3   THE COURT: He's already answered the question. You
4 can do cross-examination.
5   MR. SEILER: No further questions, Your Honor.
6   THE COURT: Now you can do it.
7 CROSS EXAMINATION BY MR. WILKA:
8 Q. Good morning, Doctor, my name is John Wilka and I am
9 working with Desmond Rouse. I just have a few questions. You
10 stated that you have testified in approximately 28 states
11 including, or plus Panama for the United States Army?
12 A. Correct.
13 Q. Is that for state and federal court?
14 A. Yes, and military.
15 Q. Approximately, just in the last five years, how many
16 times have you provided in-court testimony, roughly?
17 A. I am not sure. An estimate might, it might range between
18 25 to 50 perhaps.
19 Q. And in those --
20 A. Probably less when you say in court.
21 Q. How many times have you given testimony then?
22 A. I include deposition testimony, that's why it goes down
23 with in-court. So if it includes all types of sworn testimony
24 including depositions, hearings, trials, probably 25 to 50
25 times.

Page 488

1 Q. And of those 25 to 50 times can you give me a percentage
2 that you have testified for the party that is putting forth the
3 proposition that abuse has occurred?
4 A. For starters, not all those cases is that the issue.
5 Q. Let's just take sexual abuse, how many times have you
6 testified just generally on sexual abuse?
7 A. Most of those relate to abuse in one way or another.
8 They are not all did the abuse occur or not, they are
9 professional practice issues, other ancillary issues. So it is
10 a little bit artificial to say that, but the majority of times
11 that I am, have been asked to testify in situations where there
12 is the context or a question of abuse or not abuse, it is by
13 the side that is seeking to prove abuse.
14 Q. The majority?
15 A. The majority.
16 Q. Can you give me a percentage, sir?
17 A. Well, it would be fairly high percentage, probably 80, 90
18 percent.
19 Q. I believe in an answer to a question on direct
20 examination you were asked if you have studied the recantation
21 rates of children who have been sexually abused, correct?
22 A. I don't remember the exact words, but I did state that
23 many of these studies address probable sexually abused
24 children, and then recantation among probably sexually abused
25 children. I noted that the Practice Parameters adds the

Page 489

1 category, at least for consideration, that the child has not
2 been abused. You have to consider that when you are looking at
3 recantation.
4 Q. Because when you look at the hypothesis that a
5 recantation came about due to some sort of internal and
6 external pressure, you also, wouldn't you agree, have to look
7 at the hypothesis that the child is recanting because in fact
8 the abuse never occurred?
9 A. Correct, and that's actually one of my basic conceptual
10 principles in the framework of how I go about evaluating
11 recantation.
12 Q. I believe that, and if I jump around a bit, please excuse
13 me, I will try to follow along with my notes as much as I can,
14 but something did jump out at me. You were, when you were
15 talking about family pressure, you stated that where there was
16 a lack of support within the family that it would be very
17 unlikely that a child would be able to maintain the allegation
18 of abuse, correct?
19 A. When they are living with that family.
20 Q. Did you not cite as one of your sources the Elliott and
21 Briere article, sir?
22 A. Yes.
23 Q. Directing your attention to the page 271 of that article,
24 in that last sentence, children with nonsupportive mothers were
25 more likely to recant their original disclosure of abuse, and

Page 490

1 then you put 15.4 percent. Does that, does not that finding in
2 the Elliott and Briere article conflict with your statement
3 that children are very unlikely to maintain that abuse had
4 occurred?
5 A. That is, you only cited, perhaps I cut myself short when
6 I was testifying as I was reading as I got in to all the
7 statistical things. The comparison is 15.4 percent versus 3.3
8 percent. So what they are saying is a higher percentage
9 recanted when the mothers were nonsupportive than when they
10 were supportive, so there is quite a difference between the
11 two, that's what they are saying.
12 Q. I understand that, but does not that statement say, that
13 sentence say that nonsupportive mothers that there is 16
14 point, they found a 15.4 percent recantation rate?
15 A. With nonsupportive mothers, yes.
16 Q. The 3 percent I am not worried about, but it is 154
17 percent in the Elliott and Briere article that is nonsupportive
18 mothers, correct?
19 A. Correct.
20 Q. You stated it was very unlikely that the child would be
21 able to withstand the pressures to recant where there is
22 nonsupportive mothers?
23 A. When they are living with those families, and many of
24 these children with nonsupportive mothers, the vast majority of
25 them are not living with those mothers, they were removed

Page 491

1 because they go on to point out that the removal rate was much
2 higher.
3 Q. Actually, does it, is it not stated that where they are
4 removed that that is 31 percent versus 3.2 percent?
5 A. Correct.
6 Q. So where the children are actually in the mother's home,
7 but you stated it is highly unlikely?
8 A. Over time, you have to keep in mind this is a narrow
9 window of time in this study, which is another factor that you
10 have to look at with all these studies, is they have different
11 timeframes. That when you look at the child's ability to
12 maintain an allegation, it is also quite dependent upon the
13 time period. So that if you extend the time period in to
14 months and years, that's really what I was referring to.
15 Q. So if the time period, if there is a larger time period,
16 you are stating that it is harder for a child to maintain an
17 allegation?
18 A. If the system around them, the family system, the parents
19 are not supporting them in that, yes, the longer they are
20 subjected to that pressure, the more likely it is that they
21 will recant.
22 Q. Can you point me to an article that has passed peer
23 review and publication with known rates of error that would
24 support that contention?
25 A. Well, probably the article that comes closest is Sorenson

Page 492

1 and Snow, because they had long term, longer term exposure and
2 work with those children. So, and probably Summit's experience
3 has a longer perspective time wise. Many of these studies are
4 comparing a first interview with a second interview within a
5 week or two time, whereas the clinical observations have a
6 wider time perspective.
7 Q. What was the rate of recantation over time in the
8 Sorenson and Snow?
9 A. 22 percent.
10 Q. What was the N factor there, what was the number of
11 children studied?
12 A. 116.
13   MR. WILKA: Let me have a moment, Your Honor.
14   THE COURT: Sure. We will be in recess until 1:15.
15 (Recess at 12:07 until 1:15)
16 BY MR. WILKA:
17 Q. Good afternoon, Doctor.
18 A. Hello.
19 Q. I forgot to say welcome to South Dakota?
20 A. Thank you. My first time here.
21 Q. When we were visiting before lunch we were talking about
22 a number of the different studies and stuff, but I want to go
23 back to where you ended your direct examination where, I will
24 probably chop it up, but roughly the hypothetical was put to
25 you where you have five child witnesses who all recant. Do you

Page 493

1 recall generally that?
2 A. Yes.
3 Q. You stated that that could be an indicator that there was
4 peer pressure among those five children in that hypothetical,
5 correct?
6 A. No, I don't think that's exactly what I answered. What I
7 answered is that in that hypothetical, in addition to family
8 pressure, which was part of previous hypotheticals, there could
9 be peer pressure once a significant number of those children
10 had decided to recant. Then that becomes another form of
11 influence that children who were not yet recanting would be
12 subjected to.
13 Q. You said that could. Do you have in any of the
14 literature that you have provided us with today any statistical
15 support for that proposition?
16 A. Not in the literature that we have discussed today, that
17 is drawn from literature on social influence, peer group
18 pressure, those are well known phenomena, but it is not within
19 the literature that we have talked about here.
20 Q. You stated it is a well known phenomena social influence,
21 peer pressure, but that is just on peer pressure in general,
22 correct?
23 A. Well, social influence is the large category, peer
24 pressure being a subgroup, correct. I was answering with that
25 knowledge in my clinical experience.

Page 494

1 Q. And so the, that may be part of the clinical experience,
2 but as far as we know in the field of experimental psychology,
3 that that has not been tested for peer review publication,
4 known rate of error, et cetera, has it?
5 A. I don't have that literature with me. I am sure there
6 has been a lot of research on peer pressure.
7 Q. I am talking about the answer to the hypothetical, sir?
8 A. Has my exact precise answer been subjected to a peer
9 review research study?
10 Q. Correct?
11 A. No.
12 Q. It is just very narrow tailored?
13 A. Right, nor would most questions.
14 Q. You cited to an article by a Roland Summit, I believe it
15 was 1983 where Roland Summit came up with the child sexual
16 abuse accommodation syndrome, do you remember citing to that?
17 A. Yes, I cited that article.
18 Q. It is a fair statement, is it not, that that is not a
19 scientific article, that is merely Mr. Summit's, Dr. Summit's
20 clinical opinion?
21 A. It is not an empirical article in that it is not a
22 research study, but his opinion was his observation of
23 thousands of cases of child sexual abuse. So it was an
24 observation, science begins with observation, but it is a
25 different level, different kind.

Page 495

1 Q. As a matter of fact, in '92, as cited on page 4 of the
2 Lyon article, Dr. Summit stated, I am pointing toward the
3 bottom of the page, it should be understood without apology
4 that the CSAAS is a clinical opinion, not a scientific
5 instrument?
6 A. I see what you are referring to, yes. I think what
7 Summit was saying there, and I know because I have interviewed
8 Summit on this issue, that it is not a test, it is not a
9 diagnostic test. It was his observations and collection of
10 case knowledge distilled in to that set of factors to be
11 considered with regard to known child sexual abuse, and his
12 purpose in publishing that article was to educate judges,
13 juries, professionals about common phenomena surrounding child
14 sexual abuse that was in his view being often used to impeach
15 children's credibility, when in fact they were behaving
16 consistent with many, most children in child sexual abuse
17 cases.
18 Q. Now it is, this is a very popular stance, but again that
19 is based upon clinical intuition and not upon experimental
20 psychological data, correct?
21 A. It was based on clinical observation and data gathered
22 through his clinical consulting experience in Los Angeles.
23 That is different than psychological experiments or
24 manipulation of experimental groups, yes.
25 Q. Real briefly, just to discuss a number of the articles.

Page 496

1 For instance, the Gonzalez article that you cited to.
2 A. Yes.
3 Q. That was one where there was, what was the percentage of
4 recantation in that?
5 A. That was 27 percent.
6 Q. That is the higher rate, correct?
7 A. That was the highest of the whole series.
8 Q. In fact, the group studied in the Gonzalez study were the
9 McMartin preschool group, correct?
10 A. That's correct, and students who had been at McMartin.
11 Q. Would it not be a fair statement to say that a concern
12 with these is that, is the possibility that a number of the
13 children in these studies may not in fact have been sexually
14 abused, but the disclosures could have been the result of the
15 interviewing and therapeutic process?
16 A. That's the criticism which Tom Lyon cited in his review
17 article that could be made of that study, and it, as everyone
18 knows, it failed in criminal prosecution. What fewer people
19 remember is the jury said they felt the kids had been probably
20 sexually abused but weren't certain about by whom, in what ways
21 and what occasions.
22 Q. It would be a fair statement just to say that McMartin
23 was fraught with problems, correct?
24 A. Yes.
25 Q. Has it not been a criticism of the Snow and Sorenson

Page 497

1 article that that suffers from similar problems in that the
2 interviewing practices of Snow have been criticized in that
3 study?
4 A. Well, Snow has been criticized as a clinician in
5 subsequent instances.
6 Q. Because, wasn't the difficulty in that article is that it
7 was Snow who, in addition to ostensibly conducting the
8 research, evaluated and treated all of the cases in her study,
9 was that not one of the difficulties that has been raised with
10 the Snow article?
11 A. Well, that's the sample. I am not sure it says that she
12 treated all of them, but she or Sorenson had contact clinically
13 with them. And so one of the criticisms is that, well, it is a
14 clinical sample rather than say a substantiated child
15 protective service sample. And that's true, and I think Lyon
16 does a very good job of discussing the differences between
17 those samples and what rates of recantation and the way in
18 which those different samples might skew the amount of
19 recantation. The advantage to the clinical sample is that you
20 have a wider cross-section of cases in that in a clinical
21 sample you can also have cases that were not substantiated by
22 CPS, were not successfully prosecuted, although they used
23 criteria to select their sub sample that included those
24 conviction, confession, medical evidence. So the clinical
25 sample is broader, it also has more of a window of opportunity

Page 498

1 to watch cases over time, whereas authorities and official
2 reports tend to be more narrow in their window of observation.
3 Q. At the same time isn't it true that the broader
4 cross-section brings up methodological problems in that you
5 fail to take into account differences such as age, such as
6 race, or cultural differences, things like that?
7 A. Well, age is something that can be taken in to account.
8 I mean the sample can be selected by different age parameters
9 in either type of sample, and racial issues can be controlled
10 for, and decisions can be made about what to do with those in
11 either type of sample. All samples have their limitation, and
12 I think one of the important things to do when looking at a
13 series of studies is to try to understand the different
14 limitations of the different samples. And so it is not from a
15 single study that we can get an accurate picture of a
16 phenomena, it is by numbers of studies, and by looking at the
17 differences of findings that we get a more complete picture.
18 Q. Are you saying there have been studies where a variable
19 that can be selected and submitted to control would be racial
20 differences?
21 A. Well, often times in studies the racial make up of the
22 sample is observed, and so that is one of the factors that in
23 many studies is noted.
24 Q. Are we talking about these studies in front of us today,
25 sir?

Page 499

1 A. I don't recall specifically if many of these studies did,
2 but often the studies that are done do note how many of the
3 subjects are from different age groups, racial groups, genders.
4 Q. I will have to defer to your experience with these
5 articles, because I have not had the opportunity to read them
6 as extensively as you, but could you point out in any of these
7 articles where race was taken in to account when we are talking
8 about the recantation rates based upon any of the four models
9 you visited about during your direct examination?
10 A. I suspect because of the size of the groups, that when
11 you get down into the recantations you are going to a smaller
12 number, and as you get to smaller numbers you can't pars out
13 subsets within those groups. So I suspect that there was few
14 of these articles that analyze that, but I am looking at,
15 Elliott and Briere in particular used more extensive analyses,
16 which makes the article pretty heavy going, and they did not
17 observe differences. And I am trying to see if -- yes, here we
18 are, they did. They were looking at Hispanics versus
19 Caucasians on some of the dimensions. Let me see if I can look
20 at the recantation side. They found some ethnic differences
21 when looking at disclosing versus non-disclosing of abused
22 subjects, that's described on page 268. But this is probably
23 the most sophisticated of these studies in terms of the
24 sub-analyses, and the statistical work that they did, also a
25 large sample, and with regard to recantation they did not

Page 500

1 report any differences related to racial groups.
2 Q. Do you know of any studies involving Native Americans?
3 A. About recantation per se?
4 Q. Right.
5 A. No.
6 Q. Back to the Snow and Sorenson article. An additional
7 criticism, would it not be fair, that Snow is vocal in her
8 stance that even when the children denied the abuse they did
9 not believe them, is that not one of the criticisms of Snow, of
10 Snow' contribution?
11 A. I don't know the full detail of all of the criticism, I
12 would have to see that presented to me. I know there were some
13 concerns about the degree of zealousness that she exercised in
14 evaluating, and I don't know the fine grain detail of it.
15 Q. As a matter of fact, has it not been observed in one of
16 these criticisms that she began with the assumption that the
17 children were sexually abused?
18 A. I would have to see what you are referring to. I mean I
19 don't know that off the top of my head.
20 Q. The Elliott and Briere article, or excuse me, the study,
21 that began with 399 children, correct?
22 A. I believe that is right.
23 Q. And that was 399 children where they suspected that there
24 had been abuse?
25 A. Correct.

Page 501

1 Q. And those were broken up further in to disclosure,
2 children who disclosed and children who denied?
3 A. They actually, yes, broke them in to several different
4 groups.
5 Q. The first division was disclosure and denial, though?
6 A. Okay.
7 Q. And of the disclosure, that was further broken down in to
8 credible disclosures, partially credible disclosures, and then
9 non-credible?
10 A. Sounds correct.
11 Q. Even with all of that, and of the credible disclosures
12 there was 149, or 37.3 percent, correct?
13 A. What page are you referring to?
14 Q. Actually I am referring to my notes.
15 A. I am trying to stay with you, it is a pretty dense
16 article in terms of reading.
17 Q. If I were to say to you that that is what an analysis of
18 the article yielded, I mean you are familiar with it enough
19 that does that sound familiar enough?
20 A. It sounds like probably in the ballpark.
21 Q. And the partially credible were 60 children, or 15
22 percent?
23 A. Again it sounds reasonable, but I will be more
24 comfortable if I can actually find the place where that is
25 presented without just assenting.

Page 502

1 Q. Again the Elliott and Briere, we had 22 of the 399
2 children who recanted, or a 5 percent rate?
3 A. Over all.
4 Q. And then we look at --
5 A. I would like to see how they arrived at that 5 percent,
6 because I think they would have to take out of the 399 those
7 cases which they did not classify as likely abuse in terms of
8 calculating a recantation rate, because it would be unfair to
9 calculate that rate off of the whole group.
10 Q. But then if, wouldn't one want to keep that in there if
11 we are going to keep with our model that abuse many times often
12 starts with a denial?
13 A. Well --
14 Q. The disclosure process, excuse me?
15 A. Again I would have to look at it, I would have to study
16 it to really answer that question with precision. There was a
17 subgroup of 248 that they assessed as having been sexually
18 abused.
19 Q. And that was 149 credible and the 60 partially credible
20 and then the -- the 148 and the 60, yes.
21 A. I suspect that they used -- well, on the recantations
22 they used an N of 205, so it is a subset, not the whole group.
23 Q. Again when we look at the area of recantation, if I
24 understand you correct, we are in agreement that in some of
25 these cases the recantations may be accurate with children

Page 503

1 denying previously false allegations?

2 A. That's always a possibility, and a recantation study that

3 is studying the whole phenomena would include that possibility.

4 And my sense is that many of these studies are using

5 methodology that would lessen those, because they are using

6 other criteria for classifying their cases. They are not

7 taking the whole group, so they are probably excluding a lot of

8 cases that may be false allegations. Do you follow me on that?

9 Q. Yes, I do. So it would be safe to say that there is

10 significant debate over the range and validity of the numbers

11 we are talking about today?

12 A. The range and validity with regard to what assertion?

13 Q. From a 3 percent recantation rate in the James and Wood

14 article all the way up to 27 percent in the Gonzales article?

15 A. Right, and I think that range is well discussed in Lyon's

16 review which has been provided. And there are a variety of

17 what I think are pretty plausible good explanations for why one

18 might get a wide range based on the sample being studied.

19 Q. Again with the, some of the factors that you have visited

20 about, for instance lack of parental support, may put pressure

21 on a child to recant, correct?

22 A. Correct, it is an influence, and there is ranges. There

23 is degrees of lack of family or maternal support that go from

24 just lack of support to actual pressure.

25 Q. Do this or you don't eat?

Page 504

1 A. I mean there is all kinds of level of coercion.

2 Q. I believe the second one you said was a change in their,

3 in the situation, such as removal of the home, that would be

4 the second one, a removal?

5 A. Yes, I mean it could go either way. It is a factor to be

6 considered, and in my own framework for looking at these cases

7 as I tried to articulate it in some notes yesterday, removal or

8 return, depending upon the various environments and degree of

9 support or non-support in the different environments, could

10 have different impacts.

11 Q. So a change in the environment would be?

12 A. Is a factor to look at, yes.

13 Q. And a factor to look at, the third one as you called it,

14 the internal one, that would be feelings of guilt within a

15 child?

16 A. Right. Well, and the guilt could be very complex in

17 terms of in what way, what does it mean to a particular child?

18 Q. And many times I believe you stated that factor one

19 contributes to the genesis of factor three?

20 A. That pressures brought to bear on a child from the family

21 and parents around the child could influence a child's

22 feelings, so you would have a combination of factors.

23 Q. So what you are saying then is that children could be

24 susceptible of social influences to recant an allegation of

25 sexual abuse?

Page 505

1 A. Yes.

2 Q. And so then children wouldn't also, the alternative

3 hypotheses, sir, children also could be susceptible to social

4 influences to make an allegation of child abuse where none

5 existed?

6 A. Yes, that's true.

7 Q. When one looks at the, for instance those four factors --

8 let me back up.

9 For instance, environment could be a very motivating factor to

10 reverse an initial denial of child abuse, could it not?

11 A. It's possible, yes. Social forces can be very

12 influential.

13 Q. Let me give you a hypothetical, sir. Let us say that,

14 oh, anywhere from eight to twelve children are taken from their

15 home, and let us further assume that they are deposited in an

16 alien environment such as a foster home, are you with me so

17 far?

18 A. Okay.

19 Q. Let us further assume that they are told that they have

20 been sexually abused, and now let us further assume that those

21 children deny that they have been sexually abused, okay, are

22 you with me?

23 A. Okay.

24 Q. Then let us assume that these children after they deny

25 the sexual abuse are told that if they admit to it and if they

Page 506

1 go along with the story, they can then be returned home, are

2 you with me?

3 A. Yes.

4 Q. Would that not be a highly motivating factor for children

5 to disclose sexual abuse where none existed?

6 A. Yes.

7   MR. SEILER: Object to this, it again I think relates

8 back to the issue with respect to initial disclosure and not to

9 this Court's order which indicated this hearing was going to

10 focus on the issues of recantation and Brady. The question

11 even with the hypotheticals relates to the issue of disclosure

12 at the front end, not recantation with respect to this hearing.

13   THE COURT: Overruled.

14 A. Yes, all of those facts could generate a false allegation

15 of sexual abuse.

16 BY MR. WILKA:

17 Q. In the hypothetical that Mr. Seiler asked you, if you

18 would carry his hypothetical one more step, once the children

19 are removed from, or once the four factors are no longer

20 present, would you expect then a re-disclosure?

21 A. I can't answer the question as asked because it has got

22 internal illogic to it, you can't remove the four factors,

23 because those are just there.

24 Q. Okay, fair enough. On Summit's model of disclosure he

25 starts out with denial, correct?

Page 507

1 A. In terms of the accommodation syndrome, the elements.
2 Well, I think he started with the secrecy.
3 Q. Secrecy, then denial?
4 A. Then helplessness. Those first two conditions describe
5 the inherent vulnerability, dependence, and weakness of
6 children versus adults in the context of child sexual abuse.
7 Then the third was inconsistent, delayed unconvincing
8 disclosure, actually delayed, inconsistent. Well the third was
9 accommodation, the fourth was the delayed, inconsistent,
10 unconvincing disclosure, and the fifth was recantation.
11 Q. So the third and fourth could be called the denial phase
12 then?
13 A. Third was accommodation.
14 Q. The fourth?
15 A. The fourth and fifth, the denial really is part of the
16 accommodation. Could I take a three minute break while he is
17 going through papers?
18   THE COURT: Certainly.
19 (Whereupon, a short recess was taken.)
20 BY MR. WILKA:
21 Q. Doctor, did you review the FBI reports in this case?
22 A. Yes.
23 Q. Did you read the trial transcripts?
24 A. Yes.
25 Q. Did you hear the children testify over the last couple of

Page 508

1 days?
2 A. No.
3 Q. Are you aware of the separation of time and space for the
4 recantations of the children in this case?
5 A. Do I know the exact chronology of who recanted at what
6 point in time exactly, no.
7 Q. But you are aware that there was recantations -- strike
8 that.
9 You would agree with me that there was not a mass, simultaneous
10 recantation in this matter?
11 A. I don't know enough of the facts to -- no, I don't know.
12 Q. Would you agree with me then that the children recanted
13 at different times?
14 A. Again, I don't know the whole sequence of that.
15 Q. Are you aware that many of the children recanted their
16 stories while they were still in foster care?
17 A. Again, I don't know the whole sequence of the disclosures
18 to recantation.
19 Q. If a child, I want you to assume that a child recants the
20 disclosure, and they are still in foster care and see family
21 members only under supervised situations, might that not work
22 to remove, or lessen -- strike remove. Might that not work to
23 lessen one's concerns about factors one and two coming in to
24 play for a reason for the recantation?
25 A. Again, to really look at that you would have to look at

Page 509

1 exactly what the history in terms of when the recantation
2 occurs, what the exposure prior to that point in time was to
3 the various factors that I articulated, and then what the
4 exposure was afterwards to really look at that closely. It
5 could have an effect.
6 Q. Have you been made aware that the children are now
7 alleging that they were, for lack of a better term, physically
8 abused by a foster care provider while in foster care?
9 A. I observed the Underwager videotape interviews, and I
10 think there was something, although the audio, the voice of the
11 children was hard to discern at many of the points, at least to
12 me with the volume up on high. But it seemed like there was
13 some kind of negative statements about foster parents in those
14 interviews. I don't recall the full detail of it.
15 Q. There are two groups of interviews, being the 1996 and
16 the 1999 interviews, correct?
17 A. The tapes I looked at didn't have any date stamp on them.
18 There were two different locations, two separate tapes that I
19 reviewed, and they were made in separate locations.
20 Q. Let's just assume that two children were interviewed in
21 '96, and then those two plus other children were interviewed in
22 '99, would you do that for me?
23 A. Okay.
24 Q. Would you not agree with me that one would quite possibly
25 be more interested in the 1996 interviews with regard to

Page 510

1 recantations, because that is closer in time to when the
2 recantations started to come about?
3 A. Again, if I were reviewing all of the facts, trying to
4 look at this issue of recantation, I would look at all of the
5 history and the facts of the case, original case. Then I would
6 look at the sequence of disclosures and recantations, and then
7 look at these various factors that could be influential on the
8 children over time. So all of those points in time, with the
9 earlier having some additional importance over the later with
10 regard to some questions.
11 Q. We will leave that tributary for now. You stated that
12 you were aware that there was some vague allegations about
13 complaints about foster care?
14 A. As I recall.
15 Q. I want you to assume that -- well, let's start off with
16 an assumption that children can tell the truth about abuse,
17 okay, they do not always do, but children can tell the truth
18 about abuse?
19 A. That's a true statement, it is possible.
20 Q. Whether it be sexual abuse or physical abuse, children
21 are capable, are you with me?
22 A. Yes.
23 Q. If a child were to make a disclosure that to get rid of
24 head lice they were made to take a bath in rubbing alcohol,
25 would that cause you concern?

Page 511

1 A. Yes, that is not the treatment to remove head lice.

2 Q. You are a physician, correct?

3 A. Yes.

4 Q. A child taking a bath in rubbing alcohol, wouldn't you

5 say in your experience or what you know as a doctor, that would

6 be an unpleasant experience?

7 A. I would imagine so, I put a few drops in my ears after I

8 go swimming and that stings.

9 Q. So immersing one's body in there would?

10 A. Yeah.

11 Q. If a child were to state that they saw the little sister

12 having food shoved in her mouth because they couldn't eat,

13 would that cause, they wouldn't eat their food, would that

14 cause you concern?

15 A. Yes.

16 Q. And then if a child were to say that they saw their

17 sister pulled by her hair down a short flight of stairs, would

18 that cause you concern?

19 A. Yes.

20 Q. Now, back to our other model. If a child were, if it

21 were known that, or if it were stated by a child that they were

22 told if they go along with the story that they would be able to

23 return home, you remember that model that we visited about

24 earlier?

25 A. Okay.

Page 512

1 Q. If a child were in fact in this abusive foster care

2 environment and they were told to go along with the story, they

3 could get out of that abusive foster care environment, would

4 not that child be highly motivated to continue with the story

5 of abuse?

6 A. Yes, given the facts of that hypothetical you present,

7 then offering escape in exchange for something would be highly

8 motivating.

9 Q. Then once again it gets back to where we are in agreement

10 that when you look at the four factors, it is just a way of

11 saying that children are susceptible to social and environment

12 influence?

13 A. And internal.

14 Q. And internal?

15 A. Yes, there are three actually. Then the fourth was

16 really a somewhat different thing, it was just a broad end

17 perspective. It was including the fact that recantations can

18 be made in the service of truth and trying to correct a

19 previous false allegation, that's the number four. It is

20 really a different type of factor. There is three main; the

21 influence of parents and family around either directly or

22 indirectly; there is the consequences, things that happen after

23 sexual abuse disclosures are made, that is number two category,

24 covers a whole host of things: number three is the internal,

25 the psychological impacts within a child and effects.

Page 513

1 mechanisms.

2 Q. The fourth?

3 A. The fourth is just broadening the horizon to include the

4 acknowledgment you have to consider that recantation can be

5 motivated by a desire to correct the record to be truthful.

6 Q. It would be helpful to actually listen to the children in

7 their recantation, would it not?

8 A. One of my other principles I put down on paper yesterday

9 is that you cannot tell based on comparing the statement of

10 abuse versus the recantation in and of itself, because we don't

11 have any scientific way to look at a statement in and of itself

12 and decide whether it is true or false.

13 Q. Correct, okay. Again factor number one can cause factor

14 number three, the feeling of guilt. Is it not true that your

15 fourth factor, I will work with you and we will set it off to a

16 side as a broad category that a recantation occurred because

17 abuse did not occur, that would also generate factor three,

18 feeling of guilt?

19 A. Sure. And so in the context of a child having made a

20 false allegation and becoming aware of the consequences of

21 that, that could be a motivating thing.

22   MR. WILKA: Thank you, Doctor, that's all I have at

23 this time.

24 CROSS EXAMINATION BY MR. HAUGAARD:

25 Q. Dr. Corwin, my name is Steve Haugaard, I represent Russ

Page 514

1 Hubbeling in this matter. Doctor, I would like to go back a

2 little bit to the earliest part of your testimony and ask you

3 about your family. Are you married?

4 A. Yes.

5 Q. Children?

6 A. Yes.

7 Q. How many?

8 A. Four.

9 Q. And how old are they?

10 A. They range from twelve to twenty.

11 Q. Have you ever found your children sometimes to be

12 untruthful with you?

13 A. Yes. It is relatively uncommon in my experience with

14 them I am glad to say, but it does happen, has happened.

15 Q. You mentioned your undergraduate degree was in zoology?

16 A. Yes, pre-medical studies. That is the most closely

17 fitting major in order to do the prerequisites for medical

18 school admission. There are a lot of zoology majors at the

19 University of Michigan, four thousand in my freshman class.

20 Q. Some go in to vet science and some go in to human

21 medicine?

22 A. I think most of them were trying for human medicine, but

23 there is only 200 some places at the University of Michigan

24 medical school.

25 Q. I am curious to find out how much you are being paid per

Page 515

1 hour for your testimony?

2 A. I am being paid for my time and the time associated with

3 my being here in Sioux Falls, and the rate for being here and

4 time associated with this hearing is $400 an hour, and the rate

5 for review of records and other work that I did before coming

6 here was $300 an hour.

7 Q. You mentioned that you had been instrumental in

8 developing guidelines for practice parameters?

9 A. For the asset guidelines which are consensus generated

10 documents. The AACAP parameters I was a consultant to, and

11 gave input and testimony regarding, so I am cited as one of the

12 consultants.

13 Q. So that research in a sense revolves around your beliefs

14 based on your education, experience, and also based on your

15 internal biases?

16 A. Well, first of all you said that research, are you

17 referring to the guidelines?

18 Q. The guidelines?

19 A. The guidelines are not research in and of themselves.

20 They try to take into account the research and knowledge that

21 is in existence at the time that they are being developed, and

22 then what they add to that is the clinical experience, and

23 perspectives and insights of a broad diverse group. Thereby

24 trying to minimize individual biases by including a broad

25 cross-section of professionals working within an arena. I

Page 516

1 think I made the comment that that was specially so with the

2 AACAP practice parameters, they had a very diverse group of

3 consultants.

4 Q. Would you agree at this point in our historical

5 development we are probably more toward the end of the spectrum

6 of working with an art as opposed to a science in regard to

7 establishing validity in some of these research areas?

8 A. No, I think there is a fair amount of research, I have

9 cited quite a bit of it. There is certainly many questions

10 that remain to be asked and answered, there is a lot of

11 research that can be done, should be done, but we are not

12 purely at a stage of art. You know, that might have been more

13 true 20, 25 years ago, and I think I referred to the trickle of

14 publications versus the torrent. There is actually, there is a

15 growing and significant body of research that is relevant to

16 child sexual abuse cases, both research on sexually abused and

17 non-abused children in a variety of different dimensions,

18 research on child witnesses which I understand you heard some

19 about in the process of this trial and hearing. There are

20 growing bodies of knowledge.

21 Q. You have already discussed with Mr. Wilka today in your

22 testimony there is certainly a variety of factors that

23 researchers have not been able to adequately identify and have

24 a large enough sampling to adequately address, is that correct?

25 A. Oh, that is correct, and it will always be so for very

Page 517

1 fine questions. So there is always a place for clinical

2 experience, judgment and interpretation to build upon the

3 research knowledge, combine it with clinical experience and

4 judgment and for opinion, because we will never have research

5 studies conducted on all fine questions, it is not feasible.

6 And there is also human subjects concerns that would limit us

7 from studying many of the things that might be nice to have

8 studies on on a scientific perspective, but would be inhumane

9 and unjustifiable from a human subjects perspective.

10 Q. Those factors include all the unique personalities and

11 biases that go in to every person involved at every stage of

12 the process, is that correct?

13 A. They involve a myriad which might include many of those

14 things, and I think specifically today the questions were asked

15 about studies of Native American children. It would probably

16 be very difficult to do just studies is on that subgroup and

17 have enough subjects to ask many questions.

18 Q. And basically impossible to have such a controlled study

19 that you would always have the same initial investigation

20 methods and the same ongoing methods throughout the process,

21 correct?

22 A. Right. It is difficult, first of all, to do studies and

23 research on children, because you have extra protections, for

24 good reasons. You add to that the fact that you need large

25 populations as you get in to finer questions, because you need

Page 518

1 to maintain large enough subgroups at the end of the day to

2 have statistically valid comparisons, so it is a challenge.

3 Q. You discussed a little bit the idea of various factors,

4 and I probably didn't stay with the items one through four as

5 well as you two were doing. There was a reference made to, in

6 Mr. Seiler's hypothetical, to phone calls or letters. The

7 extent of that as being a factor certainly would be affected by

8 the contents of those phone calls and letters, wouldn't it?

9 A. Absolutely.

10 Q. Have you had an an opportunity to review audio tapes of

11 those phone calls?

12 A. No.

13 Q. Have you had an opportunity to review the letters

14 involved in those?

15 A. No. I was being asked hypothetical questions.

16 Q. Would it make a difference if a child didn't know of the

17 parents' views on the particular subject of abuse until the

18 child, until after the child had recanted, would that negate

19 that factor?

20 A. Certainly that would be something to look at.

21 Q. You indicated that you had reviewed the transcript of the

22 trial. Did you observe the fact that the questions were

23 primarily leading questions?

24 A. Yes, they were primarily referencing previous interviews

25 that the child had had with the FBI.

Page 519

1 Q. Did you have an opportunity to review audio tapes of
2 those interviews with the FBI?

3 A. No.

4 Q. So did you know the true content of that interview other
5 than reviewing reports compiled by the FBI?

6 A. No, I have not reviewed audio tapes of such interviews.

7 Q. You have no idea how the interview was done, do you?

8 A. No, beyond what is represented in the report. I have not
9 seen any other documentation from such interviews.

10 Q. The articles that Mr. Seiler presented in regard to the
11 research articles or the opinion articles, those are contained
12 in this folder we received, are those articles which you rely
13 upon as credible articles?

14 A. I reviewed them because they addressed the issue of
15 recantation. Now credible, you know, they have their strengths
16 and weaknesses each one unto itself. So on an article by
17 article basis I could discuss them. I am a little uncertain of
18 the word credible and the exact meaning that would have in this
19 context.

20 Q. In the article False Negatives in Sexual Abuse Disclosure
21 Interviews approximately in December of '92, did you find that
22 to be scientifically reliable?

23 A. It is a pretty interesting study, because it started with
24 a population of children with sexually transmitted diseases who
25 have a very high probability of having been sexually abused in

Page 520

1 that most of these sexually transmitted diseases cannot be
2 contracted in other ways at very high prevalence rates, so that
3 makes it very interesting. The two researchers are well
4 established. So respectable people, researchers, respectable
5 researchers.

6 Q. In a hypothetical sense would you, would it be your
7 observation in a case of alleged child sexual abuse that if
8 there were several adults involved and several children
9 involved, and the lack of existence of any sexually transmitted
10 disease, would you find that to be indicative of questionable
11 truth to the allegation of sexual abuse?

12 A. No, in that it is relatively uncommon for us to find
13 sexually transmitted diseases. Medical findings, medical
14 evidence as a broad category, including any kind of injuries,
15 you know, to the genital area, or changes in the hymen, and
16 also including sexually transmitted diseases is only present in
17 a relatively small percentage of sexually abused children. In
18 our own experience it ranges between your examiners from say
19 just less than 5 percent to maybe 10 to 15 percent in terms of
20 a year's experience. Sexually transmitted diseases are very
21 unusual. I mean we ask ourselves the questions periodically
22 what is the yield on doing some of these tests that are
23 relatively expensive when we have such a low discovery rate.

24 Q. Is it possible in a scientific sense that that result
25 could be due to the fact that many of the allegations would be

Page 521

1 false allegations?

2 A. What result are we talking about?

3 Q. That the presence or absence, or the absence of an STD
4 means anything in that case, that potentially there was a false
5 allegation?

6 A. The absence of an STD is pretty meaningless in the
7 question of abuse/non-abuse, because it has such a low
8 prevalence rate. In this study, though, because some of these
9 sexually transmitted diseases are so definitive with regard to
10 the question of sexual abuse, child sexual abuse, to have a
11 population that has them is probably as high a confidence group
12 as you could get without video or pictures of what happened to
13 the child, which we have in a few cases.

14 Q. Certainly that would be the preferred method of obtaining
15 initial interviews and information in regard to sexual abuse,
16 would be to videotape both the interviews and the examinations?

17 A. Well, no, very few people are videoing the examination.

18 Q. Wouldn't that be helpful, though, for someone later to
19 examine this information and assess the accuracy of someone
20 else's interpretation?

21 A. In some ways, yes. It is a balancing of privacy versus,
22 you know, the forensic value of the occasional statement made
23 during a medical exam. So there could be some potential value.
24 There is also on the other side of the issue concerns about the
25 privacy of the child during that medical procedure. The

Page 522

1 question of videotaping investigative interviews is one that I
2 am quite familiar with. I actually chaired the group called
3 the Los Angeles Task Force on Interviewing Sexually Abused
4 Children that first proposed that videotape recording be used
5 to document such interviews. We presented that nationally and
6 internationally in 1982. But it's been a highly controversial
7 issue, and only gradually are we as a field embracing
8 videotaping and overcoming the various concerns and fears and
9 reservations about it being the preferred practice.

10 Q. Why would it not be a preferred practice?

11   MR. SEILER: I object to this, it relates back to the
12 disclosure issues and not the recantation issues, and beyond
13 the scope.

14   THE COURT: Sustained.

15 BY MR. HAUGAARD:

16 Q. Dr. Corwin, there was an article you submitted in this
17 group of articles produced by Margaret Rieser, is that the
18 correct pronunciation?

19 A. Yes. I am not sure about her pronunciation, but I
20 recognize the name.

21 Q. At the outset of that article there is a, right after the
22 title and her name, there is an inset there that says this
23 article pulls together coherently a rather sparse literature on
24 children's not infrequent retraction of their earlier
25 disclosure of having been sexually abused. Evidence to date

Page 523

1 indicates that very few originally lied. Hypothetically if
2 children were asked questions about being sexually abused and
3 they say it didn't happen, and they are repeatedly asked
4 questions and they say but it didn't happen, would you find
5 that to be an initial denial of sexual abuse that would be
6 reasonably valid?
7 A. I am uncertain about the net meaning of your question, so
8 I am a little reluctant to answer it. If you could try to
9 restate it and make it a little simpler.
10 Q. Her summation was that evidence to date indicates that
11 very few originally lied.
12 A. In the cases of recantation, that's what she is saying.
13 Q. Is that based on scientific reliability?
14 A. I think that is. My view of this article and reading it
15 is it is based on clinical experience and her judgment, and
16 that no, she is not referencing that on some kind of externally
17 corroborated measure.
18 Q. Did you find that article that she wrote to be,
19 represent, to represent bias of her own position?
20 A. Well, it is her view, and her attempt to pull together
21 the literature as she reviewed it on recantation at the point
22 in time that she reviewed it, and includes a number of clinical
23 anecdotes. So it is a clinical report, but certainly it is
24 being filtered through her biases, perceptions, view of the
25 world.

Page 524

1 Q. She cites a study by Russell from 1986, she references
2 that as Russell conducted a study, a random sample of 900 women
3 regarding sexual abuse experiences. She goes on to state that
4 Russell's subjects reported numerous reasons they never told
5 anyone about the abuse such as they were afraid, or they didn't
6 think anybody would believe them. Could that, in a converse
7 context, could that be as true about children not telling
8 others that it never happened, that they might be afraid that
9 no one would believe them or they are simply afraid of the
10 people they are around?
11   MR. SEILER: Object, it goes to the initial
12 disclosure and not the issue of recantation.
13   THE COURT: Sustained as to that and form. The
14 number of negatives in there I am not sure what the ultimate
15 question was, aside from the subject matter.
16 BY MR. HAUGAARD:
17 Q. As recant would apply to initial disclosures, isn't it
18 also true that subjects might fail to recant to individuals
19 they were afraid of?
20   MR. SEILER: Object to the form of the question. A
21 double, triple negative relation back.
22   THE COURT: Sustained as to form.
23 BY MR. HAUGAARD:
24 Q. Let me give you a hypothetical. If an individual, based
25 on this Russell study, buying some of the results of that, if

Page 525

1 an individual is afraid of their caretaker or their
2 environment, might that affect whether or not they would recant
3 an earlier false disclosure?
4 A. If you separate your question from the Russell study,
5 which is really irrelevant because the dynamics are very
6 different, it makes it a simpler question.
7 Q. Alright, go ahead.
8 A. If you separate Russell out of it. The perception of the
9 child toward the care giver, taker, that is, that they are
10 dependent upon, and the perception of the child on what that
11 care taker, care giver believes is a relevant consideration,
12 yes.
13 Q. Would it also be relevant that that child might think
14 that that individual would not believe them?
15 A. Yes. I mean I have worked on cases, evaluated, in one
16 instance testified in a federal trial in Chicago, where I
17 believe children made recantations that were truthful, and were
18 not believed by the family that they were living with, and did
19 not hold to the recantations. So, yes, again the family, their
20 views, their beliefs are very powerful in their influence upon
21 a child in disclosing or not disclosing sexual abuse.
22 Q. And not just family, but care givers?
23 A. Care givers.
24 Q. And in this article, Recantation in Child Sexual Abuse
25 Cases she identifies secrecy as being a significant element in

Page 526

1 why children recant?
2 A. She listed that as one of the things to restore, the
3 secrecy, the secrecy that maintains the equanimity and the
4 peace of the family, referring again to an incest model.
5 Q. So would, in a hypothetical situation, if a child claims
6 that their mother knew of the abuse, that their grandmother and
7 aunts knew of the abuse, and all the other kids were locked in
8 an adjoining closet while one or more of the children were
9 being abused, would that demonstrate a lack of secrecy?
10 A. Certainly not within those parties. Not among those
11 individuals. I mean there is still an issue of secrecy with
12 regard to a bigger circle around those people, but within that
13 circle of those individuals there is not secrecy under that
14 hypothetical.
15 Q. Certainly open among that entire group?
16 A. Yes, and the question could be asked is what did the kids
17 that were locked in the closet know.
18 Q. And would it be characteristic of an effort to maintain
19 secrecy that an individual would abuse a child in front of
20 another child?
21   MR. SEILER: Object, irrelevant unless it relates
22 back to recantation.
23   THE COURT: Sustained.
24 BY MR. HAUGAARD:
25 Q. Another element that she cites is the lack of support and

Page 527

1 pressure to recant. If you take the converse in that setting,
2 if there is a lack of support and a pressure to maintain a
3 false disclosure, wouldn't that likewise apply that there is no
4 reason for the child to recant at that point?
5 A. Do you mean support for maintaining an allegation, you
6 said lack of support. It was inconsistent with the other
7 things.
8 Q. Support for the allegation, pressure to maintain the
9 allegation?
10 A. Maintain an allegation, could well maintain a false
11 allegation.
12 Q. Is that correct?
13 A. Yes.
14 Q. She writes that children tend to feel rather powerless
15 over their own discomfort. In addition to the absence of
16 control, the fact that children operate in a timeframe very
17 different from that of adults means having that a month of
18 having one's mother furious at one for having disrupted the
19 family may be seen by a child as unbearable. Time is important
20 to a child as far as the experiencing of abuse and the
21 potentially experiencing of false allegations?
22   MR. SEILER: Object, immaterial, irrelevant, doesn't
23 relate to recantation.
24   THE COURT: Sustained.
25 BY MR. HAUGAARD:

Page 528

1 Q. Is time a factor in the impact it would have on a child
2 as to recantation?
3 A. Yes, time is something to look at, and the events over
4 time, and how they relate to one another within time.
5 Q. If a child does not have control over their own
6 environment such as a hypothetical where children are kept from
7 their true family for as much as seven months without contact,
8 would that child feel a sense of no control over their
9 environment as to getting back to family?
10 A. If they are unable to get back to the family and they
11 want to get back to the family, and they are actively trying,
12 talking about it and asking, and they don't get back to their
13 family, yes, that would give them a sense of little control
14 with regard to that issue.
15 Q. She also identifies qualities that tend to be present in
16 incestuous families, such as strict control by the father,
17 isolation, and lack of control on the part of children, all
18 could contribute to the pressure on the victim to recant.
19 Given a hypothetical where there is no father figure in the
20 home, and isolation is limited in that the children can come
21 and go as they please in the community, and also given the fact
22 that children know that one word as to sexual abuse and they
23 could be taken out of the home whenever they wanted to, would
24 that indicate that those qualities would not be present?
25   MR. SEILER: I object to form, Your Honor.

Page 529

1   THE COURT: Sustained. I don't understand the
2 question.
3   MR. HAUGAARD: Let me try to rephrase it.
4 BY MR. HAUGAARD:
5 Q. If you have a hypothetical where there are no fathers in
6 the home, children are free to come and go, children are aware
7 of the fact that social services is available and can give them
8 quote unquote freedom from the home if they chose, given those
9 things, would that negate the existence of a quality of
10 isolation, or no control?
11 A. The fact is, is that most abused children would prefer to
12 stay with abusers.
13 Q. That isn't the question I asked?
14 A. I am trying to answer the question.
15 Q. Let me rephrase the question. Let me ask you as
16 follow-up to that. You indicate that most abused children
17 prefer to stay with the abusers. Do you have any scientific
18 studies to support that position?
19 A. That is largely based on observation, clinical
20 experience.
21 Q. So it is based on various biases of clinicians?
22 A. It is an observation, and I don't know the specific study
23 that has studied it. There are certainly many researchers who
24 have substantial biases and exercise them regularly as well.
25 Q. In the Rieser article did you observe, I found

Page 530

1 approximately four significant paragraphs where Margaret Rieser
2 was speaking about the McMartin preschool case and expressing
3 some remorse over the fact that the prosecutors simply couldn't
4 substantiate the abuse. Did you find that to affect and be a
5 significant bias in this article?
6 A. Can you tell me to what section you are referring?
7 Q. If you look at page 615, the last two paragraphs. Have
8 you had enough time to review those?
9 A. I have gotten through one of them, now I am going to the
10 second one. I think it's that second to the last paragraph
11 that relates to McMartin, it seems to me like a statement of
12 fact, a statement of historical circumstances. She is citing
13 facts of history in that paragraph.
14 Q. Look at the fourth and fifth line down from the first
15 paragraph?
16 A. On that page?
17 Q. First paragraph I referenced.
18 A. To the third paragraph on that page, fifth line down?
19 Q. Correct?
20   THE COURT: Which page are you on now.
21   MR. HAUGAARD: Page 615, Your Honor.
22   THE COURT: Thank you.
23 A. Which part, you want the sentence that starts?
24 BY MR. HAUGAARD:
25 Q. It says following the well-publicized outcomes of the

Page 531

1 Jordan, Minnesota and McMartin Preschool cases, where the
2 prosecution was unable to prove the child's allegations of
3 abuse were true?
4 A. That's a fact. She goes on to say a backlash reaction
5 occurred, that's true, that's a fact.
6 Q. Let's go to page 616, the last couple of lines on that
7 page carrying over to the next page. If you go ahead and read
8 those.
9   MR. SEILER: I object as irrelevant, Your Honor.
10 Dr. Corwin merely indicated he reviewed these articles for his
11 testimony, and the information they contained for purposes of
12 his testimony, and the literature search and the underlying
13 facts and results of the articles, and a discussion of line by
14 line review of these articles seems to be a colossal waste of
15 time and immaterial.
16   THE COURT: This is cross examination, overruled.
17 A. Could you restate what were you drawing my attention.
18 BY MR. HAUGAARD:
19 Q. If you look at 616 carrying over to 617, those couple of
20 paragraphs?
21 A. Okay. Yes, I have read this, the paragraphs.
22 Q. When you look at the last sentence in the first paragraph
23 carrying in to that next short paragraph, does that seem
24 to suggest to you any perception on her part that this
25 unfortunately could not be pursued?

Page 532

1 A. Well, she states that the children were returned home to
2 parents who had been arrested for sexually abusing them, that's
3 a true fact. I believe the, I believe there was an appellate
4 court case on this matter that actually made similar statements
5 about the facts underlying the case, but these are statements
6 of fact.
7 Q. Well, do you see any bias on her part in these comments,
8 does she try to demonstrate any objectivity as far as the
9 potential that these things were not true?
10 A. She, as I see it, she is setting forth the facts of those
11 cases, and it is consistent with some knowledge that I have
12 discerned from reading things like the appellate court that
13 reviewed some of these cases, and the Humphrey report on these
14 cases, that there were in fact other facts as she is stating
15 here that tended to support that some of the children had been
16 sexually abused by someone.
17 Q. By someone, not necessarily by those alleged to be the
18 abusers?
19 A. It gets into the question of the complexity of these
20 cases, yes. But I mean I think these are factual, historical
21 statements.
22 Q. Do you know if there was ever any subsequent prosecutions
23 of sex abuse in those McMartin cases?
24   MR. SEILER: Object, irrelevant.
25   THE COURT: Sustained.

Page 533

1 BY MR. HAUGAARD:
2 Q. Would you agree with the observation that she cites
3 concerning an article by Quinn from 1988, this is on page 618
4 right in the middle of the page. She simply cites that Quinn
5 recommends exploration during the early assessment phases of
6 the case for motivation on the part of the children to make
7 false allegations. Would you agree that would be an important
8 thing to do?
9   MR. SEILER: Object, not relevant. Doesn't address
10 the issue of recantation.
11   THE COURT: Isn't it under the heading responses to
12 recantation.
13   MR. HAUGAARD: Yes, it is.
14   THE COURT: I will make an observation, since I have
15 to decide this thing. Dr. Bruck, when she was here, criticized
16 a line by line dissection saying we should rather look at over
17 all picture or the thrust of the articles, and you can go ahead
18 because I am not going to sustain objections, I am just going
19 to tell you my view and the point she made which I think was a
20 pretty good point, but go ahead.
21   MR. HAUGAARD: With that in mind, Your Honor, I will
22 still ask this one question about Quinn which I think is an
23 isolated element of good interviewing or good early
24 investigation.
25 BY MR. HAUGAARD:

Page 534

1 Q. Would you agree that would make sense, that you would
2 want to explore the potential motivation on the part of the
3 child to make false allegations?
4 A. Yes, I think it is important to keep multiple
5 explanations and hypotheses in mind, and I think one of my
6 articles says so.
7 Q. So with that in mind, a good investigator would want to
8 challenge the allegations to a certain extent, and certainly in
9 these cases carefully, but still challenge them in some way to
10 try to find clear support?
11 A. Challenge them? It depends on what you mean by that. If
12 it means keep the alternatives in mind and think about and look
13 for evidence to prove innocence as well as guilt, yes.
14 Q. That's what I mean.
15 A. If you mean confront children, no.
16 Q. No, that's not what I mean. I do agree it is to test the
17 claim in a fashion that is appropriate to protect the child
18 both from potential for abuse and potential for false
19 allegations?
20 A. Good investigators need to keep multiple explanations,
21 alternative hypotheses in mind as they search for evidence.
22 Q. I did observe that she cited your work in that article.
23 A. Gee, I didn't even catch that.
24 Q. Congratulations. No other questions?
25   THE COURT: Mr. Binger.

Page 535

1 CROSS EXAMINATION BY MR. BINGER:
2 Q. Dr. Corwin.
3   THE WITNESS: Yes. I am looking for my name, I don't
4 see it in the reference list.
5   MR. HAUGAARD: It's on the last page, a little past
6 halfway of the page there.
7   THE WITNESS: You mean she cited me and didn't put a
8 reference in.
9   MR. HAUGAARD: Yes, she did.
10 BY MR. BINGER:
11 Q. In order to prepare your testimony today you read all the
12 transcripts from the jury trial that took place in 1994?
13 A. Not all the transcripts, just the transcripts of the
14 children's testimony.
15 Q. Did you read any of the expert testimony that was
16 produced during the trial?
17 A. No.
18 Q. Did you --
19 A. I read the affidavits that Ralph Underwager had written,
20 and Hollida Wakefield was signed on to one.
21 Q. You also have, since that, you have also watched both of
22 what we have referred to as the Underwager videotapes?
23 A. Yes.
24 Q. Did you know the dates of those interviews when you saw
25 the tapes?

Page 536

1 A. No.
2 Q. But you do know that there were two of them and they were
3 in different places and presumably at different times?
4 A. I have gathered that since watching them, yes, and it's
5 apparent, there is reference in the second to the first, but
6 they didn't have dates on them when I received them.
7 Q. Did you ever become aware of, and you may have gleaned
8 some of this from the trial transcript, but did you become
9 aware of what the chronology was of where the kids were placed
10 and what type of treatment they received after they were
11 removed from their home?
12 A. I could discern some of that, but again I didn't have
13 complete information to put the whole picture together.
14 Q. In looking at the Sorenson and Snow article, you are very
15 familiar with that study, are you not?
16 A. Yes, but I want to have it out here ready.
17 Q. There is mention in that report, actually it is a little
18 bit conflicting, on one page, on page 10 it says 93 percent of
19 recanting children eventually reaffirm, and the next page it
20 says 92 percent, on page 11 at the end of the first paragraph.
21 It says of those who recant, 92 percent reaffirmed their abuse
22 allegations over time?
23 A. Yes, I think that is a mistake, it is one or the other.
24 Q. I may have missed it, and I am just wondering if you
25 happen to know over what period of time that study showed that

Page 537

1 recanting children reaffirmed?
2 A. They don't describe in the article the period of time
3 related to recanting to reaffirmation, and the only thing we
4 know is that they had, some of these kids they were treating so
5 they had a longitudinal experience with them, but we don't have
6 the information about the range of times.
7 Q. Do you know of any scientific basis for having any
8 understanding of when you might expect a truly victimized child
9 to reaffirm or re-reaffirm a recantation?
10 A. This is the science that we have, these are the studies
11 that we have. Some of them have timeframes in them and tell
12 you what they are looking at, some don't. We don't have a
13 detailed sort of chronographic study looking specifically at
14 that question.
15 Q. Sorenson and Snow say that 92 or 93 percent of recanting
16 children will reaffirm, have you ever heard of any other study
17 that discusses that issue at all?
18 A. Well, there is one other reference here that does address
19 it, Gonzalez talks about reaffirmations in their group, the
20 majority they said.
21 Q. A majority?
22 A. Reaffirmed over time.
23 Q. Of recanting children will eventually reaffirm over time?
24 A. Right, is what they said.
25 Q. But from studying those two articles we can't tell what

Page 538

1 time, over, they are not very clear over what time we would
2 expect a truly victimized child to reaffirm, that be a fair
3 statement?
4 A. Nor could we ever predict, because there are so many
5 different variables operating, and no one I think would
6 reasonably assert that we can predict this child will recant,
7 reaffirm, that at these specific points in time, we don't have
8 that kind of precise predictive ability. We can talk about
9 factors.
10 Q. That's just because all human beings are different, some
11 children might reaffirm in six months, another child might
12 reaffirm in three years?
13 A. There is such a number of variables operating, including
14 individual differences, we can't predict that.
15 Q. Would you expect the longer period of time that we had to
16 look at the history of a case, the chances of reaffirming would
17 increase if there had actually been abuse?
18 A. Depending upon the many other factors, you know, that we
19 have talked about. The environment, the circumstances
20 surrounding the child, you would have to look at all those
21 things to try to discuss that question.
22 Q. On page 14 of Sorenson and Snow, the third full
23 paragraph, there is a reference there to the effect that time
24 can be, can prove to be a great decision making ally, since the
25 subject, subjects in these valid cases progressed almost

Page 539

1 unanimously to active disclosure. Keeping that statement in
2 mind, I mean would we not expect the passage of time to result
3 in most children who had actually, truly been abused to
4 eventually comfort and tell the truth and reaffirm the recant,
5 so to speak, over time?
6 A. It depends upon their circumstances. If we were to send
7 all abused children home to their abusive, let's say children
8 abused by parents, home to their abusive parents, very few of
9 those children probably would reaffirm or redisclose, because
10 they would be subject to influences that would make sure they
11 didn't; threats, coercion, reinforcement. It depends upon the
12 circumstances surrounding the child.
13 Q. And it would also depend on whether these children had
14 received treatment, therapy, help, would it not?
15 A. Right. I think that often in these studies treatment
16 therapy is seen as a way of providing support to a sexually
17 abused child to continue to deal with that fact.
18 Q. Would you agree that a child that has received clinical
19 treatment, and again a child that has truly been abused, is
20 less likely to recant?
21 A. I don't know that to be so. I think children are
22 children and are very susceptible and vulnerable to the
23 influences around them, and it would probably also depend upon
24 the nature of the therapy.
25 Q. Let me refer you to the Rieser article, page 618.

Page 540

1 A. Okay.
2 Q. The section entitled Responses to Recantation, the third
3 full paragraph. Where it says skilled clinical treatment for
4 both children and perpetrators of sexual abuse can also prevent
5 recantation. If a clinician is helping children to face the
6 trauma that they have undergone, as is suggested by a different
7 article, the possibility that they will recant will be greatly
8 reduced. Do you agree with that?
9 A. Yeah, as that therapy is going on, that's probably so.
10 But there is also other factors and influences that could
11 overwhelm that, particularly after it's over.
12 Q. I understand there is lots of different factors that
13 could affect and every case has to be taken on its own merits,
14 but the availability for skilled clinical treatment for these
15 children as a general concept, I realize you are not trying to
16 apply your testimony to these specific people, but as a general
17 concept the availability of skilled clinical treatment for
18 these children is going to reduce recantation if they have
19 really been abused, true?
20 A. Yes, during the time of the treatment, yes.
21 Q. When we have problems with children that change their
22 statements, I mean a lot, maybe in the beginning they deny it,
23 then they say yes, then later they say no, and perhaps you have
24 dealt with children that have changed their stories many, many
25 times, have you?

Page 541

1 A. I have dealt with a number of cases where the accounts
2 have changed. Many, many times may be an overstatement.
3 Q. Five or six times perhaps?
4 A. That's probably an overstatement. Usually less, usually
5 disclose, recant, maybe redisclose. Three, maybe, four at the
6 outside.
7 Q. So you have interviewed, you have personally interviewed
8 and clinically addressed how many cases of children that were
9 allegedly abused?
10 A. Many. I don't have an exact number.
11 Q. Hundreds?
12 A. It would probably be in the hundreds, I don't know the
13 exact number.
14 Q. In all those cases the most times you can remember
15 somebody changing their story back and forth would be roughly
16 three?
17 A. Three or four times, yeah. I am trying to think about
18 it.
19 Q. Well, again hypothetically, if you had five children that
20 were not abused, but who had been influenced in to saying they
21 were abused when no actual abuse actually took place, and then
22 you removed those children from those influences, the ones that
23 had convinced them to disclose when they really weren't abused,
24 would you logically expect that all five of those children
25 eventually would recant?

Page 542

1 A. They might well, depending upon the influences around
2 them at a later point in time.
3   MR. BINGER: Thank you, that's all I have.
4   THE COURT: Mr. Carter.
5 CROSS EXAMINATION BY MR. CARTER:
6 Q. I just have a couple of questions. I want to go back a
7 minute to your initial testimony concerning the three factors
8 and the direct pressure, and then ultimately the psychological
9 and emotional pressure, you remember those categories?
10 A. Yes.
11 Q. With respect to the matter of the direct pressure, is
12 that something that you generally see as being pretty a overt
13 kind of thing which would need to be not reading between the
14 lines kind of thing, is that what you are a addressing there?
15 A. I also added to that category or influence. So that adds
16 a broader cross-section than just direct coercion. The
17 influence can be asserted in a variety of ways, some are more
18 powerful than direct.
19 Q. I want to presume we are dealing with a situation where
20 the offenders had been sent to prison, and there are telephone
21 calls made back to the family. Would you envision talking to
22 the victims as part of that telephone conversation a form of
23 direct pressure or influence?
24 A. Of course it depends upon what is said to a degree.
25 Q. Well, let's just assume that the, in the telephone

Page 543

1 conversations it is to the effect that the offenders love the
2 kids, they just want them to tell the truth, and they think
3 about them, and not to be afraid, just tell the truth. That
4 kind of a statement, would you consider that to be in any form
5 a form of pressure or influence?
6 A. Again it depends upon the facts of the situation. I mean
7 if the child had been sexually abused by that individual and
8 they are saying I love you, and, you know, offering support,
9 and the child is, has, it's been a long time since they were
10 abused, and they are thinking well, you know, I really love
11 this person outside of the abuse, and I feel sorry where they
12 are, I mean that could have one kind of effect that would be in
13 the service of the child feeling guilty, saying I am sorry this
14 person is in prison. On the other hand, if they had not been
15 abused, that could be a supportive statement to tell the truth
16 and set the record straight.
17 Q. So your categories then, you really have to come to a
18 determination on whether the event occurred or not before you
19 can really use these factors to make any sense out of whether
20 or not it is pressure or not, is that fair?
21 A. No, but you have to consider multiple hypotheses, just
22 like a good investigator. You have to consider what the
23 meaning of some things are in different conditions.
24 Q. But again in this hypothetical situation you are not able
25 to make a determination whether this statement is pressure or

Page 544

1 influence without knowing whether they are guilty or not, isn't
2 that true?
3 A. It could have different meanings given those two
4 different possibilities.
5 Q. So how in the world then are these standards going to be
6 of any help in trying to determine whether or not a recantation
7 is valid if you have got to have the final answer in hand
8 before the question can be determined?
9 A. Because you don't, you have to consider the different
10 alternatives, and you have to consider all of the facts which
11 relate to the original case, the evidence that supported that
12 abuse had occurred versus evidence supporting other hypotheses.
13 You have to look at the timing and chronology of the
14 recantations and what factors were operating upon the children
15 at those times. You have to look ultimately at the reasons
16 that are given for the recantations, and look at those against
17 the known facts of the situation to see if they fit or don't
18 fit. And then ultimately a court or a jury has to look at the
19 credibility of a variety of witnesses, including the children
20 and others who are trying to help sort through this, and that's
21 beyond expert abilities, so that is reserved unto judges and
22 juries, and you have to put the whole picture together and see
23 what makes the most sense given all of the facts of the
24 situation that are known.
25 Q. Are you aware of any studies where there have been any

Page 545

1 efforts to present a given set of facts to a number of
2 different persons to get some sense of what percentage, or how
3 different people, what percentages would view it one way versus
4 the other?
5 A. There are have been a variety of studies that have
6 presented hypotheticals and cases using different research
7 methodologies trying to discern what factors different people
8 pay attention to, how they weight, different clinicians, how
9 they weight different factors. So there have been a number of
10 studies that attempted to do that, some are more informative
11 than others, some are sort of done by people who seem to have
12 more open minds than others with regard to the question.
13 Q. Is it fair to say that these studies have generally been
14 quite inconclusive?
15 A. Well, they are very complex, and they are also removed
16 from reality. So it is again they are limited, you have to be
17 very careful in drawing very many inferences from them.
18 Q. Within your area of professional expertise and as a
19 witness, Doctor, do you believe that you have any particular
20 biases that you bring to the situation that you are testifying
21 here to today?
22 A. Well, you know, that's a word. Bias means one thing in
23 the courts and it means another thing in psychology and in
24 research. It is a very negative term in the courtroom, it is
25 an accepted fact in psychology that everyone has certain

Page 546

1 biases, perspectives. So I would say that I have a certain
2 experience, a certain knowledge that I view the world through,
3 and that is my perception, that's my perspective. Now do I
4 have a bias that cases are always true or they are always
5 false, no, I don't. I have seen them in all sorts of different
6 presentations, and I have testified for different sides based
7 on the facts of cases that I have reviewed.
8 Q. So it is the facts again that are really the key in your
9 professional assessment?
10 A. I strive to be as objective and as neutral as I can be,
11 and to base my opinions and the testimony I give on the facts
12 and the literature and my experience.
13 Q. And the factors that you consider as being relevant to
14 determining the validity of these recantations, are those ones
15 that there is a difference on within your professional field as
16 to how various experts would view those different factors?
17 A. No, I think what I did is I gave both an overview of the
18 literature, and I described, and the Court and all the
19 attorneys have been provided a consensus document that was a
20 synthesis of that literature along with various different
21 perspectives.
22 Q. Which of those was the article that you think is the
23 synthesis or the synthetic one?
24 A. Well, the consensus document is the AACAP.
25 Q. And that's the American Academy of Child and Adolescent

Page 547

1 Psychiatry?

2 A. Right.

3 Q. That's one of the documents that you have provided here

4 today?

5 A. Yes.

6 Q. Now the Academy has had, has brought out guidelines for

7 clinical evaluation of various, for child and adolescent sexual

8 abuse, have they not?

9   MR. SEILER: I object on relevance.

10   THE COURT: Overruled.

11 A. This replaced an earlier set of guidelines that were

12 published in the late '80's by the Academy, but this is the

13 current set of parameters for the forensic evaluation in

14 suspected child abuse cases.

15 BY MR. CARTER:

16 Q. And the one that you have provided is dated what, '97?

17 A. Right.

18 Q. Now this AACAP official document here that you have

19 provided, again is this a research document, or an experience

20 oriented kind of document?

21 A. It is a document that reflects a synthesis of the

22 research findings, and there are many citations, many of which,

23 some of which we have talked about here today in the reference

24 lists that are cited in this document. And also add that to

25 the clinical experience and the knowledge of the various

Page 548

1 consultants, some of whom are researchers, including Dr. CeCe

2 is cited here as a consultant, I have already noted that I was

3 a consultant, a number of other colleagues who have somewhat

4 different perspectives and bring different perspectives to this

5 question including the lead author whose real publications have

6 been in the area of false allegations.

7 Q. Do you consider the issues of recantation and original

8 truth or falsity of charges as being flip sides of the coin?

9 A. I am not exactly sure, could you restate your question?

10 Q. Well, do you consider the recantation and the issues

11 surrounding recantation to be similar to the issues surrounding

12 the validity of the original charge?

13 A. I think in looking at a recantation one should go through

14 a process that is similar, but focused on the recantation, to

15 looking at an original charge of abuse or a version of abuse.

16 And in the model that I discussed this afternoon, in evaluating

17 a recantation, I have included looking at all the underlying

18 facts to include that as one looks at the circumstances of

19 recantations and what is known about recantation, and the

20 influence around the kids, around the time of the recantation,

21 that includes consideration of all those other facts as well,

22 because ultimately in my opinion what one has to do is try to

23 see what picture, based on all these pieces, comes together and

24 makes the most sense, that's my view of it.

25 Q. Again, so in order to really consider the validity of the

Page 549

1 recantation, would it be fair to say that you would also then

2 by definition need to consider the truthfulness of the validity

3 of the original charge?

4 A. No, because you can't assume one way or the other,

5 because you are trying to decide whether the recantation fits a

6 scenario in which it was false or it was true. So you can't

7 assume one or the other, although you can think about what it

8 means if it is one way or the other way.

9 Q. So you would put them in to separate corridors, you would

10 first of all need to consider and focus just on the recantation

11 without focusing on the issue of whether the original charge

12 was correct or not?

13 A. What I have tried to say, and I will say again, is I

14 think in my view in how I look at recantations is I look at all

15 of the known facts, including those that were known previously,

16 the facts of the case, and then look at the recantation, the

17 circumstances, the motivations to tell the truth, motivations

18 to lie, and then try to see which picture makes the most sense

19 and seems the most probable.

20 Q. Is it fair to characterize your testimony then that in

21 looking at all of the facts to assess the recantation that

22 would include all of the facts surrounding the original charge?

23 A. Right. Everything that is known about the case.

24   MR. CARTER: I have no other questions.

25   MR. SEILER: No redirect.

Page 550

1   THE COURT: Very well. Thank you, Doctor, you may

2 step down. Take a fifteen minute recess.

3 (Recess at 3:15 until 3:30)

4   THE COURT: Call your next witness.

5   MR. SEILER: Mindy Mitnick.

6

7   MINDY MITNICK,

8 called as a witness, being first duly sworn, testified and said

9 as follows:

10

11 DIRECT EXAMINATION BY MR. SEILER:

12 Q. Introduce yourself to the Court, please?

13 A. My name is Mindy Mitnick, and I am a licensed

14 psychologist in Minneapolis, Minnesota. M-I-T-N-I-C-K.

15 Q. Licensed psychologist in Minnesota. What do you do for a

16 living?

17 A. I have a private practice which I have had since 1980,

18 part time in 1983, full time where I have a clinical case load

19 for therapy and evaluations. I do a lot of training around the

20 country, I do consultation with organizations and other

21 professionals around specific issues, and I sometimes serve as

22 an expert witness.

23 Q. The name of your private practice Uptown Mental Health

24 Center?

25 A. It is.

Page 551

1 Q. Would you briefly describe your educational background?

2 A. I have a Bachelor's degree in psychology from Bryn Mawr

3 College, a Master's degree in education from Harvard

4 University, and Master's of arts in psychology from the

5 University of Minnesota.

6 Q. Are you licensed in the state of Minnesota?

7 A. I am and have been since 1980.

8 Q. As a clinical psychologist then again would you briefly

9 describe the nature of your practice?

10 A. There are two major areas of concentration in my

11 practice. One is working with children and families going

12 through divorce. The other is work with children and families

13 where there have been abuse issues, physical, sexual,

14 emotional. And then there is a small part of my practice that

15 is for general psychological issues, again therapy or

16 evaluation.

17 Q. As part of your testimony here today and part of also

18 what you do have you put together a resume or a curriculum

19 vitae in which you set forth basically your background, your

20 experience, your education and the publications you have been

21 involved in?

22 A. Yes.

23

24   (Exhibit 22 marked For identification.)

25

Page 552

1   MR. SEILER: May I approach.

2   THE COURT: You may.

3 BY MR. SEILER:

4 Q. I show you what's been marked Government's Exhibit 22 and

5 ask you if you can identify that for us?

6 A. It's my resume current to about two weeks ago.

7   MR. SEILER: We offer Government Exhibit 22. I might

8 add it is submitted, we don't intend to delve in to the major

9 specifics of her resume in the interest of time.

10   THE COURT: Good.

11   MR. WILKA: No objection.

12   THE COURT: Exhibit 22 is received.

13   MR. SEILER: May I approach again, Your Honor?

14   THE COURT: You may.

15

16   (Exhibit 23 marked For identification.)

17

18 BY MR. SEILER:

19 Q. I now show you Government Exhibit 23 which is also part

20 of the package that was distributed, can you identify that,

21 please?

22 A. Yes, that's current to about two months ago in terms of

23 my testimony history from 1996 to the present.

24 Q. Your testimonial history in courts?

25 A. Yes.

Page 553

1 Q. Would you describe whether you testified from the

2 prosecution standpoint, from the defense standpoint, or your

3 approach?

4 A. Because I have two different areas of concentration in

5 the criminal court cases I have testified, I have testified

6 disproportionately for the prosecution than for the defense.

7 In those cases in family court in which there have been

8 allegations of sexual abuse, I have testified a large number of

9 times on behalf of typically fathers who have been what I

10 believed wrongfully accused of sexually abusing their children.

11 Q. Does Government Exhibit 23 set forth a summary of your

12 testimonial experiences as you indicated over the last five

13 years?

14 A. Yes.

15   MR. SEILER: We offer Government Exhibit 23.

16   MR. WILKA: No objection.

17   THE COURT: Exhibit 23 is received.

18 BY MR. SEILER:

19 Q. In conjunction with your service to the United States

20 Attorney's office in South Dakota were you sent two videotapes

21 regarding interviews done by Ralph Underwager?

22 A. I was actually sent more than two videotapes done by

23 Ralph Underwager. There were interviews of five children and

24 there was more than two tapes. Physically more than two tapes.

25 Q. What did those tapes indicate or depict?

Page 554

1 A. With two of the children, Donovan and Thrista, there were

2 two interviews about two years apart, the dates weren't exactly

3 given. Then with three of the children there was just one

4 interview done, I believe in 1999.

5 Q. Did you have an opportunity to review and analyze those

6 tapes that contained the interviews by Dr. Underwager?

7 A. Yes.

8   MR. SEILER: Your Honor, I would represent to the

9 Court it's our understanding that those tapes are the same ones

10 that this Court has received in evidence for purposes of this

11 hearing.

12   THE COURT: Well, let me get the folder for a minute,

13 because I am going to recite the number of tapes that are in

14 there so we are all on the same page on that. I have been

15 given the folder in this case, it is, there is notation on it

16 430 which would be a docket number, video interview, Underwager

17 interview. 453 video cassettes attached to supplement slash

18 addendum to motion for new trial, volumes 1, 2 and 3. There

19 are two large VHS tapes that are with a note on them, these

20 were filed under seal with document 398 volume 6. Just a

21 minute. Alright. The one that says TDK VHS dash C

22 videoadapter is the adapter that you use when you play the five

23 smaller tapes that are the 1999 -- well, that isn't true in

24 every instance either. Three of the smaller tapes are number

25 1, Rosemary Rouse, 1-30-99. There is number 1 on it. Then

Page 555

1 there is a number 2, Rosemary Rouse, 1-30-99, those are both
2 small tapes. Then the third small tape has a number 3 on, it
3 is Lucritia, Jessica, Thrista and Donovan Rouse. Then there
4 are two more small tapes that are 1996 tapes, one of them says
5 Thrista and Donovan, the other one says Donovan Rouse. Then in
6 addition to those there is a large one that is not the adapter
7 tape housing, but rather it is the one that says Rouse Feather
8 Hubbeling case Underwager interview, and it is undated. I
9 can't remember which date that one is, even though I watched
10 it, that describes them physically too. There is a statement
11 of what is filed here in the record.
12 BY MR. SEILER:
13 Q. When you reviewed these tapes, did they contain two
14 different sets of interviews of the Rouse children?
15 A. Yes.
16 Q. One done in 1996, one done subsequent to that in 1999?
17 A. Yes.
18 Q. What did you do when you reviewed those tapes with Ralph
19 Underwager interviewing the children?
20 A. I took notes about the methods and practices that were
21 used in the interviews as I do whenever I review videotapes of
22 interviews.
23 Q. As a result of your viewing those videotapes and taking
24 notes, did you prepare a report?
25 A. I did.

Page 556

1   MR. SEILER: Approach, Your Honor.
2   THE COURT: You may.
3
4   (Exhibit 24 marked For identification.)
5
6 BY MR. SEILER:
7 Q. I show you what's been marked Government Exhibit 24 and
8 ask you if you can identify that?
9 A. That is a copy of my report that I prepared.
10 Q. Does that report contain your observations and comments
11 with respect to the Underwager videotapes?
12 A. Yes.
13   MR. SEILER: Your Honor, we offer Exhibit 24.
14   THE COURT: Hearing no objection, Exhibit 24 is
15 received.
16   MR. SEILER:
17 Q. Dr. Mitnick, does your profession recognize that there
18 are generally accepted standards for conducting forensic type
19 interviews, whether it's at the beginning of a child sexual
20 abuse in its investigation or at any point throughout the
21 investigation?
22   MR. WILKA: Objection, compound.
23   THE COURT: Sustained.
24 BY MR. SEILER:
25 Q. Does your profession recognize that there are generally

Page 557

1 accepted standards for conducting forensic type interviews in
2 child sex abuse examinations?
3 A. There are recommended practices for producing reliable
4 and accurate information from children in forensic interviews,
5 yes.
6 Q. When you reviewed the Underwager tapes, did you review
7 them with an eye toward evaluating whether those generally
8 accepted standards were followed by Ralph Underwager in
9 conducting the interviews of the children?
10   MR. WILKA: I object, the witness did not
11 specifically, did not say there were generally accepted
12 standards, stated there were recommended practices.
13   THE COURT: Well, the objection is noted but
14 overruled.
15 A. Yes.
16 BY MR. SEILER:
17 Q. Ms. Mitnick, what is your opinion with respect to whether
18 Ralph Underwager followed the general standards or the
19 recommended practices with respect to the interviews he did of
20 the Rouse children?
21   MR. WILKA: Objection as to foundation as to which
22 interview, time and manner.
23   MR. SEILER: I will rephrase, Your Honor.
24   THE COURT: Alright.
25 BY MR. SEILER:

Page 558

1 Q. First with respect to the 1996 interview of Donovan and
2 Thrista, did --
3   THE COURT: Just a moment, let me interject.
4 Possibly the question should be asked about is there any
5 difference in your view with regard to critiquing
6 Dr. Underwager's interviewing practices between 1996 and 1999,
7 because if there isn't, then we can deal with them all at one
8 time.
9 BY MR. SEILER:
10 Q. What the Judge said.
11 A. The answer is no, I don't have an opinion, my opinion is
12 that there isn't a difference in terms of the kinds of
13 practices that were used.
14 Q. In '96 versus '99?
15 A. Correct.
16 Q. Based on that then, I would ask you to answer this yes or
17 no. Do you have an opinion whether Dr. Underwager followed the
18 recommended practices, or the generally accepted standards for
19 conducting forensic type interviews in child sex abuse cases?
20 A. Yes.
21 Q. What is that opinion?
22 A. He certainly did not.
23 Q. And why do you say that?
24 A. That's a long complicated answer.
25 Q. Okay?

Page 559

1 A. The recommended practices are geared at providing an
2 atmosphere that supports children in making disclosures, if
3 there are disclosures to be made, and targeting the questions
4 to meet the developmental needs of the child being interviewed
5 to allow the child to tell as much as possible in his or her
6 own words.
7 MR. WILKA: Your Honor, excuse me, may I voir dire
8 and inquire? Did you bring a list of what they are? Of what
9 these recommended practices are?
10 A. I have an entire book here published by the American
11 Psychological Association.
12 MR. WILKA: Would you have a list of like ten or
13 eleven things that are good?
14 THE COURT: Counsel, I haven't given you an
15 opportunity to voir dire, but you are.
16 MR. WILKA: May I voir dire the witness, Your Honor?
17 THE COURT: Why don't we wait until cross
18 examination, I think, because I usually allow voir dire only
19 for purposes of making an objection.
20 MR. WILKA: I was going to voir dire for that
21 purpose.
22 THE COURT: I don't see it. So it will be cross. Go
23 ahead.
24 BY MR. SEILER:
25 Q. Are these observations set forth in your report which was

Page 560

1 just recently received in evidence?
2 A. Yes.
3 Q. When you also received the videotape, did you also
4 receive an affidavit that had been prepared by Ralph
5 Underwager?
6 A. Actually two affidavits.
7 Q. Did you have an opportunity to review them?
8 A. Yes.
9 Q. In Ralph Underwager's affidavit, did he set forth certain
10 recommended guidelines or standards for conducting interviews
11 in those affidavits?
12 A. I wouldn't say he set forth standards, but he outlined
13 certainly a part, only a partial list, but of certain things
14 that he thought were forensically relevant practices in
15 reviewing the children's interviews.
16 Q. In your review of Ralph Underwager's affidavit, did he
17 follow his own accepted standards or principles in the
18 interviews that he did with the Rouse children that you viewed
19 on the two videotapes?
20 A. No, he did not.
21 Q. And Ms. Mitnick, is it, why is it important even in this
22 type of recantation interview to follow the recommended
23 practices with respect to conducting interviews as opposed to
24 the manner in which Dr. Ralph Underwager conducted the
25 interview?

Page 561

1 MR. WILKA: Object to the form, Your Honor.
2 THE COURT: Overruled.
3 A. It is always important, if we are trying to seek
4 forensically relevant information from children, to do it in a
5 way that will seek to obtain the most accurate information
6 possible. That would be at the time of the initial disclosure,
7 that would be at the time of testimony, which could be months
8 or even years down the road, and it could be in consideration
9 of recantation, or civil litigation related to abuse. It
10 wouldn't matter what the purpose is, the goal is to obtain
11 accurate and reliable information from children.
12 BY MR. SEILER:
13 Q. Is part of the concern that you expressed, or part of
14 your opinion that you expressed in terms of Ralph Underwager
15 not following the generally recognized principles is that he
16 became an advocate for one particular point of view or side?
17 A. Yes.
18 MR. WILKA: Objection, leading.
19 THE COURT: Sustained, answer is stricken. It was
20 leading.
21 BY MR. SEILER:
22 Q. Were the interviewing practices that were used by Ralph
23 Underwager on the videotapes consistent with the statements and
24 representations that he made in his affidavit?
25 A. No.

Page 562

1 Q. And why not?
2 A. To give one example, he talked at length in one of the
3 affidavits of the importance of doing what we call alternative
4 hypothesis testing where you want to be sure that you don't
5 start your interviews with a preconceived notion and simply
6 target your interview then to obtain information from that
7 perspective, but you allow kind of a neutral, an open minded
8 approach to the interview. I did not see alternative
9 hypothesis testing in any of the videotapes that I reviewed.
10 Q. Did Ralph Underwager take a neutral approach to the
11 interviews that he conducted with the children?
12 A. Certainly not in my observation.
13 Q. What do you base that on?
14 A. Repeated statements to the children that he was there to
15 help them get their uncles out of jail. That would not be a
16 neutral stance with which we would start an evaluation or an
17 interview.
18 Q. Again these opinions and your observations are set forth
19 in your report which is received in evidence?
20 A. Yes, sir.
21 MR. SEILER: No further questions.
22 THE COURT: Cross.
23 CROSS EXAMINATION BY MR. WILKA:
24 Q. Good afternoon, Dr. Mitnick?
25 A. I am not a doctor.

Page 563

1 Q. Good afternoon, Ms. Mitnick. I am John Wilka, I am
2 working with Desmond Rouse here this afternoon. Let's focus on
3 the 1996 -- well, no, strike that.
4 You stated that the, in your opinion the practices or quality
5 of the interviews of Dr. Underwager were the same in '96 as
6 they were in '99?
7 A. They were very concerning practices both in '96 and '99,
8 yes.
9 Q. So similar quality interviews?
10 A. Yes.
11 Q. So if the '96 interviews were bad, then the '99
12 interviews were bad, correct?
13 A. Well, I am not expressing causation, I am just saying the
14 '96 interviews are bad and the '99 interviews are bad.
15 Q. So if the '96 interviews were good, the '99 interviews
16 were good, because they are of the same quality, correct?
17 A. Well, they are different concerning practices and some of
18 the same concerning practices, I am not sure exactly how to
19 answer your question.
20 Q. It is not necessary, we have established it's your
21 opinion they are of the same quality type interviews, correct?
22 A. Yes.
23 Q. Let's talk about the 1996 interview with Donovan. Now
24 did you, you took extensive notes regarding these interviews?
25 A. I don't know about whether we share a definition of

Page 564

1 extensive, I have my notes with me.
2 Q. How many pages of notes?
3 A. For '96?
4 Q. Yes, with the Donovan interview?
5 A. Four pages of notes for '96.
6 Q. Then you supplied Exhibits, a ten page Exhibit with your
7 critique, is that correct?
8 A. Yes.
9 Q. Let's look at your first one. Now it states that
10 Dr. Underwager laughs throughout the interviews?
11 A. That's a general comment about all of the interviews,
12 yes.
13 Q. In the, you stated also this would confuse children about
14 the seriousness of the interviews, correct?
15 A. Yes, it could.
16 Q. Can you show me or tell us, let's strike that and move
17 back again.
18 When you took your four pages of notes on the Donovan 1996
19 interview did you use a tape counter to say at 201 I noticed
20 this or 204 I noticed that?
21 A. No.
22 Q. Did you have anything about in the first two minutes of
23 the Donovan interview I noticed this and the last six minutes I
24 noticed that?
25 A. I didn't do it by minutes, no.

Page 565

1 Q. Did you do it chronologically?
2 A. Yes.
3 Q. Did you start writing --
4 A. Yes, sequentially.
5 Q. Sequentially, thank you. So the beginning of your notes
6 for the Donovan would be at the beginning of the interview and
7 the end would be at the end, correct?
8 A. Yes.
9 Q. Can you tell me where in the '96 Donovan interview that
10 Dr. Underwager was actually laughing?
11 A. Yes.
12 Q. Okay, tell me?
13 A. The question was asked, they were discussing about
14 Donovan how it is he got to go home, and Dr. Underwager said
15 and now you got things to do at home, and then he laughed.
16 Q. Would you characterize that as a laugh, or a chuckle, I
17 mean --
18 A. I wrote laugh. Whether it is a laugh or a chuckle, I
19 don't know.
20 Q. Would it be a fair statement to say that -- strike that.
21 When he stated that, what did you notice about Donovan that
22 appeared to confuse him about the seriousness of the interview?
23 A. I don't think I noticed anything specifically about
24 Donovan at that moment in time that would suggest he was
25 confused about the seriousness. I think it's a general

Page 566

1 statement if the interviewer is laughing it can be confusing to
2 children about whether this is something that is kind of a
3 jovial conversation, or whether it is a serious matter.
4 Q. Would you agree with me that Dr. Underwager appeared to
5 attempt to present a comfortable, non-threatening atmosphere?
6 A. At times.
7 Q. Were there times where he appeared to present an
8 uncomfortable, threatening atmosphere?
9 A. I would separate comfortable and threatening. I can't
10 know whether the atmosphere as experienced by the children as
11 uncomfortable or threatening. I have identified a number of
12 things in my report that I thought could have made the children
13 uncomfortable, that are not recommended, like touching them.
14 Q. We are just talking about the laughter here, okay?
15 A. Yes.
16 Q. I am not going to ask you about the next time he may have
17 chuckled or anything, or may have laughed, but can you tell me
18 anywhere in the Donovan 1996 interview where Dr. Underwager's
19 laughter, as you call it, appeared to confuse Donovan about the
20 seriousness of the interview?
21 A. I can't point to a specific place, no.
22 Q. Now just with the Donovan 1996 interview, I mean --
23 strike that.
24 Let's talk about the Thrista 1996 interview. Where, the same
25 question, can you point to any place in the Thrista, 1996

Page 567

1 interview where Dr. Underwager's laughter appeared to confuse
2 her about the seriousness of the interview?
3 A. It is hard to separate out the laughter and the sharing
4 of the personal information as we start to get in to this, and
5 so I can't know, and of course none of us can know what was in
6 the minds of the children. But I think my point is that it can
7 be confusing for children what the whole purpose of this was
8 when someone is repeatedly laughing, sharing a lot of personal
9 information that is not about the child. The focus of a
10 forensic interview of course being about the child.
11 Q. I am just asking about the laughter, not sharing personal
12 information.
13 A. Okay.
14 Q. Did you, for instance, you stated that he would laugh
15 throughout the interview, and for purposes of discussion let's
16 just agree that that is true. By any chance did you count the
17 number of times that Dr. Underwager laughed throughout these
18 interviews?
19 A. I did not.
20 Q. Did you note in any place in either 1996 interview that,
21 where, you know, what were the children's reactions anywhere
22 that would show confusion?
23 A. Again it is hard for me to put my mind, myself in the
24 mind of Donovan or Thrista, but it looked like more so in this
25 interview than with Donovan that one of the effects of the

Page 568

1 laughter was that it disrupted getting information from
2 Thrista. I can't know for sure that that is the case, but the
3 laughing then disrupts the sequential questioning and asking
4 for information from her, and so I don't know if she was
5 confused then if she was supposed to be laughing with
6 Dr. Underwager, chatting with Dr. Underwager, or trying to
7 recall the things that he was interspersed in her asking her to
8 recall.
9 Q. What part of that interview did laughter interrupt the
10 sequential flow of information, what particular subjects were
11 we on?
12 A. Oh, about going home.
13 Q. What answer was Thrista giving about going home where the
14 laughter interrupted that?
15 A. They were talking about the trial, and then he moved to
16 her being taken away from her mom for quite a while, and then
17 he said he was glad for her about being home, and then he
18 laughed about home being better, and then the kind of answer
19 that Thrista gave was, this is a direct quote, the place where
20 you belong, and it is not clear what is going on there, it is
21 not clear what they are talking about any more.
22 Q. Isn't it true, I know the tapes speak for themselves, but
23 Dr. Underwager said home is the place where you belong?
24 A. That may be. Let me see if I can figure out my pronoun
25 here. Yes, and she did not say anything at that point.

Page 569

1 Q. So it is your statement that her non-response to the
2 statement home is the place where you belong was an
3 interruption of the sequential flow of information from
4 Thrista?
5 A. I think it may be, yes.
6 Q. It may be?
7 A. I can't know for sure.
8 Q. We are still on the laughter, how would that technique
9 change the nature of either child's testimony?
10 A. I think the simple answer is I don't think anyone knows
11 for sure, and I was raising it as a possibility, because it
12 certainly is not a recommended practice to laugh in childrens'
13 interviews.
14 Q. Is it a recommended practice to provide a, give me a
15 moment here, a supportive atmosphere for making disclosures or
16 recantations?
17 A. Yes.
18 Q. Now if one were, if the moment were appropriate to laugh,
19 let's say if the child told a joke, is the interviewer supposed
20 to say don't joke?
21 A. No.
22 Q. So just laughter in itself is not inappropriate?
23 A. That would be laughter that was appropriately generated
24 by something the child did, not out of the interviewer's own
25 sense of humor, or joviality.

Page 570

1 Q. Joviality is inappropriate in all circumstances?
2 A. I didn't say that.
3 Q. Joviality throughout an interview is inappropriate?
4 A. I believe so, yes, in the kind that was done here.
5 Q. Okay, I think -- do you or are you in possession of any
6 literature or scientific study of child interviews that would
7 support the proposition in number one?
8 A. I am not aware of any research on that, no.
9 Q. That is your clinical opinion?
10 A. It is something, yes, I think that's a fair statement.
11 Q. Number two, Dr. Underwager shares personal information
12 with the children. Now let's start off, let's start off with
13 the hypothesis, or the statement, let me, let's agree to make
14 this a statement, that, you know, an over abundance of
15 discussion of one's age, weight, vision, marital relationship,
16 and specially the death of a grandchild would be inappropriate,
17 we can agree on that, can't we?
18 A. If we do, I am glad to hear that.
19 Q. Now, can you, and then it says that the interviews were
20 unnecessarily lengthened by these inappropriate anecdotes and
21 had an unknown impact. Can you show me where in either 1996
22 interview the child's reaction reflected that that particular
23 technique changed the nature of their testimony?
24 A. I don't know if I can. If I can take a minute.
25 Q. Please do.

Page 571

1 A. I don't see as much of the personal information, I see as
2 much personal information shared in the 1996 interviews as the
3 1999 interviews, I think again we can't know the impacts. What
4 I know is it is clearly not a recommended practice to use up
5 children's attention span and to make the interview about the
6 interviewer rather than the interviewee.
7 Q. Would that change your earlier opinion that you just
8 testified to that the quality of the '96 interviews were the
9 same as the quality of the '99 interviews?
10 A. No, because I think I said that the concerning practices
11 weren't identical across '96 and '99, but there were concerning
12 practices in both sets of interviews.
13 Q. You stated on your direct examination that Dr. Underwager
14 repeatedly said throughout the interviews that he is there to
15 help get the uncles out of prison, you recall that testimony?
16 A. I do.
17 Q. Is it not true that in the 1996 interviews that that
18 statement was not made until the end of the interviews?
19 A. I don't know, I will have to check. I believe that that
20 is correct.
21 Q. So it would be a fair statement then that at least with
22 the '96 interviews, that that technique, if you were to look at
23 it, did not change the nature of the child's testimony?
24 A. The technique of telling the child the purpose of the
25 interview?

Page 572

1 Q. Since it was at the end?
2 A. Yes.
3 Q. You would agree with me?
4 A. Yes.
5 Q. In the last sentence of paragraph two it says, for
6 instance, a child may have felt sorry for him and not wanted to
7 say anything that would upset him. You see that sentence?
8 A. I do.
9 Q. That is speculation on your part, isn't it?
10 A. Of course.
11 Q. Because we can not read a child's mind?
12 A. That's right.
13 Q. And also there is no recognized empirical studies to
14 reflect the same also?
15 A. Now I am not sure I followed you.
16   MR. WILKA: I will withdraw it.
17 BY MR. WILKA:
18 Q. Now, number four where it states that Dr. Underwager does
19 not gently challenge the veracity or the inconsistency of the
20 child's reports, are you with me there?
21 A. Yes.
22 Q. Can you show me anywhere in 19, the 1996 interview of
23 either child that the reports were inconsistent as far as being
24 fact specific?
25 A. Well, if there is recantation, by definition there is

Page 573

1 inconsistency, and so some sorting out of that inconsistency
2 would be appropriate in an interview that is looking at
3 recantation.
4 Q. Isn't it not true -- let me ask you a question.
5 Wouldn't it be a fair statement to say that in the '96
6 interviews that Dr. Underwager did not ask overly suggestive
7 questions?
8 A. Oh, no, I would not agree with that all.
9 Q. You would not agree with that?
10 A. No.
11 Q. Would it not be a fair statement to say -- okay, where
12 were there suggestive questions in the '96 Donovan interview,
13 and give me specific ones.
14 A. Well, for instance, Donovan was referring to a girl who
15 asked questions, and Dr. Underwager said the prosecutor.
16 That's an example of a suggestive practice, labeling somebody
17 that the child hasn't labeled.
18 Q. How is that suggestive again?
19 A. The child didn't say who he was talking about that asked
20 the questions, didn't give a name or identify it. So when we
21 label for the child who they are talking about, that is clearly
22 suggesting to the child who they are talking about as opposed
23 to allowing them to describe that person in their own way.
24 Q. But in that exchange, did not right before, Donovan,
25 again the tapes speak for themselves, did not Donovan identify

Page 574

1 a person called Micky, and then Dr. Underwager said oh, the
2 prosecutor. Is that not an affirmation as opposed to a
3 suggestion?
4 A. No, I think it was clear through the interviews, we are
5 focusing only on '96 now, it is clear through the interviews he
6 kept using the word prosecutor and reinforcing that word with
7 the children. They didn't have that name or identity. There
8 is no problem with him, if he called the person Micky, for
9 Dr. Underwager to call that person Micky, which is what we
10 recommend in interviews. We don't substitute our words for the
11 child's words, we simply stick with the child's words and
12 follow along in the narrative.
13 Q. By the use of the word prosecutor at that point of the
14 interview can you show me how that technique changed the nature
15 of Donovan's testimony?
16 A. I didn't say it changed the nature of his testimony. You
17 asked me if there were any suggestive practices, and I gave
18 that as an example. I can give others.
19 Q. Did the children in the '96 interviews appear to give
20 spontaneous statements at any time?
21 A. There were times that Dr. Underwager asked open-ended
22 questions, tell me about that, and they gave a narrative that
23 would be considered, I don't know if it is spontaneous or not,
24 but in response to an open-ended question as opposed to some
25 other more focused, more leading, more suggestive, more

Page 575

1 misleading question.
2 Q. I am looking at ten, paragraph ten, the last sentence on
3 page 2 where it says suggestive and coercive interviews can
4 damage the child's memory?
5 A. Yes.
6 Q. Et cetera. Are you stating that this was a suggestive
7 and coercive interview, '96 Donovan interview?
8 A. I think there were some ways it was suggestive. I would
9 not say that this one was as highly coercive as the ones that
10 happened in '99.
11 Q. How about the '96 Thrista interview, was that coercive or
12 suggestive?
13 A. Again let's go to the '99, let me get it out.
14 Q. Actually I was asking about '96, the '96 interview with
15 Thrista.
16 A. I am sorry, that's the one I am getting out. Yes.
17 Q. Can you show me where in the '96 Thrista interview that
18 there was any element of coercion?
19 A. Oh, yes. He asked questions that only have one answer,
20 like and it took months, didn't it.
21 Q. What subject were we talking about there, give me the
22 context?
23 A. About how long she was away from home.
24 Q. Can you tell me how, just talking about in the context of
25 how long someone, how long Thrista was away from home, how that

Page 576

1 affected the over all nature of her testimony?
2 A. Well, it is in the midst of other things, but there was a
3 sense of this not being just a fact finding mission, but kind
4 of identifying with her in terms of saying that what was done
5 was bad because she was kept away from home for months, and it
6 is much better to be home. He was giving his opinion about
7 these kinds of things as opposed to seeking information from
8 Thrista about what she remembers and recalls, and as we talked
9 about a little while ago, looking at the inconsistencies from
10 before and now.
11 Q. Let's talk about, do you remember, for instance with
12 Donovan, when he said it made him feel mad, do you remember him
13 talking about that?
14 A. Oh, yes.
15 Q. Then Dr. Underwager, do you remember him following up
16 with a question, well, tell me about feeling mad, do you
17 remember that question?
18 A. Yes.
19 Q. Do you find that coercive, suggestive or improper?
20 A. No.
21 Q. So some parts of it he got right?
22 A. Yes.
23 Q. In both '96 interviews Donovan and Thrista, would you
24 agree with me, unequivocally stated that their uncles did not
25 sexually abuse them, would you agree with me?

Page 577

1 A. What I would say is that the viewer of the tape has to
2 interpret what the children were saying when they said things
3 like nothing happened, and they told us what to say. There was
4 not any kind of detailed description here of what it is that
5 didn't happen, or they did say happened that didn't happen.
6 There were very broad, vague statements made both by
7 Dr. Underwager and the children. I think it is a fair
8 interpretation in the context of everything to conclude that
9 the children were agreeing with the fact that they weren't
10 abused, but there was no detailed discussion of what didn't
11 happen.
12 Q. Well, and in fact, would you not agree with me that when
13 one is interviewing a child about sexual abuse, let's say we
14 are interviewing Donovan -- or let's say Thrista, that it would
15 not be healthy for Thrista to go through each and every act in
16 detail of the abuse, because you would in fact reinjure a
17 person who had been abused?
18 A. Now I am confused, we are talking about recantation.
19 Q. But you stated, I was following up on your last answer.
20 Maybe I was confused by it. We will move on.
21 So it's your statement, you say they made vague statements that
22 nothing happened?
23 A. Yes.
24 Q. They made vague statements about they told me what to
25 say?

Page 578

1 A. Yes.
2 Q. And that they agreed that nothing happened to them, is
3 that your testimony?
4 A. Let me say this in a slightly different way. I can't
5 tell from these interviews what it is that the children are
6 denying.
7 Q. What did you, what materials, if any, did you review
8 before you watched these tapes?
9 A. I had FBI and medical reports available to me, and some
10 affidavits.
11 Q. So you knew what we were talking about here, correct?
12 A. Yes, I had to have a context to understand the tapes.
13 Q. But it is still your testimony that you don't know what
14 the kids were denying or recanting?
15 A. I want to be clear, you can't tell from the videotapes
16 what it is the kids are recanting except in a very general way.
17 Q. I am asking you, and if you have already answered, please
18 tell me you have. You, Ms. Mitnick, watching these interviews,
19 having read these FBI 302's and affidavits, et cetera, you did
20 not know what the children were denying was happening?
21 A. Not from the children's reports in these videotapes, no.
22 Q. You stated that Dr. Underwager does not challenge an
23 alternative hypotheses as he suggests should be done in
24 interviews, correct?
25 A. Yes.

Page 579

1 Q. Would it not be a fair statement to say that Donovan in
2 his quite long segment of recantation, would it not be a fair
3 statement to say that to interrupt and to challenge that would
4 interrupt the sequential flow of information that we are
5 seeking?
6 A. Yes, I didn't suggest that it be done in that way.
7 Q. But at some point it should just be gently challenged?
8 A. Yes.
9 Q. You stated that with Donovan he does not begin with open
10 end ended questions as he recommends, and begins with closed
11 questions like did you have chores and stuff, do you feel that
12 is inappropriate?
13 A. There is a more broad answer to that question, which is
14 that the interviews don't begin according to any known protocol
15 that I am familiar with in the United States. It just sort of
16 begins, and begins with these closed ended questions. It
17 doesn't go through any introduction, doesn't include any
18 instructions, it just sort of starts. And the best practices
19 that we recommend is that when we begin questioning children,
20 we begin with open-ended questions even when it is about things
21 not related to the matter at hand, the abuse, or suspected
22 abuse, or the recantation, because we want children to have the
23 experience of speaking in narratives and full sentences, and
24 not begin with yes, no, and short answer questions. So I
25 definitely would say it is not appropriate to start with the

Page 580

1 kinds of questions that it started with.
2 Q. You would have to agree with me, though, that that is,
3 that those questions did not affect the content of the
4 interviews at all?
5 A. I do not know what affect it had.
6 Q. But aren't those types of questions the warming up
7 questions that are recommended? Well, strike that.
8 At the beginning of an interview is there kind of a warm up
9 period that should be there for a child interview?
10 A. I believe that it is Dr. Underwager and Hollida Wakefield
11 his wife's own recommendations that the interviews begin with
12 an introduction and instructions, and then a practice
13 interview, and then follow-up with open-ended questions about
14 the index event or possible events, and that doesn't happen.
15 Q. But just generally should you have kind of a little warm
16 up time?
17 A. Yes, there is a phase of interviews that we call rapport
18 building.
19 Q. That question would be a rapport building question, would
20 you agree?
21 A. I am guessing that is what it was.
22 Q. But it was just phrased wrong?
23 A. It was phrased wrong, yes.
24 Q. But you don't know how it affected any content?
25 A. I know there was no ground work done to explain to

Page 581

1 Donovan what was happening to give him the rules that
2 Dr. Underwager himself recommends, so that he doesn't feel, so
3 that he does feel able to say he doesn't know, to correct the
4 interviewer, a number of rules that we provide children and
5 have them actually practice before getting in to this rapport
6 building.
7 Q. Although he may not have begun the interview with ground
8 rules, is it not true that in these 1996 interviews that
9 Dr. Underwager did in fact, for instance, tell Donovan if you
10 don't remember, you can tell me, and did in fact put out a few
11 ground rules?
12 A. Put out two ground rules in the interviews that he put
13 them out in, yes.
14 Q. On page 5, number 12, you state that, we are on Thrista
15 1, that he puts words in her mouth throughout the interview.
16 What words did Dr. Underwager put in Thrista's mouth in this
17 1996 interview?
18 A. He tells her it is hard for her to think about it, for
19 instance, doesn't ask her, tells her.
20 Q. Is that an affirmation, or putting words in their mouth?
21 A. It can't be an affirmation if the child hasn't expressed
22 it.
23 Q. Now did you make any note of Thrista's body language or
24 facial expressions at that time you put your statement that
25 appears in number 12 on page 5 of your report?

Page 582

1 A. No.
2 Q. Can you tell me what Thrista's reaction was to that?
3 A. I have it reported as I don't recall her agreeing with
4 him or disagreeing with him, I don't recall.
5 Q. Can you tell me how that particular changed the nature of
6 Thrista's testimony?
7 A. I think there was a sequence in this interview of her
8 being told kind of what the appropriate way to think and feel
9 was.
10 Q. And where was that?
11 A. Well, that was one indication. He tells her later foster
12 homes aren't good places for children to be. He tells her you
13 felt that you just didn't know what would happen if you said
14 your uncles didn't do that. I mean I can just go on.
15 Q. And can you show me how that changed the nature of her
16 testimony?
17 A. I can't show you that it changed it. What I can tell you
18 is that those are highly concerning practices for conveying to
19 a child that there are certain kinds of answers and attitudes
20 to have, because the interviewer is telling her the answers
21 rather than asking her the answers.
22 Q. Just a general question about your report. Let me ask
23 what you mean, a list of concerning practices, and so this,
24 these are just a list of the bad things?
25 A. These are a list of concerning practices, yes.

Page 583

1 Q. What do you mean by concerning practices, is concerning
2 practice a bad thing?
3 A. Yes.
4 Q. Would you define concerning practices for me, please?
5 A. They are practices that raise concern about the impact on
6 the child, they are not best practices. They are things, they
7 are practices, methods, could be a specific question, that
8 based on research we know have the potential for causing error
9 in the interview.
10 Q. There is no such thing as a perfect interview, is there?
11 A. There is not.
12 Q. And so it's a fair statement to say that you did not put
13 down or did not list in your ten page report the correct things
14 that Dr. Underwager did, did you?
15 A. That's correct.
16 Q. Because he did a lot of the things right, didn't he?
17 A. I would not use the word a lot.
18 Q. Did he not ask a number of times things like tell me what
19 else you can remember?
20 A. Yes, he did.
21 Q. Is that an appropriate question?
22 A. That is an appropriate question.
23 Q. Did he not, when talking about specific events, ask them
24 what else can you tell me about that, or open-ended questions
25 about that?

Page 584

1 A. There were times he did that, yes.
2 Q. Would it not be a fair statement that he did that
3 throughout most of the '96 Thrista and Donovan interviews?
4 A. He did that -- well, I don't know most of, he did it
5 appropriately in the '96 tapes.
6   MR. WILKA: If I may have a moment, Your Honor?
7   THE COURT: Certainly.
8   MR. WILKA: Thank you.
9 A. You are welcome.
10   THE COURT: Mr. Haugaard.
11 CROSS EXAMINATION BY MR. HAUGAARD:
12 Q. I am Steve Haugaard representing Russ Hubbeling. Can you
13 tell us, are you married?
14 A. I am.
15 Q. Children?
16 A. I do not.
17   MR. SEILER: Objection, irrelevant, Your Honor.
18   THE COURT: Well, you didn't object last time and I
19 thought you would. You are not bound by that, but actually I
20 think her husband and four children are sitting in back of you,
21 but go ahead and ask the question.
22   THE WITNESS: That would be difficult, because I
23 don't have four children.
24   MR. HAUGAARD: I think that's my Pastor.
25   THE WITNESS: He looks like a very nice man, but my

Page 585

1 husband is in Minneapolis.
2   MR. HAUGAARD: Two of those kids are my kids.
3   THE COURT: Alright, I was just curious, I thought
4 you would find out.
5 BY MR. HAUGAARD:
6 Q. How much are you being paid per hour for your work in
7 this case?
8 A. $175.
9 Q. You noted that in the one interview Dr. Underwager
10 affirmed Thrista's being out of the home for several months.
11 In an interview setting, would it be inappropriate to affirm
12 information that was already common to both of the parties in
13 the interview?
14 A. It depends first of all on whether it is indeed common to
15 both people; and second of all, it depends on how one affirms
16 it.
17 Q. Would you agree in an interview setting that it would be
18 inappropriate for an interviewer to describe what other
19 children might have said, or other alleged witnesses might have
20 said?
21 A. Generally that is inappropriate, yes.
22 Q. Would you agree that it would be inappropriate to repeat
23 information of that nature to the child, tending to suggest to
24 them the truthfulness of that information?
25 A. Now I am not sure I followed you.

Page 586

1 Q. If you repeat information expressed by other people,
2 asking for the person being interviewed to either agree or
3 disagree, would that be appropriate?
4 A. It can be problematic, it can be appropriate.
5 Q. If you repeat that information after there has been a
6 denial, would that be appropriate or inappropriate?
7 A. I would have to know more about the context.
8 Q. Is it possible for an interview subject to be impressed
9 by the question as to what the expected answer should be?
10 A. Yes.
11 Q. Would it be inappropriate in an interview situation to
12 place restrictions on whether the subject can come and go from
13 the interview?
14 A. Again it depends on how it is done. Sometimes I will ask
15 kids when they will say can I go out and see my mom in the
16 waiting room, and say can we do that when we are done, can we
17 do that in a little while. I think it is different than
18 coercing a child to stay.
19 Q. Would you agree it's inappropriate to tell a child in an
20 interview how to think or feel about a subject?
21 A. Yes.
22 Q. Would you agree that it's inappropriate to tell a child
23 that something, to preface questions such as I understand you
24 are scared?
25   MR. SEILER: I object to this line of questioning.

Page 587

1   One, it doesn't address her review of the Underwager tapes, nor
2   does it delve into the area of the best practices or generally
3   accepted standards, and therefore beyond the scope and
4   irrelevant.
5   THE COURT: Overruled.
6   A. Could you repeat the question?
7   BY MR. HAUGAARD:
8   Q. Would you agree it's inappropriate in an interview
9   setting to express to a subject of an interview that prefacing
10   a question to say I understand you are scared?
11   A. Well, it depends. If the child just told me they were
12   scared, there wouldn't be a problem with that. If it's coming
13   from somewhere where the child doesn't know it's coming from,
14   it could be inappropriate.
15   Q. Would that also presuppose the interviewer claiming some
16   understanding of what was causing the fright?
17   A. Not necessarily.
18   Q. You have indicated that it is most appropriate in an
19   interview, even though no interview is perfect, would you agree
20   in an interview setting would it be most appropriate if the
21   child was presented with some basic ground rules as to the
22   interview setting?
23   A. There is no universal agreement about doing ground rules,
24   some protocols include them, some protocols don't. I do them
25   with children who are first grade and older. I don't do them

Page 588

1   with children who are younger, because to do them properly is
2   too complicated and time consuming for young children.
3   MR. HAUGAARD: No further questions.
4   CROSS EXAMINATION BY MR. BINGER:
5   Q. My name is Steve Binger, I am the attorney for Jessie
6   Rouse, one of the defendants in this case. I believe you
7   stated earlier that you have testified in criminal cases
8   disproportionately on the side of the prosecution?
9   A. That's correct.
10   Q. Meaning ninety to a hundred percent of the time you have
11   been, you have testified for the prosecutor?
12   A. In terms of testifying, that is correct.
13   Q. Have you testified in favor of a criminal defendant?
14   A. Yes.
15   Q. Have you ever declined to work for the prosecutor in a
16   case?
17   A. I have never declined work, based on my opinion I am
18   sometimes not asked to do anything more.
19   Q. A lot of your report seems to suggest that Dr. Underwager
20   isn't following some of his own recommended practices according
21   to his own writings, or those of Ms. Wakefield?
22   A. That is absolutely correct.
23   Q. So I take it you have read all of their work?
24   A. I have not read all of their works.
25   Q. You have read a number of them concerning the practices

Page 589

1   they recommend?
2   A. I have been involved in a number of cases with
3   Ms. Wakefield where she's prepared reports. Some of their
4   writings from books, yes, let me say transcripts where
5   Dr. Underwager has testified.
6   Q. The things they have written and some of the things you
7   quote about the practices they recommend you agree with them,
8   is that true?
9   A. Generally, yes.
10   Q. You testified just a second ago that you have been
11   involved in a number of cases with Ms. Wakefield?
12   A. Yes.
13   Q. Testifying on the opposite side of her?
14   A. Yes.
15   Q. How many times?
16   A. Less than half a dozen.
17   Q. How about Dr. Underwager?
18   A. Where we actually testified, a couple.
19   Q. Well, cases where you maybe didn't testify, but you were
20   retained to give an opinion on the exact opposite side of him?
21   A. Between a half a dozen and a couple.
22   Q. He is also from Minnesota, isn't he?
23   A. They are both.
24   Q. Do you feel that as a practitioner in this field that you
25   have certain strong academic disagreements with Underwager and

Page 590

1   Wakefield?
2   A. I am not sure what you mean by academic disagreements.
3   Q. Well, are there things about the approaches they take to
4   these cases that you disagree with?
5   A. Yes.
6   Q. And how long has your history of testifying against, or
7   shall I say, I maybe don't mean against, but on the opposite
8   side of Wakefield and Underwager, how many years back does his
9   history go?
10   A. Early '80's.
11   Q. So more than twenty years you have had a practice of
12   critiquing Wakefield and Underwager, is that fair?
13   A. I would say back in the early '80's, which isn't quite
14   twenty years, just rendered different opinions. I wouldn't say
15   I critiqued their work back then.
16   Q. I just want to make sure I didn't miss here something you
17   stated in the answer to one of Mr. Haugaard's questions. Is
18   there no agreed upon protocol for starting an interview with a
19   child?
20   A. There is no universally agreed upon protocol for a
21   forensic interview of a child, that is correct.
22   Q. According to some protocols you should start out with
23   ground rules?
24   A. Yes.
25   Q. But according to other protocols you don't necessarily

Page 591

1 have to?

2 A. That is correct.

3 Q. But in your personal opinion you think you should?

4 A. And in Ms. Wakefield's own writings.

5 Q. I am talking about yours?

6 A. I want to be clear what I said was with children first

7 grade and older, yes, I think it is helpful.

8 Q. During the section of your report about sharing, this is

9 section two on the first page, sharing personal information

10 with the children. And you say this is never recommended for

11 various reasons, which you then list. Do I read that paragraph

12 correctly as saying that you believe the damage that comes from

13 that is that it unnecessarily lengthens the interview?

14 A. One of the problems, yes.

15 Q. Is there, I assume you will probably say this will vary

16 from child to child, but is there a certain length of interview

17 that just gets to be excessive, too long?

18 A. Yes, it definitely varies from child to child and varies

19 from age to age.

20 Q. How long was the interview with Donovan, do you know?

21 A. Boy, you know, I wrote it down, but I don't have that

22 information right here in front of me, I can't tell you the

23 length of each of the interviews.

24 Q. You are not prepared to tell us you think the interview

25 was too long, are you?

Page 592

1 A. I am not prepared to tell you that specific thing.

2 Q. Let's just assume -- well, maybe I better ask and not

3 assume.

4 Did you ever keep track of how long this interview was

5 lengthened because of Dr. Underwager's practice of sharing

6 personal information with the child.

7 A. The absolute number of minutes, no.

8 Q. It could have been two minutes?

9 A. It was longer than two minutes but, no, I did not keep

10 track of it.

11 Q. Well, I mean just getting right down to the nitty-gritty

12 here, if his sharing personal information caused a thirty

13 minute interview to become a thirty-five minute interview, are

14 you trying to tell me that is serious, that we should be

15 concerned about it?

16 A. What I am telling you is it can be serious, that that

17 could be five minutes of thirty. One-sixth of the time can be

18 five minutes that we didn't get forensically relevant

19 information from a child because he was wasting that child's

20 attention span sharing inappropriate information.

21 Q. Did you see any evidence that these children's attention

22 spans, you know, weakened and faded, any of that, because of

23 the time?

24 A. These were not children who were like hyperactive

25 children, so not in that way that we often see with little kids

Page 593

1 where they start flopping all over the room and doing things

2 that really tell us. So in that way, no, I didn't see that.

3 Q. You didn't see any of these children strongly showing a

4 lack of attention at any time, isn't that true?

5 A. I think that's a fair statement.

6   MR. BINGER: Thank you, that's all I have.

7 CROSS EXAMINATION BY MR. CARTER:

8 Q. In your practice, Ma'am, do you have experience in

9 working with Native American children?

10 A. I haven't myself interviewed Native American children for

11 about fifteen years, because I am not doing front line

12 interviews any more. And so I had a practice early on when

13 there weren't a lot of resources in Minneapolis for

14 interviewing children, and I was actually doing forensic

15 interviews for child protection and the police. But I would

16 say it's probably been fifteen years since I have personally

17 interviewed a Native American child.

18 Q. Did you say that you worked for the police?

19 A. I don't work for them, but there were times when children

20 were sent to me for an interview because of my specialized

21 skills in the early days before we had police and social

22 workers with forensic interview training.

23 Q. Is it your point of view that all of your criticisms in

24 your report are applicable equally to Native American children

25 and others, non-Native American children?

Page 594

1 A. As far as I know there has not been any research on the

2 specific kinds of things about the form of the question, and

3 the, you know, the leading questions and the misleading

4 questions, I am not aware of any of that being done from a

5 cross cultural perspective at all.

6 Q. In your experience in working with Native American

7 children do you think it's fair to say maybe they are a little

8 more quiet and reserved than maybe the non-Native American

9 child?

10 A. It's a general statement, but it is consistent with my

11 experience.

12 Q. Would that not then make some difference in terms of the

13 methodology that might be used by an interviewer to sort of

14 warm up the child for the interview to make them feel at ease?

15 A. What I would say is we would use the standard

16 methodology, and if it wasn't working, we would move to

17 something different. We would not begin with an assumption

18 that the methodology doesn't work, because we have no basis to

19 know that with any individual child any more than a white

20 European child might not respond to the normal methodology and

21 we might have to change it.

22 Q. Can't you tell within a matter of a few minutes whether a

23 child is going to be outgoing and bubbly and very verbal, or

24 one who is going to we staring down at his shoes?

25 A. I think that's a fair statement.

Page 595

1 Q. So that Dr. Underwager who had been at this business for
2 a few years could probably make that determination do you
3 think?
4 A. I think there is no indication in the videotapes that the
5 children were uncooperative or unable to answer the questions,
6 only that they might have been more quiet, might have taken
7 them a little bit longer to think about the answers.
8 Q. When you interview people, is it your testimony that
9 basically you don't ever laugh at any part of the proceeding?
10 A. No, certainly I wouldn't say that.
11 Q. There are times when that's appropriate?
12 A. There are times when that's appropriate.
13 Q. Do you believe that over all your letter presents fair
14 criticism of Dr. Underwager?
15 A. Absolutely.
16 Q. You don't think you are unduly nitpicky?
17 A. I do not. In fact, I did not give lists and lists and
18 lists of the kinds of errors, I gave examples of the errors. I
19 could have listed every single instance of the errors.
20 Q. So in addition to the ten pages that you did provide, you
21 probably could have given another ten if you really tried?
22 A. Wouldn't have been really trying. I don't know if it
23 would have been ten, there are certainly more examples of the
24 problems that I indicated.
25 Q. Now, and you believe that this is realistic common sense

Page 596

1 criticism?
2 A. This is the kind of critique I am asked to do all across
3 the country when I review videotapes, yes.
4 Q. That's really not the question, but is that reasonable
5 common sense criticism, or is it nitpicking?
6 A. When we are talking about the basic issues about a
7 protocol and instructions and open-ended questions and
8 inappropriate practices, I believe it is very fair criticism,
9 very even handed.
10 Q. Ten pages and maybe another ten pages over interviews
11 that took probably a couple hours?
12 A. That's why I was so concerned about the interviews.
13   MR. CARTER: I don't have any other questions.
14   THE COURT: Redirect.
15   MR. SEILER: No, Your Honor.
16   THE COURT: I have a couple questions for you. On
17 paragraph 14 of your opinion letter Exhibit 24 you reflect
18 there that Dr. Underwager and Ms. Wakefield recommend practice
19 interviews with the children before interviewing about possible
20 abuse. You observe they recommend it, but do you recommend it?
21 A. Actually I don't, Your Honor.
22   THE COURT: Actually, if you know, what do they mean
23 by a practice interview?
24 A. Oh, I do know. It is part of something called the step
25 wise protocol where before you get to the abuse you ask the

Page 597

1 child about any life events that they have had, and you
2 practice with them asking open-ended questions, and then
3 following up for details. And you do that, in that protocol
4 you do it about two different life events, so that the child
5 has familiarity with the style of the questioning they are
6 going to experience, and so they are more familiar with
7 open-ended questions when you get to the actual abuse inquiry.
8   THE COURT: Do you agree that in the instance of
9 these interviews that it was a good practice for Dr. Underwager
10 to videotape these interviews?
11 A. Yes, I do.
12   THE COURT: To be blunt about one thing,
13 Dr. Underwager is a very, very, very large man, and I watched
14 the tapes too, and of course I have seen him live here in
15 Court, but despite that, when I watched the tapes at least I
16 didn't have any sense that his bulk was intimidating the
17 children. Did you have any observation of that?
18 A. I didn't have any observation that they were specifically
19 intimidated by his physical presence, no. .
20   THE COURT: I paid attention to that since he was
21 sitting reasonably close to them, but I didn't have that
22 feeling there was any intimidation by his mere size.
23 A. No, I didn't observe that either.
24   THE COURT: Thank you, I have no other questions. Do
25 the Court's questions give rise to questions by either side?

Page 598

1   MR. SEILER: Not on behalf of the government, Your
2 Honor.
3   MR. WILKA: No, Your Honor.
4   MR. HAUGAARD: No.
5   MR. BINGER: No.
6   MR. CARTER: No.
7   THE COURT: Thank you, you may step down. We
8 finished this witness at a propitious time. Now, recognizing
9 of course that sometimes cross has taken longer than the
10 direct, and that is no criticism because we have four people to
11 cross, I mean to conduct the cross and only one person to
12 directs, none-the-less, keeping that in mind does the
13 government think that starting at 10:30 on Wednesday we are
14 going to finish this thing by five o'clock on Wednesday night?
15   MR. HOLMES: Your Honor, I am always hesitant to make
16 those representations because the Court is well aware of my
17 track record as far as accuracy of those estimations. I would
18 think we would be pushing it. We may get done.
19   THE COURT: Well, I am just trying to think about it
20 logistically. You know, I didn't anticipate this was going to
21 be going on until a while ago, I made a commitment to speak to
22 the trial lawyers convention in the Black Hills on Thursday,
23 and so I am on the program for all morning and I really can't
24 back out of that. So if you don't finish, I have a hearing on
25 Friday morning that Mr. Holmes is familiar with. How long do

Page 599

1 you think that one will last?

2 MR. HOLMES: We are not the moving party there, Your

3 Honor. I would assume in that case the two defendants will

4 testify, and both counsel have been requested by me to appear

5 and testify. I would anticipate that at most a half day

6 evidentiary matter.

7 THE COURT: That has been my, that was my estimate

8 too, I figured it was a half day deal. Well, if we don't get

9 done, I didn't schedule anything after that, because frankly

10 that's the opening day of prairie chicken hunting and I was

11 going to be out west prairie chicken hunting the next morning,

12 Saturday morning, but this obviously is a lot more important

13 than that. So once, if we don't get done on Wednesday, then

14 once we are done with the Newman hearing on Friday morning,

15 then we will continue with this hearing.

16 MR. HOLMES: Your Honor, we would ask the Court's

17 permission to call Ms. Tapken as a witness on the Brady issues

18 for very brief testimony, she is not going to be available next

19 week. She was on the defendants witness list and was not

20 called, but we believe there are just a few questions that need

21 to be responded to to have the record complete, and we would

22 ask the Court's permission to extend the hearing now to allow

23 her to testify.

24 THE COURT: Very well, proceed.

25 MR. HOLMES: Call Michelle Tapken.

Page 600

1

2 MICHELLE TAPKEN,

3 called as a witness, being first duly sworn, testified and said

4 as follows:

5

6 DIRECT EXAMINATION BY MR. HOLMES:

7 Q. Please state your name for the record?

8 A. Michelle Tapken.

9 Q. Ms. Tapken, you are currently the United States Attorney

10 for the District of South Dakota, is that correct?

11 A. I am.

12 Q. In 1994 you were an assistant United States Attorney in

13 the same district, is that correct?

14 A. That's correct.

15 Q. And did you or were you assigned this case that was

16 eventually prosecuted in this Court involving the four

17 defendants that are present today?

18 A. I was, with co-counsel.

19 Q. And who was your co-counsel in that case?

20 A. Karen Schreier.

21 Q. She was the United States Attorney at the time, is that

22 right?

23 A. That's correct.

24 Q. Can you in a general sense just inform the Court how you

25 initially became involved in the investigation?

Page 601

1 A. I can. I was actually leaving town, I was in the

2 airport, I believe, in Denver on my way to San Diego to a

3 conference, and I was called by the U. S. Attorney and asked to

4 return back to South Dakota because there had been a child

5 sexual abuse case reported, and I did so.

6 Q. Was Bill Van Roe from the FBI the case agent involved in

7 the investigation?

8 A. Yes, he was.

9 Q. Was Dan Hudspeth the Bureau of Indian Affairs

10 investigator?

11 A. Yes, he was.

12 Q. Were you generally made aware by them of how far the

13 investigation had progressed up to that point?

14 A. Yes, sir.

15 Q. Through your involvement of the case were you ever with

16 the children who ended up subsequently testifying at trial,

17 were you ever alone with them?

18 A. Never.

19 Q. How many times did you meet with the children?

20 A. I believe with the girls twice in an interview situation

21 prior to trial, and then I saw them when the guardian ad litem

22 did a visit to the courthouse, and then at the trial.

23 Q. Eva Cheney was the guardian ad litem, is that correct?

24 A. Yes, sir. And I believe I saw Donovan one time other

25 than the times before the trial, but any time I saw them it

Page 602

1 would be reflected in a 302 by the FBI, because the FBI was

2 always present when I saw them.

3 Q. Would that have been either Agent Van Roe or Agent Matt

4 Miller?

5 A. Yes, sir.

6 Q. At the time of trial what contact did you have with the

7 children other than in the courtroom?

8 A. Other than in the hallway, that was about it. The

9 guardian ad litem was with them, I believe I walked down to get

10 the guardian ad litem and walked up here with her and the

11 children. It was very limited.

12 Q. At any time when the children were in your presence did

13 they ever say that these acts of sexual abuse did not occur?

14 A. Never.

15 Q. Did you or anyone in your presence ever offer the

16 children items such as clothing, toys or money?

17 A. Nobody in my presence nor I.

18 MR. HOLMES: No further questions.

19 THE COURT: Cross.

20 MR. WILKA: I will defer, I have none.

21 MR. HAUGAARD: Thank you, Your Honor.

22 CROSS EXAMINATION BY MR. HAUGAARD:

23 Q. Ms. Tapken, are you aware of whether there were any tape

24 recordings or notes made of the interviews or the discussions

25 you had with the children?

Page 603

1 A. Yes, there should, I believe you have all of those.
2 There would be not tape recordings, but the 302's. Any time I
3 was present with the children the FBI did a 302 and those were
4 provided to defense counsel.
5 Q. And did you make notes of those interviews?
6 A. No, I did not.
7 Q. Are you aware of whether there were any notes or
8 recordings done of the interviews done by the foster parents?
9 A. No, I am not. I wouldn't have ever been present during
10 those. If they were done, they would have been turned over in
11 discovery as a 302.
12 Q. Did you ever see the children anywhere other than in the
13 federal building or in your suite of offices there in the
14 Shriver building?
15 A. No, sir.
16 Q. You indicated that the FBI was always present when you
17 were speaking with the children?
18 A. Yes, sir.
19 Q. Were they present when you were preparing for their
20 testimony here in the courthouse?
21 A. I did not prepare them here in the courthouse. I believe
22 the guardian ad litem came to my office, and the FBI would have
23 been present, yes, that's correct.
24 Q. The FBI was always present when you were in the room with
25 the children?

Page 604

1 A. Yes, sir.
2 Q. Was there ever any exception to that?
3 A. No exception, sir.
4 Q. When you were speaking with the children, were there
5 times when you were speaking with just one alone and the other
6 children were in the room off to the side?
7 A. No. The practice was when they would come to our office,
8 the FBI agent would go out and get one child and bring them
9 into the office. When the guardian ad litem was appointed,
10 then she was the one that did that, but generally there was
11 only one child interviewed at a time.
12 Q. Did you ever meet with the children in any rooms here in
13 the courthouse?
14 A. During the trial?
15 Q. Yes?
16 A. Never alone. I may have walked down to the room where
17 they were, the guardian ad litem would have always been there.
18 I think I walked down in between when we were bringing a child
19 up to testify, but the guardian ad litem was always there.
20 Q. So did you speak with the children in the room where they
21 were waiting?
22 A. I don't believe I did, other than to say it is time to
23 go, that type of thing.
24   MR. HAUGAARD: No further questions.
25   THE COURT: Mr. Binger.

Page 605

1 CROSS EXAMINATION BY MR. BINGER:
2 Q. Did there come a time in 1995 or 1996 when you got a
3 phone call from Kathleen Honomichl?
4 A. During 1995 and 1996?
5 Q. Yes.
6 A. I honestly can't tell you. I know I did see Kathleen
7 Honomichl down at the Reservation, but I can't tell you if I
8 got a phone call.
9 Q. You don't, do you recall either getting a phone call or
10 otherwise getting word from her that the children had recanted
11 their stories?
12   MR. HOLMES: Objection, not relevant to the Brady
13 issue present in the case, after the Trial.
14   THE COURT: Not relevant to Brady, that's true. This
15 is framed as a Brady issue. You were going to call her but
16 didn't, ask your next question.
17   MR. BINGER: I am sorry, sustained as to Brady?
18   THE COURT: Right, because she was proffered as a
19 Brady, she was listed as a witness of yours, and you didn't
20 call her, so cross examination of whatever the direct was.
21 BY MR. BINGER:
22 Q. At some point in time you had a meeting with Kathleen
23 Honomichl down in Wagner?
24   MR. HOLMES: Same objection.
25   THE COURT: Sustained.

Page 606

1   MR. BINGER: Well, just to clarify that subject.
2 BY MR. BINGER:
3 Q. When is the first time that you ever heard that the
4 children had recanted, or any of the children had recanted
5 their testimony?
6 A. At least probably a year after the trial. It was some
7 period of time after the trial.
8   MR. BINGER: Your Honor, just for purposes of making
9 the defense record in this case, we would argue, and I would
10 cite United States verse DeVoe, 493 F.2nd 776 from the Fifth
11 Circuit, a case that stands for the proposition that a Brady
12 violation can occur when an appeal is still in progress. I
13 believe the appeal was in progress until at least eighteen
14 months after the jury verdict.
15   THE COURT: Let me hear from the government on that.
16   MR. HOLMES: The Court has resolved this issue. The
17 Court issued an order regarding this hearing, and said that
18 Ms. Tapken's testimony was going to be limited to disclosures
19 that preceded or were during trial.
20   THE COURT: Frankly, I thought that was the issue
21 that we were dealing with, and it is your contention now that
22 there was a Brady violation some time during the appeal
23 process, is that it?
24   MR. BINGER: That was part of our original submission
25 in the case, Your Honor, was the United States Attorney's

Page 607

1 office became aware of this while the appeal was in progress.
2   THE COURT: But how would the, even if, assuming for
3 purposes of discussion that the appeal was in progress, how
4 would the record, which is already up on appeal, be
5 supplemented with that information?
6   MR. BINGER: I am looking at a footnote to this
7 opinion that I just cited to the Court. It is not a footnote,
8 I am sorry, Your Honor, in which the Court states even though
9 the government may not be required to alert the defense to
10 exculpatory developments subsequent to trial, and at this point
11 the Court is assuming that it is not, the discovery by the
12 defense of that same information may serve, in inappropriate
13 circumstances, to call in to question the fairness of the
14 earlier trial for the same reasons explicated by Mr. Justice
15 Douglas in the Brady decision. Unfairness may have crept into
16 the trial unexpectedly and should therefore be corrected in a
17 new trial if the evidence was material to the outcome. Even in
18 the Brady instance, some guidelines in this type of situation
19 are apparent. Personally I am not familiar with case law that
20 says one way or the other that the discovery of exculpatory
21 information while the case is still pending is a Brady
22 violation or not a Brady violation, but I think for purposes of
23 establishing our factual record we should be allowed to inquire
24 in to this.
25   THE COURT: Well, one concern I have about that is

Page 608

1 then if that were the case, it seems to me the flip side is
2 then that in order to have a record we would have to know when
3 the defense became otherwise aware of the first recantation,
4 whenever that was. I don't know that, because that might make
5 a difference if you accept the proposition that while a case is
6 on appeal there could be a Brady violation by not disclosing
7 information of a recantation. I am not sure about it being a
8 Brady violation. Let's just say that some violation of the
9 inherent fairness of the proceedings, I mean I am talking
10 hypothetically, it seems to me we would really need a
11 determination of that. The Court would have to know when the
12 defense first learned of a recantation. I don't know that, I
13 am not asking you to tell me at this point, all I am saying, it
14 seems to me that would be the rest of the story, because that
15 would impact whether the Court would even have to examine the
16 issue, because if the defense knew beforehand, for example,
17 that would make a difference.
18   MR. BINGER: Well, I can only, without going back
19 through every single one of our records, I can only assure the
20 Court that we are very confident it was not until some time
21 after the appeal had been decided, and it was a very lengthy
22 appeal proceeding, specially with the rehearing involved, but
23 that we did not learn of any recantation until after that had
24 occurred. But that is a whole other subject of whether you
25 want to start putting defense lawyers on the witness stand,

Page 609

1 which I don't think anybody is ready to deal with today.
2   THE COURT: I told you, I wasn't asking you, do you
3 remember.
4   MR. BINGER: Yes, I do remember that, and I can
5 understand the relevance of what the Court is saying, but at
6 the same time the Brady obligation is on the prosecutor, not
7 the defense. So for purpose of our inquiry now of this witness
8 while she is on the stand today before she leaves town I think
9 we should be allowed to proceed.
10   THE COURT: I have heard from you, now I will hear
11 from the government.
12   MR. HOLMES: Even the case cited by Mr. Binger makes
13 it clear that Brady is inapplicable, the trial is over. Even
14 if you want to accept his argument regarding an obligation,
15 what is the remedy then? Here clearly defense counsel at some
16 point in time became aware of these matters, which allowed them
17 to bring the motion that has us here today. So I guess the
18 timing of when someone knew or didn't know I would submit is of
19 absolutely no importance in the context of what we are doing
20 right now. The defense had Ms. Tapken on their witness list,
21 they chose not to call her, we called her for the purpose of
22 making our limited record regarding Brady as we see it. These
23 questions are clearly outside the scope of our examination,
24 they had their chance to call her, they didn't do it. We don't
25 believe they should be able to do a discovery inquiry at this

Page 610

1 point in time.
2   THE COURT: I want to see the Fifth Circuit case,
3 please.
4   MR. CARTER: It's in the pretrial brief packet I
5 filed with the Court.
6   THE COURT: Well, you know, the stack is about four
7 feet high. Maybe I can find it real quickly. Wait a minute.
8 If it is your brief of December 12 of 2000, I read that one and
9 the cases were attached and it is not that one.
10   MR. CARTER: The one I filed a day or so before
11 trial, 4th of September.
12   THE COURT: United States versus Frank DeVoe, I have
13 it.
14   MR. CARTER: There is a number 36 to the left of that
15 section of the case where it talks about Brady, and you can
16 probably see the highlight there of the Brady as well.
17   THE COURT: Yes. I read your brief before these
18 proceedings started, I wondered why you had DeVoe there,
19 because I saw the case, but didn't know the reason you cited
20 it. You know, the case, when you look at, I assume these are
21 headnote numbers that are in the margin. It says the Court is
22 assuming that the government may not be required to alert the
23 defense to exculpatory statements subsequent to trial. Then
24 goes on to make essentially the point that I did, I think,
25 rather one of fairness, although not a Brady violation.

Page 611

1   MR. CARTER: My reason for including it, Judge, was
2 it was one of the few, perhaps the only case I found in
3 research that found anything that really talked about Brady as
4 it related to matters after trial, and so I included it for
5 that reason as well as for the language that follows that on
6 the more general issue of fairness.
7   MR. HOLMES: Your Honor, this Court in its order of
8 March 28 directly stated the defendants shall not inquire in to
9 Ms. Tapken's knowledge of recantations after trial, as such
10 information would be irrelevant to the alleged Brady violation,
11 I think that is very clear.
12   THE COURT: I think that is pretty clear. Let's
13 assume for purposes of discussion that a year or year and a
14 half after the trial Ms. Tapken got some kind of a notification
15 that one of the children had recanted, and that the defense
16 didn't find out until say six months after that, and we are now
17 hearing the motion for new trial, which is what DeVoe really
18 considering it for, and under DeVoe even it is clear that since
19 it wasn't something that was during the trial, then there would
20 be no Giglio law automatic re-trial. How does that bear then,
21 even assuming those facts I set out, you learned it six months
22 after the government learned it, and how does that bear on the
23 new trial issue now?
24   MR. CARTER: Well, I think that when you combine the
25 issue of the recantation knowledge with the other evidence

Page 612

1 concerning the -- at the time of trial there was of course the
2 excluded testimony concerning the other sexual acts of the
3 children and so forth, and when you look at all those combined,
4 we have come to a point where there is a wide range of
5 information and evidence that we think would justify a new
6 trial. Now as to the, whether there is a remedy beyond the new
7 trial aspect of this, whether there would have been time to
8 have changed something relative to the appeals that were in the
9 Eighth Circuit at the time, I guess people that were involved
10 in that would be better able to speak than I. You know, I
11 would suggest that is probably one of the concerns that's out
12 there, that it foreclosed some of those things, and maybe this
13 motion being filed earlier, if that would have had any bearing.
14 Perhaps a motion to supplement the record, or reopen, or
15 something of that nature.
16   THE COURT: My question was, though, how does it
17 impact now the motion that is before the Court for a new trial?
18 In a hypothetical, let's say you learned six months later than
19 the government did about one of the children recanting.
20   MR. BINGER: Can I offer an answer to that, Your
21 Honor?
22   THE COURT: Sure.
23   MR. BINGER: Brady off to the side, but strictly the
24 issue of the motion for a new trial, part of our case has been
25 based upon the fact that these children recanted to Kathleen

Page 613

1 Honomichl and a few others. Kathleen Honomichl then testified
2 she got on the phone and she immediately reported that
3 information to the U. S. Attorney's office, who then told them,
4 well, too late now, we are not going to do anything about it,
5 that's been the testimony of one of our witnesses. We should
6 be allowed to find out whether that is corroborated by the
7 witness that she called.
8   THE COURT: You already did, she said she couldn't
9 remember talking to Kathleen Honomichl on the telephone.
10   MR. BINGER: I guess I thought that she had said she
11 did talk to her, but she couldn't remember exactly when.
12   THE COURT: No. Well, the record speaks for itself,
13 but just a minute.
14   MR. BINGER: Back to my point, if we are trying to
15 corroborate the testimony of our own witness, we should be able
16 to ask her if she can do so or not. If she says she doesn't
17 know or doesn't remember, then I guess we have failed at that.
18   THE COURT: In your cross examination, and I
19 recognize when somebody is cross examining, because I remember
20 when I was doing it myself, it is harder to take notes because
21 you can't and think at the same time when you are cross
22 examining, but according to my notes there was a question about
23 a telephone call from Honomichl that you asked, and the witness
24 replied she can't remember if she received a telephone call
25 from her or not.

Page 614

1   MR. HAUGAARD: There would be a question with regard
2 to whether or not she had a face-to-face conversation with her.
3   THE COURT: Didn't get to that. I think it was
4 implicitly acknowledged that there was subsequently a meeting,
5 just couldn't remember whether there was a telephone call or
6 not. There has no reason been shown to deviate from the Order
7 that I entered to begin with. And frankly, with regard to the
8 new trial motion that's before me, I can't see that that issue
9 bears on the new trial question, because even if, assuming for
10 purposes of discussion, there was some sort of requirement that
11 the prosecution a year or year and a half after trial give
12 notification of a recantation, that is not a Brady violation,
13 hasn't been shown to be one. That's what we are making inquiry
14 in now, because there is some allegations made of Brady
15 violations, but this wouldn't be one of them, so proceed.
16 BY MR. BINGER:
17 Q. I believe you did mention in your testimony that you had
18 a meeting with Kathleen Honomichl face-to-face at some point in
19 time?
20 A. Yes.
21 Q. In Wagner?
22 A. Yes.
23 Q. Do you remember where?
24 A. I do. I remember it quite well, because I had had
25 surgery, I believe a week before that, and it was maybe 22

Page 615

1 below zero, and I did not want to go to Wagner. I didn't feel
2 well, and I didn't feel like I needed to be out on the road in
3 22 below zero weather, and I called my boss, and my boss said
4 there is an MDT meeting and you will go to Wagner. I later
5 found out it was, because I was leaving for Washington, D.C.
6 the next week, and they were going to have a little goodbye
7 party, and that's why my boss was adamant. So I asked my
8 mother to ride with me, and Bill Van Roe was at the meeting,
9 and I asked Bill Van Roe to please follow me back to Sioux
10 Falls, because I was concerned about being out in that cold
11 weather. Now I can remember that much about it, which is quite
12 a bit of detail. It was January, and it was January days
13 before I left for Washington, D.C. You are going to ask me
14 what year that was, and the Judge knows I am bad with math, bad
15 with years. I believe it was 1996, January.
16 Q. At that time do you recall at this meeting Kathleen
17 Honomichl attempting to bring up to your attention --
18 A. She asked to speak to Bill Van Roe and I together, and
19 she told me at that time, and I was shocked. She told me at
20 that time that Mr. Haugaard had had the children interviewed by
21 Dr. Underwager, Donovan and Thrista, and that they were now
22 recanting, and I remember saying Mr. Haugaard, because I was
23 shocked because I thought there was a Court Order that said
24 there would not be an independent psychological exam done by
25 Dr. Underwager, and to me I remember saying to Mr. Van Roe, I

Page 616

1 was taken back by this, and I said I thought the Court order
2 said that Judge Piersol said there wouldn't be an independent
3 exam by Dr. Underwager, and now according, I said to
4 Ms. Honomichl, are you sure it was Mr. Haugaard that did this?
5 And she said yes. And at that point we left.
6 Q. Did she ever tell you the children had recanted their
7 testimony to her?
8 A. I don't believe -- I can't remember that, I can remember
9 being very surprised at this. He may have at that point said
10 and I know this, too, I honestly can't remember that. I was
11 just taken aback by the fact that they had been examined.
12 Q. So she, you can't remember well enough to say yes or no
13 to the issue of whether she directly told you that they had
14 recanted, correct?
15 A. She very possibly may have, but I can't swear to that.
16 Q. Picking out one aspect of her testimony, you recall that
17 this, that these revelations angered you and caused you to
18 pound your fist on the table and say, damn it, I will prosecute
19 somebody for perjury if they are getting somebody to change
20 their story?
21 A. No, I don't, I think it took me back, I was surprised at
22 it. I don't believe I pounded my fist on the table.
23 Q. Did you talk about possible witness tampering?
24 A. I don't believe I did. I don't remember that I did that.
25 Q. Well, on the issue of whether this would have been in

Page 617

1 1996 or perhaps '97, would there be a record of that some
2 where?
3 A. Sure, it was right before I went, days before I went to
4 Washington, D.C., and at that point I wasn't involved in the
5 case when I left. I was, I left for Washington, D.C., and I
6 was there for a year, and someone else from our office. I
7 think shortly after that time while I was gone the motion for
8 the new trial came, and I believe somebody else worked on it.
9 I am sure that date could be verified by Mr. Van Roe.
10 Q. Is it possible you received a fax at some point in time
11 from the Social Service office in Marty?
12 A. Mr. Binger, my policy is consistently that I don't, I
13 tell social service workers, and I think they, you would find
14 this is, I tell them not to fax me things, to please fax them
15 to the FBI, because I am not an investigator. The same with
16 phone calls, if they call me and they want to report something,
17 I ask them to contact an agent so there can be a 302 made of
18 it. But in my review of the records for this case, I did find
19 that I had received a fax from Kathleen Honomichl, which was
20 somewhat uncharacteristic for the way we proceed with things.
21 That fax did indicate, I can tell you there was nothing in that
22 fax that said abuse did not take place. I can tell you that it
23 talked about other abuse that had taken place. It was faxed
24 because as mandated, the Children's Home I think felt they knew
25 of further allegations and they were mandated reporters, and

Page 618

1 that is the reason I believe it was faxed.
2 Q. You have any recollection of when that fax took place?
3 A. I don't. I don't have a recollection.
4 Q. Would you remember whether it was before or after the --
5 A. It could certainly be provided to you.
6 Q. But as you are just available this week, do you have any
7 independent memory of whether it was before or after that
8 meeting you had, that MDT meeting you had down there?
9 A. I don't.
10   MR. BINGER: That's all the questions I have.
11   THE COURT: Mr. Carter.
12   MR. CARTER: Thank you.
13 CROSS EXAMINATION BY MR. CARTER:
14 Q. Micky, you were, were you involved in this case at the
15 time that the kids were down with Donna Jordan.
16 A. I became involved at the time the FBI did the interview
17 down there, yes.
18 Q. And was there a time when Donna Jordan had prepared a
19 dream book type thing that the kids were having?
20 A. I recall something to that effect.
21 Q. And were, these were written notes or statements, did you
22 ever see these written things?
23 A. I don't know if I did or not. I recall something about a
24 dream book. If I did, they would have been provided in
25 discovery. Everything that we had that was provided to us was

Page 619

1 provided in discovery. We specifically asked Agent Van Roe to
2 come over, we had two secretaries at the U. S. Attorney's
3 office, because there were some issues as to discovery in this,
4 and we wanted to be certain that we had provided everything we
5 had. So if that was the case, if we had anything like that, it
6 would have been provided.
7 Q. Well, again I was not involved in the case at that time,
8 and from the files that I have gone through I have not seen any
9 such material, nor have other counsel on the defense team to my
10 knowledge. I guess do you recall that there was ever such a
11 thing that you saw that you would have had in your possession?
12 A. If I had it in my possession, counsel would have had it,
13 that's my testimony. We provided, whatever was in our
14 possession we provided to defense counsel.
15 Q. But you were aware of this material even if you didn't
16 have it in your possession?
17 A. I believe I have heard the word dream book, but I don't
18 know any more than that about it.
19 Q. Well, in fact, didn't you make a telephone call to the
20 counselor there insisting they stop keeping this dream book?
21 A. Not that I am aware of. I can't remember, I remember the
22 word dream book, if you can tell me more about it or when and
23 where.
24 Q. Again it's my understanding that these were notes that
25 were maintained by Donna Jordan early on when Rosemary was

Page 620

1 first in her care, and that these materials were describing the
2 dreams, the bad dreams that Rosemary was having that led to
3 ultimately some of these first charges of sexual abuse. Now
4 does that sound familiar?
5 A. No.
6 Q. But if these materials were in existence, it would have
7 been your intention to have turned them over as part of
8 discovery?
9 A. We did go through, with the FBI and two people in our
10 office, through everything we had and turned it over.
11 Q. The fax that you testified to a bit ago with respect to
12 questions from Mr. Binger, was that turned over as part of the
13 discovery?
14 A. That was after the trial.
15 Q. But it was not turned over then I take it?
16 A. I don't believe any information was turned over after the
17 trial.
18 Q. Do you recall any conversations with Donna Jordan about
19 the dreams that Rosemary was having?
20 A. I never spoke to Donna Jordan independently about
21 anything. If there were any conversations with Donna Jordan,
22 the FBI would have been present and those would have been
23 recorded in 302's which would have been provided.
24 Q. What about any independent discussions with Counselor
25 Kelson?

Page 621

1 A. I don't believe, I think she was, she provided us the
2 notes that she had from her counseling sessions, and those were
3 all turned over to defense counsel.
4 Q. Did you have any discussions with her about those
5 counseling sessions?
6 A. I received the notes from her, and we talked pretrial.
7 Q. And those notes, I think that's true, Micky, I did see
8 many of those in the file, so that yes, those were turned over,
9 and I don't have a question I guess relative to it being turned
10 over as far as that goes. Were the children ever told in your
11 presence anything to the effect that if they, what it was going
12 to take for them to go home?
13 A. No, that wasn't something that was in our discretion,
14 that was up to the social service department. We had no
15 control over that.
16 Q. So I take it you don't remember any comments made to that
17 effect?
18 A. No, I don't.
19   MR. CARTER: I have no further questions.
20   MR. HOLMES: Nothing further, Your Honor.
21   THE COURT: Thank you, you may step down. I have a
22 question that I am trying to formulate, and that is that, you
23 know, Brady aside, because this is a post-trial, but assuming
24 that Ms. Tapken found out about the possibility or the fact of
25 recantation as a result of Dr. Underwager conducting the

Page 622

1 interviews, which we have the tapes of in '96, October of '96,
2 then how then, even though I recognize that the defense has to
3 explore every possibility, how then does that raise the issue
4 that you were talking about?
5   MR. BINGER: The Brady issue?
6   THE COURT: Whether you call it Brady or whether you
7 call it fairness like Justice Douglas did or what, how does it
8 raise the issue, if as a practical matter the prosecution
9 learned of the possibility of a recantation through
10 Dr. Underwager conducting the interviews with the assistance of
11 defense counsel.
12   MR. HAUGAARD: I think the record would reflect that
13 Kathleen Honomichl testified that she received a report from
14 Children's Home Society that Jessica had indicated that it
15 didn't happen, that Kathleen Honomichl then forwarded that onto
16 the U. S. Attorney's office, and that would have been the first
17 information, that was before defense found out anything about
18 it.
19   THE COURT: I am asking the question here where the
20 witness said that the first time she found out about an
21 interview and apparently a recantation was when Honomichl told
22 her down at Wagner just before the witness went to Washington,
23 and assuming that all is the case, then how does the issue
24 arise, that's my question? I mean I just want to know what
25 your position is.

Page 623

1 MR. HAUGAARD: As I said, Your Honor, I think that
2 that, I am sure the Kathleen Honomichl information that
3 Kathleen received from CHS was, as Kathleen testified,
4 forwarded onto the U. S. Attorney's office, and that was far
5 before any interviews were conducted by anyone else. That was
6 something done by Ms. Honomichl in her capacity as a social
7 worker there.
8 THE WITNESS: I didn't find anything out about that
9 until much, much later.
10 THE COURT: That isn't my question, though. My
11 question was, at least from the point of view of Kathleen's
12 testimony, was the first time, Ms. Tapken's testimony was the
13 first time she found out about interviews and about recantation
14 when she had this meetings with Honomichl in which she was told
15 that Dr. Underwager conducted interviews, and she remembered it
16 because she was flabbergasted. That being the case then, what
17 are your arguments on that point.
18 MR. CARTER: I think part of it is that even if she
19 didn't know, there is possible an argument I think with Brady
20 that if they should have known, that that isn't in the eyes of
21 the law sufficient just for the government to say that we
22 didn't actually know, if one of their branches or one of their
23 offices or whatever, has the information, the social worker,
24 whatever. I don't know that that is a rationale for not
25 producing the information, or when they do find out about it

Page 624

1 saying that it doesn't need to be turned over. If that's the
2 case, Brady doesn't mean anything.
3 THE COURT: Well, but Ms. Honomichl is a, I think she
4 is a Tribal employee, wasn't she a Tribal social worker.
5 MR. CARTER: But it was communicated on to the U. S.
6 Attorney's office I think from the testimony and as
7 Mr. Haugaard has stated.
8 THE COURT: Well, I understand your position, I
9 wanted to know what it was. Alright, we are in recess.
10 MR. BINGER: I am sorry, I forgot to do this until
11 just now. I need to bring one matter to the court's attention,
12 because you have rescheduled this hearing until 10:30 on
13 Wednesday. I cleaned out my whole schedule for that day except
14 one problem, I have an appearance in front of Judge Simko at
15 four o'clock on Wednesday regarding a defendant who is making a
16 first appearance on an indictment, and he is from Denver. So
17 should I contact Judge Simko's office and tell them that is
18 going to have to be rescheduled?
19 THE COURT: Yes.
20 MR. BINGER: I will do that.
21 MR. HAUGAARD: In regard to the writ in regard to
22 Jerome, do we need to revise that, or is it adequate the
23 Marshals are aware you directed that he be here next Wednesday?
24 THE COURT: He will be here, the Marshal did remind
25 me, at great expense, because I think they are going to charter

Page 625

1 him down in order to get him here, that's the only way they can
2 do it. One other thing, since we are doing housekeeping, I am
3 not doing anything further in regard to the Children's Home
4 records, and I am not doing anything one way or the other, I am
5 just reminding you. Thank you, we are in recess.
6 (Recess at 6:00 p.m. until 10:30 a.m. on 9-12-01.)
7 THE COURT: Government may proceed.
8
9 (Exhibit 25 marked For identification.)
10
11 MR. HOLMES: Your Honor, before calling our next
12 witness the government would like to offer into evidence a
13 declaration prepared by Ms. Tapken regarding one aspect of her
14 testimony on Friday that she, after reflection, believed was
15 partially inaccurate. The declaration has been marked as
16 Government's Exhibit 25, with the Court's permission I will
17 submit it to the clerk.
18 THE COURT: Very well.
19 MR. HOLMES: We apologize to the Court for the
20 document not being an original. I spoke to Ms. Tapken early
21 yesterday morning and we had initially planned to have the
22 original sent Federal Express for filing today, of course as
23 the Court is undoubtedly aware, Federal Express was not
24 operating last night, so the best we could have for today's
25 hearing was a fax copy of the original.

Page 626

1 THE COURT: Yes, I am well aware of it. My plane
2 took off yesterday from Reagan airport at 9:05 in the morning
3 and we got put down without much explanation in Grand Rapids,
4 Michigan, so I got here about one something this morning.
5 MR. HOLMES: We would offer Exhibit 25, Your Honor.
6 THE COURT: Any objection.
7 MR. HAUGAARD: No objection.
8 MR. WILKA: No objection.
9 MR. BINGER: No objection.
10 MR. CARTER: No objection.
11 THE COURT: Exhibit 25 is received. I want to read
12 it before we proceed. Alright, call your next witness.
13 MR. HOLMES: United States calls Donna Jordan.
14
15 MADONNA JORDAN,
16 called as a witness, being first duly sworn, testified and said
17 as follows:
18
19 DIRECT EXAMINATION BY MR. HOLMES:
20 Q. Please state your full name and spell both your first and
21 last name for the record?
22 A. Madonna Jordan, M-A-D-O-N-N-A, Jordan, J-O-R-D-A-N.
23 Q. Ms. Jordan, did you formerly live in the Jefferson, South
24 Dakota area?
25 A. Yes, I did.

Page 627

1 Q. In 1994 did you serve as a foster parent for the Yankton
2 Sioux Tribe?
3 A. Yes, I did.
4 Q. Some time in January of '94 were certain children placed
5 at your residence from the Rouse family?
6 A. Yes, they were.
7 Q. Can you tell us a little bit about your prior experience
8 prior to January of '94 as a foster parent?
9 A. I worked with the State and the Tribe for years. Is that
10 what you mean?
11 Q. Yes. How long have you been a foster parent?
12 A. Boy, at that time, guessing, maybe fifteen, sixteen
13 years. I am just guessing, I don't know exact right now.
14 Q. In order to be a foster parent did you have to go through
15 any training and evaluation?
16 A. Yes.
17 Q. Would you just briefly describe to the Court what that
18 involved?
19 A. We go through MAPP training to start, and you go through
20 twelve hours of training to keep your license, and work with
21 different counselors, or you go to training in classes, stuff
22 like that.
23 Q. What is MAPP training?
24 A. I don't even remember what it is for. It is an
25 abbreviation for the training for the State of South Dakota.

Page 628

1 You have to go 36 hours to that class.
2 Q. Prior to January of '94, can you give us an estimate of
3 how many foster children you had in your home?
4 A. Not clearly. Maybe, I don't know, maybe 80. I am not
5 sure. Can't give you an exact amount. I am guessing 80 or 90,
6 that's a guess, not to be exact.
7 Q. How long had you been working with the Yankton Sioux
8 Tribe prior to January of '94?
9 A. Maybe three or four years.
10 Q. Have you previously had Native American children in your
11 residence?
12 A. Yes, sir.
13 Q. What do you generally recall about how the children were
14 placed in your home in January of '94?
15 A. You mean how?
16 Q. Yes, how that came about?
17 A. I made a referral to the social worker of something that
18 Rosie had said, and at that time the social worker was to come
19 to talk to her and that was all turned over to them. Then they
20 placed some of the children.
21 Q. Initially it was only Rosemary who was in your care, is
22 that right?
23 A. That's right.
24 Q. Then eventually how many other children were placed in
25 your home?

Page 629

1 A. Six others, Donovan, Jerome, Thrista, Lucritia and Fury,
2 and Echo was also, then she was removed.
3 Q. Some time after the children came to your home do you
4 recall them being, or did you take them to see Dr. Kaplan for a
5 medical examination?
6 A. Yes.
7 Q. Prior to the medical examination, had you in any way
8 attempted to interview the children regarding the abuse?
9 A. No, no way.
10 Q. Why is it you did not do that?
11 A. I am not qualified to do that, for one thing.
12 Q. As a part of your training are you generally told not to
13 do that?
14 A. Yes, you are told not to do that. You are just there for
15 the care of the children and that's it.
16 Q. Some time after the children were examined by Dr. Kaplan,
17 do you remember Bill Van Roe and Dan Hudspeth coming to your
18 home to interview the children?
19 A. Yes.
20 Q. Where in your residence did the interviews take place?
21 A. In my dining room.
22 Q. During the time of those interviews did the children have
23 an opportunity to get something to drink and eat food if they
24 needed to?
25 A. Yes.

Page 630

1 Q. Did they ever complain about being hungry or needing
2 something to drink and those needs were not taken care of?
3 A. No.
4   MR. WILKA: Excuse me, Your Honor. If Agent Van Roe
5 is going to testify, I would request at least during this
6 witness that he be sequestered.
7   THE COURT: What is the government's response to
8 that?
9   MR. HOLMES: I don't understand what he means about
10 this witness, what is unique about this witness? Mr. Van Roe
11 has been here for several witnesses who testified as to matters
12 where he was involved.
13   THE COURT: That's true. The request is granted.
14 BY MR. HOLMES:
15 Q. Is that the only time you recall the children being
16 interviewed in your residence?
17 A. Yes.
18 Q. After those interviews, did you, yourself, ever make any
19 attempt to interview the children about these allegations?
20 A. No.
21 Q. Did they at times on their own talk to you about what had
22 happened to them?
23 A. No, when they would go to talk to me they were told to
24 talk to their counselor, I do not have any recollection of what
25 happened through that case, only what was turned over to their

Page 631

1 counselor.

2 Q. Did any of them in your presence ever deny that they had

3 been sexually abused by their uncles?

4 A. Never.

5 Q. Can you just generally tell us how they were in your

6 home, how they acted, and how they got along in your residence

7 from when they were brought there initially up until the time

8 they left your care?

9 A. There was a lot of changes from the time they came to the

10 time they left. I think things were more stable. The

11 children's grades had improved in school, their school was

12 doing a lot better, they were doing good at home. There was a

13 lot of fighting when they first came, a lot of they didn't want

14 to respond to any chores or responsibilities, and as a family

15 we all needed things like that.

16 Q. Approximately how long were the children in your home?

17 A. Boy, I don't remember the exact dates, maybe fifteen

18 months, I don't remember the exact dates now.

19 Q. That would have been up through the trial in this matter,

20 is that correct?

21 A. Oh, yes.

22 Q. And beyond?

23 A. Um-hum.

24 Q. Did you actually transport them up here to the trial?

25 A. Yes, I did.

Page 632

1 Q. Did any of the children in your presence ever express any

2 fear toward Michelle Tapken, Bill Van Roe, or any of the law

3 enforcement officers?

4 A. Never.

5 Q. After a period of adjustment did the children seem to get

6 along with you?

7 A. Yes, they did.

8 Q. After they left your care, did some of the children go to

9 live with Children's Home here in Sioux Falls?

10 A. Yes, they did.

11 Q. Did they ever send you cards or letters?

12 A. Yes, they did.

13 Q. What do you recall about those?

14 A. Just that they missed us, and let us know how they were

15 doing, and they made several phone calls to ask if we could

16 come and see them.

17 Q. Did you actually come and see the children?

18 A. Yes, we did. We went and spent an afternoon in the park

19 there at Children's Home Society.

20 Q. While the children were in your care or at any other time

21 do you ever recall you or anyone in your presence striking the

22 children?

23 A. No.

24 Q. I think we have heard some testimony at this hearing that

25 on one occasion you pulled Fury's hair because she wouldn't

Page 633

1 eat, did that ever happen?

2 A. No, never happened.

3 Q. I think we have also heard some testimony that Fury was

4 on one occasion pushed down a flight of stairs by you. Did

5 that ever happen?

6 A. No, never happened.

7 Q. There has also been some testimony regarding alcohol or

8 an alleged alcohol bath that some of these children had to take

9 for the treatment of lice. Did that ever happen in your

10 presence?

11 A. No, I believe that would probably be Kwell they had to

12 bathe in. Yes, they did have to be bathed in, it was

13 prescribed by a doctor.

14 Q. Tell us the circumstances that led up to that?

15 A. That would have been scabies and body lice and they had

16 to soak in that from their neck down, and after they absorbed

17 that into the skin they stay in that overnight and everything

18 has to be washed in the morning.

19 Q. When in the process of your care for the children were

20 there problems with lice?

21 A. When they first came, and then different times through

22 the visitation stuff.

23 Q. So there would be times when they would leave for a

24 visitation with their family and come back with lice?

25 A. Um-hum.

Page 634

1   MR. HAUGAARD: I object, there is not foundation as

2 to timeframe and I object on that basis.

3   THE COURT: Overruled.

4 BY MR. HOLMES:

5 Q. This time when they had to take a bath in this medicine

6 as prescribed, was that when they were initially at your

7 residence?

8 A. Yes.

9 Q. Explain to the Court how you consulted with a doctor

10 regarding that treatment?

11 A. How they went to the doctor?

12 Q. Yes.

13 A. They went for physicals and it would be on their skin, it

14 could be seen visibly on their skin.

15 Q. Did the doctor advise you that that was the treatment in

16 part that you should utilize to try to get rid of the lice?

17 A. It is prescribed, you can't get it without a

18 prescription.

19 Q. Did any of the law enforcement officials or social

20 workers in your presence ever promise these children toys or

21 new clothes in return for certain testimony in this case?

22 A. No.

23 Q. Did you ever hear anything like that?

24 A. Never.

25 Q. What do you recall the relationship being between the

Page 635

1 children and Michelle Tapken during the trial as you observed
2 it?
3   MR. WILKA: I object, asking to comment on the mental
4 state of others.
5   THE COURT: The question was what she observed. So
6 that being the question, it is overruled.
7 BY MR. HOLMES:
8 Q. How did they interact with her?
9 A. Everything was fine. We didn't see Michelle a lot during
10 the trial. I mean we would come in and say good morning or
11 things like that, but there wasn't a lot of communication with
12 Michelle during the trial.
13 Q. Following this case did you for a period of time continue
14 to serve as a foster parent?
15 A. Yes.
16 Q. In 1999 were you given an award by the Yankton Sioux
17 Tribe for being --
18   MR. HAUGAARD: Objection, relevance, Your Honor.
19   THE COURT: Overruled.
20 BY MR. HOLMES:
21 Q. Foster parent of the year?
22 A. Yes, I was.
23   MR. HOLMES: No further questions.
24 CROSS EXAMINATION BY MR. WILKA:
25 Q. My name is John Wilka. You stated that you made a

Page 636

1 referral to social services because Rosemary had made a
2 disclosure to you, is that correct?
3 A. Yes, sir, that's correct.
4 Q. Then all of the children -- strike that.
5 Then eventually six of the children came to reside there as a
6 result of the allegations in this case, correct?
7 A. Yes.
8 Q. Would it be a fair statement to say that at first more
9 than six children came?
10 A. Yes.
11 Q. Approximately how many more?
12 A. Tabetha and Christopher came, and then they were removed.
13 Q. Was not Ebony also there?
14 A. No, sir.
15 Q. How about Moses?
16 A. No.
17 Q. Jerome?
18 A. Yes, I listed Jerome.
19 Q. How many days between the time that the Rouse children
20 first arrived in 1994 was it until they went to Dr. Kaplan's?
21 A. I believe it was the next day.
22 Q. How many days from the time that they saw Dr. Kaplan did
23 they visit with Agent Van Roe and Dan Hudspeth?
24 A. I am sorry, sir, I can't give you the exact date. I
25 really can't, but it wasn't long after that.

Page 637

1 Q. Was it more or less than three days, if you remember?
2 A. I can't honestly remember.
3 Q. Do you know if it was the next day?
4 A. No, I just don't honestly remember. I know it was very,
5 it was shortly after that, but I can't exactly say one, two,
6 three days, because I don't remember.
7 Q. But what you do remember is that the children came to
8 your residence, they then saw Dr. Kaplan, they then saw Agent
9 Van Roe?
10 A. Yes.
11 Q. But is it not true that before they saw Dr. Kaplan that
12 they saw Dr. Farrell?
13 A. Dr. Farrell?
14 Q. Yes.
15 A. I don't know of any Dr. Farrell.
16 Q. You have no recollection of the children seeing a
17 pediatrician named Dr. Farrell?
18 A. Dr. Farrell, no, I don't.
19 Q. Did not the children ask you during those initial few
20 days why they had been removed en mass from their relatives
21 home on the Yankton Indian Reservation?
22 A. The social worker would have taken care of that. They
23 were brought to me and talked to by a social worker before they
24 were ever brought to me, and they explain everything to them
25 before they are ever brought to me.

Page 638

1 Q. So is it your understanding that the social worker
2 explained to them why they had been removed?
3 A. Yes, I am sure she would have. Yes, sir, I am sure she
4 would have, because that was not my job to do.
5 Q. It's your understanding this occurred before they got to
6 your residence?
7 A. I am sure it would have, she would have explained
8 something to them.
9 Q. This was explained to them before they saw Dr. Kaplan?
10 A. Before they were brought to me, why they were removed?
11 Q. Yes?
12 A. Yes.
13 Q. Matter of fact, did not Jean Brock confirm with you that
14 she had fulfilled that function?
15 A. That she had explained to them why they would be removed?
16 Q. Yes?
17 A. I am sure she would have, they usually do tell us that,
18 yes.
19 Q. You stated that the children never visited with you about
20 the sexual abuse because you told them to visit with their
21 counselor about that?
22 A. Yes.
23 Q. So you did not interview the children?
24 A. No, I did not.
25 Q. So it would be a fair statement that you did not have any

Page 639

1 documentation of any interviews of the children because no
2 interviews occurred, correct?
3 A. No, sir, I have no documentation of anything like that.
4 Q. So that would be a correct statement?
5 A. Yes, that's a correct statement.
6 Q. So if the children never made any, had any interviews or
7 discussions with you regarding this abuse, obviously then they
8 never denied that which they never talked to you about,
9 correct?
10 A. Correct.
11 Q. But isn't it true that you instructed the children to
12 keep dream journals about their abuse?
13 A. No, that's not true. No, that's not true. Rosie had a
14 dream journal when she first was there. We were trying to get
15 rid of Rosie's bad nightmares, so we come up with a dream
16 journal. There was nothing like it in this dream journal, and
17 when it came time to start going to counseling, then the
18 counselor advised that they have no dream journals. And there
19 was nothing kept track of with the dream journals, no, nothing
20 like that.
21 Q. Did you forward those dream journals on to the United
22 States Attorney's office?
23 A. I don't remember if there was anything left, if they have
24 those dream journals or not, I don't remember, sir.
25 Q. You don't know if you sent them to them?

Page 640

1 A. Pardon?
2 Q. You do not know if you sent?
3 A. I don't remember if there was anything like, if Rosie's
4 journal was sent there or not.
5 Q. You no longer live in the Jefferson, South Dakota area?
6 A. No, sir, I don't.
7 Q. Did you bring any records of the Rouse matter with you?
8 A. I have nothing. No, I don't.
9 Q. Are you still a foster parent?
10 A. No, I am not.
11 Q. What do you do?
12 A. I am working in Branson, Missouri.
13 Q. What do you do in Branson Missouri?
14 A. I manage a motel.
15 Q. You stated that the children's grades improved from the
16 time that they initially came to you until they left fifteen
17 months later?
18 A. Um-hum.
19 Q. That would be a yes?
20 A. Yes, sir.
21 Q. So you made a request for their grades and then monitored
22 them over the fifteen month period?
23 A. No, sir, but I went to teacher's conference, and that was
24 discussed in teacher's conference how much better they were
25 doing and things like that in their grades academically.

Page 641

1 Q. So if I were to -- what school did they go to?
2 A. McCook for a while, and then we consolidated with Elk
3 Point.
4 Q. So if I were to get those school records, I would see a
5 gradual and marked increase in the children's scholastic
6 performance?
7 A. I am sure you would, sir, that's what I was told.
8 Q. Is it not true that instead of the counselor that it was
9 the United States Attorney who instructed you to have the
10 children stop keeping dream journals?
11 A. No, sir, my counselor did, Ellen Kelson did.
12 Q. So if there is an FBI 302 report that states that the
13 United States Attorney instructed you to stop keeping those
14 dream journals, that would be incorrect?
15 A. I am sorry, maybe she also did, but my counselor said not
16 to keep the, the children were not to write, and that's where
17 we started with that, was the children were writing things, and
18 the counselor said it would not be advisable.
19 Q. The children were, or the child was?
20 A. Rosie was keeping a journal, and we did not go, go from
21 there any further. Rosie's journal was stopped when she
22 started counseling.
23 Q. None of the other children were asked to keep dream
24 journals?
25 A. No, sir, not that I am aware of they were asked. I don't

Page 642

1 remember a child keeping a dream journal.
2 Q. So Rosie would write these things down, and then at first
3 you would turn them over to the counselor until you were told
4 that she should no longer write these things down?
5 A. Rosie never wrote those things down. In her bad, in her
6 dream journal there was nothing pertaining to this case. We
7 were talking, I thought it was school, things like that when we
8 first come up with the dream journal. It was to get rid of the
9 nightmares. There was nothing pertaining, the morning it come
10 out she was talking to me about the dream journal, I made the
11 referral, that was the first time that anything was ever said.
12 Q. What types of things would she write down then?
13 A. She was missing her family, it was a bad day at school,
14 just things like that.
15 Q. Those are the things she wrote down?
16 A. Sure. Anything a child, you know, goes through in the
17 removal, and first coming into your home it is a big deal for
18 everyone.
19 Q. Did you find it interesting that a five year old child
20 would be able to write so extensively?
21 A. No. It is not that type of a thing, it was just like I
22 miss, you know, things like that. It was not a journal journal
23 that would be something that, you know, a big thing. It wasn't
24 a lot of writing, just things that Rosie and I would talk
25 about. It was not a big journal type deal.

Page 643

1 Q. Is it not a fair statement to say that when -- strike
2 that.
3 Is it not true that when Jessica could not remember specific
4 details about this abuse, that you produced written notes of a
5 conversation that you had with her and put them down on the
6 interview table?
7 A. No.
8 Q. That is not a true statement?
9 A. I don't remember. I can't remember all those details
10 from seven years ago, I just can't.
11 Q. So you do not remember whether or not you took notes
12 of --
13 A. As far as me taking notes, no. Maybe something happened
14 in the home pertaining to the children that I handed to
15 somebody, that would be the extent of the notes. As far as the
16 foster parent's job is to hand someone, something that was said
17 or something, yes, that might have, I might have handed that to
18 a person, but not as far as taking notes, it never happened.
19 Q. You stated that you did not observe a lot of interaction
20 with the children with Michelle Tapken at the Federal
21 Courthouse, correct?
22 A. Right.
23 Q. Did you make any observations of how the children reacted
24 with Michelle Tapken, for instance, in your home?
25 A. Michelle was never in my home.

Page 644

1 Q. How about did you ever bring the children to meet with
2 Michelle Tapken?
3 A. Yes, sir, I did.
4 Q. On how many occasions?
5 A. I can't remember anymore, several occasions, sir.
6 Q. Several?
7 A. Yes.
8 Q. On these several occasions that you brought the children
9 to meet with Michelle Tapken, then you were able to observe how
10 they interacted with her?
11 A. No, sir, because I did not sit in on the interviews.
12 Q. Would you just bring them to the United States Attorney's
13 office and then wait out in the hallway?
14 A. I would wait in that part, first part of the lobby. Yes,
15 sir, I would.
16 Q. That's right before, when you get off the elevator?
17 A. Yes, sir.
18 Q. Then you have the metal detector or whatever?
19 A. Yes, right in there.
20 Q. Did you drive the children up in a van?
21 A. Yes, sir.
22 Q. You would drive all -- well, probably for sake of economy
23 it would probably make more sense for you to drive all the
24 children up at once, is that correct?
25 A. I believe we did, sir. I am not sure it was once or a

Page 645

1 few at a time. I am really not positive on how many I brought
2 at one time. I know there was more than one, if that is what
3 you are asking, but I don't remember if I brought two, or
4 three, or what.
5 Q. I don't expect you to produce log journals and mileage
6 journals or anything like that. Do you recall if anyone helped
7 with your driving duties when you would bring the children up
8 to Michelle Tapken?
9 A. My driving duties?
10 Q. Yes, or did you drive them by yourself?
11 A. No, I drove by myself.
12 Q. On these several occasions that the children would meet
13 with Michelle Tapken, do you know if she interviewed -- no, you
14 don't, because you were out in the hallway, weren't you?
15 A. Yes, sir.
16 Q. These several occasions, do you know if, do you even
17 remember if it was more than ten or less than ten times?
18 A. Oh, been less than ten times I am sure.
19 Q. About seven or eight?
20 A. Sir, I don't remember how many times I come up here.
21 Q. Okay, that's fair. Do you recall any conversations that
22 the children may have had in the van on their way up to meet
23 with Michelle Tapken?
24 A. Do I recall?
25 Q. Yes.

Page 646

1 A. Not that I can directly say or recall, no.
2 Q. But you would tell them that it is time to go meet with
3 Micky again?
4 A. Oh, well, sure, yes.
5 Q. So they, you know, after a couple of times would it be a
6 fair statement that they appeared from what you observed to
7 know why they were going up there?
8 A. Oh, yes, sir.
9 Q. When you, after the trial when you spent an afternoon
10 with the children at the Children's Home Society, which
11 children did you spend an afternoon with?
12 A. Thrista and Donovan and Lucritia and Jessie, I believe
13 that was all.
14 Q. Since the Children's Home Society, you know, deals with
15 children who have been in a traumatic environment and literally
16 have to be protected, what steps did you have to go through to
17 get an afternoon visit approved?
18 A. I had to call and get permission and approved with them
19 to come and visit with the children right there.
20 Q. Do you recall which case worker?
21 A. No, sir, I don't, I am sorry. No, I don't.
22 Q. When you went in to -- and is this in the new Children's
23 Home Society out by Washington High School, do you recall?
24 A. No -- wait a minute. I am not familiar with the area,
25 but I know I had to turn by the Fry'n Pan and go out and go,

Page 647

1 that's the only thing I can tell you. I don't remember the
2 name of the road, I haven't been out there. Turn left, I know
3 that, and go down to the end.
4 Q. That's the new one.
5 A. I am sorry, I wasn't familiar with the area.
6 Q. Where it is kind of a campus setting?
7 A. Yes.
8 Q. Then you went into the main offices and signed the
9 requisite forms, and the children, the time that you signed
10 them out, and then when you came back in?
11 A. I wouldn't leave the building, sir. We stayed there.
12 Q. Stayed in the building?
13 A. No, we stayed right outside the building right there, we
14 didn't leave the building. We stayed in the building, visited
15 with the children and we stayed in the grounds right around
16 there, did not leave the campus or anything with the children.
17 Q. Did you have to sign any forms the children were going to
18 be with you or anything?
19 A. No, I didn't sign anything, but I didn't take the
20 children anywhere.
21 Q. You did not pull Fury's hair because she wet her pants?
22 A. No, sir, I did not.
23 Q. You did not take her and drag her down the steps?
24 A. My gosh, no, I did not. No, I did not.
25 Q. So if Jessica, Lucritia and Thrista had observed that,

Page 648

1 they must have made a mistake in their observation?
2 A. Yes, sir, I believe they did.
3 Q. You did not shove food in Fury's mouth and force her to
4 eat, did you?
5 A. No, sir, I did not.
6 Q. So if the children observed that, they must have been
7 mistaken about their observation?
8 A. I would believe they were.
9 Q. It states that the, or excuse me, I believe you stated
10 that the children had scabies or body lice when they initially
11 came into your care and that is when you got this Kwell lotion
12 for them, correct?
13 A. I am not sure, sir, if it was when they first came in to
14 my care, or -- I am not really sure when it was prescribed for
15 them.
16 Q. Do you know if it was in the first month?
17 A. It may have been. It is not unusual to have to treat a
18 child for, with this Kwell. I mean this can happen to any
19 child, so it is not an unusual thing. It would have been from
20 school, you know what I am saying, I am just not really sure
21 when they got them, I am just not.
22 Q. Which children do you recall had these?
23 A. When you treat someone in the home you have to treat
24 everyone, sir, even yourself.
25 Q. So everybody in the home took Kwell baths?

Page 649

1 A. Yes, you have to. You have to treat everything, wash
2 everything, even the clothes, all the laundry has to be done
3 completely over, all the bedding, everything has to be done.
4 Q. This Kwell lotion, did you get, have to get a
5 prescription for that?
6 A. Yes, sir, I did. You can't buy it over-the-counter.
7 Q. Did every person in the house have to get a prescription
8 for it?
9 A. Yes, sir. When they prescribe it, they take the amount
10 of people in the home, everyone, their size, everybody has to,
11 and they give you the amount to fill the prescription.
12 Q. How many children were in the home then, how many human
13 beings were in the home?
14 A. Probably seven, eight.
15 Q. So --
16 A. Including me.
17 Q. Were you married at that time?
18 A. Yes.
19 Q. Are you married?
20 A. Yes, I am.
21 Q. So it was you and your husband and the six Rouse children
22 then?
23 A. Um-hum.
24 Q. That would be yes?
25 A. Yes, sir, I am sorry.

Page 650

1 Q. So who is your pharmacist?
2 A. Elk Point Pharmacy.
3 Q. And this happened on how many occasions?
4 A. We may have had to do it twice through the time, you
5 know, that the children was there.
6 Q. I may have misunderstood you, and believe me it wouldn't
7 be the first time that I have misunderstood an answer. I
8 thought you testified on direct examination that this happened
9 a number of times, specially when the kids would go home to see
10 their folks?
11 A. I am sorry, sir, that's just for the head lice, and you
12 have got Kwell for the head lice, you have something else for
13 the head lice that you use.
14 Q. How many times did the kids get head lice?
15 A. Maybe five.
16 Q. Five times?
17 A. Um-hum.
18 Q. Did you have to get any prescription stuff for head lice?
19 A. Yes. Well, it is not prescription, you can buy it
20 over-the-counter, but there were several times where the social
21 worker brought me some.
22 Q. Do you know if that was bought at the Elk Point Pharmacy
23 also?
24 A. I am sure. From the social worker you mean, or from me?
25 Q. From you?

Page 651

1 A. From me, with the Elk Point Pharmacy, yes. Or it may
2 have been the cheapest place I could get it, Wal-Mart, K-Mart.
3 Everyone sells it, it is very expensive.
4 Q. So at some point you bought this head lice stuff at
5 Wal-Mart?
6 A. Wal-Mart or K-Mart, yes, whenever I need it.
7 Q. In Sioux Falls?
8 A. No, I didn't travel to Sioux Falls, in Sioux City.
9 Q. You travel to Sioux City?
10 A. Someplace, I am sure. I can't recall where I bought the
11 head lice stuff.
12 Q. You recall if there was a Wal-Mart in Sioux City in 1994?
13 A. Yes, there was. There is two.
14 Q. If I understand you correctly -- strike that.
15 You don't remember the first time that you had to get the Kwell
16 lotion, do you?
17 A. The Kwell lotion, no, sir, I don't.
18 Q. So you don't, so if I understand it, you don't know if it
19 is a month or a year after they first came in?
20 A. No. It would have been in the doctor's records. I just
21 don't remember, I just can't put a date to something I don't
22 remember.
23 Q. Let's see if this helps. Was it before or after the
24 trial?
25 A. Probably before. Maybe the children was there, you know,

Page 652

1 maybe before.
2 Q. You did not make Thrista or Lucritia take a bath in
3 rubbing alcohol then?
4 A. No, sir.
5 Q. So if Thrista or Lucritia stated you made them take a
6 bath in rubbing alcohol, they would be mistaken?
7 A. Yes, sir.
8 Q. So there really was no, again there was no discussion of
9 the sexual abuse by you with the children while they resided
10 with you, correct?
11 A. Correct, sir.
12 Q. How about when Jerome had to be removed for having sexual
13 relations with Thrista while he was under your care?
14 A. Yes, sir.
15 Q. That did happen?
16 A. Yes, it did.
17 Q. Then you made a referral of that?
18 A. Immediately.
19 Q. Did you ever visit with Jerome about that?
20 A. No, Jerome was removed immediately.
21 Q. Did you ever visit with Thrista about that?
22 A. No, the social worker handled that very well. In fact,
23 Thrista was removed too, sir.
24 Q. That social worker would be who?
25 A. Deena LaPointe.

Page 653

1 Q. Do you recall what month that happened?
2 A. No, sir, I am sorry. I don't.
3 Q. It is several years ago, so they all kind of blur
4 together?
5 A. Yes, sir.
6   MR. WILKA: That's all I have, thank you.
7   THE COURT: Mr. Binger.
8 CROSS EXAMINATION BY MR. BINGER:
9 Q. What exactly happened with Jerome and Thrista that caused
10 that?
11 A. Jessie and Thrista had told me that Jerome had come into
12 the bedroom and that he had tried to do things to them. I
13 immediately called a social worker and he was immediately
14 removed.
15 Q. You say he tried to do things. Did he try, or did
16 something actually happen?
17 A. Sir, I don't know, because I turned that immediately over
18 to a social worker.
19 Q. You never interviewed Jerome?
20 A. No, I did not interview him.
21 Q. So Thrista or Jessie told you in general terms that he
22 tried to do something, they didn't get specific?
23 A. Jessie told me that he was pulling the covers off her
24 trying to do things to them. And I asked her what had
25 happened. And she said Jerome was coming in the bedroom at

Page 654

1 night doing things to the girls, and I called Deena
2 immediately.
3 Q. So he was doing things to the girls?
4 A. Yes.
5 Q. You didn't ask what?
6 A. Well, he, she told me he was doing things trying to touch
7 their private area and stuff.
8 Q. Is that all?
9 A. Yes.
10 Q. So that is as specific as it got in terms of what --
11 A. Yes, it was turned over.
12 Q. You don't recall if this happened before or after the
13 trial?
14 A. After.
15 Q. And what makes you sure of that?
16 A. Because the children were removed immediately.
17 Q. Those two?
18 A. Pardon?
19 Q. Thrista and Jerome were?
20 A. No, all the children.
21 Q. All the children were removed from your residence?
22 A. Yes, sir, they were.
23 Q. Do you still do foster care work?
24 A. No, sir, I do not. I just quit in June.
25 Q. In June of 2001?

Page 655

1 A. Yes, sir.
2 Q. You just made a voluntary decision you wanted to stop
3 doing it?
4 A. We moved, sir.
5 Q. Because of your move?
6 A. Yes.
7 Q. Where do you live now?
8 A. Branson, Missouri.
9   MR. BINGER: That's all I have.
10   THE COURT: Mr. Carter.
11 CROSS EXAMINATION BY MR. CARTER:
12 Q. Donna, in your testimony you indicated and you used the
13 word a couple of times that you did not interview the children,
14 do you recall that testimony?
15 A. Yes, sir.
16 Q. Making a distinction between talking with the children
17 about these abuse issues and interviewing them, do you see any
18 difference between those terms, or are you including any
19 discussion with the children about this abuse and you are
20 saying no?
21 A. I am saying no, sir, I have no idea what happened in the
22 abuse.
23 Q. So that there were no occasions when you had discussions
24 with the children about the facts of the abuse?
25 A. That's right, sir.

Page 656

1 Q. Is it possible that your memory is not up to snuff on
2 such matters?
3 A. No, I don't believe so, because I never had interaction
4 with the children on the abuse.
5 Q. Did you have occasion to take notes?
6 A. To take notes? I had occasion to write something down
7 when something was said to me. As far as taking notes of
8 incidents, when something would be said to me I would write it
9 down and hand it to a counselor.
10 Q. How many times did you write down such matters?
11 A. Sir, I couldn't begin to tell you right now.
12 Q. Are we talking about two or three times?
13 A. I am sure with that many children it would be much more
14 than that of handing something to a counselor.
15 Q. How long did you continue this practice?
16 A. That went on, that would go on as long as you have the
17 child.
18 Q. So that went on before trial and after trial?
19 A. Yes, sir, it would have.
20 Q. You then submitted these handwritten notes to whom?
21 A. To my counselor. Just, it would not be a, just be maybe
22 a statement of something I felt she should follow up on, or
23 whatever it would be with what was going on in their life, or
24 whatever it was, that would be the end of it. I mean --
25 Q. This began then with, before the doctor's appointments?

Page 657

1 A. Before?
2 Q. Yes.
3 A. Yes. This would be an every day thing for a foster
4 parent.
5 Q. Do you remember the content of any of these things that
6 you wrote down?
7 A. No, sir.
8 Q. So it is possible that they could have been statements by
9 the child denying that the abuse occurred?
10 A. It was never denied to me.
11 Q. So you do recall something about the statements?
12 A. I would recall if I ever wrote it.
13 Q. Who did you, you said that you referred these on, I
14 believe you said to your counselor, was that a misstatement?
15 A. To my counselor.
16 Q. Yes.
17 A. Not mine, the children's counselor.
18 Q. So it went to the children's counselor?
19 A. Yes, sir.
20 Q. Who would that have been?
21 A. Ellen Kelson.
22 Q. Did you have discussions with Ms. Kelson about the
23 children then?
24 A. Yes, I did.
25 Q. Did Ms. Kelson ever indicate to you that she felt that

Page 658

1 the children were coming in with canned stories?
2 A. No.
3 Q. She did not indicate that to you?
4 A. No.
5 Q. You would have remembered that?
6 A. Yes.
7 Q. Did you ever have the sense that some of the older
8 children were speaking for all of the children, and having sort
9 of a one story that they were giving you?
10 A. About what, sir?
11 Q. About anything?
12 A. Oh, I believe the older children would speak for the
13 littler ones, sure.
14 Q. So that would have been something you could say that
15 was -- did it happen frequently?
16 A. Well, I mean the older children would always try to help
17 the littler children when they are in a foster home, coming in
18 to foster care.
19 Q. Did you then also have discussions with any of the
20 counselors at Children's Home Society?
21 A. No, sir.
22 Q. The only counselor that you had discussions with was
23 Ellen Kelson, correct?
24 A. Yes, sir.
25 Q. As far as discussions, did you ever have conversations

Page 659

1 with Mr. Van Roe of the FBI?
2 A. No, sir.
3 Q. With Michelle Tapken?
4 A. No, sir.
5 Q. With Mr. Dan Hudspeth?
6 A. No, sir.
7 Q. These individuals, a couple of these individuals were in
8 your home at the time of the one interview, isn't that correct?
9 A. Yes, sir.
10 Q. Did you speak with them on that occasion at all?
11 A. As far as?
12 Q. As far as the children, your observations of the
13 children?
14 A. No, sir.
15 Q. You didn't speak to them about these statements where you
16 were writing down about what the kids were saying and doing?
17 A. If I give them a statement, I mean, maybe I have wrote
18 something down to hand to them. We didn't have any lengthy
19 conversation over anything the children had said to me. That
20 was dealt with with their doctors, their counselors.
21 Q. It's possible that you had some discussions with them?
22 A. No, I did not have a discussion over this.
23 Q. When the, when this initial disclosure, I believe you
24 referred to it, was it by Rosemary?
25 A. Yes, sir.

Page 660

1 Q. Do you remember when that was?
2 A. The date, sir?
3 Q. Yes.
4 A. I am sorry, I just don't remember the dates.
5 Q. Before you testified here this morning have you reviewed
6 any documents or testimony of any sort?
7 A. Pardon?
8 Q. Have you reviewed any of your prior testimony?
9 A. Yes, I have. I tried to review a little bit of it.
10 Q. But you still don't recall when that would have occurred?
11 A. No, sir, I don't remember the dates.
12 Q. Was your understanding at that point when this was first
13 starting with Rosemary that you were talking to her about bad
14 dreams?
15 A. I was talking to her about bad dreams, yes. She was
16 having bad dreams, terrible nightmares.
17 Q. The allegations of abuse came out then in the context of
18 bad dreams, is that correct?
19 A. There wasn't a lot of allegation, just a few things. If
20 I recall right, that was said that I knew a social worker
21 should talk to her about, and I called her social worker
22 immediately and she went from there. I did not go any further
23 with that. The social worker did.
24 Q. But was this initial disclosure as you recall from
25 Rosemary in the context of her having bad dreams?

Page 661

1 A. Yes.
2 Q. And she had had other bad dreams before?
3 A. Yes, sir.
4 MR. CARTER: I don't have any other questions.
5 THE COURT: Redirect.
6 MR. HAUGAARD: I have not had an opportunity, Your
7 Honor.
8 THE COURT: Oh, excuse me.
9 CROSS EXAMINATION BY MR. HAUGAARD:
10 Q. My name is Steve Haugaard. You indicated that you didn't
11 have discussions with the kids about the claims of abuse, is
12 that correct?
13 A. That's correct.
14 Q. If they would say something to you, what would you do?
15 If they said something to you about abuse, what would you do?
16 A. It was handled by their counselor, sir. That is where
17 the little notations would come in that would be given to their
18 counselor.
19 Q. You have testified that you did write things down,
20 though?
21 A. Yes, sir.
22 Q. I am wondering in the course of children supposedly
23 coming up to you saying things you didn't respond at all?
24 A. Yes, sir. I told them it was to be dealt with by their
25 counselor, or the social worker, whatever the case may be.

Page 662

1 Q. Did some of those notes comprise what was referred to as
2 the dream journal?
3 A. No, sir.
4 Q. You say Rosie was keeping this dream journal herself?
5 A. Yes, but you have to imagine it was not a big type of a
6 journal, sir. It was a little kid's book. It is not like
7 there was, you know --
8 Q. How old was Rosemary at that time?
9 A. Five or six, I believe.
10 Q. And this didn't make any references to abuse?
11 A. No, sir.
12 Q. She just indicated that she was missing her family?
13 A. Missing her family and different things, just a child's
14 book. Bad day at school, or just -- I can't recall what was
15 all in it, but it was a child's book.
16 Q. When the FBI, or any other investigators came to see the
17 children at your home, did you sit in on those interviews?
18 A. No, sir. I was in the other room. My kitchen and my
19 dining area are all one big area.
20 Q. So you have no idea what was said in the context of those
21 meetings?
22 A. No, I did not sit there and listen.
23 Q. If the children would say something to you about claimed
24 abuse, who would you call?
25 A. About what, sir?

Page 663

1 Q. Any claims of abuse?

2 A. Who would I call?

3 Q. Yes.

4 A. Jean Brock, my social worker at the time.

5 Q. How many times do you think you did that?

6 A. As far as problems, sir, is that what you are saying?

7 Q. With regard to things that supposedly the kids had told

8 you about claims of abuse?

9 A. Oh, I would have made just the one referral, sir, and

10 then it would have went on with their doctor and their

11 counselor.

12 Q. So you are saying the only time you would call Jean Brock

13 about claims of abuse would be the very first time?

14 A. Well, I am sure there was -- anything that come up with

15 the children, I can't really tell you how many times I called

16 Jean Brock, but that would have been turned over to Jean Brock,

17 or the social worker.

18 Q. The kids were with you for you say, at least some of the

19 kids were with you for approximately fifteen months?

20 A. I believe about that time, sir. I am not sure on even

21 the months right now.

22 Q. Did you on any occasions ever get upset at the kids?

23 A. I am sure that that would be crazy to say I didn't get

24 upset with the kids. I mean you do that in every day life,

25 it's how you deal with it, I guess.

Page 664

1 Q. Now you are saying you don't remember if the kids had

2 lice when they came?

3 A. Pardon?

4 Q. Now your testimony is you don't really remember if the

5 kids had lice when they first came?

6 A. When they first came, no. I can't remember when the

7 children were treated, sir, I just can't.

8 Q. Did the doctor report anything about lice?

9 A. Did the doctor report it? No, I believe the school did.

10 Q. They saw the doctor right away after they got to your

11 home?

12 A. Yes. So I can't remember if they were treated for that,

13 or what they were treated for.

14 Q. After the situation with Jerome you indicated that all

15 the children were removed from your home. How long were they

16 out of the home?

17 A. Excuse me, sir, I didn't understand that.

18 Q. After the claims in regard to Jerome you say all the kids

19 were removed from your home?

20 A. Yes, sir.

21 Q. Were they returned?

22 A. To me?

23 Q. Yes?

24 A. No, sir.

25 Q. When you give these notes to Counselor Kelson, would you

Page 665

1 have any discussion with her about the content of the note?

2 A. No, sir, not usually. I didn't have a lot of discussion.

3 If there was a behavior or something, that would be the extent

4 of my discussion with Mrs. Kelson.

5 Q. Approximately how long was Rosemary in your home before

6 this claim of some kind of abuse was reported to you?

7 A. Maybe a couple of months, sir. I can't give you an

8 exact. November -- I am not sure.

9 Q. What exactly did she say to you?

10 A. I can't, I just don't remember what exactly was said to

11 me, sir.

12 Q. When you would bring the kids to the U. S. Attorney's

13 office, who else was there to interview the children?

14 A. I can't honestly say that for sure, I never went back

15 into the interviewing with the children.

16 Q. You remember speaking to Ms. Tapken when you would bring

17 the kids up for the interviews?

18 A. Yes, sir.

19 Q. Did you speak with anyone else in their office at those

20 times?

21 A. Possibly, but I am not saying positively, but possibly

22 the children's lawyer. I am not sure, sir. I am not sure any

23 more who was there.

24 Q. Did you ever speak with the children's lawyer about this

25 case?

Page 666

1 A. No, I did not, the children spoke with their own lawyer.

2   MR. HAUGAARD: No further questions, thank you.

3   THE COURT: Redirect.

4   MR. HOLMES: No redirect.

5   THE COURT: Thank you, you may step down. Call your

6 next witness.

7

8   JULIE BROWN,

9 called as a witness, being first duly sworn, testified and said

10 as follows:

11

12 DIRECT EXAMINATION BY MR. HOLMES:

13 Q. Good morning?

14 A. Good morning.

15 Q. Please state your name for the record?

16 A. Julie Brown.

17 Q. Ms. Brown, were you involved serving as a foster parent

18 between August of '96, some time in '96 through '97 for Jessica

19 and Lucritia Rouse?

20 A. Yes, I was.

21 Q. Can you explain to the Court what training you had to

22 become a foster parent?

23 A. Quite an extensive training. I think we went through

24 forty hours of initial training, and we continued to keep up

25 thirty hours after that, provided somewhat, for the most part

Page 667

1 by Children's Home Society, but then there were other trainings
2 around the community that we attended. I am also a special
3 education teacher, have a degree in elementary and special
4 education.
5 Q. During that period of time that Jessica and Lucritia were
6 in your home where were you living?
7 A. In Sioux Falls at 2709 West Oak Street.
8 Q. Could you explain to the Court the circumstances under
9 which the two girls came to your home?
10 A. Through Children's Home.
11 Q. Was I accurate on the dates as far as when the children
12 were there?
13 A. For the most part, yes, August of '96 to August of '97, I
14 believe. I don't know the exact date. There was a time in
15 transition before they were at our home permanently, so that
16 would have been even earlier, maybe July. I don't know the
17 exact dates of the transition time.
18 Q. Prior to coming to live at your residence they had been
19 at Children's Home?
20 A. Um-hum.
21 Q. Who was living in the household at the time besides
22 yourself?
23 A. My husband, and our oldest son Ryan, another son Kyle,
24 and a daughter Kara.
25 Q. How old were they at the time?

Page 668

1 A. What years, '96? Kara was ten, so that would have made
2 Kyle fourteen and Ryan sixteen.
3 Q. After August of '97 when the children left your home do
4 you know where they were placed at that time?
5 A. Yes. They were, went to the Stanford's, I believe, in
6 Brandon.
7 Q. During the period of time that the children were in your
8 home, did either Jessica or Lucritia ever tell you that they
9 had not been abused by their uncles?
10 A. No.
11 Q. Did they ever tell you that they in fact were afraid of
12 their uncles?
13   MR. WILKA: Objection, hearsay.
14   THE COURT: Foundation, sustained.
15 BY MR. HOLMES:
16 Q. Did they ever at any time while they were in your home
17 express any fear toward another person?
18   MR. HAUGAARD: Same objection, Your Honor.
19   THE COURT: Overruled.
20 A. Yes, they did.
21 BY MR. HOLMES:
22 Q. When was that?
23 A. Dates?
24 Q. Well, approximately when?
25 A. Initially they expressed some fear when they first came

Page 669

1 to our home, they wanted to make sure our home was safe for
2 them. At that time they, what they said was we --
3   MR. WILKA: Objection, hearsay, Your Honor.
4   MR. HOLMES: Well, it's a state of mind.
5   THE COURT: Overruled, go ahead.
6 BY MR. HOLMES:
7 Q. What did they tell you?
8 A. When they first came to our home, it was in August, the
9 summer time, we had a two story home and the windows were open,
10 their bedroom was on the second floor, and of course in the
11 summer we have the windows open, they insisted that we close
12 the windows. They said they were afraid that their uncles
13 would get out of jail and come and find them, and our job at
14 that time was to assure them that this was a safe place for
15 them and the home was safe, and that their uncles were in jail.
16   MR. HOLMES: No further questions.
17   THE COURT: Cross examination.
18 CROSS EXAMINATION BY MR. WILKA:
19 Q. Ms. Brown, my name is John Wilka, good morning. What
20 records did you receive before the children came to, before
21 Jessica and Lucritia came to live with you in August of 1996?
22 A. Pretty much the therapist reports that Children's Home
23 had.
24 Q. Did you review those?
25 A. Yes.

Page 670

1 Q. Anywhere in those reports did you see where Jessica had
2 in fact told one of her case workers that this abuse in fact
3 did not occur?
4 A. No.
5 Q. You did not see that anywhere?
6 A. No. You are asking me to remember a long time ago, and a
7 lot.
8 Q. Would that have been something that would have stuck out?
9 A. Probably not for me. My concern was how I can be the
10 best parent for them at that time, and be perfectly honest with
11 you, I knew practically, I knew nothing about any case or why
12 they were at Children's Home.
13 Q. Wouldn't it be a fair statement to say that your job was
14 just to provide a safe home where they would be fed, clothed
15 and sent to school, and things like that?
16 A. Exactly.
17 Q. It was not your job to inquire in to any statements as to
18 whether those statement would be true or false, correct?
19 A. Correct.
20 Q. It was not your job to inquire as to the origin of any
21 fears that the children may have had of others, correct?
22 A. Correct.
23 Q. It would be a fair statement to say that it was not your
24 job to inquire as to whether or not these fears were implanted
25 by stories that other adults may have told them, correct?

Page 671

1 A. Correct.
2   MR. WILKA: That's all I have, thank you.
3   THE COURT: Mr. Binger.
4   MR. BINGER: No questions.
5   MR. CARTER: No further questions.
6 CROSS EXAMINATION BY MR. HAUGAARD:
7 Q. Good morning.
8 A. Good morning.
9 Q. Which notes do you recall receiving prior to the kids
10 being placed with you?
11 A. Notes as in?
12 Q. You mentioned therapist notes.
13 A. Um-hum.
14 Q. Do you remember who the therapist was who signed off on
15 those notes, or was it various therapists?
16 A. There was various, and again when I was reading through
17 those it was more of a scanning just to see what I needed to
18 know as a parent, more like behavior. You know, how, if they
19 needed medications, that type of thing that as a parent you
20 would want to know for bringing someone into your home.
21 Q. Who did you have discussions with at Children's Home
22 Society prior to the kids being placed with you?
23 A. I believe Mary Weber was the, I don't know her official
24 title with the children at that time, but she was the one who
25 introduced us to them.

Page 672

1 Q. Was there anyone else that you spoke with about the kids
2 from Children's Home Society?
3 A. Initially, before the they came to our home?
4 Q. Yes, initially?
5 A. I think it was pretty much just Mary.
6 Q. Then after they were placed in your home who did you have
7 discussions with?
8 A. The therapist that we were to report and worked with the
9 girls was then Joy Christianson. I am pretty sure for the most
10 part of the time they were there. And Karla Harmon, I believe,
11 was part of that as well.
12 Q. What kind of conversations did you have with them about
13 the kids?
14 A. Pretty much it was mostly day-to-day things that I felt.
15 If they would mention something to me, then I would take the
16 information and just hand it off to one of the therapists.
17 Q. Maybe I am, I stated the question wrong. What kind of
18 questions, or what kind of things did you discuss with Joy
19 Christianson and Karla Harmon, is that what your answer was?
20 A. Yes. They wanted to know how the girls were doing, how
21 they were fitting in to our family, if they had any issues or
22 anything, those are the things we discussed.
23 Q. Prior to receiving the kids into your home, what were you
24 told as to the reason for their placement at Children's Home
25 Society?

Page 673

1 A. I don't know if we were really told all the details. If
2 we were, I didn't commit them to memory.
3 Q. Generally what were you told about the placement?
4 A. The two girls needed a home.
5 Q. Did they ever tell you that these children had been
6 sexually abused?
7 A. No. You know, and it might have been in the reports that
8 I looked over, too, but that is not something that stood out in
9 my mind.
10 Q. At some point did you become aware that there was
11 allegations that they had been sexually abused?
12 A. Oh, I am sure, I just couldn't tell you exactly when.
13 Q. And you have indicated that you received these therapist
14 notes before, did you receive them before you met the girls?
15 A. Yeah, and maybe that's why they are so fuzzy in my mind,
16 is because I hadn't met the girls, I hadn't put a face to the
17 notes.
18   MR. HAUGAARD: No further questions.
19   THE COURT: Redirect.
20   MR. HOLMES: No redirect, Your Honor.
21   THE COURT: I don't have any questions, but since
22 this isn't a jury trial, I can tell you how much, having raised
23 three children, how much I admire people that not only raise
24 their own children but have foster children in, I think you
25 should be commended. Thank you, you may step down.

Page 674

1   The matter I had in Rapid City tomorrow was canceled
2 because of what happened, so if we don't get done today we are
3 going to go straight ahead. I thought offhand, first of all,
4 at the rate we are going it looks to me like the government is
5 going to be done when, do you think?
6   MR. HOLMES: I think we will be done this afternoon.
7 We have five witnesses, but I don't think any of them are that
8 long.
9   THE COURT: Obviously you are going to get done, also
10 then there is Jerome Rouse to testify, he will testify and that
11 is going to be it?
12   MR. HAUGAARD: We will probably have some rebuttal,
13 Your Honor, from the children and a couple of the mom's.
14   THE COURT: That is going to take more time then. So
15 what you are saying is, because I told you before that we would
16 go on Friday afternoon if we didn't get done, although I
17 expected we would get done. What you are saying now is you are
18 scheduled up on Thursday, right?
19   MR. WILKA: If I may, Your Honor. I did change a
20 number of matters from --
21   THE COURT: Be specific.
22   MR. WILKA: I have a hearing in McCook County
23 tomorrow morning that, who knows, I might go, I don't know, I
24 have three or four different conferences that I had moved from
25 today and Friday to tomorrow, we bunched them all in to fit

Page 675

1 them all in tomorrow.
2   THE COURT: Conferences can be moved.
3   MR. WILKA: Yes. Then also there is a settlement
4 offer out on McCook County, but I don't know what will happen.
5   THE COURT: What kind of a hearing is it in McCook
6 County?
7   MR. WILKA: It is a visitation, custody and
8 protection order hearing.
9   THE COURT: Well, those are important. Alright, what
10 are the conflicts others have?
11   MR. CARTER: Judge, I had scheduled for some time
12 four child support hearings for tomorrow as a referee. I am
13 doing these a couple days a week, with our new law we are
14 getting quite a number of them. I did not re-schedule those
15 because of the prior discussion, of course we were going to go
16 back Friday. Obviously I can re-schedule those since I control
17 the hearing dates, but it is again you are familiar with the
18 logistics.
19   THE COURT: Yes. Mr. Haugaard?
20   MR. HAUGAARD: I have just in the office conferences.
21 It's my understanding we would go ahead and finish on Friday,
22 and the way it looks the government would be done today, and
23 certainly be my preference that we have until Friday to
24 properly prepare to respond, and I expect our response is going
25 to be relatively short.

Page 676

1   THE COURT: Office conferences just don't count, I
2 can tell you that, this is Court, the Court matters do.
3   MR. WILKA: I can check. I mean I have, I could
4 check over the noon hour, because I did communicate a proposal
5 at approximately 8:15 this morning, I don't know if it's been
6 accepted, I can definitely check over the noon hour.
7   THE COURT: The only thing I am thinking about this,
8 this is the fourth day of this and we have taken a lot of
9 testimony, and I want, once the government is done, they are
10 entitled to take whatever time it is, you are entitled to take
11 what ever time on cross examination that is necessary, and now
12 we have some rebuttal, and which is not unanticipated, but if
13 we wind up being pinched on Friday, that's what I was thinking
14 about.
15   MR. WILKA: I could be back, the hearing is in the
16 morning, so I would be available tomorrow afternoon.
17   THE COURT: What about your hearings, Dave?
18   MR. CARTER: Again, there are four separate ones, I
19 would need to have my secretary call and re-schedule those that
20 we would need to today, that can be done.
21   THE COURT: I know, but what about if we were, you
22 know, let's say that John had his hearing and was available
23 tomorrow afternoon, would you be available tomorrow afternoon?
24   MR. CARTER: Again, I would have to re-schedule some
25 of them, I schedule one at 8:30, one at 10:00, one at 1:30, and

Page 677

1 one at 3:00, so that is the regimen that I am faced with.
2   THE COURT: Let's say the government gets done today,
3 and how lengthy is Jerome's testimony going to be?
4   MR. HAUGAARD: I haven't had an opportunity to speak
5 with him yet. He has been here in Sioux Falls, he was in the
6 county jail, I was hoping to speak with him this morning, but
7 they didn't bring him up here. So I would talk to him tonight,
8 I would expect it wouldn't be more than twenty minutes
9 probably.
10   THE COURT: How long do you think your rebuttal will
11 last?
12   MR. WILKA: We would expect fifteen, twenty minutes,
13 short rebuttal, Your Honor.
14   MR. HAUGAARD: Per person.
15   THE COURT: You have three people?
16   MR. WILKA: Right now we are anticipating three.
17   MR. HAUGAARD: I think our total with Jerome and
18 rebuttal, probably two hours.
19   THE COURT: That is just direct. I see problems on
20 Friday afternoon. I told you I will take Friday afternoon as
21 much as it takes to get it done, but we are going to get done.
22 Dave, let me ask you, on yours, are those short fuse things?
23 In other words, they come up on short notice and you need to
24 have them done quickly?
25   MR. CARTER: Well, yeah, we do have some timing

Page 678

1 requirements that the UJS puts on us, we have to process them
2 within a certain number of days or what happens is that the
3 feds then change their reimbursement schedule back to the
4 state. It is one of the ways in which there are some timing
5 requirements in there for the state to process those through.
6   THE COURT: I know, but if the two that you have
7 tomorrow afternoon were moved to Friday morning, you see I have
8 another hearing that is going to take me all Friday morning,
9 could you move the two you had on tomorrow afternoon to Friday
10 morning.
11   MR. CARTER: That would be a possibility, assuming we
12 can get ahold of everybody. I will talk to Mary and get her on
13 the phone.
14   THE COURT: Let's see if we can do that so we can go
15 tomorrow afternoon, and then if we don't get done tomorrow
16 afternoon then we will go Friday afternoon. That will allow
17 John to go tomorrow morning to McCook County and allow you to
18 have your two hearings tomorrow morning, and the other two
19 hearings you can have Friday morning, because I am going to be
20 having yet another hearing Friday morning, see if you can do
21 that.
22   MR. CARTER: Okay.
23   THE COURT: Thank you, we are in recess.
24 (Recess from 12:05 until 1:00.)
25

Page 679

1   INDEX TO WITNESS

2

3   DR. DAVID CORWIN

4 DIRECT EXAMINATION BY MR. SEILER 457
    CROSS EXAMINATION BY MR. WILKA 487
5 CROSS EXAMINATION BY MR. HAUGAARD 513
    CROSS EXAMINATION BY MR. BINGER 535
6 CROSS EXAMINATION BY MR. CARTER 542

7

8   MINDY MITNICK

    DIRECT EXAMINATION BY MR. SEILER 550
9 CROSS EXAMINATION BY MR. WILKA 562
    CROSS EXAMINATION BY MR. HAUGAARD 584
10 CROSS EXAMINATION BY MR. BINGER 588
    CROSS EXAMINATION BY MR. CARTER 593

11

12   MICHELLE TAPKEN

13 DIRECT EXAMINATION BY MR. HOLMES 600
    CROSS EXAMINATION BY MR. HAUGAARD 602
14 CROSS EXAMINATION BY MR. BINGER 605
    CROSS EXAMINATION BY MR. CARTER 618

15

16   MADONNA JORDAN

17 DIRECT EXAMINATION BY MR. HOLMES 626
    CROSS EXAMINATION BY MR. WILKA 635
18 CROSS EXAMINATION BY MR. BINGER 653
    CROSS EXAMINATION BY MR. CARTER 655
19 CROSS EXAMINATION BY MR. HAUGAARD 661

20

21   JULIE BROWN

    DIRECT EXAMINATION BY MR. HOLMES 666
22 CROSS EXAMINATION BY MR. WILKA 669
    CROSS EXAMINATION BY MR. HAUGAARD 671

23

24

25

Page 680

1   INDEX TO GOVERNMENT EXHIBITS

2 Exhibit 21 Marked 461
    21 Offered 462
3
      21 Received 462
    Exhibit 22 Marked 551
4 22 Offered 552
5
      22 Received 552
    Exhibit 23 Marked 552
6 23 Offered 553
7
      23 Received 553
    Exhibit 24 Marked 556
8 24 Offered 556
9
      24 Received 556
    Exhibit 25 Marked 625
10 25 Offered 626
11
      25 Received 626

12

13

14

15

16

17

18

19

20

21

22

23

24

25

Page 679

```
 1        UNITED STATES DISTRICT COURT
 2        DISTRICT OF SOUTH DAKOTA
 3            SOUTHERN DIVISION
          · · · · · · · · · · · · · · · · · ·
 4                        ·
   UNITED STATES OF AMERICA,   ·
 5                        ·
          Plaintiff,   ·    Volume IV
 6                        ·
   ·vs·           ·  CR. 94-40015
 7                        ·  MOTION FOR NEW TRIAL
   DESMOND ROUSE, JESSIE ROUSE  ·
 8 GARFIELD FEATHER, RUSSELL   ·
   HUBBELING,            ·
 9                        ·
10        Defendants.  ·
11 · · · · · · · · · · · · · · · · · ·

12

13 BEFORE:    The Honorable Lawrence L. Piersol
            Chief United States District Judge
14           For the District of South Dakota
            Sioux Falls, South Dakota
15

16
   PROCEEDINGS:    The above-entitled matter came on for
17     hearing on the 5th day of September, 2001
       commencing at the hour of 9:00 a.m. in the
18     courtroom of the Federal Building, Sioux
       Falls, South Dakota.
19
   Proceedings recorded by mechanical stenography, transcript
20 produced by computer.

21

22

23

24

25
```

Page 680

```
 1 APPEARANCES:

 2     Mr. Randy Seiler
       Ms. Michelle Tapken
 3     Mr. Dennis Holmes
       Assistant United States Attorneys
 4     Pierre, South Dakota
       Sioux Falls, South Dakota
 5
          Attorneys for the United States;
 6

 7     Mr. John Wilka
       Attorney at Law
 8     Sioux Falls, South Dakota

 9        Attorney for Desmond Rouse;

10
       Mr. Steven Binger
11     Attorney at Law
       Sioux Falls, South Dakota
12
          Attorney for Jessie Rouse;
13

14     Mr. David Carter
       Attorney at Law
15     Sioux Falls, South Dakota

16        Attorney for Garfield Feather;

17
       Mr. Steve Haugaard
18     Attorney at Law
       Sioux Falls, South Dakota
19
          Attorney for Russell Hubbeling.
20

21

22

23

24

25
```

Page 681

```
 1        MR. HOLMES:  United States calls Eva Cheney.
 2        MR. BINGER:  Your Honor, I would like to make a
 3 motion on behalf of the defendants regarding this witness.
 4        THE COURT:  Alright.
 5        MR. BINGER:  We would move to exclude any testimony
 6 from this witness on the grounds that her, and I can't know
 7 exactly what she is going to be asked or what she might exactly
 8 say, but we feel that she is being called for the purposes of
 9 impeaching the testimony of the children.  She was originally
10 appointed by the Court to act as their attorney and guardian.
11 Our research does not disclose any specific case law one way or
12 the other.  We think this testimony raises some very serious
13 attorney/client privilege issues.  We also think that this
14 witness is being called for the express purpose of impeaching
15 her own client's testimony, and I think there is something
16 contrary to the rules regarding that.  I think there is just
17 something about her role in the case that we find disturbing
18 when she, at the request of the government, is appointed by
19 this Court to represent the children as their guardian, and now
20 she is being called as a witness by the government to impeach
21 their testimony.  She is being, rather than the neutral role of
22 guardian that she was originally assigned to have in this case,
23 she is now being used as an advocate witness by the government.
24 Therefore, again I can't pretend to know exactly what the
25 government intends to question her about today, but whatever
```

Page 682

```
 1 extent she is being offered as a witness to impeach the
 2 testimony of the children, we submit that violates the
 3 attorney/client privilege and contrary to the public policy of
 4 this Court's role when it originally appointed her as guardian
 5 for the children, and now she is being used as a witness
 6 against them.
 7        THE COURT:  When you say we, you are speaking for all
 8 the defendants?
 9        MR. BINGER:  Yes, I am.  I know I am.
10        THE COURT:  Mr. Holmes, what do you have to say about
11 that?
12        MR. HOLMES:  Counsel hasn't cited any authority for
13 the position that he is taking, and I guess I am really not
14 clear what the argument is.  He seems to be stating that
15 somehow this witness is an advocate for one side or the other,
16 that is clearly not the role of any witness in this proceeding.
17 They were served a subpoena and compelled to come here and
18 testify as to what is within their personal knowledge.  And so
19 I guess I am at a loss to understand what the basis would be
20 for excluding this witness's testimony.  I guess at best they
21 could be trying to argue that there was some privilege here
22 regarding communications, but I don't think that the situation
23 under which Ms. Cheney was appointed really had the makings of
24 an attorney/client privilege.  This was a guardian situation,
25 and she simply happens to be an attorney, and was so at the
```

Page 683

1 time. I don't think there are any privilege concerns. Any
2 testimony regarding what the children said or didn't say to her
3 necessarily would have been in the presence of others, and I
4 don't think there would even be any attorney/client privilege
5 in that regard. We simply don't see any basis for the Court
6 excluding this witness's testimony.
7   THE COURT: Anything in rebuttal before I rule?
8   MR. BINGER: Nothing specific except for the fact
9 that I guess I just ask the Court to consider that that, it was
10 this Court that appointed her to this role, and I don't think
11 this Court ever contemplated she would ever be used by either
12 party as a witness for anything.
13   THE COURT: Well, it's true that this Court appointed
14 her as the guardian for the purposes of that litigation, which
15 is the criminal charges against these defendants. I guess
16 whether I contemplated she would be called in some subsequent
17 proceedings, didn't really contemplate that. But in analyzing
18 it, there is no attorney/client privilege involved in that, she
19 was their guardian for purposes of litigation, and given the
20 litigation that was going on it was desirable to have somebody
21 who was a lawyer to serve in that capacity. But I don't see
22 any privilege that is there. She has been subpoenaed and has
23 an obligation to testify to the truth, whatever is asked by
24 which ever side. I am not done yet, did you have argument you
25 wanted to take, Mr. Haugaard.

Page 684

1   MR. HAUGAARD: I wanted to make a comment that as I
2 recall --
3   THE COURT: I don't ask for comment in the middle of
4 my ruling. If you have argument, go ahead and make it.
5   MR. HAUGAARD: During the course of proceedings
6 Ms. Cheney has been referred to as the children's attorney
7 often times.
8   THE COURT: I am aware of that, because she is a
9 lawyer, I recognize that, but I know what capacity I appointed
10 her in and why I appointed her. It was to be a guardian ad
11 litem for the children. What you say is so, Mr. Haugaard, that
12 the fact that she is a lawyer I think was referred to. I am
13 talking about before today, but back when, which is what I
14 think you were referring to also. But I don't see an
15 attorney/client privilege, because she was in a different
16 capacity, she was in a capacity as a guardian. I don't know
17 whether or not she is going to impeach her own charges. The
18 summary that the government gave said will testify as to her
19 presence at all interviews conducted after her appointment, and
20 that she was with the victims during the trial and present
21 during all the discussions with the victims. What will come
22 out of that we will see, but there is no privilege, and if her
23 testimony is contrary to the recantation of the victims, then
24 that is not necessarily contrary to their interest. She is
25 under oath, and I am going to make the decision as to

Page 685

1 credibility as to the victims and their recantations, as well
2 as the other decisions I have to make in ruling one way or the
3 other on this motion. Because, as we all know, my
4 determination as to the victims' credibility is not the final
5 issue I have to rule upon. It is what impact will the evidence
6 that came before me, including the recantation, in my judgment
7 have upon a jury if a retrial were to be granted. So even if
8 her testimony does impeach the children, that doesn't mean that
9 it is necessarily contrary to the children's interests. So she
10 is here, there is no privilege as far as I am concerned, and
11 she just has to testify to the truth. Your motion is denied,
12 proceed.
13
14   EVA CHENEY,
15 called as a witness, being first duly sworn, testified and said
16 as follows:
17
18 DIRECT EXAMINATION BY MR. HOLMES:
19 Q. Would you briefly describe for the Court your educational
20 and professional background?
21 A. I was licensed, I graduated from the University of South
22 Dakota school of law, I was licensed to practice law in South
23 Dakota in 1991. I am also licensed in Pennsylvania, and most
24 recently licensed in Minnesota. I have been a practicing
25 attorney for ten years.

Page 686

1 Q. In May of 1994 were you appointed guardian ad litem for
2 the children in this case?
3 A. Yes, I was.
4 Q. Can you generally describe what you understood your role
5 to be as guardian ad litem for the children in the case?
6 A. It was my understanding that my role was to be the
7 guardian ad litem, my understanding of that role is that the
8 guardian is to look out for the children's interests throughout
9 the process of the proceedings from the time they are appointed
10 forward. There are competing interests on both sides, and the
11 guardian ad litem is supposed to insure that neither the
12 prosecution nor the defense does anything that would cause more
13 injury or trauma to the children than need be. Often times
14 when children are involved in the judicial process, it is
15 confusing for them. Often times children can be more
16 traumatized by the actual judicial proceedings than the initial
17 abuse, so a guardian ad litem, it is my understanding, is to
18 make sure the children get through the process in a safe
19 manner, and it is the guardian's responsibility to do whatever
20 it takes to ensure that that happens.
21 Q. How did you become acquainted with the children after you
22 were appointed guardian ad litem?
23 A. My initial contact with the children was at their
24 counselor's office. I thought it would be best for the
25 children if they were introduced to me, rather than just

Page 687

1 meeting me alone for the first time, I had their counselor
2 introduce me to them. We did that at the counselor's office in
3 surroundings that were familiar with the children. I
4 introduced myself to the children, and I explained in very
5 simple terms for them that the Judge in the case was, wanted to
6 make sure that their voice was heard. I explained to them that
7 grown-ups make a lot of noise and talk a lot, and a lot of
8 times children's voices can't get heard, and that Judge Piersol
9 wanted to make sure if there was anything they wanted him to
10 know, that all they would have to do is tell me and I would use
11 my big voice to make sure the Judge heard what it was that they
12 wanted him to know. Also it was important for them to know if
13 anything bothered them, or if they had any questions, it was my
14 job to explain things to them, they could ask me about it. I
15 explained to them that I was their lawyer, that I didn't work
16 for the government or for the defense, that I was just for
17 them. And I wanted to create an environment for them that made
18 them feel like it was safe to talk to me if they had concerns.
19 Not necessarily about the abuse, because they had counselors,
20 they had foster parents, they had plenty of people to take care
21 of those needs, and I am not qualified to do that. So I was,
22 tried to be real clear with them what my narrow role was, and
23 that was to help them through the jury, and the events before
24 it up to that time.
25 Q. Do you recall approximately how many times you met with

Page 688

1 them initially in an effort to become acquainted with them?
2 A. Yes, I met with them that first time in the counselor's
3 office, and that wasn't a real long meeting. All of the
4 children were there, and it was kind of in a big room and kind
5 of a play room, and I never went in to, I never did ask real
6 specifics about the case, because that wasn't my role, but that
7 initial meeting was a half an hour. I did meet with them
8 again, I drove back down to Sioux City, which is where the
9 counselor's office is, and I picked them up from the
10 counselor's office when I took them, I think the only place I
11 could find in Elk Point where I could meet with them alone was
12 a Dairy Queen, and we met there. Again I was trying to
13 establish a relationship with the children, not at the
14 counselor's office, not associated with any of the other
15 people, but just me and them. So we went there and just had
16 conversation again about my role, and pretty informal
17 conversation. Again the purpose was for them to just get to
18 know me and feel comfortable with me, again that was maybe a
19 half an hour meeting, not real long. I believe the next time
20 that I saw the children was here in Sioux Falls. I believe
21 that they came up to meet with the U. S. Attorney, Michelle
22 Tapken, and I was there, again I saw my role as being there
23 with the children to make sure that there were no abuses of any
24 sort, just make sure that there was no questioning or anything
25 out of line. We brought them up to the courthouse, met Judge

Page 689

1 Piersol, things like that, to make them comfortable with the
2 process, and to answer any questions they had about what a
3 courtroom looks like, where they would sit, what the process
4 was. I also met with them during the course of the trial. We
5 had them in a room here in the courthouse, and so I would be
6 either with them in the room or I would accompany them up here
7 to the courthouse, or courtroom when they testified.
8 Q. After your appointment, at least to your knowledge, were
9 these children ever interviewed by either a government
10 investigator or a prosecutor without you being present.
11 A. No. In fact, that reminds me, there was one other time I
12 was with the children. There was an interview of I think it
13 was maybe Jerome down in the park in Yankton. But no, there
14 was never a time that they met with the U. S. Attorney or the
15 FBI agent that I wasn't with them.
16 Q. During these times when you were present when they were
17 interviewed either by the Assistant United States Attorney or
18 an investigator, did anyone in your presence ever promise these
19 children any clothing, or toys, or anything else of value in
20 return for their testimony?
21 A. No.
22 Q. Did anyone ever in your presence threaten the children in
23 any way?
24 A. No.
25 Q. Did you hear either Ms. Tapken or any of the

Page 690

1 investigators ever in effect tell these children what to say
2 when they testified?
3 A. No.
4 Q. How would you describe these interviews that you were
5 present at?
6 A. Well, the interview at the park in Yankton was very
7 informal, very, I hate to use the word casual, but it was very
8 child oriented. And that I don't believe was an interview of
9 one of the alleged victims, it was of Jerome, I believe, and I
10 think that the FBI agent asked the questions, and they were in
11 my mind real non-threatening questions. The next time that
12 they were interviewed by the U. S. Attorney was when they were
13 up here in preparation of the trial, and again when I use the
14 word interview, I should maybe be more clear about that. Donna
15 Jordan brought them up here to the U. S. Attorney's office, and
16 there was a big room and she just stayed there with all the
17 kids, and the children one by one would go in and meet with the
18 U. S. Attorney. When I say interview, they weren't necessarily
19 questioned about the allegations so much as it was going over
20 what to expect from, about what was going to happen. And I
21 remember Ms. Tapken telling them to, you know, tell the truth,
22 but I don't remember it being like an interrogation interview.
23 It was just going over what was going to happen at the jury
24 trial, and they would talk about the things they talked about
25 with the FBI agents, and reminding them to tell the truth and

Page 691

1 things of that nature.

2 Q. During the trial itself were you with the children either
3 in the witness room or individually when each one of them came
4 up to testify?

5 A. Both, yes.

6 Q. And when they were in the witness room, what kind of
7 environment was present there as far as their ability to get
8 something to drink, or eat, or use the restroom?

9 A. It was a fairly large room downstairs in this building.
10 It was downstairs, but there are windows in it, it is in the
11 lower level, but there are windows, so it was a big, sunny
12 room. I remember there was a TV there, and they had movies for
13 the children to watch, because I believe they were here for
14 several days. There was food there for them, there was drink
15 there for them. I don't recall if anybody asked to go to the
16 bathroom when I was there, but I don't recall anyone denying
17 them the ability to go to the bathroom. But I would go there
18 at the beginning of each day and check in with them and make
19 sure they were okay, and I didn't see any problem with the
20 room.

21 Q. In either these pretrial interviews or during the course
22 of the trial did you ever hear anyone say in the presence of
23 the children words to the effect that the sooner you cooperate,
24 the sooner you will get to go home?

25 A. No.

Page 692

1 Q. I think there has been some testimony here during the
2 course of this hearing about some comment to the effect that
3 after these guys go to prison we are going to party. Do you
4 recall anything like that ever being said?

5 A. No.

6 Q. Do you think you would have remembered such a comment?

7 A. Well, yeah, I would have, because that is, I mean the
8 people that I was around were, I can't imagine any of them
9 making that kind of statement, it would be out of character.

10 Q. What do you recall about the atmosphere in the courthouse
11 during the course of the trial proceedings when the children
12 were actually here at the courthouse?

13   MR. WILKA: Objection, foundation.

14   THE COURT: What is the basis for the foundation

15 objection?

16   MR. WILKA: Well, what part of the courtroom, who was
17 present. Also I add relevancy to it.

18   THE COURT: I will overrule the relevancy. I think
19 with regard to the question, it could be more specific. I will
20 sustain that part of it.

21 BY MR. HOLMES:

22 Q. I believe you testified that you were present here in the
23 courthouse during the time that the children testified and the
24 times that they were waiting to testify, is that correct?

25 A. Yes.

Page 693

1 Q. During that period of time were you aware of some
2 incidents here in the courthouse that involved individuals
3 either making loud noises or doing other things that caused you
4 to have some concern regarding the children?

5 A. Well, yeah. There were a couple of things I think that I
6 requested. One thing I was concerned about, and mentioned to
7 the U. S. Attorney, was before the trial even started there
8 were large numbers of people. We had thought about having the
9 children in a hotel room rather than here in the courthouse,
10 but realized they would have to walk through large groups of
11 people and that might be intimidating to them. So that was the
12 first thing, was making a different decision about where they
13 would actually be while they were waiting to testify. I also
14 remember, I think I made a request directly to the Court to
15 have the hallways be cleared when it came time for the children
16 to testify, because I recall that there were a lot of people
17 standing in the hallway, and they would have had to walk down a
18 corridor that was lined along both sides with people. I
19 remember there just being a lot of people. So when the kids
20 were called to testify, the hallways were cleared at that time
21 I remember the children being afraid, and so that was the
22 motivation behind my wanting to make sure that they had a
23 non-intimidating route to the courtroom to testify, because
24 they were already afraid.

25 Q. Was there an incident where some individuals banged on a

Page 694

1 vehicle that the children were being transported in?

2 A. Well, the guardian ad litem --

3   MR. HAUGAARD: Objection, that calls for a yes or no
4 answer.

5   THE COURT: Sustained.

6 A. Yes.

7 BY MR. HOLMES:

8 Q. What do you recall about that?

9 A. The foster mother spoke to me --

10   MR. HAUGAARD: Objection, hearsay.

11   THE COURT: It is hearsay. I view it as preparatory,
12 I will assume, I will accept it. If it isn't, you can renew
13 your motion and I will view it substantively rather than
14 preparatory. Go ahead.

15 BY MR. HOLMES:

16 Q. What do you recall?

17 A. The foster mother spoke to me and requested that I do
18 something security wise, that when they had left Court the
19 evening before some individuals had --

20   MR. HAUGAARD: Objection, hearsay.

21   MR. WILKA: I will join in that objection, Your
22 Honor.

23   THE COURT: I am going to, with regard to what is
24 going to be said, I am going to sustain that objection, but I
25 am going to at the same time receive the testimony, not for the

Page 695

1 truth of the matter stated, but rather to see what the
2 predicate is. I assume it's a predicate to something else she
3 is going to say, but if not, you can move to strike it and I
4 will strike the whole thing. I am going to receive it for this
5 limited purpose at this point, sustained to that extent.
6 BY MR. HOLMES:
7 Q. Continue with your answer, please.
8 A. It had been brought to my attention, because I was their
9 guardian ad litem, she felt it was necessary to bring it to my
10 attention to ask for some security measures, because that had
11 happened.
12 Q. What did you do after receiving that information?
13 A. Boy, I am trying to remember, because it seemed to me
14 like there was a motion where that was brought up as part of
15 the basis for a motion, but I can't remember what that motion
16 was. It was brought to the Court's attention.
17 Q. During the period of time that you were guardian ad litem
18 for these children did they ever express to you any fear toward
19 anyone?
20   MR. WILKA: Your Honor, at this time I am going to
21 object and I renew Mr. Binger's objection. My basis for that,
22 if I may, is that three things were explained by this witness
23 to the children. One, that their voice was to be heard; two,
24 that she was to explain things to them; but three, and whether
25 this Court intended it or not, she explained that she was their

Page 696

1 lawyer. Even though the Court may have appointed Ms. Cheney
2 the guardian ad litem under the CJA, by stating that she was
3 their lawyer she did de facto create an attorney/client
4 relationship.
5   THE COURT: Well, the Court's intention was to create
6 a guardianship for purposes of the trial, and the only reason
7 the CJA was used at all was as a funding mechanism so somebody
8 could be paid to do it, that's what it amounted to. As far as
9 the Court was concerned then and now, there was no
10 attorney/client relationship established, so your objection is
11 noted but overruled. Go ahead.
12 BY MR. HOLMES:
13 Q. Did any of the children ever state to you that they had a
14 fear toward any individual or individuals?
15 A. The children were afraid of their uncles. They were also
16 afraid of some individuals during the course of the trial and
17 before they testified, I don't know what individuals, but
18 individuals had gone to the foster parent's home, and the kids
19 thought that they were relatives, so they were afraid of a lot
20 of people.
21 Q. They ever express to you any fear toward Ms. Tapken or
22 the investigators in the case?
23 A. No.
24 Q. Did any of the children ever in your presence say any
25 words to the effect that this alleged sexual abuse had not

Page 697

1 occurred?
2 A. No.
3   MR. HOLMES: No further questions.
4   THE COURT: Cross examination.
5 CROSS EXAMINATION BY MR. WILKA:
6 Q. Good afternoon, Ms. Cheney?
7 A. Good afternoon.
8 Q. Welcome back to Sioux Falls. Now a couple of preliminary
9 matters, you are a white person, correct?
10 A. Correct.
11 Q. Donna Jordan is a white person?
12 A. Yes.
13 Q. Ellen Kelson is a white person?
14 A. To my knowledge.
15 Q. Kids are Native American, right?
16 A. Yes.
17 Q. You stated that the children were afraid of their uncles?
18 A. That is what they said to me.
19 Q. They never recanted the alleged sexual abuse to you?
20 A. They never recanted, but I need to also say that I didn't
21 discuss the alleged abuse with the children, that wasn't my
22 role. I think I created a safe environment for them, if they
23 felt they needed to say something to me that they could, but I
24 didn't ask them specific questions about that, I didn't see
25 that as my role.

Page 698

1 Q. So you are not here to state whether or not you have any
2 independent observational knowledge as to whether or not these
3 statements, the current statements by the children were
4 coerced, do you?
5 A. I am not sure what you mean by current statements?
6 Q. Are you aware the children are currently stating that
7 this did not happen?
8 A. Right.
9 Q. You are?
10 A. I am aware of that, yes.
11 Q. Have you interviewed the children, or spoken to them
12 within the last couple of weeks?
13 A. No.
14 Q. But you are aware that they are claiming the abuse didn't
15 happen?
16 A. Yes, I am aware of that.
17 Q. You are aware that they are claiming that these, that the
18 adults surrounding them in their environment gave them the
19 impression that if they went along with the story of abuse that
20 they would be able to be returned to their mothers?
21 A. I can't say that I am real aware of that. I was just
22 aware they had recanted, but as to the specifics, no, I am not
23 aware of what exactly they are saying.
24 Q. This interview in a park in Yankton, did that take place
25 prior to the trial?

Page 699

1 A. Yes, it did.
2 Q. And the children were present?
3 A. Well, they were present in the sense that they were at
4 the park, but the children were off playing over at the swings
5 in the playground part. I believe that they were talking with
6 Jerome, I can't remember for sure, but the other children were
7 off in another area of the park playing.
8 Q. Do you know how long before the trial this interview took
9 place?
10 A. No.
11 Q. You don't know if it was a month, or a week?
12 A. Well, I don't recall. Remember, I was appointed in May
13 and I believe the trial was in July. But I don't think that it
14 was -- I know that it was before the children came up here to
15 speak with the U. S. Attorney in preparation for trial, I know
16 it was before that.
17 Q. You stated that the children were off swinging on the
18 swing set, so were you sitting -- strike that.
19 Who conducted the interview?
20 A. I don't remember Matt's last name, but Matt was there, an
21 FBI agent.
22 Q. Special Agent Miller?
23 A. Yes, Matt Miller. Matt Miller was there, and Assistant
24 U. S. Attorney Michelle Tapken was there, but I believe it was
25 Matt Miller. I can't recall for sure, but it seemed to me that

Page 700

1 Matt had asked the questions.
2 Q. Were you there as Jerome's guardian ad litem also?
3 A. I don't remember that Jerome was one of the children.
4 First of all, I don't remember if it was Jerome. I was there
5 because all of the children were there, and they were
6 interviewing a child, so I was there for that reason. I don't
7 believe that I was technically appointed, don't remember if
8 Jerome was, I don't remember if it was Jerome, and I don't
9 remember if he was even one of the children that I was
10 appointed to represent, but that is why I was there, because
11 all of the children were there.
12 Q. Were you alerted or instructed by somebody to bring the
13 children to Yankton?
14 A. I didn't bring the children to Yankton. I was notified
15 that they were going to interview a child, and I was advised
16 when, and I went to observe that.
17 Q. Were Jerome and Special Agent Miller seated at a picnic
18 table or on a bench?
19 A. First of all, I hesitate to say it was Jerome. That's my
20 recollection, but I am not real sure who it was. Yeah, there
21 was a picnic table there, and we were seated at the picnic
22 table. Real informal.
23 Q. So you were in a proximity to hear the questions given by
24 the agents and the answers given by the child?
25 A. Yeah, I was there to make sure that none of the children

Page 701

1 were traumatized by any of the events that would occur as far
2 as this process. So yes, I was there.
3 Q. Do you recall what the interview was about?
4 A. You know, I don't. It wasn't very lengthy, and I can't
5 even remember. I can't remember now.
6 Q. Was it about, for instance, any sexual activity on behalf
7 of Jerome, on the part of Jerome?
8 A. I can't remember. Honestly, I can't remember.
9 Q. Do you recall if the agent was taking notes while this
10 interview was going on?
11 A. I can't recall that either.
12 Q. So you would have no idea if an FBI 302 report was
13 prepared, do you?
14 A. No, I wouldn't know.
15 Q. Are there any other places that you were informed to go
16 aside from Yankton, or strike that.
17 Let me see if I have you here. You met with the children at
18 the counselors in Elk Point, at a Dairy Queen in Elk Point?
19 A. Yes.
20 Q. And at a park in Yankton?
21 A. Yes.
22 Q. At the U. S. Attorney's office in Sioux Falls?
23 A. Yes.
24 Q. At the courthouse in Sioux Falls?
25 A. During the trial, yes.

Page 702

1 Q. Were there any other places that you met with the
2 children?
3 A. Not that I can remember.
4 Q. Did you and the Assistant U. S. Attorney ever go to lunch
5 with the children?
6 A. No. You know, I hesitate because I am trying to remember
7 during the course of the trial, we had the room downstairs and
8 we had food there for the children, but I don't recall that
9 either of us ate there with the children. So I don't think so,
10 no.
11 Q. The children were all in a basement, or not in the
12 basement, but in a room on the lower level of the courthouse?
13 A. Yes.
14 Q. Would the process be that a child would be removed from
15 the room, the rest of the children would stay in that room, and
16 that child would be brought to the courtroom, right?
17 A. Yes.
18 Q. Then after that child's testimony, that child would go
19 back to that room and then a different child would come up?
20 A. Yes, but I didn't take them immediately down. I would,
21 you know, visit with them just a little bit. I think there was
22 a room down at the end of the corridor, and I would just talk
23 with them a few minutes and make sure they were okay and then
24 we would go back downstairs, yes.
25 Q. You were I believe present during all of the children's

Page 703

1 testimony at the trial, correct?

2 A. Yes.

3 Q. While you were up here who was with the children

4 downstairs?

5 A. Donna Jordan, their foster parent, and I believe, I don't

6 know the name of the person, but the person who is the victim

7 witness person for the U. S. Attorney's office, you know, that

8 made arrangements to get the food, the movies, and the

9 accommodations for the children.

10 Q. So the U. S. Attorney's office was in charge of not

11 housing, but rooming and feeding the children during the trial,

12 correct?

13 A. Well, yeah. I mean we needed to make some accommodations

14 they had something to eat and drink. I think they were here

15 for two days, maybe, even before they were able to testify, and

16 so we had to have them somewhere. Yes, they made the

17 arrangements to have the food there, I believe.

18 Q. Do you know if anyone was keeping notes while the

19 children were visiting with each other downstairs?

20 A. No, I don't know that.

21 Q. Do you know if there was -- strike that.

22   MR. WILKA: That's all I have, Your Honor.

23   THE COURT: Mr. Binger.

24 CROSS EXAMINATION BY MR. BINGER:

25 Q. Ms. Cheney, during this contact down in Yankton, I know

Page 704

1 you mentioned the name Jerome twice, but are you now kind of

2 not so sure who they interviewed?

3 A. I think I said from the very beginning I think it was

4 Jerome, but I don't remember for sure.

5 Q. When Jerome was interviewed it would have been you, Agent

6 Miller and Jerome and no one else, the other kids were off

7 somewhere else playing?

8 A. Right. Assistant U. S. Attorney Michelle Tapken was

9 there also.

10 Q. Did she participate in asking questions?

11 A. Not in asking questions. I think that she did say a

12 little bit like, you know, we are here to ask you some

13 questions, or to tell the truth, but it was more introductory,

14 explaining who she was, but I don't recall her asking

15 questions.

16 Q. You don't remember much of the content of what was asked?

17 A. It was really short, I don't even remember why they were

18 talking to him, I honestly don't.

19 Q. You say really short, you mean five minutes or less?

20 A. Maybe ten minutes. It just really -- wasn't there very

21 long.

22 Q. So they interviewed who you think was Jerome, but then

23 they interviewed no other ones?

24 A. No, no one else.

25 Q. You drove from Sioux Falls to Yankton for this?

Page 705

1 A. Yes, I did.

2 Q. And the kids were brought to Yankton?

3 A. Yes, their foster mother brought them over.

4 Q. So all these people traveled to Yankton, including all

5 the children and their foster parent and yourself, for one

6 roughly five minute interview?

7 A. Well, we all traveled there.

8 Q. And that's all that happened?

9 A. Yeah.

10 Q. The trial concluded as I recall some time in the middle

11 of October, 1994. After that date did you ever see the kids

12 again?

13 A. No, I didn't.

14   MR. BINGER: That's all I have.

15 CROSS EXAMINATION BY MR. CARTER:

16 Q. Eva, during the time that you were involved as guardian,

17 whatever, for the attorney, or attorney for the children, did

18 you ever, did the family ever have access to the children

19 during that time?

20 A. Well, I believe that they were having visits with their

21 mothers, but that wasn't something I was a part of. That was,

22 you know, that was the Tribal Social Services, that was a

23 totally separate situation than this. So I didn't have any

24 involvement in that, but it was my understanding they were

25 having visits with their mothers.

Page 706

1 Q. Were you present for those events?

2 A. No, I wasn't.

3 Q. Did you find the children to be fairly quiet, or were

4 they bubbly and very verbal, how would you describe that?

5 A. Actually they were very verbal in a quiet way, but they

6 were all very talkative with me. They seemed comfortable with

7 their foster mother. They were talkative. One was, I

8 remember, I don't remember if her name was Jessica or Lucritia,

9 but she had glasses, and she was just very verbal, they were

10 all fairly comfortable in speaking with me.

11 Q. During the time that you were involved did the children

12 ever make any statements to you that they missed their family

13 and they wanted to go home?

14 A. Sure.

15 Q. How frequently was that a comment that you remember being

16 made?

17 A. I wouldn't say it was frequent, I would say that that was

18 something they had said in passing.

19 Q. So you didn't think it was something that was

20 particularly important?

21 A. I thought it was something that was fairly common for

22 children who are in foster care. It would be a natural thing

23 for them, I wasn't surprised that they wanted to be with their

24 mothers.

25 Q. You were present then for the -- strike that.

Page 707

1 What sort of materials did you, did you review any materials
2 from the counselors, or their social workers, or anybody like
3 that, relative to the kids while you were working for them?
4 A. Yes, I did.
5 Q. Can you tell me what sort of materials that you would
6 have received and reviewed?
7 A. I am trying to remember, I don't know that I got to see
8 the counselor notes. I think I reviewed, may have reviewed the
9 302's which were the interviews with the children. I can't
10 recall for sure.
11 Q. It's possible that you reviewed the 302's with the
12 children?
13 A. You know, I might have, but I can't say for sure.
14 Q. Do you remember in what, any specifics?
15   THE COURT: I want to make sure I understand
16 something. When you say with the children, the 302's were
17 taken regarding interviews with the children, or 302's, take
18 them and go over them with the children? I want to make sure I
19 understand that.
20   MR. CARTER: The latter.
21 A. Oh, I didn't go over them with the children.
22 BY MR. CARTER:
23 Q. You did not?
24 A. No.
25 Q. You reviewed them for your own background?

Page 708

1 A. Yes.
2 Q. Did you have discussions ever then with FBI, Mr. Van Roe
3 or anybody with the FBI about those 302's?
4 A. No. I was given, you know, I was given some material, I
5 can't remember exactly what materials, but they were to
6 familiarize me with who the children were, what the
7 circumstances were, just for my own knowledge, because I was
8 going to be working with the children.
9 Q. Did you ever review any materials from the Children's
10 Home Society?
11 A. No.
12 Q. Did you ever speak to their counselor about their
13 counseling situation?
14 A. The only time I spoke with their counselor was when I
15 made arrangements for her to meet the children for the first
16 time in her office, because I thought that would be best for
17 her to be present so that it would be easier for them, and that
18 was my discussion with her basically, and not really anything
19 beyond that.
20 Q. Did you ever get the sense from the children that the
21 older children were essentially speaking for the whole group
22 and they kind of told you what they wanted you to hear?
23 A. No. In fact, like I said earlier, I remember one of the
24 younger being probably more vocal than some of the older ones.
25 Q. And you never had any discussions with Ellen Kelson about

Page 709

1 anything of that sort with the kids?
2 A. Anything of what sort, I not sure?
3 Q. Where the older children were speaking for the younger
4 ones, and basically deciding, they got the same story from all
5 of the children essentially?
6 A. I never spoke to Ellen Kelson about that.
7 Q. Did you ever have any discussion with anyone regarding
8 dream journals of Rosemary?
9 A. No.
10 Q. Were you aware of there being such a journal?
11 A. I really don't recall.
12 Q. In preparation for your being a witness in this matter,
13 Eva, have you gone over any records to refresh your memory on
14 any of these matters?
15 A. I reviewed an affidavit that I prepared a few months ago,
16 and I reviewed a transcript of some testimony that I had given
17 in Court in support of a motion. I did that a couple weeks
18 ago.
19   MR. CARTER: No further questions.
20   THE COURT: Mr. Haugaard.
21 CROSS EXAMINATION BY MR. HAUGAARD:
22 Q. Ms. Cheney, did you keep notes of your contact with the
23 children?
24 A. No.
25 Q. How did you document your time involved in this case?

Page 710

1 A. I kept a time, I kept track of my time, but I didn't take
2 specific note taking notes of my conversations with them or
3 anything.
4 Q. Did you take any notes as to people that you would have
5 met with on given dates?
6 A. I would have been keeping track of that, yes.
7 Q. Would you be able to go back and find exactly what date
8 and who is present at the Yankton interview?
9 A. No.
10 Q. You didn't keep notes about those types of things?
11 A. I am not saying I didn't keep notes, I am saying I don't
12 know that I would be able to find them.
13 Q. Did you keep notes about who was at a given meeting?
14 A. I always keep notes of what I am doing when I am working
15 on a case. Did I specifically write down who was there, that I
16 can't answer. I don't know that I would have been that
17 specific. It probably would have been more that I went to
18 Yankton and back.
19 Q. Did you maintain a file in regard to the Rouse children?
20 A. Yes, I did.
21 Q. Do you have it in your possession yet?
22 A. Yes. I believe I do.
23 Q. Would you be willing to provide that to us for review?
24 A. If the Court ordered me to, and if I was able to locate
25 it. I have moved twice since I had that case, and it has been

Page 711

1 over seven years ago. I believe I do have it, I believe that I
2 could find it if the Court wanted me to do that. But I say
3 that with hesitation, because I have moved twice. I am pretty
4 sure I have it, but I would need to locate it.
5 Q. Are you asserting any attorney/client privilege in regard
6 to that file?
7 A. I would leave that up to the Court. I believe the Court
8 has already told me there is no attorney/client privilege, so I
9 would rely on the Court's advice to that. I wouldn't turn over
10 anything unless the Court told me to.
11 Q. You indicated that you brought the kids to, I am not
12 sure, did you bring the kids to Sioux Falls to meet with
13 Ms. Tapken?
14 A. No, their foster mother, Donna Jordan, transported them.
15 Q. So when that meeting took place, you mentioned that you
16 brought the children over to the courthouse, familiarized them
17 with the courthouse, is that right?
18 A. Yes.
19 Q. Do you remember approximately when that was?
20 A. I would guess it was, you know, within a week or two
21 before the trial, because I wanted to do it closer to trial.
22 You know, with little kids, time is much longer for them than
23 it is for us, so it was much better to do that closer to the
24 time of trial.
25 Q. Did you indicate that they had an opportunity to meet the

Page 712

1 Judge that day?
2 A. By accident, yes. We were walking up the street and he
3 was coming down the street, and so we took the opportunity to
4 introduce them to him.
5 Q. Did the questioning that you heard from any of the
6 investigators, counselors, or Ms. Tapken ever begin with the
7 preface something to the effect that don't worry, you will be
8 safe?
9 A. No.
10 Q. Did they ever assure the kids that they would be safe?
11 A. I think that in the course of things that I probably
12 reassured them that they would be okay. I don't recall
13 specifically whether anyone else did or not. It wouldn't
14 surprise me if they did, because the kids were very concerned
15 about their safety, so it wouldn't surprise me in general
16 terms. I know I did, I assured them it would be okay, not to
17 be afraid, tried to assure them as much as I could because they
18 were very afraid.
19 Q. Now you are saying it could very well have happened that
20 others assured them they would be safe?
21 A. I don't know if I would use the word assured. I am
22 saying I did. Your question was did anyone predicate a
23 question with that. I am saying no, to my knowledge no one
24 predicated a question with that. Did people assure them from
25 time to time they would be safe? I know I did. I wouldn't be

Page 713

1 surprised if other people told them that also, but I can't
2 recall a specific observation of that.
3 Q. Do you recall when Jessica was in the Judge's chambers
4 prior to the time when she was called as a witness the Judge
5 asked her a question about what does it mean to tell the truth,
6 and her response was we get to go home, do you recall that?
7 A. I don't recall that specific testimony, no.
8 Q. If it is in the transcript you would not dispute that?
9 A. I wouldn't dispute it. No, I just don't recall. It has
10 been seven years ago, I couldn't testify to what any of their
11 testimony was.
12 Q. The time that you met, maybe there was more than one
13 time, I am not sure, the time or times that you met with the
14 children at the U. S. Attorney's office, how many times?
15 A. Once. I believe it was just when they were up here prior
16 to trial.
17 Q. And you indicate that Donna Jordan brought the kids to
18 Sioux Falls?
19 A. Yes.
20 Q. When Donna Jordan brought the kids to the U. S.
21 Attorney's office were you already at the U. S. Attorney's
22 office?
23 A. I don't know who got there first, I can't remember.
24 Q. Did you have the opportunity to speak with Ms. Tapken
25 independently of the kids about this case?

Page 714

1 A. Yes.
2 Q. So you discussed the content of the claims?
3 A. Not necessarily the allegations. I believe that there
4 were, there was at least one motion, maybe two motions where, I
5 don't remember if they made the motion and I supported the
6 government's motion or vice versa, but I would have talked with
7 her about that.
8   MR. HAUGAARD: No further questions, thank you.
9   THE COURT: Redirect.
10   MR. HOLMES: No redirect.
11   THE COURT: You may step down. Call your next
12 witness.
13   MR. HOLMES: United States calls Mary Weber.
14
15   MARY WEBER,
16 called as a witness, being first duly sworn, testified and said
17 as follows:
18
19 DIRECT EXAMINATION BY MR. HOLMES:
20 Q. Good afternoon.
21 A. Good afternoon.
22 Q. Please state your full name and spell your last name for
23 the record?
24 A. Mary Weber, W-E-B-E-R.
25 Q. Ms. Weber, how are you currently employed?

Page 715

1 A. I work at Children's Inn in Sioux Falls.

2 Q. In the years of, I believe 1995, beginning in 1995 for

3 approximately a year and a half were you involved in dealing

4 with some of the Rouse children at the Children's Home Society

5 here in Sioux Falls?

6 A. Yes, I was.

7 Q. What position did you hold at Children's Home at that

8 time?

9 A. I was a unit director on the upstairs unit, and then I

10 was also a family therapist.

11 Q. Would you briefly describe for us what your educational

12 background is?

13 A. Sure. I have a Bachelors Degree in child development and

14 family relations and a Masters Degree in counseling from SDSU,

15 and I have two licensures, I am a licensed professional

16 counselor and a licensed marriage and family therapist.

17 Q. Let's go back to '95, will you describe what your

18 positions were there at Children's Home, can you give us a

19 little more of a description as to what those positions

20 involved, what you had to do there in those positions?

21 A. I was a unit director in the upstairs residential unit,

22 so 21 children stayed there. So I supervised the coordinators

23 who then supervised the child care staff that was in charge of

24 day-to-day activities. I oversaw the therapy components of the

25 children on the unit, and then I was also a family therapist,

Page 716

1 and so that meant that I had a small case load myself that I

2 helped with the individual group and family therapy with.

3 Q. Were you specifically involved in therapy with Lucritia

4 and Thrista Rouse?

5 A. Yes, I was.

6 Q. There were some of the other Rouse children at Children's

7 Home at that time, is that right?

8 A. That is right.

9 Q. Would they have had a different individual involved in

10 their therapy sessions?

11 A. Yes. I did work a little bit in group therapy with the

12 other Rouse children, and I can't remember, I think Jessica I

13 did a little bit of the work at the end, but mainly it was

14 Lucritia and Thrista that I worked with.

15 Q. What type of therapy was this where you worked with

16 Lucritia and Thrista, what were those sessions like and who

17 would be involved in them?

18 A. Well, the individual sessions it was usually then just

19 myself and the child. They would range from a variety of

20 discussions, maybe activities, maybe when they would draw they

21 would share things, we would visit. Some were just chit-chats,

22 how their day was, were they having any tough times. The group

23 sessions, sometimes they were the four Rouse children together,

24 sometimes the girls were in a girls group with just girls on

25 the unit talking about how to get along, how to make good

Page 717

1 choices, be a good friend. Then sometimes there was family

2 therapy sessions, sometimes I was the therapist, sometimes

3 there were other therapists, and that could have been with

4 either one of the mothers we were working with and their

5 children.

6 Q. Was one of the mothers that would come up Beta Rouse?

7 A. Yes.

8 Q. Do you recall her actually coming up to some of these

9 family sessions?

10 A. She came to a few, yes.

11 Q. How would you describe her attitude toward the

12 allegations of abuse?

13   MR. WILKA: Your Honor, may I voir dire.

14   THE COURT: No.

15   MR. WILKA: I will object on the basis of commenting

16 on the mental state of another.

17   THE COURT: Overruled.

18 BY MR. HOLMES:

19 Q. You can answer the question.

20 A. She was pretty hesitant to share a lot of information

21 with us, she was very guarded. She shared that she did not

22 believe the abuse occurred by the uncles. She shared some of

23 her own theories on what happened. She at one time said she

24 didn't believe it happened, because the children never shared

25 the information directly with her. But then when they did on

Page 718

1 different occasions she still felt that it wasn't the truth,

2 because she felt that the children didn't look her in the eyes.

3 So throughout the course of the time that we worked with her

4 she continuously felt that the abuse did not happen by the

5 uncles.

6 Q. What about Lucritia and Thrista, did they ever in your

7 presence deny that the abuse occurred?

8 A. No, they did not.

9 Q. Did they in fact describe the abuse during these

10 sessions?

11 A. I can't remember the specifics of what they described,

12 but I remember them both clearly talking about being hurt by

13 their uncles.

14 Q. What involvement did you have with the social worker,

15 Kathleen Honomichl?

16 A. Well, initially when the children were placed at

17 Children's Home Society she wasn't the worker, and then I think

18 she came on that fall, and so we would have periodic contact.

19 I think sometimes she was the one that transported maybe the

20 mothers up for visits or for therapy sessions, sometimes there

21 would be phone calls. She would be the one that decided the

22 long term plan for the children. Then there was a period of

23 time that she wasn't involved, and she was involved again, and

24 then at the end she was involved again.

25 Q. Did you ever tell Kathleen Honomichl that you had an

                                         Page 715 - Page 718

Page 719

1 opinion that this abuse did not occur?

2 A. I never said that.

3   MR. HOLMES: No further questions.

4   THE COURT: Cross exam.

5 CROSS EXAMINATION BY MR. WILKA:

6 Q. Good afternoon, Mrs. Weber, my name is John Wilka. Just

7 a few questions.

8 A. Good afternoon.

9 Q. You are a licensed counselor?

10 A. Yes.

11 Q. You are a licensed therapist?

12 A. Licensed professional counselor, and then a licensed

13 marriage and family therapist.

14 Q. These sessions that you had with some of the Rouse

15 children was in your role as a counselor?

16 A. Yes.

17 Q. So that was the type of relationship that you established

18 with them?

19 A. Yes.

20 Q. You are here testifying at the request of the government,

21 correct?

22 A. Yes.

23 Q. Before you testified did you review your notes?

24 A. A couple months ago I went through some of the files, and

25 another supervisor went through one of the children's files and

Page 720

1 then kind of told me any highlights that she saw in those

2 notes.

3 Q. Before providing testimony about substance of the

4 sessions that you had with these children in your role as their

5 counselor, did you seek their permission to reveal what was

6 stated in those sessions from the children?

7 A. Reveal to who?

8 Q. Testify today, did you seek the children's permission?

9 A. No, I responded to my subpoena.

10 Q. Did you seek the parents' permission that you testify

11 about the substance of the conversations?

12 A. No, I did not.

13   MR. WILKA: Your Honor, I would ask that her

14 testimony be stricken as privileged.

15   THE COURT: Let me hear from the government on that.

16   MR. HOLMES: I guess I don't understand the basis of

17 the privilege claim here.

18   MR. WILKA: She is their therapist, Your Honor. I

19 mean there is a recognized, she is not a physician, but there

20 is a recognized privilege that when someone is counseling that

21 that is, those are privileged communications.

22   THE COURT: What is your authority? I think there

23 is, but I would like you to have the citation for me.

24   MR. WILKA: I don't have the code with me.

25   THE COURT: You should have had.

Page 721

1   MR. WILKA: I didn't anticipate this, Your Honor.

2   THE COURT: Wait a minute now, when you are going to

3 do something, she is listed down here, this thing was filed,

4 defendant's objection, Docket 463 filed on January 26, and it

5 says with regard to Mary Weber will testify that at no time did

6 she tell Kathleen Honomichl she did not believe the children

7 had been abused. So you know she is going to testify. You

8 know, so what is your authority? If you are going to spring

9 something on me, I want to look at the cite. I believe, like

10 you do, there is a statute, but I want to know about it.

11   MR. WILKA: I did read their affidavit and she wants

12 to testify what she believes Honomichl said, you know, I had

13 notice of that, that's one thing, Your Honor. I would say the

14 privilege statute under the rules of evidence, if I can --

15   THE COURT: I am going to go find it, it will be in

16 recess, but I expect you to do it, but I will.

17 (Recess at 2:10 until 2:35.)

18   THE COURT: Alright, I will trace this for you, an

19 interesting objection, but you know that courts always like to

20 have objections ahead of time so they can think about them.

21 Here is how it basically comes out. Federal Rule 501, Federal

22 Rule of Evidence with regard to privileges, which you have to

23 look at. Then you go to Jaffee versus Redmond, which is a

24 Supreme Court case, 116 Supreme Court 1923, a 1996 case, and

25 which I have read before, and what they do is in a civil case

Page 722

1 there they opine that in Rule 501 the state law was adopted,

2 they declined to take the position that a few courts, a few

3 states have, of a balancing. In other words, you wouldn't know

4 if you had a privilege until the Judge had ruled on it one way

5 or the other in a particular instance, they declined to follow

6 such a rule, and they say, likewise that with regard to

7 adopting the privilege, that they go on to say at 1931, we have

8 no hesitation in concluding in this case that the federal

9 privilege should also extend to confidential communications

10 made to licensed social workers in the course of psychotherapy.

11 The reasons for recognizing a privilege for treatment by

12 psychiatrists and psychologists apply with equal force to

13 treatment by a clinical social worker such as Karen Beyer,

14 B-E-Y-E-R. I don't think this was psychotherapy in this case,

15 but none-the-less, to trace it on, and the privilege statutes

16 that counsel was thinking about I think are 19-13, SDCL 19-13-6

17 to 19-13-11 which are in the evidence code there, 13-6 is Rule

18 503(a), that's the physician-patient privilege, and 13-7 goes

19 on to psychotherapists. Also I looked at Weinstein's Federal

20 Evidence 501.03(3), but then you go over to SDCL 36-26-30,

21 which is South Dakota's separate social worker-client

22 privilege, and that statute is its exceptions, sub 3 of that

23 says when the person is a minor under the laws of this state

24 and the information acquired by the licensed certified social

25 worker, licensed social worker, or licensed social work

Page 719 - Page 722

Page 723

1 associate indicated that the minor was the victim or subject of
2 a crime, the certified social worker, the social worker, or the
3 social work associate may be required to testify fully in any
4 examination, trial, or other proceedings in which the
5 commission of such a crime is the subject of inquiry. That's
6 exactly what we have here, the motion is denied, proceed.
7 BY MR. WILKA:
8 Q. Did you regularly keep notes and records when you were at
9 Children's Home Society?
10 A. Yes, I did.
11 Q. Were those handwritten notes?
12 A. No, we dictated them in to a microphone and then someone
13 transcribed them.
14 Q. Did you have case meetings with, I may be using the term
15 wrong, but case review meetings with other counselors regarding
16 the Rouse children?
17 A. Well, like weekly we would have therapists meetings, and
18 so if there was other therapists working with other kids, with
19 the other Rouse children, I am sure there would be periodic
20 times that we would discuss them. Otherwise, we had like
21 quarterly meetings that involved like the family members, and
22 the social workers really came and reviewed how children were
23 doing on a quarterly basis.
24 Q. At some point did it come to your attention that Jessica
25 Rouse -- you had some meetings with Jessica, correct?

Page 724

1 A. I know I had her in group periodically. I was thinking
2 at the end of her treatment that I did a little bit of work
3 with her, but for the most part I wasn't her primary therapist.
4 Q. Who was her primary therapist, if you recall?
5 A. When she was at Madsen House, which is the evaluation
6 unit at Children's Hospital, I am not sure who her therapist
7 was at that time, but when she moved to Van Demark House, which
8 is the longer term treatment where I was at, was Norma Finnell.
9 Q. Was Judy Zimbelman, are you familiar with her?
10 A. You know, the name is familiar, but I don't remember
11 meeting with her. I think she was maybe there on a contractual
12 basis at Madsen House, and I wasn't involved in that part of
13 the program.
14 Q. Did you, did it ever come to your attention that Jessica
15 Rouse disclosed to Judy Zimbelman that the abuse did not take
16 place?
17 A. Just when I was reviewing the files a few months ago I
18 saw some of those pieces.
19 Q. That Jessica had stated that it did not occur?
20 A. I don't remember if I ever read anything from Judy
21 Zimbelman, I think I read something from Norma Finnell.
22   THE COURT: Is that Mona Finnell?
23   THE WITNESS: Norma Finnell.
24 BY MR. WILKA:
25 Q. Did you read the interview FBI reports in this case

Page 725

1 before you started any counseling with the Rouse children?
2 A. Boy, I don't remember. We usually, when children came to
3 Children's Home Society, there was some pre-placement
4 information, but I don't remember what that was on these
5 children.
6 Q. Do you recall having concerns with the children that the
7 nature and extent of what they were reporting with regard to
8 abuse was taking place?
9 A. I don't understand your question.
10 Q. I don't blame you. That their stories were inconsistent,
11 do you recall having, do you recall having a concern about
12 that?
13 A. No, I do not. What I do remember is I know it was a
14 struggle for the mother's, specially Beta, to listen to what
15 the children had to say. So my hope was to try and engage her
16 in family therapy, because I knew the goal was to try and
17 reunite the children with their mothers. So I tried to be
18 empathetic and say I know this is hard to believe, this is hard
19 to understand, but it was never in a context that I doubted the
20 children, it was trying to be empathetic with mom.
21 Q. I am not asking whether you doubted them or not. Let's
22 go to case meetings, do you recall any concerns being voiced
23 that the children's stories were inconsistent?
24 A. No, I don't recall that.
25 Q. What I mean by inconsistent here, is that for instance --

Page 726

1 let me back up a bit. Are you aware that at the trial, or
2 there was a report, that Donovan claimed that he was tied up,
3 or that he was locked in a closet, are you aware of that?
4 A. That doesn't sound familiar to me. I didn't work very
5 much with Donovan except in some of the group settings.
6 Q. Are you aware or were there any reports in your review of
7 the file that one of the girls were claiming that they were
8 locked in a closet?
9 A. I remember something about that, but I don't remember
10 which child or what the context was.
11 Q. Are you, did you see any reports that described a bedroom
12 down in the basement of grandma Rouse's house?
13 A. I don't remember reviewing that.
14 Q. One of the difficulties, or not difficulties, one of the
15 main thrusts of your work with the children had to do with the
16 presence of alcohol in their mothers' lives, correct?
17 A. Yes.
18 Q. And would it not be a fair statement to say that most of
19 the conversations with the kids regarding fears and angers had
20 to do with the use of alcohol by their mothers?
21 A. I think that was quite a bit, but I would say maybe it
22 would be 50/50 concerns about the alcohol and concerns that mom
23 didn't believe them about the abuse.
24 Q. And now with abuse, is it not also alleged that Jessica
25 and Lucritia had been sexually abused by Jerome?

Page 723 - Page 726

Page 727

1   A. That sounds accurate.

2   Q. Would you, would the counselors at the Children's Home

3   Society, when you had your -- you had weekly therapist

4   meetings?

5   A. Yes.

6   Q. At these weekly therapists meetings would you review

7   typed records with each other regarding children?

8   A. No, we did not.

9   Q. That's where you go over your handwritten notes you may

10   have dictated?

11   A. No, we didn't even review handwritten notes. It's more

12   how the week has been, what's going on with kids, how are staff

13   doing.

14   Q. More day-to-day immediate concerns with --

15   A. Yes.

16   Q. When you had quarterly reviews would you go over the

17   typed notes?

18   A. We didn't go over the typed notes. It would be, what we

19   would have in front of us was a summary of how they were doing

20   in therapy, how they were doing in school, how they were doing

21   in the new setting, how they were doing on the goals and

22   objectives, what the plan was for them.

23   Q. When were you at Children's Home society?

24   A. Me personally?

25   Q. Yes?

Page 728

1   A. From 1988 until 1996.

2   Q. So when, if I were to tell you that in July of '95 that

3   Jessica was working with Judy Zimbelman, you would have no

4   reason to doubt me then, would you?

5   A. Right.

6   Q. Did you ever review any -- now again, you reviewed the

7   file in preparation for your testimony?

8   A. I briefly went through the file.

9

10   (Exhibit C marked For identification.)

11

12   MR. WILKA: May I approach the witness, Your Honor?

13   THE COURT: Certainly.

14 BY MR. WILKA:

15   Q. I am showing you what has been marked as Defendant's

16   Exhibit C, would you identify that, please?

17   A. This looks like an individual therapy note on Jessica

18   Rouse on 7-7 of '95 by Judy Zimbelman.

19   Q. Does that appear to be the type of individual therapy

20   note that was kept in the regular course of the business of the

21   Children's Home Society?

22   A. Yes.

23   Q. You have seen those types of reports before?

24   A. Yes. I don't remember reading this or any of Judy

25   Zimbelman's reports, but mine probably look similar, and

Page 729

1   Norma's.

2   Q. Again, Judy Zimbelman was a therapist during 1995 out to

3   the Children's Home Society?

4   A. I think, yes.

5   Q. Would you please read the last sentence of the first

6   paragraph of that?

7   MR. HOLMES: I object, unless the Exhibit is

8   introduced.

9   MR. WILKA: I offer Exhibit C, Your Honor.

10   MR. HOLMES: We object unless the entire file is

11   produced and is produced as the complete record of these

12   therapy sessions. We believe it is inappropriate to offer one

13   portion of the file without counsel having access to the file.

14   We don't know what else is in there. Apparently defense

15   counsel has read the file.

16   THE COURT: Well, let me see the document.

17   Overruled, Exhibit C is received.

18 BY MR. WILKA:

19   Q. Would you please read the last sentence of the first

20   paragraph?

21   A. She was very quiet and put her head down as she answered.

22   She told me that no, she had not been touched before. And as

23   she discussed this further, she then looked at me and very

24   quietly in a whisper said it never happened.

25   MR. WILKA: I have nothing further.

Page 730

1 CROSS EXAMINATION BY MR. BINGER:

2   Q. Ma'am, I believe you stated that you were not familiar

3   with the report by Judy Zimbelman, but you had heard of a

4   report somewhat similar that had come from Norma?

5   A. Yes.

6   Q. And that is, what is her full name again?

7   A. Norma's full name?

8   Q. Yes?

9   A. Norma Finnell.

10   Q. She was a case worker at the Children's Home Society

11   also?

12   A. She was a family therapist.

13   Q. That report that you refer to in your answer, who did

14   that relate to?

15   A. Jessica.

16   Q. What do you recall about that report?

17   A. The one that I am recollecting that I reviewed and just

18   took a brief note on is Norma talking with Jessica, stating

19   that sometimes Jessica had said the abuse didn't happen and

20   sometimes she said it did, and Norma was just talking with

21   Jessica and clarifying, and Jessica shared that when she said

22   it didn't happen, it was the time she didn't want to talk about

23   it with anybody, but that it actually had happened.

24   Q. That was reflected in a written report?

25   A. In Norma Finnell's documenting.

Page 731

1 Q. And when, when do you recall this happening?

2 A. I don't have my notes in front of me.

3   MR. BINGER: Nothing further.

4   THE COURT: Mr. Carter.

5 CROSS EXAMINATION BY MR. CARTER:

6 Q. Ms. Weber, my name is David Carter. I had a question

7 here regarding the -- as I understand it, your role in this was

8 that of a counselor, would that be correct?

9 A. Yes.

10 Q. Would you agree with me that that role is really more one

11 of being supportive of the child and giving them an opportunity

12 to talk out things rather than determining what did or didn't

13 happen?

14 A. Yes.

15 Q. Again then with that in mind, would you adopt a sort of a

16 sympathetic kind of posture with the child when you were

17 working with them?

18 A. Well, I was kind and supportive.

19 Q. Would it be a fair statement to say that your attitude

20 toward this is that the abuse occurred, and your role is to

21 help counsel the children through it?

22 A. I felt that I needed to listen to the children, be a safe

23 and trusting person that they could talk to, share their

24 feelings, share their thoughts, and then help process those

25 things with them.

Page 732

1 Q. As part of that process would that entail a mind set and

2 an approach where you presumed the abuse took place?

3 A. Yes, I believed the children.

4 Q. So again, you would have approached this whole matter

5 from the standpoint the abuse did take place?

6 A. Yes.

7 Q. Now would that be something that the children would

8 perceive, do you think, in your attitude toward your questions

9 and your approach in working with them as a therapist?

10 A. I guess I wouldn't probably want to say how the children

11 would perceive things. My hope would be I was someone they

12 could listen to, they could talk to. I was not a detective, I

13 wasn't there to say this happened or didn't happen. I was

14 there to support them and let them take the lead in what they

15 shared.

16 Q. Is it your experience that children are interested in

17 pleasing adults?

18 A. I suppose some children, and some not.

19 Q. You don't think that would be a fair characterization of

20 children that you work with generally?

21 A. Well, at Children's Home Society I worked with lots of

22 children that had lots of defiance and oppositional behavior,

23 and lots of anger, and lots of mistrust, so I don't think so.

24 Q. Do you believe that these children were interested in

25 trying to please you?

Page 733

1 A. I guess I can't say that. I don't know.

2 Q. You don't know. But it is possible that that can happen?

3 A. I suppose.

4   MR. CARTER: I have no further questions.

5   THE COURT: Redirect -- excuse me, I keep on thinking

6 you are first.

7   MR. HAUGAARD: We got our sequence out of order.

8 CROSS EXAMINATION BY MR. HAUGAARD:

9 Q. My name is Steve Haugaard, Ms. Weber. During the course

10 of your counseling with the Rouse children you had occasion to

11 do both individual sessions and group sessions, is that

12 correct?

13 A. Yes.

14 Q. I think I missed it when you were talking about when you

15 were involved. What timeframe you were involved, could you

16 tell me that again?

17 A. Where I was the therapist, the entire time once Lucritia

18 and Thrista were at the Van Demark House in Children's Home

19 Society, and I did some of the group work. Donovan, just if I

20 only saw him in group, and involved a little bit with the other

21 therapists in the family situations.

22 Q. You also saw Jessica individually, though, is that

23 correct?

24 A. I think I did a little bit at the end, I can't recall a

25 hundred percent.

Page 734

1 Q. Do you recall in a group session with the children,

2 including their mother Beta, a time when you observed and made

3 reference in your notes that Beta was quite reserved, and that

4 she would not look at you during the sessions?

5 A. I don't remember that specific therapy note, but that

6 would, yes, I remember those times.

7 Q. Do you remember noting that although you understood this

8 could be a Native American issue, you still thought that she

9 was not having enough eye contact?

10 A. I remember feeling that she was very guarded, and

11 mistrustful and angry.

12 Q. Did you also observe that to be a possible Native

13 American issue, not looking at someone else?

14 A. I guess I would try and be sensitive to maybe that was

15 it.

16 Q. If you reflect that in your notes, or if that is

17 reflected in your notes, would you believe that was probably

18 your present impression at that time?

19 A. Yes.

20 Q. Also in that counseling session with the family

21 counseling where the children are involved and Beta was

22 involved, do you remember Beta explaining that she wasn't

23 closing out the idea that there was possible sexual abuse, but

24 she was just observing it might have been the two neighbor

25 cousins, do you remember that?

Page 735

1 A. Yes.

2 Q. Then also the fact that Jerome had been involved in some
3 of the sexual abuse, is that correct?

4 A. I think so. I remember something about Jerome, just not
5 the specifics.

6   MR. HAUGAARD: Your Honor, May I approach the
7 witness?

8   THE COURT: Certainly.

9

10   (Exhibit D marked For identification.)

11

12 BY MR. HAUGAARD:

13 Q. Did you have occasion to make therapy notes in regard to
14 both group sessions and individual sessions?

15 A. Yes.

16 Q. Were you counseling with Jessica during May of 1996?

17 A. I am not sure. I know I had involvement with her, I
18 don't remember the exact dates.

19 Q. If you did, you would have made some kind of therapy
20 notes?

21 A. Yes.

22 Q. I ask you to take a look at Exhibit D and tell me if that
23 appears to be a therapy note that you would have made?

24 A. Yes.

25 Q. And was this toward the end of your therapy sessions with

Page 736

1 Jessica?

2 A. I didn't look at the date. That is May, and I think they
3 left August.

4 Q. I would ask you to read to the Court the third sentence
5 of this paragraph?

6   MR. HOLMES: Objection, it's not been received.

7   THE COURT: Sustained.

8   MR. HAUGAARD: I will offer Exhibit D, Your Honor.

9   MR. HOLMES: May I see it? No objection.

10   THE COURT: Exhibit D is received.

11 BY MR. HAUGAARD:

12 Q. Ask you to read the sentence?

13 A. Jessica's first response was my wish came true, and she
14 then asked what will happen if her mom starts drinking again.

15 Q. I probably should have asked you to read the preceding
16 sentence also.

17 A. Her social worker decided that on August 1st she and her
18 sister Lucritia will be discharged from Sioux Falls Children's
19 Home Society and returned home to her mom. Jessica's first
20 response was my wish came true, and she then asked what will
21 happen if her mom starts drinking again.

22 Q. You indicated that during your sessions with the
23 children, your time involved in this case, that you believed
24 the children. If all the children now independently say that
25 this did not happen, would you also believe them now?

Page 737

1   MR. HOLMES: Objection, calls for an improper
2 conclusion.

3   THE COURT: I don't think there is adequate
4 foundation, sustain it on that basis.

5 BY MR. HAUGAARD:

6 Q. You indicated that during the time that you were involved
7 with this case you believed the children. If the children
8 presently state that these allegations were not true, would you
9 believe the children now?

10   MR. HOLMES: Same objection, Your Honor.

11   THE COURT: I am not sustaining it on that basis, I
12 am sustaining it based upon -- I tell you what --

13   MR. HAUGAARD: I will just withdraw the question.

14   THE COURT: I will tell you what my reason is because
15 I don't think that, it isn't that simple. It would take more
16 foundation I think to have that be admissible.

17   MR. HAUGAARD: No further questions, thank you.

18   THE COURT: Redirect.

19 REDIRECT EXAMINATION BY MR. HOLMES:

20 Q. Ms. Weber, I think you previously identified another
21 employee at Children's Home there by the name of Norma Finnell,
22 is that correct?

23 A. Norma Finnell.

24 Q. She was involved in doing therapy with some of the other
25 children, is that correct?

Page 738

1 A. She primarily did the work with Jessica, and some of the
2 family work, and then there was a different therapist involved
3 with Donovan.

4 Q. Ms. Finnell has since passed away, is that right?

5 A. Yes, last December.

6 Q. You were asked some questions about reviewing notes, and
7 in fact were asked about notes that apparently Ms. Zimbelman
8 had generated. Did you also review notes that Ms. Finnell had
9 generated during her sessions with Jessica?

10 A. Yes, I was able to review some of them.

11 Q. I think you made reference to at least one, or maybe more
12 notations, where Ms. Finnell had noted that Jessica later
13 indicated that the abuse had happened, is that correct?

14 A. Yes. And after that one session that I shared with you
15 where it seemed to be some dialogue back and forth between
16 Jessica and Norma, then the rest of the stay that Jessica had
17 at Children's Home her stories were consistent, or the message
18 that her uncles had hurt her, it hadn't fluctuated again during
19 her time with us.

20 Q. In fact, in one of those notes it was, or at least noted
21 by Ms. Finnell, that Jessica had said that when she had said
22 her uncles did not hurt her, it was because she did not want to
23 talk about it?

24 A. Yes, that's what I recall reading.

25 Q. But she said that the truth was that her uncles hurt her?

Page 739

1 A. Yes, that's what I recall.

2   MR. HOLMES: Nothing further.

3   THE COURT: Anything further?

4   MR. WILKA: Briefly, Your Honor.

5   MR. HAUGAARD: Your Honor, if I might, I know this is

6 delayed, but I would object to the last question based on

7 foundation and ask it be stricken. There was no specific

8 timeframe referenced in regard to when those comments may or

9 may not have been made.

10   THE COURT: Too late. You can cross on it if you

11 want to. Can't start backing up all the time and having

12 objections and so on.

13 RECROSS EXAMINATION BY MR. WILKA:

14 Q. You reviewed Norma Finnell's notes?

15 A. Some of them. I mean I went through everything kind of

16 briefly.

17 Q. One of the concerns that she had was that Jessica was all

18 over the place about whether or not this abuse happened,

19 correct?

20 A. I guess I don't remember reading something in those

21 words.

22 Q. You don't remember it in those words, what do you

23 remember?

24 A. Well, what I had shared. I remembered something about

25 Norma talking with Jessica about at times you had said this did

Page 740

1 not happen, and I can't speak for Norma, but I wondered if she

2 was referring to maybe working with Judy, and then, but saying

3 that it had happened, and just kind of trying to feel out with

4 Jessica what is that about. And then my, what I remember

5 reading is that Jessica shared there were times that she didn't

6 want to talk about it, so she would say nothing happened, but

7 in actuality it did happen, and that was the truth.

8   MR. WILKA: May I have a moment, Your Honor?

9   THE COURT: Certainly.

10 BY MR. WILKA:

11 Q. So if I understand you correctly, Ms. Weber, that last

12 statement is based upon a brief review of your notes and other

13 person's notes and their impressions, correct?

14 A. Yes.

15   MR. WILKA: That's all I have.

16 RECROSS EXAMINATION BY MR. BINGER:

17 Q. Ms. Weber, your answers today about Jessica saying it

18 happened and then it didn't happen, and kind of being all over

19 the place or whatever, it is based upon, I think you said it

20 was a brief review, and you reviewed some of Norma Finnell's

21 reports but you didn't review each one, one by one?

22 A. What I did was I sat at a table and had the files and

23 kind of quickly paged through like Jessica's files, some would

24 have been from Norma, some from me, maybe some from other

25 people.

Page 741

1 Q. Basically you were skimming the reports, would that be

2 fair?

3 A. Maybe a little more than skimming, but I didn't study

4 them every page in great detail.

5 Q. Did you make an attempt to actually sit down and pin down

6 how many times Jessica changed back and forth?

7 A. No, I did not.

8 Q. But it was multiple times, is that a fair statement?

9 A. That isn't my recollection. I was thinking that it was

10 after Norma had that conversation with her, then I thought then

11 the rest of the, throughout the rest of her therapy it stayed

12 consistent.

13 Q. Well, we know she told Judy it didn't happen, right?

14 A. And that was I think maybe the time that Norma was

15 referring to. It is hard because I wasn't the therapist, but

16 my thought is when Norma, because what happened is Judy was

17 working with Jessica probably thirty days at the Madsen House,

18 or however long Jessica stayed there, then when she moved to

19 the Van Demark House Norma became her therapist. My guess is,

20 and this is only a guess, my guess is Norma reviewed the

21 documentation from the Madsen House and was probably clarifying

22 that with Jessica, but I don't remember reading that that

23 happened throughout the course. I thought once that happened

24 it didn't continuously get repeated.

25 Q. Well, you didn't, you never saw a report that said that

Page 742

1 both Judy and Norma talked to her at the same time?

2 A. I don't remember that.

3 Q. So if there are reports of her denying the allegations to

4 each of them, then they had to have been made on separate

5 occasions, didn't they?

6 A. I guess I wasn't sure, though, that with Norma she was

7 denying the abuse. I thought maybe it was Norma saying I had,

8 you know, with Judy or someone else you said it didn't happen,

9 now you are saying it did, let's talk about that. So I guess I

10 am not sure if she told Norma initially it didn't happen or

11 not.

12 Q. You don't mean to tell me that she denied it to Judy and

13 then Norma came along and by the time she was done talking to

14 Norma she changed her story?

15 A. You know what, that would be wrong of me to make any

16 assumptions.

17 Q. Did you ever hear, read any notes, or hear any

18 conversation about Thrista and Jessica having sexual touching

19 with each other?

20 A. I don't remember specific children, but there might have

21 been something vaguely with the children, but I am not sure

22 specifically which ones or what had happened.

23   MR. BINGER: Thank you, that's all I have.

24 RECROSS EXAMINATION BY MR. CARTER:

25 Q. As I understood from your redirect, there were occasions

Page 743

1 when the child made the statement something to the effect that

2 she didn't want to talk about it any more?

3 A. That was in my review of a document from Norma.

4 Q. And is that something that you personally also heard from

5 her?

6 A. No, I did not.

7   MR. CARTER: I have no further questions.

8   THE COURT: Mr. Haugaard.

9   MR. HAUGAARD: Thank you, Your Honor. Thank you for

10 remembering.

11 RECROSS EXAMINATION BY MR. HAUGAARD:

12 Q. Ms. Weber, isn't it true that when Jessica responded that

13 the basis for the placement was because of mom, or because --

14 because of mom?

15   MR. HOLMES: I object, outside the scope of redirect,

16 which is limited to Ms. Finnell's notes.

17   THE COURT: Read the question back, please?

18

19 (Whereupon, the requested portion of the Record was read by the

20 Reporter.)

21

22   THE COURT: Sustained.

23 BY MR. HAUGAARD:

24 Q. In reviewing Ms. Finnell's notes, did you observe that

25 some notes where Norma had probed the basis for placement, at

Page 744

1 least at times, maybe several times, the response from Jessica

2 was it was because of mom's behavior?

3 A. I don't remember a specific part about reason for

4 placement, but I know the children, including Jessica, talked

5 about that.

6 Q. When you reviewed the file, isn't it true that some of

7 Norma's notes would be individual therapy notes and some would

8 be group counseling notes?

9 A. Individual for sure. I am not sure if Norma did some of

10 the groups or not, but for sure individual, maybe some family.

11   MR. HAUGAARD: No further questions, thank you.

12   MR. HOLMES: Nothing further, Your Honor.

13   THE COURT: You may step down. Call your next

14 witness.

15   MR. HOLMES: United States calls Karla Harmon.

16

17   KARLA HARMON,

18 called as a witness, being first duly sworn, testified and said

19 as follows:

20

21 DIRECT EXAMINATION BY MR. HOLMES:

22 Q. Good afternoon?

23 A. Good afternoon.

24 Q. Would you please state for the record, your full name and

25 spell your first and last name?

Page 745

1 A. My name is Karla Harmon, K-A-R-L-A, H-A-R-M-O-N.

2 Q. Ms. Harmon, how are you currently employed?

3 A. I work for Sioux Valley Behavioral Health Services.

4 Q. In 1995 through 1996 how were you employed?

5 A. I worked at Children's Home Society.

6 Q. What position did you hold at Children's Home at that

7 time?

8 A. I went from a unit manager, I think I was program

9 director at that time.

10 Q. And at that time could you tell us what your educational

11 and professional background was?

12 A. I have a Masters Degree in social work from the

13 University of Iowa, and I had a licensure of a licensed

14 certified social worker at that time.

15 Q. Can you describe what your duties were there at

16 Children's Home in 1995 and 1996 as clinical supervisor?

17 A. I supervised Madsen House, which was an assessment unit,

18 thirty day assessment unit for twelve children, and I also

19 supervised a portion of the foster care program.

20 Q. Did you have any involvement with Lucritia and Jessica

21 Rouse during their placement at Children's Home?

22 A. Yes, I did. It was very limited initially when they were

23 at Madsen House, and then toward the end as they were getting

24 ready to go home I did therapy with they and their mom in an

25 effort to reunite them.

Page 746

1 Q. And can you describe how frequently the family therapy

2 sessions with the mother would have been prior to their leaving

3 Children's Home?

4 A. We tried to increase them and then compliment them with

5 home visits, and I think they went from either once a month or

6 twice a month, I think we tried for either one. I don't know

7 the exact frequency of what actually happened.

8 Q. What typically would take place in one of these family

9 counseling sessions?

10 A. Typically we talked about how the girls were doing, and

11 how Beta was doing, and we also talked about the home visits.

12 It was a time for them to kind of plan activities, what they

13 were going to do once they got home. We also discussed safety

14 plans, what would happen if they wouldn't have supervision, or

15 if something got them scared, and we would always go, they

16 would always go home with some kind of a plan in mind of what

17 they could do if that happened.

18 Q. During the period of time that you were involved with

19 Jessica and Lucritia, did they at any time ever deny that the

20 sexual abuse had taken place?

21 A. No.

22 Q. Was Kathleen Honomichl involved in any way in these

23 sessions when you were involved with the girls and their

24 mother?

25 A. Kathleen was the social worker involved, and she became

Page 747

1 part of the plan to, she helped with transportation, getting
2 Beta to counseling, and helping with transportation home.
3 Q. Would there be times when she would sit in with Beta
4 during the course of these family therapy sessions?
5 A. Initially. In fact, I invited her to sit in because I
6 didn't know Beta well, and I wanted her to feel comfortable, so
7 she sat in initially. Then it got to the point where I got the
8 feeling that Beta was looking at Kathleen to kind of answer the
9 questions. Kathleen got very, very involved in the case, and
10 so I asked to just meet with Beta privately.
11 Q. So some point in time Kathleen was either asked or told
12 not to come into the family therapy sessions?
13 A. Yes.
14 Q. Did you ever talk to her about the case where she
15 expressed any concern about being too close or too involved in
16 the case?
17 A. Toward the end, I think it was the last time I actually
18 saw her as part, as a social worker for that case, she was
19 quite upset and said she was very nervous and scared, and that
20 she was losing sleep, and she felt she might need to have
21 representation about this case.
22 Q. Did she say that she felt she was too close to the case?
23   MR. WILKA: Objection, asked and answered, Your
24 Honor.
25   MR. BINGER: Also object it's leading and suggestive

Page 748

1 of the answer.
2   THE COURT: Sustained on the latter.
3 BY MR. HOLMES:
4 Q. What did she say besides -- did she say anything else
5 about her involvement in the case?
6 A. She said that -- let me remember. She said that she was
7 scared about the case, and that her involvement, she was
8 questioning what her involvement was. I think that's the most
9 accurate way to put it.
10 Q. You recall approximately when that would have been that
11 she made those statements to you?
12 A. It was, I think it was mid summer or latter summer, like
13 July or August, somewhere in there, because I only had the case
14 for a very short time.
15 Q. Of what year, if you recall?
16 A. The year that the girls went home, was it '96?
17   MR. HOLMES: No further questions.
18   THE COURT: Cross.
19   MR. WILKA: No questions, Your Honor.
20   MR. BINGER: No questions.
21 CROSS EXAMINATION BY MR. CARTER:
22 Q. What would be the approximate number of times that you
23 would have personally counseled with the children?
24 A. With just the children, or in family counseling?
25 Q. Let's start with just the children?

Page 749

1 A. You know, I don't think I could say for sure, because
2 like I said, my goal was re-integration, and so I worked mostly
3 with mom and the children. I know I transported them back from
4 foster care, I did some of that stuff.
5 Q. So it would be fair to say then your role was really more
6 in the family counseling area than with personal counseling
7 with the kids?
8 A. Yes.
9 Q. I believe you indicated that the children did not ever
10 personally deny the sexual abuse to you, is that your
11 testimony?
12 A. Yes.
13 Q. Were you aware, however, from your position there at
14 Children's Home Society, that they had denied the abuse to
15 other members there at the Children's Home Society?
16 A. No, I was never aware of that.
17   MR. CARTER: Nothing further.
18   MR. HAUGAARD: No further questions.
19   THE COURT: Redirect.
20   MR. HOLMES: No redirect, Your Honor.
21   THE COURT: Thank you, you may step down. Call your
22 next witness.
23   MR. HOLMES: United States calls Terryl Cadwell.
24
25   TERRYL CADWELL,

Page 750

1 called as a witness, being first duly sworn, testified and said
2 as follows:
3
4 DIRECT EXAMINATION BY MR. HOLMES:
5 Q. Good afternoon?
6 A. Good afternoon.
7 Q. Please state your name for the record?
8 A. Terryl Cadwell.
9 Q. Ms. Cadwell, how are you currently employed?
10 A. I am employed as a senior U.S. probation officer in the
11 District of South Dakota in Sioux Falls.
12 Q. In 1994 were you also a U.S. probation officer, and
13 specifically were you assigned to prepare a pre-sentence
14 investigation report regarding Jessie Rouse and Desmond Rouse?
15 A. Yes, I was.
16 Q. And that followed their conviction here in Federal Court
17 on certain federal charges involving sexual abuse of children,
18 is that your memory?
19 A. That's correct.
20 Q. As part of the investigation to prepare the pre-sentence
21 report did you speak to any of the children?
22 A. Yes, I did.
23 Q. Who do you recall speaking?
24 A. I recall speaking to I believe they were children that
25 were in age between about seven and three years old, the ones

Page 747 - Page 750

Page 751

1 that were in the foster home at Elk Point. I believe there was
2 also a little boy was in that group of children as well.
3 Q. Did you actually go down to the foster parent's home to
4 do that interview?
5 A. Yes, I did.
6 Q. What do you generally recall talking to the children
7 about on that occasion?
8 A. Generally I wanted to satisfy myself and to report to the
9 Court very accurately whatever information, beyond the
10 investigative reports and the collateral investigation I did, I
11 wanted to satisfy myself of any information that the Court may
12 need to have about what happened to the children.
13 Q. And as long as -- let me backtrack. We should have the
14 record clear.
15 These children included the victims in the case, is that
16 correct?
17 A. Yes.
18 Q. During your discussion with any of the children, did any
19 of them tell you that the alleged abuse had not occurred?
20   MR. BINGER: Objection, Your Honor. Could I ask a
21 question for purposes of objection?
22   THE COURT: Yes.
23   MR. BINGER: Ma'am, your only contact with the
24 alleged, or with the children in this case was prior to the
25 sentencing, is that correct?

Page 752

1 A. That's correct.
2   MR. BINGER: The sentencing, if I remember right, was
3 in roughly January of 1995?
4 A. I am not sure of the exact sentencing date.
5   MR. BINGER: After the sentencing you never spoke to
6 the kids again?
7 A. No, I did not.
8   MR. BINGER: This is not relevant to whether the
9 children subsequent to January of '95 recanted, which is what
10 our whole motion is about, and the fact they didn't recant
11 during that contact with the pre-sentence report is irrelevant.
12   THE COURT: Overruled.
13 BY MR. HOLMES:
14 Q. Did any of the children express to you any fear toward
15 any of the defendants?
16 A. Yes, they did.
17 Q. What do you recall regarding those statements?
18   MR. WILKA: Objection, hearsay.
19   THE COURT: I think it is a state of mind exception,
20 but let me take a look. 803(3) with regard to then existing
21 mental, or emotional condition, and I am going to receive it
22 for that purpose, because it bears on what the children are
23 reporting their state of mind was at that time, which is
24 relevant to the issues in this case, so the objection is
25 overruled.

Page 753

1 BY MR. HOLMES:
2 Q. What do you recall in that regard?
3 A. Would you repeat the question again?
4 Q. Did any of them state to you in any way that they were
5 afraid of the defendants in the case?
6 A. Generally the children told me that they were fearful of
7 the defendants, most particularly Jessie Rouse, and that they
8 were relieved that they were going to be in prison.
9 Q. Were you present at the sentencing hearing in this case?
10 A. Yes, I was.
11 Q. Did that hearing in fact take place down in what is
12 commonly referred TO AS the Bankruptcy Courtroom here in the
13 courthouse?
14 A. Yes, on first floor.
15 Q. Do you recall the children's mothers being present during
16 that hearing?
17 A. Yes, I do.
18 Q. Following that hearing, what do you remember happening
19 regarding any statements that were directed toward you by them?
20   MR. WILKA: Objection, hearsay and relevance.
21   THE COURT: I find it is relevant.
22   MR. BINGER: May I ask that when he said by them, is
23 he referring to the children or to the mother?
24   THE COURT: I clearly understood it was the mothers.
25   MR. HAUGAARD: I would likewise join in the

Page 754

1 objection.
2   THE COURT: Overruled, go ahead.
3 A. What I recall is that there was a scuffle with the
4 defendants after the sentencing and the Marshals as they were
5 taking the defendants out, I wanted to leave the Court room. I
6 had to testify, and I wanted to get out of the face of
7 everybody that was in the courtroom, and as I was walking down
8 the hall I believe it was three women, I know Lori Smith was
9 one of them, I don't know the exact names of the other two
10 women, called at me something about the effect of being a honky
11 bitch, come back here, or something like that. It was
12 something to that effect before I entered our offices on first
13 floor.
14 BY MR. HOLMES:
15 Q. During the course of the preparation of the pre-sentence
16 had you been down to the Rosemary Rouse residence?
17 A. Yes, I was. Rosemary Rouse being the grandmother I
18 believe.
19 Q. Yes.
20 A. Yes.
21 Q. What do you recall about the situation within the home
22 there as you observed it regarding Rosemary Rouse's attitude
23 toward the charges in this case?
24 A. Well, I remember that the adult family members of the
25 defendants were generally very angry, generally pretty hostile

Page 755

1 about the investigation and toward me during the investigation.
2 That day in the home I remember feeling a little intimidated
3 and a little concerned about my safety. Not necessarily from
4 Mrs. Rouse, but there was another male in the home that day and
5 there was a small child in the home, and I just remember
6 thinking it was a bad situation.
7   MR. BINGER: Object, move to strike, not relevant
8 whether she felt fear of some unnamed person. How could that
9 bear on any of the witnesses in this hearing?
10   THE COURT: Overruled.
11   MR. HOLMES: Nothing further.
12   THE COURT: Cross.
13 CROSS EXAMINATION BY MR. WILKA:
14 Q. Good afternoon.
15 A. Good afternoon.
16 Q. Have you visited with the children within the past two
17 weeks?
18 A. No, I have not.
19 Q. So you have no idea, for instance, that Thrista provided
20 testimony that she wanted to come over here and sit with her
21 uncles and hug them?
22 A. No, I didn't know that.
23 Q. Are you aware that the children are alleging physical
24 abuse at the hands of the foster mother?
25 A. No.

Page 756

1 Q. You interviewed the children approximately when, what --
2 A. I believe it would have been in the timeframe of between
3 maybe August and October of 1994 would have been about the
4 time.
5 Q. And that would have been to the best of your recollection
6 almost a year since the children had been removed from their
7 home?
8 A. I don't know when they were removed from their home
9 without checking my pre-sentence report, but that could be
10 accurate.
11 Q. Did the children make any statements to you that they
12 wanted to go home to their mothers?
13 A. They said they missed their mothers and their grandma.
14 Q. Are you aware that 100 percent of the child witnesses
15 have now stated that they were pressured in to alleging abuse?
16 A. No.
17   MR. WILKA: That's all I have.
18   MR. BINGER: No questions.
19 CROSS EXAMINATION BY MR. CARTER:
20 Q. Terryl, do you know where the children actually were in
21 terms of where they were residing all of the time before trial?
22 A. No, I am not aware of where they were the entire time.
23 Q. Did you review foster parents at all as part of your
24 pre-sentence investigation?
25 A. I interviewed the Jordan family in Elk Point as part of

Page 757

1 my report.
2 Q. Were there ever any disclosures to you by anyone prior to
3 you doing your pre-sentence report that the children had
4 recanted?
5 A. Not that I recall.
6 Q. When you went to the children and did your interview with
7 them, am I correct that you would have identified who you were
8 and that you worked for the United States government?
9 A. I am sure I told them I worked for the Judge, that would
10 be normally what I would say.
11 Q. Would the children have understood that you did not work
12 for the defendant?
13   MR. HOLMES: Objection, calls for a improper
14 conclusion from this witness.
15   THE COURT: Sustained.
16 BY MR. CARTER:
17 Q. Your testimony concerning the remarks and so forth that
18 were made, that was out in the hall after the sentencing?
19 A. That's correct.
20 Q. Do you remember who all was present at that occasion?
21 A. Do you mean in the hall?
22 Q. Yes.
23 A. I believe there were three women. I know Lori Smith was
24 one, and I believe there were two other women, but I am not a
25 hundred percent sure who they were, I don't remember who they

Page 758

1 were.
2 Q. Do you know who made the statement about supposedly being
3 a honky to you?
4 A. No. I don't know which one of them said that. There
5 were several different, there were several of them calling out
6 or yelling at me as I was walking down the hall, but I don't
7 remember who said what.
8 Q. So you don't really know whether the remarks came from
9 any particular person in the hallway then?
10 A. No. I know that it came from some of the else in the hallway
11 the sentencing hearing. There was no one else in the hallway
12 that day but myself and people that came out of the courtroom
13 after me. As far as I know, it was just about four of us in
14 the hall, myself and about three other women.
15 Q. But in terms of addressing that, or focusing those
16 remarks to be somehow attributable to the family of the
17 defendants, you can't really do that, can you?
18 A. Well, I know that Lori Smith was one, and I believe she
19 was Jessie Rouse's either common law wife or his spouse.
20 Q. And what race is she?
21 A. I believe she is non-Indian, I am not sure.
22 Q. You don't know if she made the statement or someone else
23 did?
24 A. I am not sure which woman made the comment.
25 Q. Would it be possible that there would have been other

Page 755 - Page 758

Page 759

1 people there that were not necessarily connected to these
2 defendants by way of family or relation?
3 A. I don't believe so.
4 Q. The children were not there in the hall?
5 A. I don't know -- no, I don't think the children were
6 there. Sir, I don't recall that the children were there, I
7 want to say that, I don't believe they were.
8   MR. CARTER: No further questions.
9   THE COURT: Mr. Haugaard.
10 CROSS EXAMINATION BY MR. HAUGAARD:
11 Q. Are you Native American, Ms. Cadwell?
12 A. No, I am not.
13 Q. When you went to the foster home did you record the
14 interviews with the children?
15 A. No, I did not.
16 Q. Was the foster mother at home that day?
17 A. Yes, she was.
18   MR. HAUGAARD: No further questions.
19   MR. HOLMES: No redirect, Your Honor.
20   THE COURT: Thank you, you may step down. Take a
21 fifteen minute recess.
22 (Recess from 3:50 until 4:05)
23   THE COURT: Call your next witness.
24   MR. HOLMES: United States calls William Van Roe.
25

Page 760

1   WILLIAM VAN ROE,
2 called as a witness, being first duly sworn, testified and said
3 as follows:
4
5 DIRECT EXAMINATION BY MR. HOLMES:
6 Q. Please state your name for the record?
7 A. William Van Roe.
8 Q. Mr. Van Roe, you are retired from the Federal Bureau of
9 Investigation, is that correct?
10 A. Yes.
11 Q. When did you retire from the FBI?
12 A. The end of July, 2000.
13 Q. How many years of service did you have with the FBI at
14 the time of your retirement?
15 A. Thirty-one years.
16 Q. You were the case agent from the FBI in this
17 investigation, were you not?
18 A. Yes.
19 Q. Was Dan Hudspeth a criminal investigator with the Bureau
20 of Indian Affairs, or the investigator from the BIA on the
21 case?
22 A. Yes, he was.
23 Q. Can you just generally tell the Court how you initially
24 became involved in the investigation, or I should say became
25 aware of it?

Page 761

1 A. Dan Hudspeth contacted me I think around January 13th of
2 '94 to advise me that there was an allegation that he was
3 starting an investigation, asked for our help.
4 Q. Were you aware that some time prior to your contact with
5 the children that they were taken to see Dr. Kaplan?
6 A. I found that out I think through discussion with Dan
7 Hudspeth and Micky Tapken.
8 Q. Did you have any involvement in taking the children to
9 see Dr. Kaplan?
10 A. None.
11 Q. Was the FBI to your knowledge in any way involved in
12 removing the children from the residence with Rosemary Rouse,
13 the grandmother?
14 A. The FBI was not involved in any way.
15 Q. When was the first time as you recall that you had
16 contact with the children who were the victims in this case?
17 A. I believe it was around January the 19th when criminal
18 investigator Hudspeth and myself went down to Elk Point.
19 Q. Did you meet with the children in Donna Jordan's
20 residence?
21 A. We did.
22 Q. Can you generally tell us what you did with the children
23 there without going through any of the details regarding what
24 the children said to you?
25 A. I had met Dan Hudspeth, and due to the allegations and

Page 762

1 the numerous allegations, numerous defendants, all involving
2 Native Americans, we agreed that Dan should do the interviewing
3 since he is Native American, and that I would try to record the
4 interviews. That's how we split up the assignment
5 responsibility.
6 Q. Where in the residence did the interviews take place?
7 A. I believe it was the dining room.
8 Q. Did you interview the children together, or individually?
9 A. Individual.
10 Q. What involvement, if any, did Donna Jordan have in the
11 interview?
12 A. She was seated back I believe in the kitchen area of the
13 residence. She may have been holding one of the babies and
14 keeping the children under control.
15 Q. Where were the children who were not being interviewed at
16 the time, where were they in the home?
17 A. I think some of them may have been in the basement, and
18 maybe one was in a separate room away from the living room area
19 and dining room area.
20 Q. Do you recall approximately how long the individual
21 interviews of the children were?
22 A. They varied. I would say Thrista probably was the
23 longest, and it has been a long time ago, but it might have
24 been, her interview may have been 45 minutes. Each one of the
25 other children were something less than that maybe.

1 Q. During these interviews did the children have access or
2 an opportunity to get something to drink or eat if they needed
3 that?
4 A. Yes, they did.
5 Q. Was the same true regarding their ability to use the
6 bathroom if they needed to?
7 A. Yes.
8 Q. When was the next time you had any contact with the
9 children?
10 A. I think it was around January 21st when they were brought
11 up to visit Micky Tapken.
12 Q. Where do you recall they met with Ms. Tapken?
13 A. At the United States Attorney's office.
14 Q. Explain to the Court what was done on that occasion with
15 the children?
16 A. I think Ms. Tapken just wanted to meet the children,
17 introduce herself, explain her role in the matter. Maybe, it
18 has been a long time ago, but I think maybe one of the children
19 was interviewed for the first time, and that is basically what
20 happened.
21 Q. To your knowledge, Mr. Van Roe, were you present at all
22 times when Ms. Tapken would have seen and talked to the
23 children with the exception of one time when Agent Matt Miller
24 went with her to talk to one of the children?
25 A. I was with her every time except the time in Yankton.

1 Q. You recall that occasion when Agent Miller was involved
2 being on July 30th of 1994?
3 A. I don't know the circumstances. I don't think I was
4 here. That may have been the time that my son was married and
5 I may have been in Aberdeen for a day or two.
6 Q. Did you become aware that Eva Cheney had been appointed
7 guardian ad litem for the children?
8 A. Yes.
9 Q. Is it your recollection that occurred some time around
10 May of 1994?
11 A. I don't know the date. It was early on in the
12 investigation.
13 Q. After her appointment did you have any contact as far as
14 interviewing or talking to the children other than when she was
15 present?
16 A. No, none.
17 Q. To your knowledge did Ms. Tapken?
18 A. She did not.
19 Q. What do you recall regarding the trial preparation for
20 the case insofar as meeting with the children, either yourself
21 or with Ms. Tapken?
22 A. Arrangements would be made with Donna Jordan to bring the
23 children up, I think I usually made those arrangements. She
24 would bring them up, I think she had a van, and she would bring
25 them to the United States Attorney's office.

1 Q. How were the children, or what was said to the children
2 regarding or during these trial preparation meetings?
3 A. Just certain aspects of their testimony would be gone
4 over.
5 Q. Was that done by Ms. Tapken?
6 A. Yes.
7 Q. What do you recall about contact with the children during
8 the course of the trial of the case?
9 A. I know they were in a separate room in this building. We
10 had limited contact with them. We may have gone down -- maybe
11 I went as they were witnesses to bring them physically or help
12 them into the courtroom, but that was it.
13 Q. During the period of time that you were with the
14 children, either with Ms. Tapken or during the initial
15 interview of the children, did you or anyone in their presence
16 ever promise them clothing, toys or money?
17 A. We made no promises to them.
18 Q. During those same timeframes did you or anyone in your
19 presence ever tell them words to the effect that the sooner
20 they would cooperate the sooner they would go home?
21 A. No.
22 Q. During the time that you had contact with the children,
23 did you or anyone in their presence ever tell them what they
24 should say?
25 A. No, that never happened.

1 Q. Did you ever, or anyone in your presence ever threaten
2 the children in any way?
3 A. No, that never happened either.
4 Q. Did the children ever in your presence recant their
5 allegations of sexual abuse at the hands of the defendant?
6 A. They never did.
7 Q. What did you observe as far as how the children got along
8 with Donna Jordan?
9 A. Seeing them in the Jordan residence on the 19th and
10 seeing them up here in the United States Attorney's office they
11 were always very consistent, always bubbly, upbeat, appeared to
12 be happy.
13 Q. Did you ever hear from them or from any other source that
14 Ms. Jordan had physically abused any of the children?
15 A. No, I didn't.
16 Q. If you had been made a aware of that, would you have
17 reported it to social services?
18   MR. BINGER: That's not relevant, objection, Your
19 Honor.
20   THE COURT: Overruled.
21 A. Yes, we would have reported it.
22 BY MR. HOLMES:
23 Q. You were present during most of the witness testimony in
24 this hearing, is that correct?
25 A. That's correct.

Page 767

1 Q. Do you recall Ms. Tapken testifying about an occasion
2 when I believe you and her were down on the Reservation prior
3 to the trial -- or after the trial, excuse me -- when Kathleen
4 Honomichl made some statements regarding the children seeing
5 Dr. Underwager?
6 A. Yes, I do.
7 Q. I believe Ms. Tapken indicated that she believed that
8 that occurred in January of '96. Is your recollection of the
9 date of that event different?
10 A. Yes, it is.
11 Q. When do you recall that happening?
12 A. I believe it was January of '97.
13 Q. What do you recall about that occasion when Ms. Honomichl
14 made those statements?
15 A. We had participated in an MDT meeting at Fort Randall
16 Casino west of Wagner that day, and after that MDT meeting
17 Ms. Honomichl was very excited and she asked to talk to Micky
18 Tapken. After the meeting was over with we had that meeting
19 with her. She was very excited and wanted to tell us that, and
20 she told us that Haugaard had told her that the kids were now
21 saying that the sexual abuse did not happen. Micky was, Micky
22 Tapken was surprised, I was surprised, and Ms. Tapken asked
23 Kathleen how did this happen? She said either she had taken
24 the children up to Sioux Falls to see Underwager, or she had
25 had someone take the children up to see Underwager.

Page 768

1 Q. Prior to hearing that from Kathleen Honomichl, were you
2 aware that the children had been seen by Dr. Underwager?
3 A. No, I wasn't aware of it.
4 Q. Prior to that had you been made aware that the children
5 had recanted?
6 A. Yes.
7 Q. How was that?
8 A. The only thing I knew was what Kathleen Honomichl told me
9 in January of '97.
10 Q. That was the first you had learned that the children had
11 recanted?
12 A. Absolutely.
13   MR. HOLMES: No further questions.
14   THE COURT: Cross.
15   MR. WILKA: I have no questions.
16 CROSS EXAMINATION BY MR. BINGER:
17 Q. Do you know where Dan Hudspeth is nowadays, or where he
18 works?
19 A. He is fortunate enough to be retired like I am.
20 Q. Is that fortunate?
21 A. Yes, sir.
22 Q. You specified that during your first contact down there
23 where he interviewed them because he was Native American you
24 would let him do the interviewing and you would try to record
25 the interviews, is that correct?

Page 769

1 A. That was the agreement, yes. Since he was Native
2 American and the allegations involved a lot of big men, I think
3 at that time the two of us probably weighed 650 pounds
4 together, and he was Native American, it would be easier for
5 him.
6 Q. What did you do to try to record the interview?
7 A. I took notes.
8   MR. BINGER: Thank you, that's all I have.
9 CROSS EXAMINATION BY MR. CARTER:
10 Q. Mr. Van Roe, my name is David Carter, I represent
11 Garfield Feather. As I recall reading the transcript from the
12 time of trial there was some reference in your testimony to the
13 number of times that the children were interviewed at the time
14 before trial, do you recall any of that testimony?
15 A. I remember someone asking me how many times did you talk
16 to the kids.
17 Q. Do you remember how many times you stated that the kids
18 had been interviewed?
19 A. Today I don't, no.
20 Q. And you don't remember how many times today as you are
21 sitting here how many times they were interviewed by you before
22 trial?
23 A. On the January 19th, January 21st, and they may have been
24 brought up to see Ms. Tapken one or two times in addition to
25 that. I just can't give you any specifics at this date and

Page 770

1 time.
2 Q. Would you think that nine times would be correct or
3 incorrect?
4 A. Nine times each, or total? What are you asking?
5 Q. Nine times the children were interviewed each?
6 A. I don't think that's accurate.
7 Q. You think they were interviewed nine times between all of
8 them?
9 A. I wouldn't say that either.
10 Q. I believe you indicated that you were present all the
11 times that Michelle Tapken interviewed the children?
12 A. I was except with the one exception.
13 Q. Is there any way that you would know if Micky Tapken
14 interviewed them without you being present?
15 A. Didn't happen.
16 Q. Is there any way you would know?
17 A. Yes.
18 Q. If she didn't tell you, how would you know?
19 A. She would tell me.
20 Q. That wasn't my question. If she didn't tell you, would
21 you know?
22 A. If she didn't tell me?
23 Q. If she didn't tell you that she had interviewed the
24 children, would you know?
25 A. Yes, I think I would.

Page 771

1 Q. Really.

2 A. Yes.

3 Q. You don't have your offices in the same floor over at the

4 Shriver's Building, do you, as Micky Tapken?

5 A. I think at that time we were in the Shriver's Building.

6 Q. On the same floor?

7 A. No. Close proximity, though.

8 Q. You are not saying you would know everything that

9 Michelle Tapken does, are you?

10 A. I did in this case, I am very clear about that.

11 Q. In terms of your testimony here today, what have you

12 reviewed prior to you testifying here this afternoon?

13 A. I looked at my court testimony to see the date and who

14 referred this case to me.

15 Q. Did you review any of your 302's?

16 A. I looked at the children's interviews, I believe the one

17 at Elk Point on January 19th and maybe January 21st.

18   MR. CARTER: May I approach?

19   THE COURT: Yes.

20

21   (Exhibit E marked For identification.)

22

23 BY MR. CARTER:

24 Q. Mr. Van Roe, I am going to show you what has been marked

25 here as Defendants' Exhibit E, is that a document that you can

Page 772

1 identify?

2 A. It is.

3 Q. What is it?

4 A. It is an interview of Jean Brock on January 19th.

5 Q. This would be one of your 302 report forms?

6 A. It would.

7   MR. CARTER: We offer Exhibit E.

8   MR. HOLMES: No objection.

9   THE COURT: Exhibit E is received.

10 BY MR. CARTER:

11 Q. I want to call your attention to the second page of

12 Exhibit E, the section at the bottom that has Donna Jordan's

13 name in capital letters, you see that?

14 A. There is three different.

15 Q. It would be the third one from the bottom.

16 A. Yes.

17 Q. Do you remember anything about the dream journals that

18 are referenced in that section?

19 A. Well, there is no reference to dream journal in that

20 paragraph, counsel.

21 Q. Well, let me just see it here a minute. What about Donna

22 Jordan's notes, I guess?

23 A. Yes.

24 Q. Do you remember having had some discussion with Donna

25 Jordan about those notes before you wrote that 302?

Page 773

1 A. I think, and it's been a long time ago, that she was

2 concerned that the children wanted to talk about these

3 allegations, and she didn't know what to do about it. And that

4 she had, I believe, rather than ask some questions, if they

5 wanted to talk about it, they should write them down themselves

6 in some type of notebook, maybe that is what you are referring

7 to.

8 Q. Well, in the Exhibit it makes reference, does it not, to

9 the fact that these notes from Donna Jordan are going to be

10 made available at some later date?

11 A. That's what it says.

12 Q. And that was your understanding at the time?

13 A. That's what it says.

14 Q. Did you ever see those notes?

15 A. I don't remember today ever seeing them.

16 Q. Mr. Van Roe, you indicated on your direct testimony that

17 you did not ever threaten the children, I believe, wasn't that

18 what you testified to?

19 A. That's accurate.

20 Q. And these children at the time that you were dealing with

21 them were quite young, isn't that true?

22 A. Well, they were I think Fury, and there were a couple

23 little babies involved, and then there were older children,

24 five, six, seven, eight, maybe nine years.

25 Q. Would you agree with me that even though you may not have

Page 774

1 intended to threaten the children, that being a large man and a

2 man in an important position that that could perhaps be

3 threatening to these children?

4 A. No, I don't think so. I was never that close to them, I

5 was in the same room when Mr. Hudspeth

6 interviewed them, I was never in there alone. Eva Cheney was

7 there after she was appointed, Micky was there, Donna was

8 there, at times Jean Brock was there. No, I have to disagree

9 with that.

10 Q. But you had many different occasions throughout the time

11 that you were involved in this file that you, including appear

12 preparing for trial, that you were with the children and

13 preparing for some of these testimonies, isn't that correct?

14 A. Sure.

15 Q. As far as the, you indicated that you had made notes of

16 these interviews with the children down at Donna Jordan's,

17 correct?

18 A. That's right.

19 Q. Is there some reason that you did not tape record these

20 interviews?

21 A. Well, it was 1994, it wasn't 2001, and it wasn't our

22 policy back in 1994.

23 Q. Did you have a policy against taping them at that time?

24 A. Basically, yes.

25 Q. Do you know why?

Page 775

1   MR. HOLMES: Objection, that's not relevant.
2   THE COURT: Sustained.
3 BY MR. CARTER:
4 Q. Did you have discussions with the counselors of the
5 children?
6 A. Not that I can recall.
7 Q. Given the amount of time that has occurred since this
8 trial and the investigations, is it fair to say that your
9 memory at this point has got a few holes in it?
10 A. What does a few holes mean?
11 Q. Well, are there things that you recall exactly everything
12 that occurred in this file?
13 A. Oh, probably not.
14 Q. You probably, your memory today is not as good as it was
15 a few years ago on it?
16 A. Given my age today, and it was six or seven years ago, I
17 am sure I have forgotten some things.
18   MR. CARTER: No further questions.
19   THE COURT: Mr. Haugaard.
20 CROSS EXAMINATION BY MR. HAUGAARD:
21 Q. Mr. Van Roe, how old are you?
22 A. I will be, I am 57, I will be 58 this month.
23 Q. It looks like the time has been good to you, you have a
24 tan?
25 A. It's been wonderful.

Page 776

1 Q. Could you tell us approximately in 1994 what your height
2 and weight was?
3 A. I would say it's pretty much what you see today.
4 Q. What is that?
5 A. About six two, six two and a half, 208 pounds maybe.
6 Q. At the time, Mr. Hudspeth, was he a large man?
7 A. Very large man at the time.
8 Q. How much would you estimate he weighed at that time?
9 A. Oh, goodness. I would say in excess of 300 pounds.
10 Q. And he is Native American?
11 A. Yes.
12 Q. Was it common for him to wear cowboy clothes?
13 A. Yes.
14 Q. Was it common for you to wear cowboy clothes?
15 A. No.
16 Q. At that time did you have a nice tan?
17 A. It was January.
18 Q. So the answer is no?
19 A. The answer is no.
20 Q. You indicated that the interviews took place in a main
21 floor room at Donna Jordan's house originally, I believe
22 January 19th interview?
23 A. January 19th, '94, I believe it was in a dining room.
24 Q. You said Donna Jordan was in the kitchen area?
25 A. Yes. It was the main floor, a wide open area, so the

Page 777

1 dining room and the kitchen were connected, but they were large
2 rooms.
3 Q. You could see Donna Jordan from where you were sitting?
4 A. Maybe out of the corner of my eye.
5 Q. The January 21st, 1994 interview at the United States
6 Attorney's office, is that where it took place?
7 A. The interviews on the 21st.
8 Q. On the 21st?
9 A. Yes.
10 Q. Which room did that take place in?
11 A. That would be Micky Tapken's office.
12 Q. Was that interview recorded?
13 A. Are you talking about video, or audio?
14 Q. Video or audio recorded?
15 A. No.
16 Q. When Eva Cheney was involved in this matter were there
17 times when Ms. Tapken would interview the kids in your presence
18 and Eva Cheney was in the general area?
19 A. She would be in the room.
20 Q. Were these individual interviews, or were all the kids
21 present?
22 A. When the interviews were conducted it would be, to my
23 recollection, that they were individual interviews.
24 Q. During the course of the trial did you have occasion to
25 have, make casual comments to the children as you would walk

Page 778

1 back and forth from the Court room?
2 A. I know the children were very concerned --
3 Q. I just asked you a question. I ask you if you had
4 occasion to make comment to the kids, yes or no.
5 A. I think so, yes.
6 Q. Are you aware of any conversations Donna Jordan had with
7 the children prior to your being there at Donna Jordan's home?
8 A. I don't know how I could.
9 Q. You have no idea about that, do you?
10 A. I don't know how I could.
11 Q. Were you aware of whether or not the five year olds were
12 able to write?
13 A. Who were the five year olds?
14 Q. Lucritia and Jessica and Rosemary?
15 A. I don't know if they could or not.
16   MR. HAUGAARD: No further questions.
17   MR. HOLMES: No redirect, Your Honor.
18   THE COURT: Thank you, you may step down. Call your
19 next witness.
20   MR. HOLMES: We have no further witnesses, Your
21 Honor.
22   THE COURT: Well, we will start then at one o'clock
23 tomorrow and proceed ahead. Thank you, we are in recess.
24 (Recess at 4:50 p.m.) (9-13-01 1:00 p.m.)
25   THE COURT: Defense may proceed.

1   MR. HAUGAARD: We call Jerome Rouse, Your Honor.

2

3   JEROME ROUSE,

4 called as a witness, being first duly sworn, testified and said

5 as follows:

6

7 DIRECT EXAMINATION BY MR. HAUGAARD:

8 Q. Good morning, Jerome, please state for the record your

9 name?

10 A. Jerome Michael Rouse.

11 Q. How old are you?

12 A. Nineteen.

13 Q. Where do you presently live?

14 A. Dickinson, North Dakota.

15 Q. What put you in Dickinson, North Dakota?

16 A. I got in to a fight at another placement.

17 Q. Jerome, who is your mother?

18 A. Beta Rouse.

19 Q. Who are your brothers and sisters?

20 A. Donovan, Lucritia, Jessica, Fury and Ebony.

21 Q. Do you remember when you and your brothers and sisters

22 were taken to foster homes back in 1994?

23 A. Yes.

24 Q. Tell us what happened when you were taken?

25 A. Me and my brother and a couple cousins were in my room,

1 we listened to the radio and saw some cops pull up.

2 Q. Your brother who?

3 A. My brother Donovan and two cousins of mine were in my

4 room, and we saw the cops pull up, and I walked out into the

5 living room, kitchen area, and asked what was going on, and one

6 of my aunts told me that they were taking us away. So we

7 really couldn't grab anything, they just told us to go out in

8 the cop car, and they, that was it, they took us to the BIA

9 station that day.

10 Q. Let's back up. What is your age right now?

11 A. Nineteen.

12 Q. Your birth date?

13 A. January 23, 1982.

14 Q. Did you know why you were being taken away?

15 A. No, I didn't.

16 Q. Did you know where you were being taken to?

17 A. No, I didn't.

18   MR. LANGLEY: Your Honor, may I be heard.

19   THE COURT: Yes.

20   MR. LANGLEY: Your Honor, my name is Tim Langley from

21 the Federal Public Defender's office, and I represented

22 Mr. Rouse on a previous juvenile matter. I met with him

23 earlier this morning, and based on the questions that I expect

24 to be elicited today, I advised him not to testify and to rely

25 on the 5th Amendment, because I believe incriminating answers

1 may be elicited from him. Obviously he is not taking my

2 advice, I wanted to advise the Court that was my advice, and he

3 indicated at the time that we talked that that was his desire

4 also.

5   THE COURT: Mr. Rouse, you understand of course what

6 your lawyer has just said?

7   THE WITNESS: Yes.

8   THE COURT: Alright. Mr. Langley, you are going to

9 remain in attendance so that if some question may give rise to

10 your concerns you will be able to so advise your client?

11   MR. LANGLEY: I will, Your Honor.

12   THE COURT: Very well, proceed.

13 BY MR. HAUGAARD:

14 Q. Where were you taken to?

15 A. A foster home in between Elk Point and Jefferson, Donna

16 and Roger Jordan's.

17 Q. How long did you reside there?

18 A. For about a couple of years.

19 Q. When you first got there did you know why you were there

20 yet? Let me ask you this. On the way down had anyone told you

21 why you were going there?

22 A. No.

23 Q. When you first got there did you and your brother talk

24 about anything?

25 A. When we first got there we talked about running away from

1 the foster home.

2 Q. Why would you want to run away?

3 A. Because I didn't want to be there.

4 Q. Did you know why you were there at that point?

5 A. No.

6 Q. When did you first find out why you were there?

7 A. Probably a couple of days later.

8 Q. How did you find out?

9 A. I think one of my cousins told me that someone told that

10 we were being neglected, and that there was drinking going on

11 in the house.

12 Q. Did investigators eventually come and speak with you?

13 A. Later on, a year and a half later.

14 Q. What questions did they ask?

15   MR. LANGLEY: Your Honor, I hate to intervene again,

16 I appreciate the Court's indulgence, may I have two minutes

17 with my client?

18   THE COURT: You may.

19

20   (Whereupon, an off the record discussion

21   was held.)

22

23   THE COURT: You may proceed.

24 BY MR. HAUGAARD:

25 Q. What kind of questions were you asked by investigators?

Page 783

1 A. I remember being asked that if I saw my uncles touch any
2 one of my cousins or sisters, and asked that if they touched
3 me.
4 Q. What did you say originally?
5 A. I said no.
6 Q. Did you say no more than once?
7 A. On, yes, a couple of times.
8 Q. Did they keep asking you the same types of questions?
9   MR. HOLMES: Objection, leading.
10   THE COURT: Sustained.
11 BY MR. HAUGAARD:
12 Q. Did their questions change significantly?
13 A. Yes, over time, after two or three times that they asked
14 me.
15 Q. Did you eventually agree with their questions?
16 A. Yes, I did.
17 Q. Were you telling the truth?
18 A. No.
19 Q. Did your uncles ever abuse you?
20 A. No, they didn't.
21 Q. Did you ever hear of any of the girls being abused by any
22 of your uncles?
23 A. No, I didn't.
24 Q. Did you ever suspect that any of your uncles or Garfield
25 or Russ had ever abused any of the girls?

Page 784

1   MR. HOLMES: Objection, calls for an improper
2 conclusion.
3   THE COURT: Overruled.
4 A. No, I didn't.
5 BY MR. HAUGAARD:
6 Q. Did you ever see any of your uncles try to arrange to be
7 alone with the girls?
8 A. No.
9 Q. Did you ever see your uncles do anything to any of the
10 girls that would be considered abuse or sexual abuse?
11 A. No.
12 Q. Why did you eventually agree with the investigators that
13 something had happened?
14 A. I felt that is what they wanted to hear.
15 Q. Do you remember what they looked like, the people who
16 asked you questions?
17 A. No. I remember a lady with red hair and that's it.
18 Q. Were these Indian people who asked you questions?
19 A. No.
20 Q. Did you feel that you could trust them?
21 A. No.
22 Q. Why not?
23 A. Because they were white.
24 Q. What difference did that make to you as a ten or twelve
25 year old?

Page 785

1 A. I only knew my family and the people on the Reservation
2 that were Native American, and I didn't feel that it was right
3 to tell someone about the family.
4 Q. Did you ever make up any stories about what might have
5 happened?
6 A. Yes.
7 Q. Was that in response to the questions you were being
8 asked by the investigators?
9 A. Yes.
10 Q. Why did you do that?
11 A. Like I said, I felt that is what they wanted to hear.
12 Q. Did it appear to you when you were in the foster home
13 that you were going to be able to go home?
14 A. No.
15 Q. Did you want to go home at that point?
16 A. Yes.
17 Q. What did you think it was going to take for you to be
18 able to go home to your mother?
19 A. I didn't know exactly what it would take.
20 Q. Did the investigators ever ask if you had committed any
21 acts of abuse against your sisters or cousins?
22 A. No, they didn't.
23 Q. Did you ever have sexual contact with any of your
24 cousins?
25 A. I refuse to answer that on the 5th Amendment.

Page 786

1 Q. Did you ever have any sexual contact with your sisters?
2 A. I refuse to answer that based on the 5th Amendment.
3 Q. While you have been in custody have you gone through sex
4 offender treatment?
5 A. Yes.
6 Q. Did you trust Donna Jordan?
7 A. No, I didn't.
8 Q. Why didn't you tell her that this abuse hadn't ever taken
9 place?
10 A. Because she was not part of the family, and she was
11 white.
12 Q. Did you go to a counselor for a while, while you were
13 staying with Donna Jordan?
14 A. Yes.
15 Q. Why didn't you tell the counselor that none of this abuse
16 happened?
17 A. For the same reason.
18 Q. Did you like staying at Donna Jordan's?
19 A. No, I didn't.
20 Q. Why not?
21 A. It was not home.
22 Q. Was Donna good to you?
23 A. Not exactly.
24 Q. What did you ever observe her do that -- what did you
25 ever observe her do that you thought was inappropriate?

Page 783 - Page 786

Page 787

1 A. I remember seeing her grab my sister's hair.

2 Q. Which sister?

3 A. Fury. She grabbed her by the pony tail and pulled her
4 head back, and I remember her yelling at her about either
5 peeing in her pants or not eating, one of those two situations,
6 and I remember her pushing her head forward after she yelled at
7 her and told her to go lay down.

8 Q. Did Donna sometimes do this in front of her husband?

9 A. Not that I recall.

10 Q. Would she sometimes do this in front of her son?

11 A. No.

12 Q. When you came to Sioux Falls to testify at the trial, why
13 didn't you tell someone that this didn't happen?

14 A. I didn't talk to anyone else.

15 Q. What did you say?

16 A. I did not talk to anyone else.

17 Q. Why didn't you tell Eva Cheney?

18 A. I don't know who that is.

19 Q. Do you remember a lady who had dark hair and about
20 shoulder length?

21 A. Yes, vaguely.

22 Q. Do you remember who that was?

23 A. No, I don't remember her name or her face.

24 Q. Was she with you while you were waiting to testify?

25 A. I don't remember.

Page 788

1 Q. When you came to testify do you remember all of you kids
2 being paid something to come to Sioux Falls?

3 A. Yes.

4 Q. Was that because of the subpoena to have you come to
5 testify?

6 A. I think so.

7 Q. Do you remember how much you were supposed to be paid?

8 A. Somewhere like two hundred some dollars.

9 Q. Did Donna control that money?

10 A. Yes.

11 Q. How much did you receive?

12 A. Twenty dollars.

13 Q. How much did any of the other children receive?

14 A. The same.

15 Q. When you were asked questions about your uncles, who did
16 you think of as your uncles?

17 A. Desmond, Rod, Jessie.

18 Q. Are those your mother's brothers?

19 A. Yes.

20 Q. When you think about Garfield and Russ Hubbeling, what do
21 you see as their relationship to your family?

22 A. As friends to the family.

23 Q. Were you aware that each of these men had girlfriends or
24 spouses at that time?

25 A. Yes.

Page 789

1   MR. HAUGAARD: If I may have a moment, Your Honor,
2 just to review my notes?

3   THE COURT: Sure.

4 BY MR. HAUGAARD:

5 Q. Jerome, before you were taken away from your mother's
6 home in 1994, were you acquainted with the actions involved in
7 sexual intercourse?

8 A. Yes.

9 Q. Had you ever observed your mother involved in that?

10 A. No.

11 Q. Had you ever observed any of these men here in the
12 courtroom involved in sexual activity with anyone?

13 A. No.

14 Q. Had you ever seen any of your cousins involved in that?

15 A. No.

16 Q. Were you involved in sexual activity with cousins or
17 siblings?

18 A. I refuse to answer that on the 5th Amendment.

19 Q. Were you involved in sexual activity with Thrista?

20 A. I refuse to answer that on the 5th Amendment.

21   MR. HAUGAARD: No further questions.

22   MR. WILKA: I have no questions, Your Honor.

23   MR. BINGER: Nothing.

24   MR. CARTER: No questions.

25   THE COURT: Cross examination.

Page 790

1 CROSS EXAMINATION BY MR. HOLMES:

2 Q. Jerome, it's your memory that you were first interviewed
3 a year and a half after you were taken away from your home?

4 A. I really don't know the time, but I think it was a year
5 and a half later.

6 Q. Who interviewed you?

7 A. Some lady and two agents, I guess.

8 Q. What did they talk to you about?

9 A. They asked me questions.

10 Q. About what?

11 A. About the abuse that was going on in the home.

12 Q. Were you interviewed at all after that?

13 A. No.

14 Q. You were interviewed one time?

15 A. Yes.

16 Q. I think you were asked by Mr. Haugaard some questions
17 about why you didn't tell other people that this did not
18 happen, and you said you didn't feel right because, didn't feel
19 right to talk to people about something that happened in the
20 family, you remember that?

21 A. Yes.

22 Q. You also said that you were not willing to talk to some
23 people because they were not Native American, you remember
24 saying that?

25 A. Yes.

Page 791

1 Q. So it's your testimony that you were not willing to
2 confide in other people about things that happened in the
3 family, is that right?
4 A. Yes.
5 Q. And that you did not have a trust for people that were
6 non-Indians?
7 A. Yes.
8 Q. But you would have this Court believe that you were
9 willing to lie to a female, non-Indian person about this sexual
10 abuse when she interviewed you one time, is that what you want
11 this Court to believe?
12 A. It's like I said, I thought that is what they wanted to
13 hear, so I told them.
14 Q. You were willing, according to you and your testimony, to
15 tell this female, non-Indian family secrets just because you
16 thought that is what they wanted to hear?
17   MR. HAUGAARD: Objection, asked and answered.
18   THE COURT: Overruled.
19 A. It wasn't a family secret.
20   MR. HOLMES: Nothing further.
21   THE COURT: Redirect?
22   MR. HAUGAARD: Yes, Your Honor.
23 REDIRECT EXAMINATION BY MR. HAUGAARD:
24 Q. Jerome, the answers you eventually gave to the
25 investigator, were they made up stories?

Page 792

1 A. Yes.
2 Q. As I asked you before, did any of your uncles or any of
3 your mom, or aunts, grandma, anyone in the family to that
4 extent, Russ, Garfield, did any of them have sexual contact
5 with your siblings, or your cousins, or yourself?
6 A. No.
7   MR. HAUGAARD: No further questions.
8   MR. HOLMES: Nothing further, Your Honor.
9   THE COURT: Mr. Rouse, this interview that you talked
10 about, was that an interview before or after these defendants
11 were tried?
12 A. That was before.
13   THE COURT: Thank you. Do the Court's questions give
14 rise to questions by either side?
15   MR. HOLMES: Not from the government.
16   MR. HAUGAARD: Nothing further, Your Honor.
17   THE COURT: Thank you, you may step down. Call your
18 next witness.
19   THE COURT: Call your next witness.
20
21   JESSICA ROUSE,
22 recalled as a witness, being first duly sworn, deposed and said
23 as follows:
24
25 DIRECT EXAMINATION BY MR. HAUGAARD:

Page 793

1 Q. Jessica, please state your name again?
2 A. Jessica Rouse.
3 Q. I just want to ask you questions about a lady by the name
4 of Sherry, Sherry Fridel at Wagner school, do you remember her?
5 A. Yes.
6 Q. Do you remember telling her that you wanted to talk to
7 her one time a couple of years ago?
8 A. Yeah.
9 Q. And did you tell her that you were afraid of your uncles?
10 A. Yeah.
11 Q. Why did you say that?
12 A. Because I didn't know em.
13 Q. Pardon?
14 A. I didn't know em.
15 Q. Didn't know your uncles?
16 A. I didn't know them all that good.
17 Q. You said that you didn't know them very well, or at all?
18 A. I didn't know them very well.
19 Q. How did you remember them when you thought back on them,
20 what could you remember about your uncles?
21 A. They were big.
22 Q. Had they ever done anything to hurt you?
23 A. No.
24 Q. Had you ever seen them hurt any of your cousins, or
25 sisters, or brothers?

Page 794

1 A. No.
2 Q. Do you remember what you told Sherry Fridel?
3 A. No.
4   MR. HAUGAARD: No further questions.
5 DIRECT EXAMINATION BY MR. WILKA:
6 Q. Good afternoon, Jessica. My name is John, and I am just
7 going to ask you a few questions, okay? You remember Donna
8 Jordan?
9 A. Yeah.
10 Q. Do you remember when you testified that she made you take
11 a bath in rubbing alcohol, or to bathe with rubbing alcohol?
12 A. Yes.
13 Q. How do you know it was rubbing alcohol?
14 A. Because it smelled just like alcohol.
15 Q. What is your mother's name?
16 A. Beta Rouse.
17 Q. Did Beta Rouse ever tell you that you had to lie to get
18 your uncles out of prison?
19 A. No.
20 Q. How old were you in 1994, do you remember? How old are
21 you now?
22 A. Twelve.
23 Q. So you were about four or five years old then? Would
24 that be yes?
25 A. Yes.

Page 795

1 Q. If your uncles would have hurt you, would you be here
2 today?
3 A. No.
4   MR. WILKA: Thank you, that's all I have, dear.
5   MR. BINGER: No questions.
6   MR. CARTER: No questions.
7   THE COURT: Cross examination.
8 CROSS EXAMINATION BY MR. HOLMES:
9 Q. Jessica, did you know Sherry Fridel very well?
10 A. Not really.
11 Q. Why did you go talk to her some time right before
12 Christmas?
13 A. Don't know.
14 Q. You don't remember?
15 A. No.
16 Q. You remember telling her that you were afraid your uncles
17 were going to get out of prison?
18 A. Yeah.
19 Q. You remember that?
20 A. Yes.
21 Q. Do you remember telling Sherry Fridel that you were
22 afraid of your uncles?
23 A. Yes.
24 Q. Do you remember telling Sherry Fridel that your uncle had
25 touched you in your private parts?

Page 796

1 A. No.
2 Q. Do you remember telling her that you and your sister the
3 summer before had to go tell a social worker that someone had
4 made up stories about your uncles?
5 A. No.
6 Q. What else do you remember telling Sherry Fridel?
7 A. Nothing.
8 Q. Do you remember her a few days after you went to talk to
9 her meeting with you a second time?
10 A. Yes.
11 Q. What did you tell her that time?
12 A. I don't remember. I just remember going back and talking
13 to her.
14 Q. Did she tell you anything?
15 A. Yeah.
16 Q. What did she tell you?
17 A. That my uncles weren't coming home.
18 Q. Do you remember telling her that second time that your
19 uncle had crawled in bed with you and had touched you in the
20 private parts?
21 A. No.
22 Q. You remember telling her that your mom had told you to
23 lie also?
24 A. No.
25 Q. After she talked to you, were you still afraid of your

Page 797

1 uncles?
2 A. No.
3 Q. Because you knew they weren't getting out of prison,
4 right?
5 A. No.
6 Q. Well, she told you that, didn't she?
7 A. Yes.
8   MR. HOLMES: Nothing further.
9   THE COURT: Anything further?
10 REDIRECT EXAMINATION BY MR. HAUGAARD:
11 Q. Jessica, as you sit here today do you recall being kind
12 of afraid of your uncles back then?
13 A. Back when I was talking to Sherry?
14 Q. Yes.
15 A. Yes.
16 Q. Now that you have seen your uncles again face-to-face,
17 does that remind you of anything that they have done bad to you
18 before?
19 A. No.
20 Q. Have they ever done anything bad to you before?
21 A. No.
22 Q. Do you remember them being in your grandma's house?
23 A. Yeah.
24 Q. Do you remember them drinking sometimes?
25 A. Yeah.

Page 798

1 Q. Did that sometimes scare you?
2 A. No.
3 Q. Did you like it when they drank?
4 A. No.
5 Q. Are you afraid of them today?
6 A. No.
7   MR. HAUGAARD: No further questions.
8 REDIRECT EXAMINATION BY MR. WILKA:
9 Q. I want you to, if you can, remember back to when you were
10 four or five years old, Jessica, and when you agreed with
11 people that your uncles had done bad things to you. Do you
12 remember agreeing with them that your uncles had done bad
13 things to you?
14   MR. HOLMES: Objection, outside the scope of cross.
15   THE COURT: Sustained.
16 BY MR. WILKA:
17 Q. As you sit here today, probably the last time that you
18 will sit in that chair, is there anything else that you think
19 Judge Piersol should know?
20 A. Yes.
21 Q. What is that?
22 A. That my uncles didn't do nothing wrong.
23   MR. WILKA: That's all I have, thank you.
24   MR. BINGER: No questions.
25   MR. CARTER: No other questions.

Page 795 - Page 798

Page 799

1   MR. HOLMES: Nothing further, Your Honor.

2   THE COURT: Thank you, you may step down. Call your

3 next witness.

4

5   DONOVAN ROUSE,

6 recalled as a witness, being first duly sworn, testified and

7 said as follows:

8

9 DIRECT EXAMINATION BY MR. HAUGAARD:

10 Q. Donovan, please state your name for the record?

11 A. Donovan Rouse.

12 Q. Donovan, you were here the other day and testified, do

13 you remember that?

14 A. Yes.

15 Q. Do you remember when you were first in Donna Jordan's

16 home?

17 A. Yes.

18 Q. Do you remember talking to Jerome?

19 A. Yeah, all the time.

20 Q. He was there with you?

21 A. Yeah.

22 Q. Did you two talk about running away?

23 A. Yes.

24 Q. When people asked you questions when you first got there,

25 why didn't you tell them the truth?

Page 800

1   MR. HOLMES: Your Honor, this is not proper rebuttal.

2   THE COURT: Sustained.

3 A. Am I telling the truth.

4   THE COURT: The objection to the question is

5 sustained, you don't have to answer that one.

6 BY MR. HAUGAARD:

7 Q. Did you trust the white people there?

8   MR. HOLMES: Objection, same objection.

9   THE COURT: Sustained.

10 BY MR. HAUGAARD:

11 Q. You remember being at Children's Home Society?

12 A. Yes.

13 Q. Do you remember talking to some ladies about these claims

14 of sexual abuse?

15 A. Yes.

16 Q. Why didn't you tell them that it didn't happen?

17 A. Because I wanted to go home still.

18 Q. So why didn't you tell them?

19 A. Because I wanted to go home.

20 Q. Did you think that was the only way you could go home was

21 if you went along with the story?

22 A. Yes.

23 Q. Is there anything else you can think of you would like to

24 tell the Judge today?

25   MR. HOLMES: Objection, this isn't proper rebuttal.

Page 801

1   THE COURT: Sustained.

2   MR. HAUGAARD: No further questions.

3 DIRECT EXAMINATION BY MR. WILKA:

4 Q. Good afternoon, Donovan?

5 A. Good afternoon.

6 Q. My name is John, I am working with Desmond Rouse, I just

7 have a couple of questions, okay?

8 A. Alright.

9 Q. How old are you again?

10 A. Sixteen.

11 Q. At the time that you were taken out of your folks' house

12 down in Marty how old were you?

13 A. Eight or nine.

14 Q. When Mr. Haugaard was asking you some questions about the

15 Children's Home Society, do you remember your years there?

16 A. Yes.

17 Q. And do you remember answering Mr. Haugaard's questions

18 about talking to the ladies that worked there about this sexual

19 abuse story?

20 A. Yes.

21 Q. What were you afraid of that would happen if you told

22 them these things didn't happen?

23 A. That I would have been, that they would have kept me

24 there longer.

25 Q. Do you remember Donna Jordan?

Page 802

1 A. Yes.

2 Q. Did Donna Jordan talk to you about this sexual abuse?

3   MR. HOLMES: Objection, improper rebuttal, he asked

4 that in his direct and cross.

5   THE COURT: Overruled.

6 BY MR. WILKA:

7 Q. Donovan, did Donna Jordan talk to you about these alleged

8 acts of sexual abuse?

9 A. Yes. She just mostly just said you don't have to be

10 scared, you can tell the truth and stuff like that.

11   MR. WILKA: Thank you, Donovan, that's all the

12 questions I have for you today, young man.

13   MR. BINGER: No questions.

14   MR. CARTER: No questions.

15   MR. HOLMES: No cross.

16   THE COURT: Thank you, you may step down. Call your

17 next witness.

18

19   THRISTA ROUSE,

20 recalled as a witness, being first duly sworn, testified and

21 said as follows:

22

23 DIRECT EXAMINATION BY MR. HAUGAARD:

24 Q. Thrista, would you please state for the record your name?

25 A. Thrista.

Page 803

1   Q.   Last name?

2   A.   Rouse.

3   Q.   Just so Mr. May has it spelled properly, spell your first

4   name?

5   A.   T-H-R-I-S-T-A.

6   Q.   Thrista, we asked you questions the other day about your

7   time at Donna Jordan's place. Do you remember when I asked you

8   about the alcohol bath?

9   A.   Um-hum.

10   Q.   How did you know that was alcohol?

11   A.   Because it had rubbing alcohol, and it burned whenever we

12   sat in it.

13   Q.   What did you see that said rubbing alcohol?

14   A.   Rubbing alcohol bottle, those bottles. I know what a

15   rubbing alcohol bottle looks like, and I know what it smells

16   like.

17   Q.   Jerome has been here to testify this morning, do you

18   remember being in the foster home with Jerome?

19   A.   Yeah.

20   Q.   While you were in the foster home with Jerome did there

21   come a time when you and Jerome were in bed together?

22   A.   Yeah.

23   Q.   Did that happen a lot of times?

24   A.   Not really.

25   Q.   Did it happen a few times a week?

Page 804

1   A.   Yeah.

2   Q.   Before you were taken out of the home, Thrista, had you

3   been with your cousin Moses?

4   A.   Yes.

5   MR. HOLMES: Objection, move to strike, improper

6   rebuttal.

7   THE COURT: Sustained, the answer is stricken.

8   BY MR. HAUGAARD:

9   Q.   When you ended up in the foster home, were you familiar

10   with sexual activity?

11   MR. HOLMES: Same objection.

12   A.   Yes.

13   MR. HOLMES: Move to strike.

14   THE COURT: Overruled.

15   BY MR. HAUGAARD:

16   Q.   So you knew about sexual activity before you were taken

17   out of the home?

18   A.   Yes.

19   Q.   Did you ever see your -- let me ask you this, who do you

20   consider are your uncles in this courtroom?

21   A.   Uncle Jess and uncle Des.

22   Q.   And Garfield and Russell are who to you?

23   A.   Garfield is my uncle, too, I think.

24   Q.   And Russell, is he a friend of the family?

25   A.   Yeah.

Page 805

1   Q.   Did any of those men ever have any sexual contact with

2   you?

3   MR. HOLMES: Objection, improper rebuttal.

4   A.   No.

5   MR. HOLMES: Move to strike.

6   THE COURT: Just a moment. The answer is stricken

7   while I look at my notes. The answer is stricken, the

8   objection is sustained, ask your next question.

9   BY MR. HAUGAARD:

10   Q.   Thrista, as you sit here today, is it difficult to talk

11   about these things?

12   A.   Kind of.

13   Q.   Is this embarrassing to talk about these things that

14   happened between you and your cousins?

15   A.   Yes.

16   Q.   Were those things that were going through your mind when

17   you were in the foster home and being asked questions by other

18   people?

19   A.   Yes.

20   Q.   Are you afraid of your uncles?

21   A.   No.

22   Q.   If they were sexual abusers would you be here today?

23   A.   No.

24   MR. HOLMES: I object, this isn't relevant, it's not

25   rebuttal, just argument by counsel.

Page 806

1   THE COURT: Sustained.

2   MR. HAUGAARD: No further questions.

3   THE COURT: The last answer is stricken, go ahead.

4   DIRECT EXAMINATION BY MR. WILKA:

5   Q.   My name is John, I have a couple of questions for you.

6   Do you remember testifying about your time at Donna Jordan's?

7   A.   Yeah, yes.

8   Q.   There has been some testimony from Donna Jordan about how

9   she did not pull Fury's hair, or drag her down the stairs. Do

10   you agree or disagree with Donna Jordan on that?

11   A.   Disagree.

12   Q.   And why is that?

13   A.   Because she did.

14   Q.   Did you see that happen?

15   A.   I seen it happen once.

16   Q.   I am not sure if I heard you correctly when you were

17   answering a question from Mr. Haugaard. How do you know that

18   it was rubbing alcohol that you took a bath in?

19   A.   How do I know?

20   Q.   Yes.

21   A.   Because I know what rubbing alcohol is, and it stinks,

22   and it burns when you put it on sores.

23   Q.   Did you see any labels on any bottles or anything like

24   that?

25   A.   Yeah, I seen a whole bunch of bottles.

Page 807

1 Q. On these bottles -- at that time were you able to read?

2 A. Yep.

3 Q. And you were able to read in the English language?

4 A. Yes.

5 Q. Were you able to see words on these labels?

6 A. Yes.

7 Q. What do you remember the words on these labels saying on

8 these bottles?

9 A. Rubbing alcohol.

10 Q. Do you remember being at the Children's Home Society?

11 A. Yes.

12 Q. Do you remember when you were at the Children's Home

13 Society, did you want to go home to your mother's?

14 A. Yes.

15 Q. Do you remember talking to some ladies at the Children's

16 Home Society?

17 A. Yes.

18 Q. There has been some testimony after you left here --

19   MR. HOLMES: Your Honor, I object to counsel

20 characterizing testimony for a witness.

21   THE COURT: Well, let him finish asking the question.

22 Go ahead.

23 BY MR. WILKA:

24 Q. There has been some testimony after you left here that

25 while you were at the Children's Home Society that you would

Page 808

1 state that the abuse from your uncles did take place, okay. Do

2 you remember talking to these ladies at the Children's Home

3 Society about how abuse from your uncles took place?

4 A. No.

5 Q. Did you trust these ladies?

6 A. No, I didn't really talk to them about my uncles.

7 Q. What did you, what do you remember you really talking to

8 them about? Is that difficult for you to answer?

9 A. No.

10 Q. You don't remember?

11 A. I remember, but I know we didn't talk about my uncles a

12 lot.

13 Q. Let's go back to Donna Jordan's house, okay? Did Donna

14 Jordan talk to you about the alleged acts of abuse by your

15 uncles against you?

16 A. Yes.

17 Q. Did your grandma or any of the other grown up women in

18 your family, relatives, tell you that you had to lie to get

19 your uncles out of prison?

20 A. No.

21 Q. Did they ever tell you that they wouldn't love you if you

22 didn't lie to get your uncles out of prison?

23 A. No.

24 Q. Are you afraid of your uncles?

25 A. No.

Page 809

1 Q. Why not?

2 A. Because nothing, they never did nothing to me.

3   MR. WILKA: Thank you Thrista, that's all that I

4 have.

5   MR. BINGER: No questions.

6   MR. CARTER: No questions.

7   THE COURT: Cross.

8   MR. HOLMES: No cross.

9   THE COURT: Thank you, you may step down. Call your

10 next witness.

11   MR. HAUGAARD: Your Honor, may I have a moment with

12 counsel?

13   THE COURT: Yes, certainly.

14

15   (Whereupon, an off the record discussion

16   was held.)

17

18   MR. HAUGAARD: Your Honor, it had been my intention

19 to call Rosemary back for a brief question, but she is not

20 available right now, so I think we will just pass on that

21 particular item. Other counsel do have an offer to make.

22   MR. WILKA: If I may, Your Honor. May it please the

23 Court and Mr. Holmes. In this Court's previous order on the

24 witness list this Court stated that counsel for the defendants

25 could not call Moses Rouse. We would like to make the

Page 810

1 following offer of proof and would renew that request. It is

2 our belief that Moses Rouse would testify that before the

3 children were removed from the residence in Marty, South

4 Dakota, that he had more than occasional sexual contact with

5 one or more of the minor children involved, and so that is the

6 offer of proof that we believe that Moses Rouse would testify

7 to if he were allowed to, and so we would renew our request

8 that Moses Rouse be allowed to testify.

9   THE COURT: What does the government have to say

10 about that?

11   MR. HOLMES: Well, the government's position is the

12 same as before. That this is not newly discovered evidence, it

13 was dealt with at trial, there is a transcript, I believe at

14 least six pages of transcript on it, it was available to

15 counsel at that time, and it was presented, and the Court has

16 ruled upon whether he could be called or not, and there is

17 nothing new that's developed here that would mandate any

18 altering from that course that the Court has already set

19 regarding this witness.

20   THE COURT: I have ruled earlier on this issue, and I

21 haven't gone back now again and re-read what I worked on when I

22 ruled earlier with regard to the new trial proceedings when I

23 ruled that way, but my recollection from the trial is that the

24 offer there was just about as hazy as it is now, and for the

25 reasons that were previously stated in my ruling on this issue,

Page 811

1 the offer is received, of course, it is in the record, but I am

2 not going to have Moses testify.

3   MR. WILKA: May I make, I understand that ruling, may

4 I make one final argument for the record so I feel safe?

5   THE COURT: Certainly.

6   MR. WILKA: The United States has stated that it is

7 not newly discovered evidence. The defense would submit that

8 while it may not be newly discovered testimony, in this context

9 of a recantation that does render that evidence of a nature

10 that is newly discovered.

11   THE COURT: How is that?

12   MR. WILKA: Because at the trial in itself the

13 recantations hadn't taken place, and so that in that context,

14 Your Honor, it is our position that just the rendering about

15 how it fits into the whole context of these proceedings would

16 be newly discovered. It would fit within that. The United

17 States says that nothing has developed here that has changed

18 anything. And, well, we obviously have been here for several

19 days, and it may be relevant to the Court's exercise in

20 assessing the credibility of the recantations.

21   MR. HAUGAARD: Your Honor, argument?

22   THE COURT: Yes.

23   MR. HAUGAARD: Along that same line, maybe I wasn't

24 catching it as John intended it to be, but the point would be

25 that at the time of trial we weren't aware of the recantations,

Page 812

1 now we are aware they were recanting right away, or that they

2 were denying right away, and they are recanting within time

3 after that, and so those things affected the manner in which we

4 approached witnesses throughout the proceedings. We weren't

5 aware of that. Had we been aware of these things that we know

6 now, we certainly would have crafted our questions much

7 differently and called witnesses differently.

8   THE COURT: There hadn't been any recantations at the

9 time of trial, that hasn't been shown, so what are you talking

10 about if you would have known what you know now, what you know

11 now wasn't in existence at that time.

12   MR. HAUGAARD: What existed at that time was the

13 initial denial.

14   THE COURT: Your argument was that, as I heard it

15 anyway, was that you didn't know of the recantations, and my

16 question back to you is, well, there weren't any recantations

17 then, so you couldn't have known of recantations with which to

18 frame your questions differently.

19   MR. HAUGAARD: Maybe I can clarify. I believe the

20 record does reflect that Rosemary recanted to Derrick during

21 that summer prior to trial is my recollection.

22   THE COURT: I have re-reviewed pages 31 through 40 of

23 the trial transcript which I had reviewed before ruling on this

24 issue again in March, and Docket Number 466, and the proffered

25 testimony is not newly discovered evidence, and you have your

Page 813

1 record with regard to your proffer that you have made now. The

2 proffer is denied. Call your next witness.

3   MR. WILKA: Defense rests, Your Honor.

4   THE COURT: Any surrebuttal from the government?

5   MR. HOLMES: No, Your Honor.

6   THE COURT: Alright. We all know what the standard

7 is for granting a new trial. Of course I tried this case to

8 begin with, now this is the fifth day of evidence in the case,

9 65 pages of notes this time in the case, that's not counting

10 the notes from reviewing Dr. Underwager's tapes which are in

11 evidence and which I have reviewed. There is a point, frankly,

12 that I have not researched. I will, but I assume I know the

13 answer to it, that is this is a multiple count indictment, 24

14 counts, one of which was not sent to the jury, so 23 counts

15 went to the jury, and there were some findings of guilty and

16 some not guilty to the various counts. Obviously the ones that

17 there were findings of guilty are the ones we are here about.

18 There were eleven counts in which guilt was found, and twelve

19 upon which guilt was not found. Given the test that I have to

20 apply in this case, it seems to me that rather than considering

21 these as a whole, I have to go down for each count and analyze

22 each count in ultimately determining in view of the testimony

23 my view as to the probability of the jury returning a not

24 guilty verdict in the event of a re-trial. So I am going to

25 have to engage in that analysis to each count. Does anybody

Page 814

1 disagree that that is the approach that the Court has to take?

2 Hearing no disagreement, that is what I will do. I am not

3 prepared, of course, at this point, because I didn't know what

4 the testimony would be until we had it all, so I will review

5 all that and enter an opinion accordingly. Frankly, I don't

6 think I need any briefs, I have heard the evidence, and I have

7 to review the evidence. If there is anything that anybody

8 wants to say, now is the time to say it. I don't think I need

9 any argument, but if there is something that you think that I

10 may have overlooked, you can say so now.

11   MR. HAUGAARD: Your Honor, I would request we be

12 allowed to brief the very thing, I was thinking about the

13 distinction between the defendants, I would like to be able to

14 brief that, and you can put a cap on pages or something so you

15 don't end up with volumes. I would like to be able to argue, a

16 closing essentially, to the Court with supporting case sites.

17   THE COURT: Yes, and of course once you get down to

18 that point, each defendant is for himself, so to speak, because

19 each of the counts of course are defendant and victim specific,

20 there is no joint counts. I am going to be considering

21 everything count by count. So certainly you can do that. How

22 soon would you submit it?

23   MR. HAUGAARD: The way the past couple of weeks has

24 gone, I would ask that I have at least two weeks to prepare

25 that.

Page 815

1 THE COURT: I understand how the last two weeks have
2 gone, because we didn't think we were going to be here for five
3 days. But how much time does the government want then for
4 response?

5 MR. HOLMES: A week.

6 THE COURT: Alright. Does anybody else want to do
7 the same? I am not looking for bids, but if you want to, you
8 can.

9 MR. BINGER: What I am thinking of doing, and I
10 realize there is a vast amount of material here and I am not
11 going to be writing a 25 page brief, but what I am thinking of
12 doing is maybe write a brief two or three pages in length where
13 I try to emphasize what I have seen to be some of the most
14 important points in the case that would relate to the counts of
15 conviction against my client.

16 THE COURT: It narrows down pretty well with regard
17 to each defendant. Because Garfield Feather has four counts,
18 Russell Hubbeling has two counts, Desmond Rouse has three
19 counts, Jessie Rouse has two counts, that's it. Frankly, I
20 would like, because this is all very fresh in my mind, I would
21 like to do it as quickly as I can when everything is fresh in
22 my mind. Let me see where three weeks takes us. Could I look
23 at my schedule?

24 MR. HAUGAARD: Your Honor, about the timeframes, this
25 is essentially like closing argument, and I would ask maybe

Page 816

1 that the briefs from both sides be submitted at the same
2 expected date.

3 THE COURT: It is more helpful to me if I get the
4 benefit of an advocacy where one comes in and then there is a
5 response, I think it would be more helpful to me.

6 MR. HAUGAARD: Would you expect surrebuttal to that
7 then?

8 THE COURT: Yes, if you get it in before I decide it,
9 because I want to work on it when it is really fresh in my
10 mind.

11 MR. HAUGAARD: The other attorneys are indicating
12 they would like to see it done in a week then, I guess I will
13 pursue that.

14 THE COURT: If you could, I think that would be
15 desirable, a week for the defense. In other words, next
16 Thursday I will have your response, which would be the 20th,
17 then the government's reply would be on the 27th, and --

18 MR. CARTER: Could I be heard on just a brief matter.

19 THE COURT: Yes.

20 MR. CARTER: In my situation, I am kind of on the
21 bubble here for a while, my father-in-law is very near death in
22 Rochester, I am frankly expecting it could be about any day.
23 And so there will be that matter for me to deal with I am sure
24 within the next couple of weeks, and so therefore I think I
25 really need to raise that as an issue if I am tied down to one

Page 817

1 week. If something happens, I am going to have to be gone for
2 a while.

3 THE COURT: If something happens, then I will just
4 have to view yours separately, because Mr. Feather's case, just
5 like each one of them, is separate. If that happens, obviously
6 you can contact the Court and we will give you the additional
7 time that you need. And the government's time with responding
8 to yours would move accordingly. That's one of those things we
9 can't do anything about. Obviously I would rather do them all
10 at the same time, but I will adjust as necessary because
11 obviously if your father-in-law passes away you are going to
12 have all kinds of personal obligations.

13 MR. CARTER: Thank you.

14 THE COURT: Once again I am not taking bids for a
15 rebuttal, but Mr. Haugaard indicated that he wanted to have
16 rebuttal. Let me see the 27th is when the replies would be in,
17 so the rebuttal should be in by the 2nd of October. As I did
18 before, I want to thank counsel, because you are all Court
19 appointed counsel, and as I told you after the end of the
20 trial, it is in the finest tradition of the Bar that you are
21 serving, and I know working hard with regard to these serious
22 matters on behalf of your clients, it is in the best traditions
23 of the Bar, the Court thanks you, we are in recess.

24
25

Page 818

1 STATE OF SOUTH DAKOTA)
2   :SS   CERTIFICATE
3 COUNTY OF MINNEHAHA)
4
5
6
7
8 This is to certify that I, JERRY MAY, Court Reporter in the
9 above-named County and State, took the proceedings of the
10 United States District Court, and the forgoing pages 1-817,
11 inclusive, are a true and correct transcript of my stenotype
12 notes.

13 I FURTHER CERTIFY that I am not an attorney for, nor related to
14 the parties to this action and that I am in no way interested
15 in the outcome of this action.

16 Dated at Sioux Falls, South Dakota, this 21st day of December,
17 2001.
18
19
20
21
22
23 COURT REPORTER
24
25

Page 815 - Page 818

Page 819

1   INDEX TO WITNESS

2

3   EVA CHENEY

4   DIRECT EXAMINATION BY MR. HOLMES 685
    CROSS EXAMINATION BY MR. WILKA 697
5   CROSS EXAMINATION BY MR. BINGER 703
    CROSS EXAMINATION BY MR. CARTER 705
6   CROSS EXAMINATION BY MR. HAUGAARD 709

7   MARY WEBER

8   DIRECT EXAMINATION BY MR. HOLMES 714
    CROSS EXAMINATION BY MR. WILKA 719
9   CROSS EXAMINATION BY MR. BINGER 730
    CROSS EXAMINATION BY MR. CARTER 731
10   CROSS EXAMINATION BY MR. HAUGAARD 733
    REDIRECT EXAMINATION BY MR. HOLMES 737
11   RECROSS EXAMINATION BY MR. WILKA 739
    RECROSS EXAMINATION BY MR. BINGER 740
12   RECROSS EXAMINATION BY MR. CARTER 742
    RECROSS EXAMINATION BY MR. HAUGAARD 743

13

14   KARLA HARMON

15   DIRECT EXAMINATION BY MR. HOLMES 744
    CROSS EXAMINATION BY MR. CARTER 748

16

17   TERRYL CADWELL

18   DIRECT EXAMINATION BY MR. HOLMES 750
    CROSS EXAMINATION BY MR. WILKA 755
19   CROSS EXAMINATION BY MR. CARTER 756
    CROSS EXAMINATION BY MR. HAUGAARD 759

20

21   WILLIAM VAN ROE

22   DIRECT EXAMINATION BY MR. HOLMES 760
    CROSS EXAMINATION BY MR. BINGER 768
23   CROSS EXAMINATION BY MR. CARTER 769
    CROSS EXAMINATION BY MR. HAUGAARD 775

24

25

Page 820

1   JEROME ROUSE

2   DIRECT EXAMINATION BY MR. HAUGAARD 779
    CROSS EXAMINATION BY MR. HOLMES 790
3   REDIRECT EXAMINATION BY MR. HAUGAARD 791

4

5   JESSICA ROUSE

6   DIRECT EXAMINATION BY MR. HAUGAARD 792
    DIRECT EXAMINATION BY MR. WILKA 794
    CROSS EXAMINATION BY MR. HOLMES 795
7   REDIRECT EXAMINATION BY MR. HAUGAARD 797
    REDIRECT EXAMINATION BY MR. WILKA 798

8

9   DONOVAN ROUSE

10   DIRECT EXAMINATION BY MR. HAUGAARD 799
    DIRECT EXAMINATION BY MR. WILKA 801

11

12   THRISTA ROUSE

13   DIRECT EXAMINATION BY MR. HAUGAARD 802
    DIRECT EXAMINATION BY MR. WILKA 806

14

15

16   INDEX TO DEFENDANT EXHIBITS

17   Exhibit C Marked 728
      C Offered 729
18   C Received 729

19   Exhibit D Marked
      D Offered 736
20   D received 736

21   Exhibit E Marked
      E Offered 772
22   E Received 772

23

24   MISCELLANEOUS INDEX
    Government Rests 778
25   Defense Rests 813